# Kids on Meds

# Kids on Meds

*Up-to-Date Information about
the Most Commonly Prescribed
Psychiatric Medications*

## Kevin T. Kalikow, MD

W. W. Norton & Company
New York • London

For information about permission to reproduce selections from this book, write to
Permissions, W. W. Norton & Company, Inc., 500 Fifth Avenue, New York, NY 10110

For information about special discounts for bulk purchases, please contact W. W. Norton
Special Sales at specialsales@wwnorton.com or 800-233-4830

Manufacturing by Quad, Fairfield Graphics
Book design by Paradigm Graphics
Production manager: Leeann Graham

Library of Congress Cataloging-in-Publication Data

Kalikow, Kevin T.
 Kids on meds : up-to-date information about the most commonly prescribed psychiatric
medications / Kevin T. Kalikow, MD. -- 1st ed.
    p. cm.
 Includes bibliographical references and index.
 ISBN 978-0-393-70637-6 (hardcover)
 1. Pediatric psychopharmacology--Handbooks, manuals, etc. I. Title.
 RJ504.7.K34 2011
 618.92'8918--dc23
                              2011017985

ISBN: 978-0-393-70637-6

W. W. Norton & Company, Inc., 500 Fifth Avenue, New York, N.Y. 10110
                        www.wwnorton.com
W. W. Norton & Company Ltd., Castle House, 75/76 Wells Street, London W1T 3QT

1 2 3 4 5 6 7 8 9 0

All case studies presented here are composites. Please consult your health care professional
for detailed treatment interventions.

To Ellie

# Kids on Meds: At a Glance

# Kids on Meds: The Details

## Table of Contents

**Saving Paper: Help with Acronyms**

Categories of psychiatric medicines are often abbreviated. Here's an alphabetical list of the frequently used acronyms for various groups of medicines:

| | |
|---|---|
| FGA | First-Generation Antipsychotic |
| MAOI | Monoamine Oxidase Inhibitor |
| SGA | Second-Generation Antipsychotic |
| SSRI | Selective Serotonin Reuptake Inhibitor |
| TCA | Tricyclic Antidepressant |

# Acknowledgements

Many people supported me in writing this book. I am indebted to them all. The faith of Deborah Malmud at W. W. Norton prompted this project. Libby Burton, Vani Kannan, Amanda Heller, and Kevin Olsen at Norton all provided expert guidance.

I am appreciative to my friends and colleagues Ronald Emerson, MD, Alan Kantor, MD, Michael Gewitz, MD, and Jamie Greene, PhD, for reading sections of the book. I am particularly thankful to Boris Birmaher, MD, and Judith Owens, MD, who reviewed chapters. Their stepping up to help a colleague they do not know well was an inspiring example of collegiality.

I thank my agent, Danny Baror, who tends to the details necessary to keep this book on bookshelves. And, I thank my friends Robert Seaver, MD, and Mark Banschick, MD, for their ongoing support

I thank my home team—Lauren, Josh, Jeff, Kate and Adam—who provided everything from editorial advice to tech support. And, finally, I am grateful to Adrian who encouraged me to write this book, but more importantly has been with me for every step.

# Prologue

Although arguments abound as to whether psychiatric medicines are over- or under prescribed, their use in childhood and adolescence has become commonplace. For those who work with troubled youth, whether psychologists, social workers, nurses, teachers, or the many others who help children, a working knowledge of these medicines is mandatory. Many of those with whom these professionals work already take medicines such as Ritalin, Adderall, Prozac, Risperdal, Abilify, and the like. Knowing how the medicine works, its side effects, and its doses will help the professional understand the child's experience. And in treating those who do not take medicine, an almost inevitable question is "Could medicine help?"

This book aims to educate those who are not medically trained about the current use of psychiatric medicines in children and adolescents. I have tried to give more than a simple list of benefits and side effects, instead providing the reader with a little more depth about each. First, however, the stage is set so that information about medicines can be seen in context.

The first five chapters of the book address topics that underlie any discussion of medicines. These topics include how medicines are named, how the brain works, what the life cycle of medicine is as it travels through the body, how diagnosis in child psychiatry has evolved, and how a medicine's benefits and risks are evaluated. While many readers may be tempted to skip right over these chapters and jump to the specifics about certain medicines, unless the reader is already familiar with the chapter's topic, I highly recommend looking at these chapters, since they are crucial to understanding the information in the chapters that follow.

The next eight chapters are about specific groups of medicines or about the treatment of specific areas that are not neatly associated with a specific family of medicines. The first four of these eight chapters review specific families of medicine and are generally divided into sections that include the way these medicines work, the proof that they work in treating certain disorders, the day-to-day basics of how to use these medicines, and the side effects of the medicines. Last, the specific medicines in that family are listed with a short blurb about each. Because different families of medicines are used for a variety of disorders, each chapter is divided in a slightly different manner.

These chapters are not just about the "how to" of medicine, although that important topic is certainly included. In addition, I mention some of the research that supports using these medicines. Too often, as we'll see, medicines are prescribed more on a hope that they'll work than with an understanding of the probability with which they will work. In addition, I have not simply listed side effects. Instead, each is briefly discussed to give the reader a sense of the probability with which they occur and their overall significance.

The next two chapters review the decision-making process that surrounds any patient's decision to use medicine and the communication between interested parties during this process. The final chapter examines the incendiary topic of whether psychiatric medicines are over- or underprescribed to children and adolescents.

While this book contains plenty of specifics about certain medicines, the underlying principles are more enduring. Future editions of this book will undoubtedly cover medicines yet to be created or approved, and many of the medicines currently included are sure to be tossed from the medicine cabinet only to be replaced by others. Nevertheless, the way in which one approaches the decision whether a patient should take medicine, or any treatment, is timeless and independent of specifics.

One of the difficulties in writing this book is that childhood is a period of rapid development, and so a 5-year-old's response to a medicine might be different from that of a 15-year-old. Prepubescent children differ from adolescents. The physical differences include the obvious external signs of puberty but also the less obvious differences in the way their bodies handle medicine. When the difference is crucial, I use the words *children* or *adolescents* to distinguish the two.

Another difficulty is that treating young people means treating those whose diagnostic categories are not fully understood. I discuss the evolution of the psychiatric disorders of childhood and adolescence. But for now, let's simply put the truth on the table. Our understanding of the myriad factors that affect the psychological health of young people is growing but still young itself. And the manner in which we place young people into diagnostic categories is an evolving science.

The book offers my best advice on how to evaluate and treat young people with medicine, but I readily acknowledge that sometimes I don't follow my own best advice. In the real world of treating real people, one must sometimes flex to the demands of time, money, family dynamics, and the like. In that sense, my advice assumes a best-case scenario. In addition, I acknowledge that different clinicians, many of whom I respect and with whom I work, have different styles of approaching clinical problems. For example, many colleagues typically start children on long-acting stimulants, whereas, especially for younger children, I prefer short-acting stimulants. These simply reflect differences of opinion when there is no clearly indicated correct answer.

Since I'm discussing the hard reality about personal style, a word about myself, the clinician leading this tour of pediatric psychopharmacology. I am, by nature, conservative and cautious. I tend not to be the first doctor on the block to prescribe the latest medicine, instead waiting for the initial results to be reviewed before jumping in. After being in private practice for close to 30 years, I find that the words of the clinicians I learned from still ring true. Namely, when a medicine is introduced, it carries the promise of treating all the disorders it was intended to treat, treating some of the disorders it was not intended to treat, and bringing peace to the most troubled areas of the world. After the first of the rare side effects are reported, as they inevitably are, the media rage and the medicine is assumed to be heading toward the dung heap of pharmacohistory. Then the dust settles, and clinicians and patients find a reasonable place for the medicine, allowing for both its potential benefits and side effects.

As a result, I am always suspicious of the drug *du jour*, the medicine that "everyone is using for everything." I am equally suspicious of the medicine that garners banner headlines for killing anyone who even considers using it. I try to maintain an evenhanded and analytical approach in evaluating whether any specific medicine is right for any particular patient, while following the time-honored maxim "First do no harm."

I must also acknowledge that I do not use every treatment mentioned in this book. I discuss some of them, such as a few of the alternative treatments, because people often have questions about them. Others are treatments used more by clinicians with a hospital-based practice. These clinicians are more often faced with patients whose difficulties mandate some treatment, even if the evidence supporting the treatment is not available.

Before moving into the body of book, I offer the following caveats that characterize my understanding of the diagnosis and treatment of the psychological difficulties of children.

• Children are very sensitive to their environments. These range from the impact of a mother's depression on her 5-year-old, to the teasing inflicted on a middle schooler, to the chronic academic stress of a high schooler. And we haven't even mentioned conflicts with parents, conflicts between parents, breakups with girlfriends or boyfriends, the question of being gay, family financial stress, worry about how to handle friends who drink on Saturday night, worry about a mother who drinks every night, and the like. Major or chronic life stress might become a chronic disorder that requires medicine, but life stresses do not necessarily require medication. The normal, if significant, stresses of life should be opportunities for personal growth, not pharmacological intervention. These are better treated by helping the patient cope with, or remove, the stress.

- Temperament, the biological canvas onto which personality is painted, is a powerful, but not determinative, force. The slow-to-warm child might have a greater chance of becoming an adult with social anxiety disorder but does not yet have that disorder. As a result, parenting is a compelling influence and should be given the opportunity to impact the child's development. At what point temperament becomes disorder and whether medicine can prevent a particular temperament from developing into a psychiatric disorder are sticky issues that require more research.

- Although we know a lot about the medicines we use, there is far more to learn about their use in children. Long-term information about many medicines is lacking, as are data regarding specific populations, such as preschoolers. So although one wants to help the suffering patient, it is often wise to resist the initial urge to treat pharmacologically, then to consider carefully the benefits and risks. In short, stay humble and treat cautiously.

- Set reasonable expectations for medicine. As we'll see, medicine can benefit many patients. But whether because of environmental stressors or complex biological comorbidities not as yet understood, medicine does not cure every problem. Some patients are diagnostic enigmas, and while they might be treated with medicine, the prescriber must acknowledge that this is a calculated shot in the dark. In these cases, medicine should not replace the need for other treatment goals such as ongoing evaluation or the need to minimize family conflict. Yet the prescriber must also acknowledge that sometimes one gets lucky and, while aiming to treat one symptom with medicine, treats another.

- Medicine should not be used to treat the clinician's frustration. Let's admit that some patients are difficult—very difficult—to treat. Sometimes we must be content to stay with the patient through the difficulty. Therapists who call with vague requests for medication, such as to "help loosen him up," should carefully examine the motivation for their request.

- Because the first medicine used is not always effective, follow-up is crucial. The patient might be diagnostically confusing or might simply be unresponsive to the medicine prescribed. Follow-up allows one to evaluate the chosen intervention and then change it if necessary.

• Although I discuss side effects and the importance of knowing their frequency, in the real world patients report all sorts of reactions. Sometimes they're describing a known side effect but using words that the clinician interprets differently. Other times they're clearly reporting a side effect that's not on the list. It's worth remembering that rare events do happen, if rarely.

• The often used pseudologic that the patient who has a mild problem merits a little bit of medicine does not make sense. As we'll see, an effective dose is determined by the amount of medicine required to change effectively the neurons in the brain. This is often independent of the extent of the patient's problem.

• Some patients, despite the clinician's well-thought-out efforts, do not improve. When that happens, one must consider whether the patient's diagnosis is correct, whether comorbid diagnoses are complicating the picture, whether the patient is taking the medicine at all or as prescribed, and whether environmental issues, such as family chaos, are overriding the effect of the medicine.

• Who holds the medicine will vary from family to family. Obviously, medicine must be kept secure from the curiosity of young patients and their siblings, as well as suicidal adolescents. Different families, however, feel differently about whether the patient or parent should dispense the medicine. Although the clinician feels a sense of security when a parent is in charge, some parents are more disorganized than their responsible children, and other parents want to promote the child's independence and ownership of taking medicine.

• People who take medicine can begin to see every subsequent experience as tied to the medicine. This can lead to inaccurately labeling any reaction a side effect and any improvement as due to the medicine. When a patient reports being sad because he forgot to take his antidepressant, he is seeing his mood as determined only by the medicine, even though many other factors might impact his mood. The point is that for many, especially parents, taking or giving medicine can be a powerfully important experience through which hopes, fears, and a multitude of feelings are played out.

Throughout the book I tell the stories of many patients. These stories are either composites of many patients or are fictitious characters being used to convey a particular point.

Last, in discussing diagnosis I generally reference *DSM-IV* with the understanding, as we'll see, that it is an evolving document. *DSM-V* is due out in 2013 and is sure to provide some changes to the criteria used to diagnose the psychiatric disorders of children and adolescents. When discussing medicines, I generally use the generic name. However, sometimes I will use the brand name because I think it is more familiar to the reader.

So with these guidelines, let's get started.

# Kids on Meds

*CHAPTER 1*

# Getting Started

Writing a prescription for medicine is the last in a series of steps. It represents one, and rarely the only, choice of treatment that follows a careful evaluation of the patient who has presented with a complaint. Before beginning my discussion of general psychopharmacology and then the specific groups of medicines, I summarize the steps that should precede treatment with medication so that the use of medicine is couched in the reasonable expectations of patient and physician. These steps include taking a complete history and arriving at a tentative understanding of the problem.

## Signs and Symptoms

In most cases the patient initiates contact with the clinician regarding a specific complaint. These complaints are called symptoms. They are by definition subjective and include aches and itches, blurry vision and double vision, urinary hesitancy and urinary urgency, feeling hot and feeling cold, and all the other complaints that bring the patient to seek medical attention. In child psychiatry these complaints include feeling worried or sad, being full of rage or apathy, having racing thoughts and disorganized thoughts, and much more.

An interesting rub of child psychiatry is that the inherently subjective complaint usually comes from a person other than the patient, namely the parent or caregiver. This raises a number of issues. For example, the clinician must ascertain the subjective experience of the young child, who often does not understand the parent's motivation for the consultation or cannot easily articulate his or her own feelings. Or the clinician must hear from the very articulate adolescent who only wants to assert his or her independence or guard his or her self-image by denying that the parent's complaint has any resemblance to reality.

Signs, by contrast, are distinct from symptoms in that they are the physician's clinical findings and are, ideally, objective. The signs of clinical medicine include what the physician sees, hears, feels, and finds by various tests, whether taking a blood pressure or viewing a magnetic resonance imaging (MRI). These findings can be described and measured. So while the patient might complain of the symptom of feeling hot, the physician describes the patient's sign as a fever of 103 degrees. The signs of child psychiatry are more difficult to measure than those of general medicine, but they include such observations as a sad face, fidgetiness, lack of eye contact, fast speech, and lack of focus. As can be seen, mental health professionals are at a distinct disadvantage in not being able to quantify these signs easily.

For thousands of years, diagnosis and treatment were based solely on a careful evaluation of symptoms and signs. With the advent of modern technology, the world of signs available to the physician has expanded dramatically from the simple measurement of blood sugar to the measurement of images on an MRI and beyond. In clinical child psychiatry, however, we are largely without the technology that has been such a help to the rest of medicine. The high-tech instruments that measure the anatomy and functioning of the brain are used as the tools of research, not usually for patient care. Besides those, our most sophisticated tools, beyond our observational skills, are rating scales completed by patients, parents, teachers, and clinicians and the psychological tests performed by psychologists. While these can be valuable aids in understanding the patient, there is still a premium on carefully watching and listening to the patient and his or her family. Admittedly, however, the lack of clear standards of measurement leaves gray zones around the diagnosis of psychiatric disorders in children and makes the clinician vulnerable to using a diagnosis reached on a less-than-objective basis. This can ultimately affect the treatment plan, including whether medicine is prescribed.

# The Evaluation

Taking a careful history of the patient's symptoms and comparing them with the signs observed by the clinician is the essence of the psychiatric evaluation of the child and adolescent and should precede the decision to use any treatment, obviously including medicine. The difficult task of trying to understand the mental life of a maturing and ever-changing child demands a careful evaluation of the many spheres of the child's life. Most experienced clinicians hold that a careful initial history is the single most important element of the evaluation.

Different clinicians have different styles of accomplishing this task, and every clinician will vary his or her style depending on the age of the child and the specifics of a given situation. In general, however, for preadolescent children, I initially speak with parents for an extended period. During this meeting I ascertain the details of the current problem as well as a history of the other areas of the child's life, including topics such as early development, moods, friendships, and family relationships. School history includes information about both academics and behavior and is obtained by speaking directly with and sometimes through consulting school staff or parents, and completing a rating scale. The baseline feedback of school staff can be very important to the clinician later in deciding whether a particular treatment is effective.

Reviewing the family's history of psychiatric disorders is also important, since it is becoming increasingly clear that although rates vary for different disorders, having a close blood relative with a given psychiatric disorder increases the possibility that a child will have that same disorder. In addition, knowing which family members have a psychiatric disorder helps the clinician understand the environment and family legacy with which a child lives. It is also helpful to know other family members' responses, both positive and negative, to different medicines, as this might help determine which medicine to prescribe to the child if medicine is indicated. Although my general rule is to start with a medicine approved by the U.S. Food and Drug Administration (FDA), if a parent or sibling has had a strongly positive response to a nonapproved medicine or a strongly negative response to an FDA-approved medicine, I reconsider that rule.

The child's medical history is also particularly important to any discussion of treatment with medicine. First, medical difficulties are unfortunately an important part of the life experience of some children and need to be noted if one is going to understand the child. Second, one needs to understand whether the child's presenting difficulties are caused by an underlying medical problem. For example, is the child's depression due to an underactive thyroid gland? Psychological explanations are sometimes too easily given, leaving the admittedly infrequent medical cause of psychiatric symptoms undiscovered. Biological problems can also be manifestations of psychiatric disorders. For example, sleep, appetite, and energy level can all be affected by depression. And finally, if medicine is going to be prescribed, the clinician must know whether any medical contraindications rule out the use of a specific medicine. For example, does a child's cardiac arrhythmia contraindicate the use of a stimulant for attention deficit hyperactivity disorder (ADHD)? Or does a history of obesity argue against the use of a second-generation antipsychotic?

In addition, if medicine is to be used, knowing the child's baseline medical functioning gives the clinician a means of comparison in case the child should develop side effects. In this regard, knowing the child's baseline sleep schedule and eating habits is particularly important. Knowing whether the patient had insomnia prior to starting medicine is important in evaluating insomnia while he or she is using medicine.

In particular, children with frequent physical complaints, especially those with underlying anxiety, are prone to report side effects from medicine. These children are excessively sensitive to the many minor bodily sensations we all frequently experience, but they too quickly jump to the conclusion that these are side effects of medicine. They then often use the alleged side effects as a reason to resist taking the medicine. Knowing that the patient has a tendency to overinterpret these sensations is crucial.

> Twelve-year-old Justin is a chronic worrier. His concerns range from why his dad comes home 20 minutes late from work to whether he's prepared sufficiently for tomorrow's math test. Justin complains frequently about vague bellyaches and head aches. Despite his reluctance, Justin is started on a minimal dose of sertraline. Minutes after taking the medicine he feels dizzy. His doctor does not see this as a side effect of the medicine and helps Justin work through his anxiety about taking medicine.

Part of the medical history includes asking about medicines the patient is taking, since these might cause psychiatric symptoms, such as agitation, or interact with other medicine the patient may take. Parents will usually share that the child is taking prescription medicines; but over-the-counter medicines or other substances, such as herbal remedies from the health food store, are also pertinent and sometimes are not seen as medicine by patients or their parents. Often patients incorrectly believe that substances purchased in a health food store offer potential benefits without risk. In addition, asking adolescent girls about their sexual history, including the use of birth control pills, is germane, since birth control pills can interact with other medicines. This is also a logical introduction to a discussion of the use of medicines during pregnancy.

After obtaining a complete history from the parents, I usually speak with the child. This allows me to gain a better understanding of the child and compare my view of the patient to that of the parents. Not infrequently, a child can appear very different from what the parents described, and parents are often upset that the clinician is not seeing the "real" child. I generally reassure parents that I believe their description and inform them that children often put their best foot forward for a stranger, in particular an authority figure. This phenomenon is especially true, I find, of children described as very defiant by their parents, who, because of their tendency to embarrass easily, want to appear in control in public.

In evaluating adolescents, I usually speak to the patient before obtaining historical information from the parents. This helps establish a relationship and aims to prevent adolescents from feeling as if they are talking with someone already biased by their parents' point of view. This relationship can be crucial when the clinician eventually discusses the treatment plan, especially with regard to medicine. In addition, parents are often unreliable in assessing an adolescent's moods, for example, underestimating the extent of the depression.

Part of the routine evaluation, particularly if one is considering the use of medicine, is a recent physical examination. Again, this helps establish whether there is a medical cause of the patient's difficulties and assures the prescriber that there are no contraindications to the patient's taking a particular medicine. While sometimes this should be done at the time of the psychiatric evaluation or immediately preceding the use of medicine, in most cases simply knowing the patient has had a physical exam within the past year is sufficient.

For many medicines, however, certain measurements should be ascertained at the time the medicine is started. These include, for example, height, weight, blood pressure, and pulse prior to the use of stimulants, and weight and certain blood levels (e.g., cholesterol, triglycerides, fasting blood sugar) before the use of "second-generation" antipsychotics (SGAs). These will be more fully noted when specific families of medicine are discussed.

## The Diagnosis

The purpose of the evaluation, as I've just detailed, is to arrive at the most complete understanding of the child's mental life relative to his or her complaints or symptoms. The emotions, thoughts, and behaviors of a child are multidetermined, that is, they reflect many causes, and sometimes understanding and explaining those causes is sufficient treatment. As we'll see, at other times, more important than understanding the causes of behavior is diagnosing a disorder that is lessened by a particular treatment. First we'll look at the causes of behavior, and then we'll look at viewing behavior as a disorder. To simplify the discussion, I refer to emotions, thoughts, and behaviors simply as behaviors. In a sense this is not only simpler but also accurate in that one can think of thoughts and feelings as the unseen behaviors of the brain.

Causes of signs and symptoms can be immediate or distant. For example, the excitement of an upcoming party might be an immediate cause of one child's fidgetiness, or the screaming between parents might be an immediate cause of another child's withdrawing into immobility. Distant causes are exemplified by the child who nearly drowns and, 10 years later, still refuses to return to the pool.

An interesting aspect of distant causes is that they are rarely only distant events but typically include the numerous events that follow the original one. So, in our example, the distant event is the near drowning, but the more proximal events include the way the parents have dealt with that event through numerous interactions over subsequent years. Perhaps, after the original event, they refused to allow the child near any body of water or, at a more subtle level, became tense and anxious whenever the subject arose. These constitute an accumulating series of events that all become causal. Some psychiatric treatments focus on understanding these causal events. For example, Freud's psychoanalysis put the most distant alleged causes, the traumas of infancy, on the psychological map.

Philosophers and scientists have speculated about the causes of people's behaviors for millennia. In ancient Greece, behavior was thought to be a function of the four bodily humors. Another respected theory of the time, astrology, held that if one knew the alignment of the constellations at the exact time of a person's birth, one could understand that person's behavior. Centuries later, in an era dominated by religious thought, bad behavior was understood as being caused by supernatural factors, in particular the devil. During the Enlightenment of the 18th century, philosophers saw children as inherently good beings whose misbehavior was caused by the negative influence of society.

Through the centuries, while philosophers speculated about the causes of adult behavior, there was minimal focus on understanding the causes of childhood behavior and how childhood experiences caused adult behavior. This changed at the beginning of the 20th century with the theories of Sigmund Freud, who hypothesized about the many ways infant and childhood experiences influence later adult behavior. His followers went on to theorize about other causes of behavior, such as how family relationships influence the behavior of the individual. The overall goal of this effort was to explain all human behavior, dysfunctional or not. Whether it was the symptom of a complaining patient or the everyday behavior of a completely functional non-patient mattered little.

While Freud's theories powerfully influenced the field of psychology, in one sense their most important impact was simply the focus on the causes of behavior. Discussions about patients among most mental health professionals during the mid-20th century were predominantly discussions of what psychological factors, whether in childhood or adulthood, caused the current behavior. This might have included looking at the person's early feelings about his or her parents or current relationships with family members. The point is that explaining behavior, dysfunctional or not, was the goal, and causal factors held center stage.

Over recent decades, biological causes have pushed their way onto the stage, indeed grabbing the spotlight. This change has been aided by technological advances involving machinery, such as MRIs and PET (positron emission tomography) scans, and concepts such as our understanding of the human genome and the workings of neurons. This is apparent in the current tendency to see genetic and other biological influences as paramount, a trend that gives credibility to the use of medicine to change that biology.

The shift of focus onto biological causes was aided, though not caused, by a paradigm shift in psychiatry in 1980. In that year the focus switched from searching out the psychological causes of the patient's difficulties to a more empirical approach of observing the patient's symptoms and signs and finding a diagnosis. The focus on psychological causes receded, while searching for the biological causes of well-defined disorders took precedence.

The publication of the third edition of the *Diagnostic and Statistical Manual of Mental Disorders* (DSM-III), a book that is essentially devoid of any mention of causes, marked this momentous change from psychologically centered to empirically centered psychiatry. DSM-I (1952) and DSM-II (1968) had previously described psychiatric disorders, but during those years most clinicians were preoccupied with determining the psychological causes of behavior, not establishing whether the patient had a disorder. In 1980 the focus shifted to determining the patient's disorder, a group of symptoms and signs that occur together more frequently than by chance and that cause clinically significant dysfunction.

In addition, a group of signs and symptoms merits the label "disorder" if they show a tendency to run in families, correlate with biological markers, run a somewhat predictable course, and respond to treatment in a certain way. The point is that the focus changed from understanding the psychological causes of behavior to diagnosing disorders. With this shift in thinking, another, sometimes dominating goal of the psychiatric evaluation became diagnosing a disorder or disorders.

A disorder is not a cause of behavior. It is simply a shorthand label for describing a certain group of symptoms and signs. If a child has attention deficit hyperactivity disorder, the ADHD does not cause the child to be hyperactive and inattentive. Rather, labeling the child with ADHD is a way of saying that he has these symptoms and signs at a certain level and that they are interfering with his functioning. The cause of the ADHD might be one or a combination of factors, ranging from the environmental, such as lead poisoning, to the biological, such as being genetically predisposed.

We should not lose sight of the goal of the psychiatric evaluation of the child, which is to understand the child's behavior so that one can decide the proper treatment. Knowing the cause of the behavior may or may not be necessary. The patient comes to the clinician with complaints, looking for relief. The patient is not necessarily interested in the cause. The diagnosis of a disorder is simply a way of organizing the patient's symptoms so that one can compare the patient to other patients with the same group of symptoms and signs. By comparing, the clinician can arrive at the most accurate prognosis and treatment plan, which is what the patient expects. Some patients find reassurance in receiving the label of a disorder, since with the label comes knowledge of treatment and outcome. Others are left anxious because a diagnosis often sounds more ominous than simply having symptoms.

One must be careful in this process of diagnosing disorders, however. Just as psychological causes are easily, but not always accurately, hypothesized by the imaginative clinician, so can nonexistent disorders be diagnosed by the overzealous or frustrated clinician, who is looking to impose order and understanding on the patient's symptoms. Like DSM-III, DSM-IV (1994) offers the clinician a diagnosis based on clinical judgment rather than the patient's explicit presenting symptoms and signs. In DSM-IV this is noted by the term "not otherwise specified" (NOS), which can be used as a modifier with most diagnoses. So, for example, if a patient fits only some of the criteria for depression, but in the clinician's judgment the correct diagnosis is depression, then depression, NOS, can be diagnosed.

While the sentiment behind this appendage is understandable, and while the authors of DSM-IV acknowledge the inherent subjectivity in the NOS diagnosis, the danger of this diagnosis must also be acknowledged. Using NOS, clinicians are free to diagnose patients who are diagnostic orphans by stretching the borders of what is considered a sign, thus leaving the confines of researched criteria, yet using an official diagnosis, albeit one that perhaps reflects an inaccurate understanding of the patient. This forced diagnosis can hamper the clinician's ability to predict the effect of different treatments, in particular, medicine. The expected efficacy of medicine or any other treatment derives from research done on patients who fit the strict diagnostic criteria for a particular disorder. This might include patients with an NOS diagnosis, but if so, the diagnosis is used only after a patient's signs and symptoms have crossed a high enough threshold.

> *It's late in the winter, and 13-year-old Matthew has been more irritable than usual for the past two or three months. The school year seems interminable. He owes overdue homework in three subjects. His teachers are on his case. His parents are on his case. He doesn't seem to be enjoying his friends, but he loves going skiing on the weekends. He sleeps well and eats like a horse. He can't see far enough into the future to know if the summer will offer a much-needed respite.*
>
> *Matthew doesn't fit the criteria for depression, but his parents think that an antidepressant might help him. Matthew's mother had a hard time a couple of years ago and seems to have responded nicely to the Lexapro her internist started her*

*on. Matthew's doctor wonders if Matthew has depression, NOS. Lexapro is begun, and a month later Matthew is doing better. Was it the medicine? Was it that the cute girl with the ponytail who sits next to him in band started talking with him? Was it the start of baseball season? Was it the beginning of a beautiful sunny spring? It's hard to know.*

We can argue about whether Matthew has depression, NOS. If he does, however, the chances that he'll respond to a selective serotonin reuptake inhibitor (SSRI) like Lexapro are unpredictable. Matthew is distant enough from the patients with DSM-IV depression on whom the SSRIs were tested to make predicting a treatment response only a guess. In years to come, Matthew's gray zone diagnosis may be clarified. Like many others, however, his case illustrates the need to use NOS diagnoses cautiously.

Even the non-NOS diagnoses should be seen as simply representing our best current understanding of which symptoms and signs hold together as a distinctive entity. Roughly every 15 or 20 years the DSM is updated to reflect more recent research. The DSM system of psychiatric diagnosis should be seen for what it is, an evolving nomenclature that is important but not canonized. The fifth edition, DSM-V, is due out in the spring of 2013.

# Treatment

How is this inability of a diagnostic nomenclature to clearly capture some patients relevant to the use of medicine as a treatment? First, it emphasizes the need for a careful evaluation of the multitude of causes of a child's behavioral dysfunction. Second, it reveals the importance of clearly diagnosed disorders in determining the possibility that medicine will be effective. Third, it acknowledges that while a diagnosed disorder helps predict the effectiveness of medicine for a given patient, some medicines do improve the symptoms of patients who do not strictly fit the criteria of a disorder, albeit with less certainty.

Labeling a moody adolescent who does not fit the criteria for depression with depression, NOS, does not ensure that an SSRI will be effective. Yet perhaps it will. Weighing the risks and benefits of the medicine against the risks and benefits of other treatments as opposed to the risks and (rarely) benefits of continuing to suffer with the symptoms or disorder is the culmination of the evaluation.

Ultimately, understanding the patient's dysfunction leads to choosing the best treatment. With the understanding that the proper treatment is not always medicine, let's begin to look at the psychiatric medicines and how they are classified.

## CHAPTER 2

# What's in a Name?

People often talk about psychiatric medicines as if they were all alike, without appreciating that they are very different from one another. Just as a discussion of vehicles would begin by distinguishing 18-wheelers from bicycles, an objective discussion of psychiatric medicines should begin by distinguishing the different types.

## The Characters

The main characters in this book are the psychiatric medicines. They are as different from one another as are various vehicles. We might group them together at times, but the groups are different from one another, and even the medicines within any group are different from one another. For example, although fluoxetine and sertraline are both SSRIs, they are different medicines. Some patients will respond to fluoxetine and others to sertraline.

There is no organized system to the names of the different groups of psychiatric medicines. The names have evolved for a variety of reasons.

Sometimes the names have historical significance. For example, the atypical antipsychotics, such as Risperdal and Zyprexa, are atypical only relative to the antipsychotics that preceded them for 30 years. The typical antipsychotics, such as Thorazine and Haldol, were not called typicals until the next generation of so-called atypical antipsychotics arrived. They had been referred to as major tranquilizers or, because of their association with neurological side effects, as neuroleptics. For this reason, the typicals are sometimes called the first-generation antipsychotics (FGAs) and the atypicals the second-generation antipsychotics (SGAs). The antipsychotics that followed the second generation, such as Abilify and Geodon, are sometimes referred to as the third-generation antipsychotics, but for our purposes, I'll keep them lumped with the SGAs.

Other families of medicines are named for their chemical structure or their effect at the synapse between neurons. For example, the tricyclic antidepressants (TCAs), such as Tofranil and Elavil, are called tricyclic because they have a three-ring molecular structure. The selective serotonin reuptake inhibitors (SSRIs), such as Prozac and Zoloft, work at the synapse by inhibiting the reuptake of the neurotransmitter serotonin. And the monoamine oxidase inhibitors (MAOIs) inhibit the enzyme monoamine oxidase in the synapse.

The stimulants, such as Ritalin and Adderall, are known for their effects of stimulating a physical response. This harks back to one of the first noted effects of amphetamine, namely, to stimulate breathing by dilating the bronchi, and to their first clinical use on those with narcolepsy, a disorder of untimely sleep (Goodman & Gilman, 1975). The family name "stimulants" will also seem a logical choice to anyone who has witnessed a patient who has taken an excessive dose of amphetamine tearing apart an emergency room and needing to be held down by three security officers.

Sometimes psychiatric medicines are grouped by the disorders they treat, for example, the antidepressants or the antipsychotics. This would also seem a logical way to categorize medicines, except that it assumes a clean distinction among the parts of the brain affected by each group of medicines. It would be as if the part of the brain involved in depression were distinct from the part involved with anxiety and that antidepressants went only to the former. This is simply not the case. Understanding the biology of psychiatric disorders is a field still in its infancy, so the exact location of depression cannot be neatly distinguished from that of anxiety. And in any case, we cannot tell any medicine exactly where we want it to go and what symptoms to treat. Instead, medicine travels throughout the body and throughout the brain, affecting many different regions. In short, the effect of antidepressants, whether the SSRIs, the TCAs, or the MAOIs, cannot be reduced to treating depression. They are also very effective at treating anxiety.

Similarly, some of the first-generation antipsychotics, such as Haldol, are effective antipsychotics and are also effective in reducing the tics of Tourette's disorder. In child and adolescent psychiatry, the SGAs, despite being labeled antipsychotics, are used far more often to treat bipolar disorder and extreme agitation than they are used for treating psychosis.

The alpha agonists, such as Catapres, named for their proactive effect on alpha receptors at noradrenergic receptors (don't worry; this will become clear in Chapter 3), are marketed for treating high blood pressure in adults and now for ADHD. But they are also used in child psychiatry to lessen tics, to treat attention deficit hyperactivity disorder, and to help children with insomnia. The point is not to restrict a medicine's use to the name under which it is classified.

Another factor necessary to understanding the classification, if not the naming, of medicines is the concept of isomers. Molecules are isomers of each other if they are the same molecule but oriented differently in space. For example, my two hands are identical, except that one is oriented with the thumb on the right and the other with the thumb on the left. Similarly, molecules can have a "right-handed" version (called *dextro*, which is from the Latin for "right") and a "left-handed" version (called *levo*, which is from the Latin for "left"). Sometimes one isomer is responsible for more of the medicine's clinical effect and the other is responsible for more of the side effects.

Some medicines are composed of both the right- and left-handed molecules. Others are composed of only one isomer (i.e., only the left or only the right). Sometimes a company will market the medicine that contains both isomers and also a medicine that contains only one isomer. For example, Ritalin contains both isomers of methylphenidate, while

Focalin, produced by the same manufacturer, contains only right-handed methylphenidate, namely dexmethylphenidate.

## The FDA

In addition to not making assumptions based on the medicine's family name, one should not assume that the Food and Drug Administration's approval defines exactly what a medicine treats. FDA approval reflects only the FDA's answer to a specific request by a drug company.

A drug company introduces a medicine only after many, many years of development costing hundreds of millions of dollars. It is not a simple process, and only one or two of about 10,000 compounds pass all the hurdles for approval (Upadhyaya, Gault, & Allen, 2009). After a medicine is developed, it is tested for short- and long-term safety on animals. If it passes that hurdle, it is tested for short-term safety on typically a few hundred healthy, non-disordered adults. If it passes that hurdle, it is tested for both safety and efficacy on a few thousand patients who have the disorder it is intended to treat. (After FDA approval, use continues to be monitored so that, as a larger number of patients are treated, rare side effects can be discovered.)

When the drug company has two double-blind, placebo-controlled studies of sufficient size to prove the medicine is effective in treating a specific disorder in a specific age group and adequate safety data, it requests FDA approval to market the medicine for that disorder in that age group. If approval is given, the company can advertise the medicine as treating that disorder in that age group. For example, if approval is given for a medicine to treat depression, the medicine can be advertised only to treat depression. And if a medicine is approved for the treatment of depression in adults, it cannot be advertised for the treatment of depression in children or adolescents.

Just as category names do not limit how a medicine functions, however, neither does FDA approval. A medicine might be effective in treating a disorder or an age group for which the drug company does not have approval. For example, some of the SSRI antidepressants are approved to treat depression in children older than 8 (Prozac) or 13 (Lexapro). But they and other SSRIs are probably even more effective in treating certain anxiety disorders in children, even though they do not have FDA approval for the treatment of anxiety. The manufacturer may simply have decided not to request FDA approval.

If a medicine is not FDA approved to be marketed for treating a specific disorder in a specific age group, physicians can still prescribe the medicine for that disorder or age group. This is called off-label prescribing, and it is legal, ethical, and commonly done. In fact, up to approximately 70% of the medicines prescribed in all pediatrics are prescribed off-label. Although the pediatrician thinks the medicine is effective on the basis of anecdotal evidence or research studies, the drug is not FDA approved for use in children. Different physicians, often on the basis of their own experience or their own personality traits (for example, cautious versus daring), have different thresholds for using medicines off-label.

If a medicine is effective in treating disorders in children, why wouldn't the drug company seek FDA approval to market it as such? Very simply, that is a business decision made by the company. The drug company may feel that the cost of proving to the FDA that the medicine is safe and effective in that age group is simply not worth the possible financial return, especially because doctors might prescribe it off-label anyway.

In 1997 the government initiated the Pediatric Exclusivity Program, offering companies financial incentives to perform clinical trials in children and adolescents. This has resulted in the approval of more medicines for use in this age group. The process, however, remains slow, arduous, and expensive. In addition, in the past, not all of the information garnered from this research made it into the public eye. Studies failing to prove the efficacy of a drug, in other words, might not have been shared. Putting these results on the FDA Web site was mandated in 2007.

# Generics

The last issue to discuss about types of medicines is the issue of generics. After a pharmaceutical company's patent for a particular medicine expires, other companies can produce their own version of that medicine. While the active molecule from the original medicine is used, the rest of what composes the medicine (the coloring, preservatives, and so on) might be different from the original medicine. The manufacturer must prove to the FDA that the generic is adequately absorbed and the like, albeit in a normal population of volunteers, not those with a disorder, and with some margin of difference from the original. The FDA assumes that the generic is as effective and safe as the original; therefore the manufacturer does not have to prove efficacy or safety of the generic.

While generic drugs are often equivalent to the brand-name drug, differences can exist, and so a person taking a brand-name drug might find, after switching to the generic, that the medicine is no longer effective or that the dose needs to be changed. The same can happen after a switch from one generic to another. Therefore it is wise for patients to learn to identify their medicine and, if they are taking a generic, to know which company produces it, so they can stay with the same, (with luck) effective generic.

## CHAPTER 3

# The Brain

N ow that we've discussed the classification of medicines, let's look at the field in which they work, namely, the brain.

## A Little History

Although Freud was trained as a neurologist in the late 19th century, his psychoanalytic theory of the early 20th century drifted far from his biological roots. As we saw in Chapter 1, by the mid-20th century, so much emphasis was placed on the psychological causes of human behavior, including psychosexual stages, defense mechanisms, and the theories of interpersonal relationships spawned by Freud's followers, that it was as if these processes of mind existed outside the person's body.

The 1950s and 1960s saw the advent of significant new psychiatric medicines, such as antipsychotics like Thorazine, and tricyclic anti-depressants like Norpramin. Within a few more decades, technology surged ahead with the development of such tools as computerized axial tomography (CAT), MRI, and PET scans. What had been the study of psychological processes was being transformed into the study of the brain, the organ within which these processes take place.

The late 20th century saw another leap forward in the development of new medicines that acted on the brain. By the early 21st century, it was clear to everyone from the research scientist to the psychoanalyst that whether the treatment was pharmacologic or psychological, it was acting on the brain. So before I explain the medicines used in treating children and adolescents, it is necessary to understand the basics of how the brain works.

# The Big Picture

Let's first take a look at the major parts of the brain. The brain sits fairly well protected in its lockbox, the skull, surrounded by three layers of coverings, the meninges, which lie between the brain and the skull. The outermost and toughest covering is the dura mater. The middle covering is the arachnoid mater, and the innermost covering is the pia mater, which clings, like plastic wrap, to the brain itself. The brain essentially floats in a fluid, called cerebrospinal fluid (CSF), which bathes the space between the arachnoid and pia mater. Researchers measure levels of chemicals produced in the brain, such as enzymes and neurotransmitter metabolites, by taking a small sample of CSF through a lumbar puncture, or spinal tap.

The brain itself is divided into different areas. I'll mention the functions of these different areas as if they were simple and straightforward. They are not. They are highly complex, multifunctioning, and interrelated.

The simplest way to approach the brain is to start at its lowest part, just above the spinal cord (see Figure 3.1). Here sits the brainstem, the most primitive part of the brain, which controls such vital functions as heart rate, breathing, and, through the reticular activating system, arousal.

Just above the brainstem is the diencephalon, containing such important structures as the hypothalamus, the thalamus, the limbic system, and the pituitary gland. Each of these plays an important role in regulating body function. The hypothalamus sits above the pituitary gland at the base of the front of the brain just behind the eyeballs. It

Figure 3.1 Diagram of the human brain

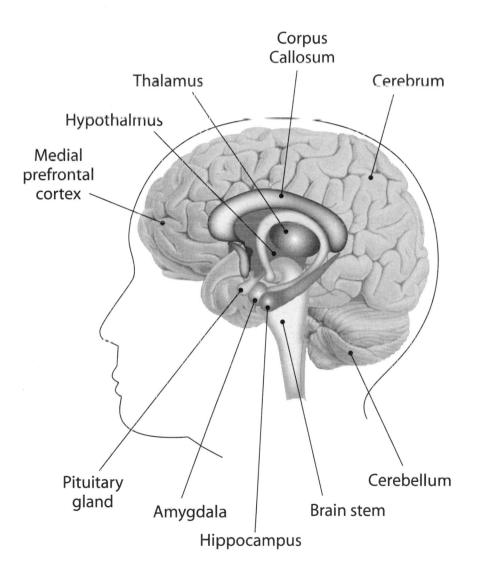

Corpus
Callosum

Thalamus

Cerebrum

Hypothalmus

Medial
prefrontal
cortex

Pituitary
gland

Amygdala

Hippocampus

Brain stem

Cerebellum

controls the pituitary gland by sending different releasing factors, which tell it when to release its hormones. These hormones in turn regulate such functions as temperature control, sleep, food intake, sexual functioning, and lactation. Medicines, such as the SGAs, can interfere with this connection between the hypothalamus and the pituitary, causing the side effects of breast enlargement and milk letdown. Just behind the hypothalamus, and deep within the cerebral hemispheres, is the limbic system, the most notable parts of which are the amygdala, involved in emotional states, and the hippocampus, involved in memory.

Around the thalamus is the basal ganglia system. This group of structures includes the substantia nigra and the caudate nucleus. The basal ganglia are part of the system known as the extrapyramidal system, which is crucial to controlling movement. Some psychiatric medicines, particularly the antipsychotic medicines, affect this system, causing debilitating side effects of movement.

Covering all these relatively primitive parts of the brain, and forming the outermost portion of the hemispheres, is the cerebral cortex; the cortex has many folds, or convolutions, giving it a very large surface area. The complex cerebral cortex is the part of the brain that most distinguishes humans from other animals. The two sides of the brain, the right and left hemispheres, are connected by a bundle of nerves called the corpus callosum, and each is further divided into lobes: the frontal lobes up front, the parietal lobes on the sides, the occipital lobes in the rear, and the temporal lobes below the parietal lobes.

The cortex is involved with many basic functions, such as vision, muscle action, and sensory perception. The cortex is also responsible for the higher functions that distinguish human beings from other species, including language and thought. Some regions of the cerebral cortex are responsible for particular functions. For example, the ability to use language to express oneself is located in the left temporal lobe. The frontal lobe, in particular the most forward (anterior) portion, called the prefrontal cortex, is involved in inhibitory behavior and other executive functioning, which is why it is implicated in certain deficits of children with attention deficit hyperactivity disorder, such as inhibiting impulses and planning ahead. The cortex is also involved in memory, attention span, and many other functions.

The cerebellum is nestled behind and below the cerebral hemispheres. Traditionally it has been seen as being important in coordinating movement. Recent research, however, is expanding that view of its functioning.

Last, the autonomic nervous system (ANS) is composed of two sets of neurons, the parasympathetic nervous system and the sympathetic nervous system, which are involved in flight-or-fight reactions and other automatic bodily functions. These include such functions as heart rate, artery tone, pupil dilation, bronchial constriction, and gastrointestinal movement.

## The Neuron

The most basic component of the brain and spinal cord is the nerve cell, or neuron. There are a few types of neurons, which differ structurally from one another. The easiest way to picture the model of a neuron is to imagine a child's stick figure of a man without arms but with thousands of legs of various lengths. Now add the dendrites, the thousands of projections coming out from the head of the figure, something like the coiffure of Jimi Hendrix, but with each hair having a multitude of split ends. These are neurons, and they come in lengths ranging from under an inch to a few feet.

The "head" of the stick figure is the cell body, housing most of the hardware that runs the cell and producing the neurotransmitters (see below). The long "body" of the neuron is called the axon, and the tip of each of the thousands of "legs" of the neuron is called the axon terminal.

The brain is composed of literally billions of neurons, perhaps 100 to 200 billion. Electricity flows from the tip of each dendrite down to the cell body, where a specialized part of the cell exists, the axon hillock. The electricity flowing down the dendrites all ends up in the axon hillock, which acts as a kind of central station. If sufficient electricity comes into the axon hillock, it sends the signal down the axon to the thousands of axon terminals.

Each axon terminal communicates the electrical message to a dendrite of the next neuron. The nature of this communication is key to understanding neurons and the way psychiatric medicines work. The axon terminal does not actually touch the next dendrite. There is a space between the two called the synapse. At the synapse, the electrical energy that comes down the axon is transformed into chemical energy, which crosses the synapse and then is transformed back into electrical energy at the dendrite on the far side of the synapse (see Figure 3.2).

Figure 3.2 Idealized mamalian neuron

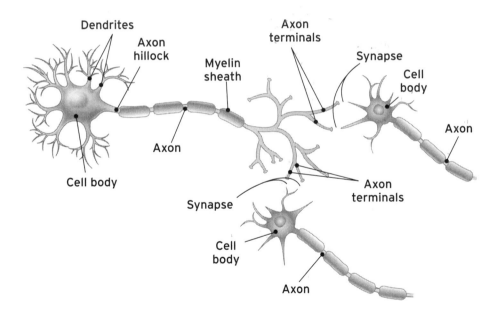

How is the electrical energy running down the axon transformed into chemical energy to cross the synapse? At the axon terminals are vesicles storing chemicals called neurotransmitters. The most famous of these neurotransmitters are norepinephrine, serotonin, and dopamine, but there are at least dozens of others, some already known and many more being discovered. These chemicals are released from the axon terminal of the presynaptic neuron, that is, the neuron "before" the synapse. The neurotransmitters cross the synapse and plug into receptor sites, like sockets, on the dendrite of the postsynaptic neuron. The chemical message is then transformed back into an electrical message, which continues down the next neuron.

After the message has been sent, the neurotransmitters detach from the receptor sites and are either broken down by enzymes or reabsorbed into the presynaptic neuron and "repackaged" in the vesicles, to be used again.

One complicating factor (there are many) is that sometimes a neuron will send one of its axon terminals not to communicate with the next neuron but back to itself. In this way the neuron is giving itself a message. The receptors on the neuron are called presynaptic receptors or auto-receptors. These receptors are responsive to a variety of neurotransmitters, which generally cause the neuron to inhibit itself.

That is the basic functioning of the brain: electrical energy continuously flowing down billions of neurons throughout the brain. One should not forget that each of these billions of neurons has thousands of dendrites and thousands of axon terminals. With a little multiplication one can begin to appreciate the enormous complexity of the brain with its trillions of connections.

## Neurotransmitters and Receptor Sites

Most psychiatric medicines work by changing brain chemistry at the synapse. This is called pharmacodynamics. Using different mechanisms, medicine alters the manner in which the presynaptic neuron communicates with the postsynaptic neuron. First we'll look at how neurons communicate across the synapse. Then we'll examine the neurotransmitters and the receptor sites on the postsynaptic neuron. Later chapters will address how specific medicines alter the neurotransmitters and the receptor sites.

There are dozens of different neurotransmitters, many as yet unidentified. The most recognized names include serotonin, dopamine, acetylcholine, histamine, norepinephrine (also called noradrenaline), and epinephrine (also called adrenaline). Less recognized neurotransmitters that are the subject of much current research are GABA (gamma-amino-butyric acid) and glutamate. As mentioned above, the neurotransmitters are produced in the cell body of the neuron, then travel down the axon through microtubules and are stored in vesicles in the axon terminal. Any particular neuron produces and stores one neurotransmitter. So, for example, some neurons are dopamine-producing neurons, also called dopaminergic. When signaled, the neuron releases the neurotransmitter into the synapse, which the neurotransmitter crosses, before plugging into a receptor site on the postsynaptic neuron.

The receptor site is composed of a protein on the dendrite of the postsynaptic neuron. Each receptor site receives only a particular neurotransmitter. For example, a histamine receptor accepts only histamine. There are, however, many different types of receptor sites for each neurotransmitter, and any particular postsynaptic neuron might have receptor sites for many neurotransmitters (e.g., for dopamine as well as for serotonin and norepinephrine). These neurotransmitter-specific sites serve different functions and are distinguished by number. So histamine receptor sites include an H1 site and an H2 site, both accepting histamine, but different from each other. When histamine crosses the synapse, it can recognize either of these sites. The complexity increases when one realizes that each neurotransmitter has not just two but multiple receptor sites. For example, at least 15 serotonin receptor sites have been identified.

In addition, the receptor sites on the dendrites are not static but can increase or decrease in number, thus changing the message sent. When receptor sites increase in number, the process is called upregulation. When they decrease in number, it is called downregulation. If this is becoming just a tad confusing or at least daunting, it serves as a well-deserved reminder that the brain is a very complicated and not nearly fully understood place. But given that it houses our entire experience of life, we should expect nothing less.

The brain's great flexibility is accomplished through having a variety of receptor sites but only a relatively small number of neurotransmitters. The brain uses up neurotransmitters the way old-time accountants used up pencils. Over the course of evolution, the brain developed a versatile system of producing neurotransmitters efficiently and putting its resources into developing specialized receptor sites.

Once the neurotransmitter has finished its task at the receptor site, it is released back into the synapse. In the synapse it has one of two fates. Either it is broken down, or metabolized, by enzymes in the synapse and prepared for excretion, or it is reabsorbed into the presynaptic neuron and repackaged for its next mission. Different enzymes are used to break down specific neurotransmitters. For example, one enzyme is mono-amine oxidase, which metabolizes neurotransmitters with a single amine group (monoamines), such as norepinephrine.

Recent research has suggested that genetically determined differences in certain synaptic enzyme levels and receptors are likely to be important to the development of some psychiatric disorders as well as the responses of individual patients to particular medicines. On the horizon is the possibility that knowledge of one's genetic code will aid both diagnosing a disorder and selecting the most effective medication.

## How Psychiatric Medicines Work

As mentioned above, most psychiatric medicines work at the synapse, either stimulating or blocking the effect of a given neurotransmitter-receptor combination. A medicine that blocks a particular neurotransmitter is said to be an antagonist. One that stimulates the effect of a neurotransmitter is said to be an agonist.

Medicines accomplish their tasks at different points in the communication across the synapse. The most common manner in which medicines block transmission is by blocking the receptor site. For example, antipsychotic medicines have their antipsychotic effect by blocking the D2 receptor of dopamine. Medicines can have an agonist effect by increasing the amount of a neurotransmitter or the time that neurotransmitter sits in the synapse. This can be accomplished either by stimulating the presynaptic neuron to release more of a neurotransmitter or by blocking the reuptake of the neurotransmitter back into the presynaptic neuron. For example, amphetamine stimulates the release of dopamine into the synapse, while the SSRIs, or selective serotonin reuptake inhibitors, block the reuptake of serotonin. Medicines can also inhibit the enzymes used to break down a neurotransmitter. For example, the monoamine oxidase inhibitors, or MAOIs, are antidepressants that inhibit this enzyme, thus allowing more norepinephrine to accumulate in the synapse.

## The Specific Neurotransmitters

The various regions of the brain are interconnected by bundles of neurons, often called tracks or pathways, each using a particular neurotransmitter. There are many more pathways than there are neurotransmitters, however, and so a particular neurotransmitter will commonly be used for multiple unrelated purposes. For example, one bundle of dopamine-containing neurons (the nigrostriatal pathway) runs from the substantia nigra to the striatum and affects certain muscle movements. Another bundle of dopamine-containing neurons (the mesolimbic pathway) runs from the brainstem at the bottom of the brain to the limbic system of the brain and affects pleasure seeking and other functions. Another bundle runs from the hypothalamus to the pituitary gland at the base of the brain and affects a lactating woman's milk letdown. And still another (the mesocortical pathway) runs from the brainstem up to the cerebral cortex and affects cognition and still other functions.

This use of one neurotransmitter by many pathways has a few important implications. When a medicine that blocks dopamine at the D2 receptor is used, the medicine cannot distinguish one pathway from another and so affects all dopamine-containing pathways of neurons. Because the medicine affects all the pathways, it causes many different effects. Some of these are desired, and others we label side effects. The more specific a medicine is at pinpointing only certain receptors or certain pathways, the more control the prescribing physician has. In our dopamine example, blocking the D2 receptors of some pathways stops hallucinations, but blocking others might cause a movement disorder.

Not only do medicines affect all the pathways of a given neurotransmitter, but also a particular medicine might affect a number of different neurotransmitters in a number of different pathways. Medicines that affect many neurotransmitters are said to be "dirty." This is not an insult, just a way of saying that a medicine is nonspecific in what it affects. So, for example, the tricyclic antidepressants block norepinephrine reuptake, serotonin reuptake, postsynaptic histamine receptors, and postsynaptic acetylcholine receptors. Each of these blockades causes benefits or side effects.

Being "dirty" is not necessarily bad. Sometimes it's a way for one medicine to have many effects. But forfeiting control is often the cost.

Let's return to the specific neurotransmitters. As noted above, there are dozens of neurotransmitters, and more are being discovered. Some are very involved in our current understanding of psychiatric illness and therefore the development of psychiatric medicines. I list here the most commonly studied neurotransmitters.

### Serotonin

Serotonin is also called 5-hydoxytryptamine, or 5-HT. It is produced from the amino acid tryptamine. It is located not just in the brain but in many parts of the body, especially the gastrointestinal (GI) tract, where it increases GI contractions. It affects many of the body's functions including mood, sleep, sex, and body temperature. Interestingly, during fetal development, serotonin acts not as a neurotransmitter but as an organizing signal to neural development in parts of the brain in which it does not act during adulthood (Weller, AACAP, January 2007).

There are many different receptor sites for serotonin. These are divided into families, designated as 5-HT1, 5-HT2, 5-HT3, and so on. These families are further subdivided. After it functions at the synapse, serotonin is either reabsorbed or metabolized into 5-hydroxyindoleacetic acid (5-HIAA). This substance is sometimes measured as a means of determining the brain's level of serotonin activity, although one can appreciate that it is difficult to distinguish how much 5-HIAA originated from the brain and how much from the plentiful serotonin in the gut. The involvement of serotonin in psychiatric disorders revolves mostly around depression, anxiety disorders, and obsessive-compulsive disorder. The selective serotonin reuptake inhibitors (SSRIs) are medicines that block the reuptake of serotonin into the presynaptic neuron.

## Dopamine

Dopamine is a catecholamine (meaning its chemical structure contains a catechol group and an amine group) and is the product of the transformation of tyrosine, an amino acid. As noted already, it is located in different parts of the brain and, depending on the pathway, is involved in everything from psychosis to attention span to response to rewards to milk letdown during lactation. The effect of dopamine at the D2 receptor, especially in the mesolimbic pathway, is crucial in the formation of psychotic symptoms such as hallucinations and delusions. Antipsychotic medicines block the D2 receptor. Substances that stimulate the D2 receptor, such as cocaine, can cause these psychotic symptoms. After it has been released from the receptor site, dopamine, like norepinephrine, is metabolized by either monoamine oxidase (MAO) or catechol-o-methyltransferase (COMT).

## Norepinephrine

Like dopamine, norepinephrine (or noradrenaline) is a catecholamine and also the product of the transformation of tyrosine. After tyrosine is metabolized into dopamine, some of the dopamine is further metabolized into norepinephrine. The cell bodies that produce norepinephrine are said to be noradrenergic and are located in the locus coeruleus in the center of the brain. The axons of these neurons project widely throughout the brain, including to the cortex, the cerebellum, and the limbic system, down into the spinal cord and through the autonomic nervous system. The receptors affected by norepinephrine (and epinephrine) are divided into the alpha and beta receptors, each of which has subsets. Medicines labeled beta blockers block the effect of norepinephrine at the beta receptor, thus slowing the heart and decreasing blood pressure. After norepinephrine is released from the receptor, some is reabsorbed into the presynaptic neuron, and some is metabolized by the enzymes MAO and COMT.

## Epinephrine

Epinephrine (or adrenaline) is another catecholamine and is derived from norepinephrine. Like norepinephrine, epinephrine is a neurotransmitter used by the autonomic nervous system. The neurons that release epinephrine are said to be adrenergic. Epinephrine is particularly important in the fight-or-flight response we are programmed to use in emergencies, speeding our heart rate, dilating our pupils, increasing blood flow to muscles, and decreasing blood flow to organs not useful in emergencies. Most of the body's epinephrine is released not from neurons, however, but from the adrenal medulla of the adrenal glands, located over the kidneys. Like norepinephrine, epinephrine affects the alpha and beta receptors of the autonomic nervous system.

## Acetylcholine

Acetylcholine (ACh) is the product of the combination of acetate and choline. It is located at synapses throughout the parasympathetic nervous system of the autonomic nervous system, the system responsible for the body's automatic functions, such as causing the heart to beat and the bowels to contract. These neurons are said to be cholinergic. Acetylcholine is also the chemical that transmits messages from the ends of neurons to muscles, so that a lack of ACh impairs the ability of neurons to communicate effectively with muscles.

In psychiatry ACh is of importance in two ways. First, it is the neurotransmitter used in many of the neurons important in cognition. Medicines used to treat Alzheimer's disease attempt to increase the level of ACh to impede the loss of cognitive function plaguing Alzheimer's patients. ACh is also important because, as we'll see, many of the medicines used in psychiatry over the years have been anticholinergic; that is, they block ACh at the synapse. This leads to many side effects such as dry mouth and constipation. When ACh has finished its work at the synapse, it is metabolized by an enzyme called acetylcholinesterase. The medicines used to treat Alzheimer's, such as donepezil (Aricept), increase the level of ACh by inhibiting acetylcholinesterase. These medicines function reversibly, meaning that they inhibit the enzyme temporarily. Notably, chemicals that are irreversible inhibitors of acetylcholinesterase interfere with neuron control of muscles, causing paralysis. These have been used as insecticides and as nerve gas (Sarin) by the military.

## Histamine

Histamine is formed from the amino acid histidine. The histamine located in mast cells and basophils, a type of white blood cell, is released during allergic reactions, causing inflammation with its pain, swelling, and itching. Histamine is also located in the lining of the stomach. In some of the brain's neuronal pathways, histamine also acts as a neurotransmitter. Its blockade in the brain, such as by antihistamines, causes sedation.

## Glutamate

Glutamate is an excitatory neurotransmitter. It affects different sites, the best known of which is the NMDA (N-methyl-d-aspartate) receptor, which is being investigated for its role in schizophrenia. Phencyclidine (PCP), a drug of abuse, is thought to have its effect by binding the NMDA receptor.

## Gamma-Aminobutyric Acid

Gamma-aminobutyric acid (GABA) is an inhibitory neurotransmitter in that it decreases neuron activity. It is made from glutamate and appears in many locations in the brain, including the cortex, cerebellum, and hippocampus. There are different GABA receptors located throughout the brain. Medicines that are GABA agonists include the benzodiazepines, such as diazepam (Valium); the hypnotics, such as a zolpidem (Ambien); and the barbiturates.

That, in short, is a bird's-eye view of the most complex and least understood object on earth—the brain. Billions of neurons and trillions of connections all throb with electrical energy. I'll go on to discuss the medicines that affect the way electrical energy is changed to chemical energy and back to electrical energy at the synapse.

## CHAPTER 4

# The Life Cycle of a Medicine

Like most people, I experience a sense of magic whenever I take a medicine. My awareness of, or even concern for, the medicine's whereabouts stops after I put it in my mouth and drink the water that sends it on its way. As if by magic, it does its work and I am relieved of pain or infection or whatever.

But magic is a state of mind and cures nothing beyond its placebo effect. In reality, after the medicine disappears in my mouth, it voyages through my body to destinations of my choosing and some that, if asked, I would prefer it avoid. Ultimately it leaves my body a changed substance. Appreciating this life cycle of medicine is important in understanding its benefits and dangers.

This movement of any medicine through the body over the course of time is called pharmacokinetics. The process can be divided into four phases: the absorption of the medicine into the body; its distribution through the body; its metabolism, or the way it is broken down; and its elimination from the body.

## Absorption and Distribution

Unless medicine is placed directly into the target organ, it must access the bloodstream, which acts like an interstate highway system. Although the patient often wants the medicine to reach only one particular organ, this circulatory system carries the medicine throughout the body. There are a number of ways to get medicine into the bloodstream. One can shoot it directly into the bloodstream, such as when a hospitalized patient is given intravenous medicine. One can inhale the medicine so it is absorbed through the blood vessels of the nose. Most commonly, however, medicine is swallowed.

When it arrives in the stomach, and especially the small intestine, the medicine is absorbed through the cells that line the gut wall and into the blood vessels of the gut. If the medicine is a tablet, it first breaks up, and its molecules are absorbed. If the medicine is a liquid, it is absorbed more quickly. Different people absorb medicine at different rates, adding to each person's unique experience with medicine. In addition, medicine is generally absorbed faster, albeit sometimes with gastrointestinal distress, when taken on an empty stomach. Food can minimize the stomachache some children complain of when taking certain medicines. But food also sometimes affects absorption. For example, methylphenidate is better absorbed when there is food in the stomach. By contrast, Seroquel SR is long acting only if it is taken on an empty stomach.

As the medicine is absorbed through the gut lining, it is sometimes changed by some of the enzymes in the cells of that lining, so that the amount of medicine ingested is lessened even before it reaches the bloodstream.

In the bloodstream, some of the medicine is bound to proteins and some remains free of protein. The larger size of the protein-bound molecules prevents them from leaving the bloodstream; only the free medicine is able to leave the bloodstream and enter the target organ. Throughout most of the body there is enough space between cells of the capillaries, the smallest blood vessels, for the medicine to squeeze through and gain access to the cell. The brain, however, is different. Within the brain, capillary cells are lined up shoulder to shoulder, preventing many substances from entering. This is called the blood-brain barrier (BBB), and only some substances can cross it. Medicines that are fat soluble enter more quickly.

## Metabolism

Within a minute of being absorbed into the bloodstream, the medicine has been carried throughout the body—but not before it makes an important stop. One of the first places where the blood takes the medicine is to the liver, the organ in charge of clearing the body of toxins and foreign substances. Unaware that you have chosen to put this helpful substance into your body, the liver immediately tries to protect the body by metabolizing some of the medicine into other substances. This metabolism before the medicine makes it to its destination is called first-pass metabolism, and it leaves you with a bit less medicine than you started with.

The distribution and metabolism of medicine in children is affected by their unique body structure. For example, compared to those of adults, children's livers account for a greater proportion of their body weight. In addition, children have more body water, less body fat, and less of the protein albumin to bind the molecules of medicine. All these differences help children metabolize medicines faster than adults. This makes it difficult to use body weight simply to extrapolate an adult dose to one for a child and raises the risk of underdosing the child, who is processing the medicine faster than an adult. It also means that children are more prone to the withdrawal symptoms that occur when a medicine is stopped abruptly or when a short-acting medicine is simply metabolized quickly. As we'll see in future chapters, these considerations must be balanced against the tendency of young children to be more sensitive than adults to certain medicines, such as stimulants.

When children reach adolescence, the sexes go through obvious changes, some of which affect the life cycle of medicine. In particular, girls increase their percentage of body fat and decrease their percentage of body water. Boys do the opposite.

Adults, adolescents, and children, however, share much about the basics of metabolism. In general, there are two metabolic systems: the Phase I system, or cytochrome P450 system (P450), which changes the molecule of medicine, and the Phase II system, in which the metabolized medicine is attached to other molecules in preparation for excretion. Some medicines undergo both Phase I and Phase II, and others undergo only one or the other. Currently, much research is focused on the cytochrome P450 system. Most psychiatric medicines are metabolized, at least in part, by this complex system of enzymes, and knowledge of its workings impacts the way psychiatric medicines are prescribed.

The metabolic pathways of medicines are also important because these are often the bases through which medicines interact. That is, if one medicine affects the metabolic pathway of another, it can increase or decrease the amount of the second medicine in the bloodstream.

The P450 system is a group of at least a few hundred enzymes that originated in living things about 3.5 billion years ago and are coded for genetically in each of us. Their purpose is to help metabolize substances that arise directly within our bodies, such as steroids, as well as foreign substances, such as the toxins in the plants eaten by our ancestors. This enzyme system fairly indiscriminately metabolizes all foreign substances, medicine being a relatively recent addition in human history. While it is not fully matured at birth, by the time we reach three years of age, it is well developed.

The P450 enzymes are coded for by our genes. There are families and subfamilies of these enzymes based on their similarity to one another, and their names convey this similarity. For example, the cytochrome P450 enzymes 1A1 and 1B1 are in the same family, indicated by the first 1, but different subfamilies, indicated by the A and B. The second 1s indicate further subfamilies. While humans have dozens of these enzymes, six do the lion's share of the work of metabolizing the medicines discussed here. These enzymes are 1A2, 3A4, 2C9, 2C19, 2D6, and 2E1. These enzymes influence the life cycle of many psychiatric medicines and, it is very important to note, the way medicines impact one another.

Different medicines are metabolized by different P450 enzymes. For example, fluvoxamine (Luvox) is metabolized by the enzymes 1A2 and 2D6. Paroxetine (Paxil) is metabolized by only one enzyme, and sertraline (Zoloft) is metabolized by five enzymes. The more enzymes the medicine is metabolized by, the more assured the patient should be that if anything happens to one of those enzymes, others will pick up the slack and metabolize the medicine.

While medicines are changed by the P450 enzymes, many medicines also change these enzymes in turn. They are either enzyme inducers, causing an increase in the amount and therefore the efficiency of the enzyme, or enzyme inhibitors, which cause a decrease in their efficiency. Each medicine has its own profile concerning the degree to which it has these inducing or inhibiting effects on different enzymes. For example, fluoxetine is a weak inhibitor of 1A2 but a strong inhibitor of 2D6. Carbamazepine is a strong inducer of 3A4. Even "natural" substances and foods impact this process. For example, St. John's wort is an inducer of 3A4, and broccoli is an inducer of 1A2. Chronic smoking is also an inducer of 1A2.

To complicate matters, some psychiatric medicines either inhibit or induce the enzymes by which they are metabolized. For example, fluoxetine is metabolized by many enzymes, including 2D6. Fluoxetine is also an inhibitor of 2D6. Therefore fluoxetine is inhibiting one of the enzymes that should be metabolizing it. The longer one takes fluoxetine, the more 2D6 is inhibited, and the more likely it is that the level of fluoxetine in the body will rise. Luckily other enzymes also metabolize fluoxetine. Nevertheless, the confusing nature of drug metabolism is evident.

It is virtually impossible to remember all the effects of all the medicines and all the foods on all the enzymes. And in fact, because they are only weak effects, many of them are negligible. Sometimes, however, they are more potent and impact the dose and effect of the medicine.

*Melissa, who is 18 years old, is diagnosed with bipolar disorder. Her doctor starts Melissa on lamotrigine (Lamictal) for depression. After about three months, the medicine is seen as ineffective. A consultant suggests that the birth control pills Melissa is taking might be inducing (increasing) the enzymes that metabolize lamotrigine, thus effectively lowering the blood concentration of the medicine. Melissa's physician increases the dose of lamotrigine, thus increasing its concentration, and after a few weeks Melissa is less depressed.*

An additional lesson to draw from these interactions is that if one medicine is discontinued, its effect on enzyme levels ceases, so the blood level of the medicine metabolized by those enzymes changes. For example, if a patient is doing well on atomoxetine and fluoxetine, the proper dose of each having been adjusted, but then fluoxetine is stopped, the fluoxetine will no longer be inhibiting 2D6, and the atomoxetine will be metabolized more quickly, thus lowering its blood levels. The point is that starting and stopping other medicines must be monitored.

There's an important rub to understanding the P450 enzymes and their efficiencies. Although most people will have a fairly standard amount of each of these enzymes, some people, depending on race, sex, and the like, might have much more or less of the enzyme than other people. That is, their genes have coded for more or less of that enzyme. If one has a lot of the enzyme, the enzyme works very efficiently, and one is said to be an ultraextensive or ultrarapid metabolizer. If one is relatively deficient in that enzyme, the enzyme works slowly, and one is said to be a poor metabolizer.

For example, 7–10% of the Caucasian population are thought to be poor metabolizers at 2D6. That is, they have less, or at least less functional, 2D6 than most other Caucasians. The same is true of 1–8% of Africans and 1–3% of East Asians (Vitiello, 2008). If they are taking a medicine that is metabolized by 2D6, the medicine will be metabolized much more slowly, and they will therefore require a lower dose. For these people, the usual dose might be toxic. By contrast, if one is an ultraextensive metabolizer at a particular enzyme, one might require a higher dose of a medicine metabolized at that enzyme. Some laboratories are beginning to offer patients the opportunity to discover whether they are poor or ultraextensive metabolizers at different P450 enzymes.

The duration for which one takes medicine and the dose might also impact how it is metabolized. For example, a dose of sertraline stays in the bloodstream longer when given at higher doses. So initially, when sertraline is started at lower doses in children and adolescents, it should be given twice daily, but when doses have increased, it can be changed to once daily.

To put aside the details of the different enzyme systems, when a medicine is metabolized, it is changed into a different chemical or metabolite of the original medicine. While many of the metabolites are inactive substances that are simply more readily excreted than the original, some metabolites might be as pharmacologically effective as the original medicine. For example, the tricyclic antidepressant imipramine

(Tofranil) is metabolized to, among other things, desipramine. The metabolite desipramine is itself an active molecule and is marketed separately as Norpramin.

# Elimination

After medicine is metabolized, it is excreted from the body, usually via urine, but also through feces and sweat. This represents the elimination phase. The number of hours it takes half the medicine in the body to be eliminated is called the elimination half-life. Because their liver is a greater percentage of their body weight, children metabolize medicines faster than adults. Therefore the half-life of a medicine is usually shorter in a child than in an adult.

Allow me a brief aside about half-life. The half-life is important in determining not only how long it takes the body to eliminate a medicine but also how long, once the medicine is started, it takes the body to build up a functional amount of medicine. In other words, imagine that at 6 A.M. you give a patient medicine with a half-life of 6 hours. That means that after 6 hours, at noon, only 50% of the medicine is still present; after 12 hours, at 6 P.M., only 25% of the original medicine is present; and after 18 hours, at midnight, only 12.5% of the original medicine is present. Now, suppose you simultaneously had given the same medicine to another patient at 6 A.M., but to this patient you gave a second dose of the medicine at noon, just as the first dose was at its 50% level. Suddenly the blood level would jump to about the 150% level. That is, 100% of the second dose would be present plus 50% of the first dose. Now, suppose you gave a third dose at 6 P.M. This would bump the blood level yet again.

When all is said and done, if you give a medicine at every half-life milestone (i.e., every 6 hours for a medicine whose half-life is 6 hours), then it takes five doses of medicine to reach a steady level of medicine, or a plateau. This is an important consideration, because medicines that require a constant level need to be given for five half-lives before they reach that level.

The medicines used in child psychiatry range from short-elimination half-lives of about 3–4 hours (methylphenidate) to the very long-elimination half-life of about 10–14 days of fluoxetine and norfluoxetine (the very active metabolite of fluoxetine). Practically speaking, this means, on the one hand, that if one wanted continued activity from a medicine such as methylphenidate, one would have to take it again after just a few hours. On the other hand, if one forgot to take fluoxetine on Thursday, there is sufficient medicine in one's bloodstream from Wednesday to work through Thursday and into Friday, when, one hopes, you'd remember to take the medicine. Of course, these numbers are averages. Even if a given individual is not a slow or ultraextensive metabolizer, he or she still might be different from the average.

Another practical difference among medicines with different half-lives is that those with short half-lives are more likely to cause a rebound after they wear off. That is, after a short-acting medicine wears off, the patient might return to his or her original symptoms and then some. For example, those taking a short-acting benzodiazepine to help them fall asleep might fall asleep readily, but a few hours later experience a rebound increase in wakefulness. Longer-acting medicines are less likely to cause that rebound.

Half-life, however, is not synonymous with the length of time in which the medicine is effective. Nor is it synonymous with the length of time in which side effects can be observed. That is, even though the half-life of a medicine is 8 hours, enough receptor sites might be occupied at 12 hours to cause a side effect. Half-life is simply a reasonable approximation of how long side effects may occur. For example, one patient of mine experienced improved focus for about 8 hours while on Focalin XR but decreased appetite for about 12 hours.

If one graphs the dose of medicine on the x-axis and the response to the medicine on the y-axis, one usually finds that the results can be expressed in one of two graphs. Some—for example, the effect of the stimulants, such as methylphenidate, on hyperactivity—are linear. That is, as the dose increases, the response increases. A small dose leads to a small response, and a larger dose leads to a larger response. If one weren't stopped by side effects, one would simply keep increasing the dose. The other graph is like an inverted U. That is, there is little response at low doses and at high doses but maximum response at the middle doses. These medicines, such as nortriptyline, are said to have a therapeutic window. That is, the middle blood level of medicine leads to the optimal effect of the medicine.

For most medicines, readily available assays to determine the level of medicine in the blood are not available. Or if they are available, the blood level that corresponds to optimal response to the medicine has not been determined. For some medicines, however, these blood levels are available, and there is research that supports a particular blood level of the medicine as the most effective. When this information is available, for example, as it is for lithium, the blood level is a major help in determining the proper dose. In fact the crucial factor is not really blood level or dose but rather the number of receptor sites (or other local effects) affected by the medicine. A blood level of medicine is only a proxy for the neuronal change, and the dose given is only a proxy for blood level.

While finding the correct dose is important, for many medicines used in psychiatry the amount of time one takes the medicine is equally important. Some medicines rapidly enter the brain and cause the neurochemical changes at the synapse that lead to the desired clinical changes. Others, however, take lots of time, often weeks or even months, to change the synapse enough to cause clinical effects. For example, the SSRIs typically take weeks to effect clinical change.

Sometimes, whether out of frustration or because the number of days allowed in the hospital is minimal, doses are increased quickly. This does not cause the medicine to work any faster. In fact this overly zealous intervention can cause the best dose to be bypassed, resulting in the patient's being on an unnecessarily high dose and thus more prone to side effects that lead to the patient's discontinuing the medicine altogether. Fitting to psychiatry, its medicines, like psychotherapy, often take some time and patience.

At the level of the synapse, it is also important to note that the changes that took so long to develop can take a while to dismantle. Clinically, this means that even though a medicine is stopped, the side effects caused by the medicine, which are also a function of the synaptic changes, might go on for a while. It also means, however, that the beneficial neuronal changes caused by the medicine might not change back as soon as the medicine is discontinued. They may endure for a few weeks or months. This is not true of all medicines, but it is true of some.

To return to blood levels, whether routinely ascertained or not, they are also crucial in determining a medicine's therapeutic index. This is the ratio of a toxic dose of the medicine to the therapeutic dose. In other words, if a medicine had a therapeutic index of 1.0, that would mean the toxic level of medicine and the therapeutic level were equal, implying obviously that the medicine could not be used. Some medicines, such as the SSRIs, have very high therapeutic indices, meaning that the blood level required for the medicine to be toxic is thankfully much higher than the therapeutic dose. Other medicines, however, such as lithium, have a low therapeutic index, implying that the toxic level of the medicine is just a tad above the therapeutic level. These are medicines that need to be used with great caution.

In terms of elimination, it is also important to note that when one takes a second dose of medicine after half of the first dose of medicine is eliminated from the body, the second dose enters the body with half the first dose still present. That means that even if the second dose is lower, it can still reach the same blood level as the first. This is pertinent when a patient is using short-acting medicines, like methylphenidate, in which the second dose of the day, taken at noon, can be lower than the dose taken earlier that day because it enters the body while half of the first dose is still present.

## CHAPTER 5

# Deciding to Use a Medicine

As we've seen, the decision to take medicine, whether prescribed or not, has a magical quality. In the best-case scenario, the physician brings knowledge, experience, and authority, while the patient brings hope and expectation for success. These factors alone will result in some degree of effectiveness in treating many ailments with almost any treatment. This is the placebo response, or the success of sham treatments, and as we'll see, it can be a powerful force in child psychiatry, as it is in all of medicine.

While the experienced clinician knows that factors other than the actual treatment are instrumental in causing any treatment to be effective, the responsible clinician does not rely solely on these factors, but should also understand and explain to the patient the chances that a given treatment will be effective and the chances that the treatment will cause side effects. These become the basis of the risk-benefit ratio, the basic tool underlying all clinical decisions in the treatment of all patients.

Ultimately, the risks and benefits of a treatment are weighed against those of other treatments and against the risks and benefits of not pursuing any treatment. First, however, one must measure the potential benefits and risks for a particular treatment, in this case, medicine. This chapter reviews how that is done.

## Measuring Benefit

Many factors that affect a treatment's efficacy cannot be quantified. Nevertheless, the extent to which a treatment is better than a sham treatment can and, when possible, should be quantified. This is the basis for establishing the benefit that will be weighed against the risk of that treatment.

For centuries, physicians prescribed treatments that seemed correct in their time. From incantations to herbal ointments to bloodletting, physicians have tried them all. Some patients improved. Others did not. Those who improved often did so because of all the intangible factors that go into accruing benefit, whether trust in the clinician, the drama of the healing event, or the wish that the treatment might be effective. These hopes and expectations bring with them not yet understood changes in brain chemistry that underlie the placebo response.

The advent of the scientific method, however, has demanded that physicians use more than their powers of persuasion in convincing a patient that medicine will work. It is expected that the clinician will use treatments that are more effective than placebo and can roughly quantify the chance that the treatment will be effective. Unfortunately, this is a standard that, until recent decades, was rarely met in child psychiatry. Instead, child psychiatrists, bereft of controlled data, were left to decide that a treatment was beneficial on the basis of their philosophical orientation and the common wisdom. When I was in training in the early 1980s, the program in which I trained was oriented toward psychoanalytic psychotherapy. So that was the treatment most children and adolescents received. No great body of controlled data supported or disputed those decisions. Rather, we made an almost philosophical decision supported by belief in the theory that underlay the treatment approach and detailed case studies by those who believed the underlying theory. In truth, some researchers did try to put those treatments to the scientific test. The research was complicated and difficult, however, and the results were often vague.

Over recent decades, with the increased use of medicine, the tradition within psychiatry of proving that a treatment is more effective than placebo has grown. It has even broadened to include efforts to prove the effectiveness of various types of psychotherapy. Now, given these quantitative data, the different therapies can be compared with one another and with combinations of therapies. This is a huge step forward in finding the most effective treatment for a given disorder.

So, how is any treatment's benefit suspected, and how is it then proven? Different roads lead to proving the benefit of a treatment.

Sometimes a drug company develops a medicine for a particular purpose. This usually takes many years, even decades, from start to finish. The drug company then must show that the medicine is effective and safe before the FDA approves it to be advertised and sold to treat a particular disorder in a particular age group.

Other times a medicine is already being marketed for a particular disorder, but the drug company might not want to pursue approval to use the medicine for treating other disorders or age groups. Doctors, however, might prescribe the medicine off-label, that is, to an age group or for a disorder for which the medicine does not have FDA approval. As I've discussed, this is legal and ethical and is done every day by virtually all doctors.

When a medicine is first prescribed off-label, the clinician might be impressed with the result and write a report about a case or small series of cases that show the medicine is effective. This is the beginning of building a database to prove a medicine's benefit. It is, however, only the beginning. It is no more the final proof than the unhatched egg of an eagle is the adult eagle that soars overhead.

Many factors stand in the way of reaching the hoped-for conclusion. The "proof" of the psychotherapy prescribed when I was in training usually consisted of case reports by well-known clinicians with illustrious professional backgrounds. Case reports can be dramatic, hopeful, and convincing. But they are not conclusive. In fact they are often ultimately proven to be incorrect.

When a number of cases garner sufficient interest, a researcher might do a chart review. This consists of reviewing the medical records of a large number of patients who were treated off-label with a particular medicine and seeing how they fared. The benefit of this research is that it is chart based, and so one can gather information on a lot of patients fairly easily. The negative side of this research is that one has to hope the diagnoses and assessments of progress made on these patients were accurate. The results can also be confounded because many patients probably had diagnoses other than the one being studied and were taking other medicines and treatments. Maybe one of the other disorders improved, or perhaps one of the other medicines was effective.

If a chart review shows that a medicine may possibly have been effective, a researcher might then do an open trial of the medicine. That consists of gathering a group of subjects who are diagnosed with a particular disorder in a standardized way so there's little argument afterward about whether the presumed diagnosis was accurate. The researcher also tries to minimize the other medicines being taken simultaneously. The patients are then treated with the medicine in question, and the researchers observe and assess the patients' progress. The problem with open trials is that the researcher and the patient know that the patient is receiving the medicine in question. So when assessing the patient's progress, the researcher and the patient are influenced by their desire for the medicine to be effective. People tend to see what they want to see, and researchers are no different. Open trials can result in overly optimistic results.

If open trials are effective, the medicine is then put to a more rigorous test, namely, the double-blind, placebo-controlled (DBPC) trial. This trial gathers a group of patients all diagnosed with the same disorder in a standardized manner, then randomly divides them into two groups, so that the two groups are of about the same age, intelligence, social stratum, and all other factors that might influence the outcome of the trial. One group is then treated with the medicine (or other treatment to be tested), and the other group receives placebo, a pill identical to the medicine but not containing the actual medicine. Neither researchers nor patients, however, know who is taking active medicine or placebo. Both groups are said to be "blind"; hence the term *double-blind*.

Because treatment with placebo leads to varying degrees of improvement for patients with different disorders, the importance of comparing medicine to placebo cannot be overemphasized. A medicine needs to prove itself better than placebo to be worth the risk of side effects. If the medicine is no better than placebo, doctors might as well rely on their powers of persuasion and treat with an innocuous substance or procedure, and the patients can forgo the risk of medicine.

The importance of the placebo trial is demonstrated by the history of child psychiatry with the SSRI antidepressants. In many trials these medicines decrease the depression of perhaps 60% of patients. In those same trials, however, about 40–50% of patients improved by taking placebo. This difference is often not statistically significant, thus leaving open to question whether some of these medicines are effective in youth depression or if placebo is sufficient to treat many cases.

The double-blind trial is the gold standard of scientific proofs. But even it is not infallible. As we've seen, patients with some disorders frequently respond to placebo, raising the intriguing question of how that happens. Has the study proven that medicine isn't effective or that placebo is? The underlying issues that lead to the efficacy of placebo beg to be understood, as they become important in designing studies that effectively prove a medicine's worth.

Another difficulty with the DBPC trial lies in the diagnostic complexity of the subjects and the number of patients. Many patients with psychiatric illnesses are complex, meaning that they have more than one diagnosis. Which disorder improved? Finding patients who have only one diagnosis is challenging. Also a DBPC trial with 10 subjects in each group is far less convincing than a trial with 100 subjects in each group. Chance plays a greater role with 10 subjects but is far less likely to do so with 100 subjects. In addition, there's no accounting for unknown factors. Two research centers studying the same medicine can arrive at different conclusions. A DBPC trial proving the efficacy of a medicine at one research center gathers great weight if the results are repeated at another center.

A host of other factors influence research results as well. These include who is funding the study, as it has been shown that research paid for by drug companies is more likely to favor medicine over placebo. The duration of treatment and dose of medicine are also important factors. If medicine takes four weeks to act, then a two-week trial puts the medicine at an unfair disadvantage. And if an insufficient dose of medicine is used, the medicine is again unfairly penalized.

It is also worth remembering that the results are based on whatever is being measured. Researchers use rating scales to measure general improvement and the improvement of specific symptoms. These scales are completed by the patient, the physician, and in child psychiatry the parents and sometimes teachers. Who completes the rating scales can have a significant effect on whether the medicine is shown to be effective.

The discerning reader also wants to ask what constitutes a response. Is a 20% improvement in rating scale scores sufficient, or is a more demanding 50% improvement used? How many subjects improve, and how much do they improve? Is the improvement noted on all rating scales or only on those completed by teachers or parents? For how long did the response last? Many studies proving the efficacy of medications used in child psychiatry last only a month or two.

As can be seen, even the DBPC trial is not a walk in the park. It is the best standard by which we decide if medicine is effective, but it has its difficulties. And given that the DBPC trial is not available for every treatment, clinicians must often rely on current clinical wisdom and their best judgment. In addition, a DBPC trial might prove that a given medicine is better than placebo, but it does not prove that one medicine is better than another. That requires a head-to-head trial of two different medicines.

Also, it is important to note, although the DBPC trial might prove that a medicine is more effective than placebo, this does not mean that everyone who takes the medicine will improve. For example, a medicine can be seen as very effective in treating obsessive-compulsive disorder if research has shown that it substantially helps 40% of patients while placebo helps only 3% of patients. A response rate of 40%, however, means that the patient has a 60% chance of not being helped.

Parents are often little interested in research, its fallibilities, and its tentative conclusions. They are raising their children now and want to know what to do today. Therefore they often use the "if the shoe fits, wear it" approach to evaluating benefit. If they try an untested treatment and their child improves by their subjective standard, they are content. The problem with this approach is that there can be substantial costs in time and money to some procedures that are no better than placebo; the durability of the response can be in question; and physical side effects of some substances, even over-the-counter or so-called natural ones, are possible.

## Evaluating Risk

How do we evaluate the risks of any treatment, medicine in particular? For now I'll focus on the physical risks of medicine and defer a discussion of other costs of treatment, such as the time and money spent, the chance of unrealized hopes, and the psychological and societal consequences. But to be sure, although parents are understandably concerned about physical side effects, they are often equally worried about psychological side effects, such as whether using Adderall to help a child focus on homework will cause the child to grow dependent on medicine, thus negating the role of self-discipline and effort.

First, a word on perspective. Side effects do not exist in the absolute sense. That is, the goal of taking a medicine defines what is benefit and therefore what is side effect. For example, in the 1960s a medicine named Obetrol was marketed as an appetite suppressant to help people lose weight. Weight reduction was the goal and hoped-for benefit of taking this medicine. Thirty years later Obetrol was renamed Adderall. The goal became increasing attention span. Weight reduction, previously a benefit, became a side effect. Perspective matters.

This discussion of side effects is also not limited to prescribed medicines. All medicines, whether prescribed or over-the-counter, have side effects, as do all supplements, herbal remedies, "natural" substances, and the like. It is worth remembering that nicotine, caffeine, and alcohol are all natural and all have significant side effects.

The first way of approaching side effects is to note whether they are short-term or long-term. Unfortunately these terms are not as precise as we would like them to be. Short-term side effects usually refer to those side effects that begin shortly after a medicine is begun and cease shortly after the medicine is stopped. This heading typically includes what I call the usual suspects, the many side effects that are possible from taking most medicines. For example, virtually any medicine can cause an allergic rash or an upset stomach. In psychiatry, many medicines cause some patients to become tired, and other medicines cause some patients insomnia. Sometimes the same medicine will cause tiredness in some and insomnia in others. These short-term side effects are the standard outcome of prescribing medicines and are generally briefly uncomfortable but ultimately inconsequential, unless they prevent the patient from taking the medicine.

Just because a side effect begins shortly after the medicine is begun, however, doesn't mean the side effect is benign. For example, if shortly after starting a medicine the patient suffers a cardiac rhythm disturbance, or arrhythmia, and dies, the short-term side effect would have obvious long-term consequences.

Side effects are also sometimes classified as long-term, another vague label. It can imply that the side effect will be noticed in years or that the medicine must be taken for years before one notices the side effect. A dreaded example of the former is the pregnant woman who takes a medicine, even briefly, which has a deleterious effect on her child 20 years later. The use of diethylstilbestrol (DES) by pregnant women during the early 1950s, which led to an increased rate of cervical cancer in their adult daughters, is the classic example. An example of the latter is tardive dyskinesia, a movement disorder suffered by some patients who used the first-generation antipsychotics, such as chlorpromazine, for many years. This side effect correlated with the cumulative amount of medicine taken by the patient over months or years.

Discovering these kinds of long-term side effects is challenging. Determining if an effect is a side effect requires comparing children who took a given medicine, preferably at a given dose for a given number of years, to a comparable group who took placebo or no medicine. Understandably, parents are loath to commit their children to such long-term plans. Therefore other means of determining side effects must be sought.

In evaluating side effects, as in evaluating benefit, one must always ask what is the chance that the patient will experience the side effect. A side effect that occurs in 1% of patients is of far less concern than one that occurs in 25% of patients. One also wants to compare this number to the number of patients who experience that side effect when taking placebo. Just as some patients experience symptom relief from placebo, they also experience side effects. Side effects such as sedation, headache, and stomach distress are common consequences of taking placebo. But even unusual side effects, such as rash or ejaculatory failure, are seen. In evaluating the risk of a medicine, one must consider any side effects caused by taking placebo.

To determine whether an event constitutes a side effect, one must also compare the rate at which that event occurs to the rate for those not taking medicine. For example, over recent years the stimulants have come under fire for possibly being linked to sudden cardiac death. Obviously this is a most important issue. The first question that must be asked, however, is whether the rate of sudden cardiac death in those taking stimulants is any higher than the rate of such death in those who do not take stimulants. The point is that terrible events happen even to those not taking medicine, and before one concludes that the medicine carries risk, one must know that the same risk was not present in those not taking the medicine.

In addition to the percentage of people experiencing a side effect, the severity of the side effect must be evaluated. A mild decrease in appetite that one can work around is very different from a severe loss of appetite that leads to significant weight loss.

Different factors affect whether taking a medicine leads to having a side effect. First, the dose of the medicine is important. In general, higher doses lead to a greater risk of side effects. The age of the patient also matters. Sometimes younger children can be more sensitive to a particular dose of medicine. For example, preschoolers are more likely than older children to become irritable when taking a stimulant.

Next, the duration for which one takes the medicine might matter, although as we've seen, some dangerous side effects can occur after only a short time on the medicine, and taking a medicine for a long time does not necessarily increase risk.

The other medicines taken concomitantly are also important factors. As we saw in Chapter 4, medicines, whether prescription or over-the-counter, can affect one another, for example, through the P450 enzyme system.

From a clinical point of view, the last and, I find, most important point about side effects is my LIV rule. In short, if side effects are lethal, irreversible, or very painful (LIV), I consider more carefully whether the potential benefit is worth the risk. If side effects are not LIV, while I hope the patient doesn't experience them, I worry less about them. For example, when parents fear starting Ritalin because their child might lose her appetite, a common side effect, I explain that if appetite diminishes, the medicine can be discontinued, and no harm will have befallen the child. Obviously, over a long duration, this might be more medically significant, and therefore appetite must be monitored. But over the short run, this is not a dangerous side effect, and it is reversible without negative consequences.

If a medicine has a possibly lethal side effect, however, even if rare, I carefully consider with parents whether the possible benefit is worth the slight risk. Sometimes it is and other times it is not. For example, the slight risk of a potentially fatal rash with lamotrigine might be outweighed by successfully treating the depression of the child with bipolar disorder, since the untreated depression carries significant risk itself. Nevertheless, the potentially fatal side effects of some medicines always provide reason for careful consideration.

And what if a side effect occurs? While some side effects, such as those that are LIV, mandate the immediate discontinuation of the medicine, such is not always the case. Sometimes a simple reduction of dose solves the problem, and the patient can continue to accrue benefit from the medicine.

In summary, the decision to prescribe medicine rests on weighing its risks against its potential benefits, then weighing those against the risks and benefits of other treatments and against the risks and benefits of not treating. Here I've focused on the medical risks. In a later chapter I'll point out some of the personal and societal consequences of using medicine, as well as some of the pitfalls of using this ratio. For example, whenever a medicine is prescribed, there is the perennial risk that it could be used in an intentional or unintentional overdose by the patient or, as too often happens, by an unwitting younger sibling.

As a final point, predicting which individual patient will benefit or experience a side effect from medicine A or its sister, medicine B, from the same family is usually only a guess. Once a family of medicine is chosen, there is no way to know which medicine in that family will provide benefit or precipitate a side effect. For example, a patient might have decreased appetite on one stimulant but not another. This may simply be unpredictable.

## CHAPTER 6

# The Stimulants and Other Medicines for ADHD

Despite being neither the most common nor the most dangerous of child psychiatric disorders, no topic garners as many questions, comments, and opinions as the use of medicine to treat the seemingly ubiquitous attention deficit hyperactivity disorder (ADHD).

## What Is ADHD?

ADHD is currently seen as a disorder of excessive motor activity, impulsivity, and inattention. These are not all-or-nothing symptoms, however. The excessive motor activity ranges from squirminess to the inability to stay in one place and tends to diminish as the child gets older. Difficulty with inattention is rarely pervasive, as children with ADHD can often stay focused, sometimes very focused, on tasks that are stimulating or very interesting to them.

It is important to recall that the criteria for the psychiatric disorders of childhood are evolving. Although children who would fit the criteria for ADHD were described in world literature well before any DSM, the concept that impulsivity, hyperactivity and inattention constituted a medical disorder has been evolving since 1902. In that year George Still, a famous British pediatrician, described a group of children with these symptoms, as well as defiance and the inability to learn from experience.

The role of neurobiology in causing these symptoms was solidified when children were noted to have developed hyperactivity as a result of encephalitis suffered during the influenza pandemic of 1917. Fast-forward a few decades to a point when doctors noted hyperactive children who had no history of viral infection, or of any other obvious neurological disorder for that matter. During the 1950s these children were labeled as having minimal brain damage or minimal brain dysfunction (MBD), presumably because they had brain dysfunction (hence the hyperactivity) but no other signs of obvious neurological dysfunction (hence the condition was minimal). Fast-forward again to the early 1960s, and the name changes from the vague and unsatisfying MBD to one that simply describes the observed symptom, namely hyperactivity, or as stated in the DSM-II (1968), hyperkinetic reaction of childhood. Fast-forward one last time to 1980, when, to give greater weight to the symptom of inattention often displayed by these children, DSM-III switches the name to attention deficit disorder, some children having ADD with hyperactivity and some without hyperactivity. The change in DSM-IV (1994) was a more minor change to attention deficit hyperactivity disorder (ADHD), acknowledging that most children had some degree of each symptom. Nevertheless, DSM-IV allows for three subtypes—ADHD, predominantly inattentive type; ADHD, predominantly hyperactive-impulsive type; and ADHD, combined type.

The point of this short historical review is to remind us that ongoing research elucidates our conception of the symptoms of the disorder and perhaps the name of the disorder. In DSM-II, what is currently called ADHD was described very simply and without many of the signs and symptoms listed in DSM-IV.

Over recent years, research has focused on a variety of other signs and symptoms of those with ADHD. For example, the biological measurements indicate that the outer layer of their brain, the cortex, is thinner, as measured on MRIs, especially in areas important in the control of attention (Shaw et al., 2006). Interestingly, in this study the cortical thinning of parts of the brain concerned with attention improved in those subjects who clinically improved over the course of about five years, but not in those who did not clinically improve. This finding is not yet used clinically to diagnose, but does demonstrate an increasing understanding of ADHD.

Research has also focused on the variety of these children's clinical difficulties, many of which were not appreciated by DSM-II. For example, over recent years the spotlight has been on these children's deficits in executive functioning, such as planning, organizing, working memory, delaying rewards, controlling temper, modulating interest levels, and the like.

As more information is gathered about children with ADHD, different nuances of the disorder will be better understood. For our current purposes, this is very important because the medicines we use to treat ADHD may effectively treat some of the symptoms of ADHD and not others. In other words, as the diagnostic criteria evolve with research, some patients might fit the criteria for ADHD but have symptoms that do not respond to the stimulants that are the mainstay of treatment.

For example, Abikoff and colleagues (2009), in using Concerta to treat a small group of children with ADHD, found that improvement in organization, time management, and planning correlated with improvement in ADHD. Nevertheless, more than half the children continued to have difficulty with those executive skills. So while stimulant medicine might diminish the patient's impulsivity or help the patient focus, it might not be the complete answer to helping him organize his time or possessions, a skill very necessary in the classroom.

In any case, the current conception of ADHD is that it is made up of a hyperactivity-impulsivity component and an inattentiveness component, although different patients might have more symptoms of inattention or of hyperactivity-impulsivity. Many of those with ADHD have predominantly inattention and many have symptoms of both inattention and impulsivity-hyperactivity. The smallest group, consisting of about 10% of those diagnosed with ADHD, have only symptoms of impulsivity-hyperactivity.

These subtypes are not necessarily static. A patient might evolve from one to another. Lahey and colleagues (2005) found almost one third of a group of 4- to 6-year-olds with ADHD, combined type, changed subtypes over the subsequent eight years.

It is important to note that the symptoms of ADHD must interfere with the patient's functioning to a clinically significant level, admittedly a subjective call. According to the criteria of DSM-IV, there must also be a minimum number of symptoms. It is fairly easy to lower this threshold and make a diagnosis of borderline ADHD by allowing a diagnosis based on fewer criteria. DSM-V, scheduled for publication in 2013, might reconceptualize ADHD so that it is seen as existing on a spectrum with the rest of the population.

In addition to there being a requisite number of symptoms, the symptoms must be present in more than one setting, namely school and home, not one or the other, thus pointing to the importance of getting input from the school staff. This also becomes important in terms of monitoring any changes caused by medicine. The symptoms must be of some duration as well. Currently this duration is six months. While this criterion might change, the point is that one does not diagnose ADHD in someone whose symptoms have developed only over the past few weeks.

Another current criterion is that the symptoms begin prior to age 7. Interestingly, Faraone and colleagues (2006) have shown that those diagnosed between 7 and 12 years of age had similar outcomes to those diagnosed earlier. Clinicians are often faced with the question whether to diagnose ADHD in a child who had minimal or no symptoms of ADHD in elementary school but began to manifest symptoms in middle school. Does this represent ADHD manifesting only as the academic and organizational demands of school have increased? Or is this simply a normally disorganized child or early adolescent for whom school is not a top priority?

A final criterion is that another disorder does not account for the symptoms of ADHD. That is, a depressed child with inattention does not necessarily have ADHD. The child might more accurately be seen as having depression, which is causing inattention. That said, about two thirds of children with ADHD have a comorbid (or co-occuring) diagnosis. Most commonly this is oppositional defiant disorder (ODD), occurring in about 60%, but many children also have an anxiety disorder, depression, and other disorders. The comorbidity of ADHD with ODD increases the risk for more dangerous diagnoses, such as conduct disorder.

When one applies these criteria for ADHD rigorously, the disorder is not as ubiquitous as it seems. The prevalence of ADHD in the United States for years was given as 3–5%. Over recent decades, with the greater recognition of ADHD, predominantly inattentive type, the prevalence is cited at about 8%. Fairly common, but not ubiquitous. Studies from around the world indicate that ADHD is not an American disorder. Rather it is seen as having a worldwide prevalence rate of about 5%, with some countries having a higher prevalence than the United States and some lower (Polanczyk et al., 2007).

Boys with ADHD outnumber girls. Nevertheless, girls, if often overlooked, also suffer from ADHD. The undercounting is probably the result of these girls tending to be less rambunctious and their symptoms interfering less in the lives of others, thus causing them to fall through the cracks. Nevertheless, as do boys, girls with ADHD have significant difficulties at follow-up.

In the 1970s the common wisdom was that patients outgrew ADHD during adolescence. Follow-up studies proved this to be incorrect. About one third of children will outgrow ADHD during adolescence. About half, however, will continue to have many symptoms of ADHD as adolescents and adults, and more that one third will have significant difficulties in life.

Lest one think that ADHD is simply the new label for what used to be called being a boy, one should remember that those with ADHD make more visits to the emergency room and the outpatient medical department, spend more money on inpatient hospital stays, smoke cigarettes earlier and more frequently, have more sexually transmitted diseases, earlier pregnancies, more school cuts, a greater high school dropout rate, more job changes, more divorces, more traffic accidents, more arrests, more family difficulties, and more social difficulties. Looking specifically at girls, Biederman (2010) found an increased risk for antisocial disorders, mood disorders, anxiety disorders, eating disorders, and addictive disorders. In short, ADHD is not simply about being a boy (or girl), and it is not innocuous.

Children with ADHD also have a high likelihood of continuing to experience ADHD as they get older. And while the symptom of hyperactivity tends to diminish through the childhood years, as adults many will continue to have a subjective sense of restlessness and the need to multitask or keep busy. For some, impulsivity continues, as seen in the difficulty of modulating one's emotions, for example, as angry outbursts.

> Nineteen-year-old Robbie is an impatient driver. He drives too fast and is constantly playing with the buttons on the car radio, unable to find a station he likes for more than five seconds. Robbie is happily cruising around town in his red sports car when a little old lady driving a 15-year-old beige sedan, without realizing it, cuts Robbie off. Robbie suddenly lowers his window, angrily sticks his hand in the air, and makes an obscene gesture. Two minutes later Robbie is again contentedly driving and playing with his radio.

Inattention and distractibility are other important features that continue, so as adults these people tend to be forgetful and leave tasks half done, prematurely moving on to the next. More significantly, many of those who continue to have ADHD will experience significant difficulties in life, including arrests, frequent job changes, divorce, injuries, and drug and alcohol use. Again, while the diagnosis of ADHD can be stretched to include many otherwise high-functioning, multitasking, successful people, for many others ADHD is a malignant, life-altering disorder.

The diagnosis of ADHD is made clinically by taking a history from caregivers, getting information from teachers, and meeting the child. The interview can be deceptive, because many children with ADHD will appear fine for most of an interview (or the entire interview, if it is brief). Getting information from parents and teachers can also be tricky in that they do not always agree. That may be because they are seeing the child in different settings with different expectations or because they have different levels of knowledge regarding normal childhood behavior. Some studies have shown significant disagreement in diagnostic rates of ADHD depending on whether one gets information from a parent or a teacher, which is why getting the teacher's input is very important.

There is no blood test, brainwave test, or psychological test that can replace making a diagnosis by history taking. A medical history and physical exam, perhaps with accompanying blood tests, is necessary to rule out medical causes of symptoms, although usually one does not find a medical cause of ADHD. Nevertheless, one wants to be sure to rule out the possibility of ailments such as lead poisoning, thyroid disease, seizure disorder, substance abuse, and head injury.

Before starting medication, a recent physical is also necessary to make sure there are no contraindications to medicine. As we'll see when I discuss the stimulants, the child's pulse, blood pressure, height, and weight should be taken at baseline and then monitored.

Psychological testing can be very useful in assessing the patient's intellect, cognitive strengths and weaknesses, and academic functioning. This is, however, not mandatory. Rating scales such as the Conners and the SNAP-IV (Swanson, Nolan, and Pelham-IV) are useful ways of trying to quantify the observations of parent and teacher, but these are simply tools to confirm, not establish, a diagnosis. They also serve as a way of objectively documenting the patient's baseline functioning prior to starting medicine.

## The Treatment of ADHD

ADHD can be treated with either behavioral interventions or medication. Treatment with medication, particularly the stimulants, is the mainstay of the treatment of ADHD. Nevertheless, the use of behavioral interventions includes a wide variety of methods that are dictated by both controlled studies and common sense. I will not review all the possible behavioral interventions of ADHD. Nevertheless, because they can be easily overshadowed by the pursuit of the right medicine, a few comments are in order before I discuss the pharmacological treatment of ADHD.

### Behavioral Methods

The goal of behavioral interventions is not to eradicate the symptoms of ADHD but rather to minimize their effect on the patient and his or her environment. In other words, behavioral treatment does not necessarily lessen the child's hyperactivity, although it might. Rather it provides an approach that smooths the interaction between the child and his or her environment. Psychologically this is in the child's best interest.

In general, parents should learn to see ADHD, not as willful behavior, but as the result of a neurological process. Just as one wouldn't yell at an asthmatic child for wheezing, one shouldn't lose one's temper at the poor judgments of the impulsive or hyperactive child. It is difficult to see misbehavior as analogous to involuntary bodily processes such as breathing, and to be sure, they are not completely analogous. Nevertheless, they are more alike than many appreciate, and understanding this helps parents see the need to relinquish their reactive screaming as a method of discipline and instead embrace a proactive system of behavior modification.

I teach parents about the short feedback loop, namely, that a cornerstone of parenting these children is to follow up one's instructions in a timely manner. For example, if one tells Jonny to put on his pajamas, one can't follow up with Jonny 20 minutes later, only to find out that he hasn't met any of the expectations. This leads to parental frustration, exasperation, and perhaps screaming. Instead, after giving Jonny the instruction, the parent should check in with Jonny two minutes later. If two minutes is too long, she should check in after one minute or even sooner. The same principle of frequent feedback can be used in school.

Parents also need to use time out effectively, reinforce the child's compliant behavior, manage the environment to prevent difficulties, and the like. In addition, parents need to foster working relationships with school staff so that the feedback each of them provides to the child is in synchrony. For example, the child who forgets to hand in homework regularly needs the teacher to sign off on the child's memo pad at the end of the day that the child's homework assignments have been written down and that his books are in his book bag. His parents then need to sign off that the work has been completed and placed back in the proper place in his book bag.

Teachers need to keep the environment stimulating and provide support to help the patient with organization and planning, especially on homework assignments. An emphasis on homework often adds a major stress for children with ADHD, and I frequently wonder if the benefit of homework is worth the cost of filling households with conflict, frustration, and tension.

Like parents, teachers must also be educated about ADHD and not see it as laziness or a moral failing. Teachers who say, "He's in middle school now. He needs to be able to . . ." are not appreciating that what the child needs to be able to do and what the child is able to do are two different things. The asthmatic child should be able to breathe easily, but his biology prevents that, and so adults intervene to make it more possible.

Again, this is by no means a comprehensive summary of the behavioral interventions of ADHD. The point is that although medicine is the mainstay of treatment, behavioral treatment should not be ignored, though it is very easy for parents and the clinician to do so once the focus is on medication. To neglect the importance of environmental interventions is to increase the risk of chronic academic failure, conflict at home, and subsequent demoralization and low self-esteem. In addition, it places unfair expectations on medicine to solve a complicated set of problems, some of which are beyond its influence.

Although parents often desperately seek other treatments of ADHD so as to avoid medicine, these treatments are generally of unproven efficacy. Dietary modifications, such as a sugar-free diet, and EEG feedback are not established as efficacious. Again, to reiterate a basic premise of this book, that is not to say that an individual patient will not improve after having undergone these or any other treatments. Rather it is to say that the scientific method of placebo-controlled, double-blind trials have not proven their efficacy in large groups of patients.

## Medicine

I find it helpful to approach the medicines used to treat ADHD as four groups. The first two groups are both FDA approved. The first group is the stimulants, namely methylphenidate (MPH) and amphetamine (AMPH), and the second group includes atomoxetine and guanfacine extended release. I see these two groups of FDA-approved medicines as two tiers because in fact, most clinicians use the stimulants as the first line of treatment and reserve the others for specific situations or to be used if the stimulants fail. The third group of medicines is not FDA approved for the treatment of ADHD, but its use is supported by some evidence of efficacy, if not as high a level of evidence as for the stimulants. This group includes the alpha agonists, guanfacine (not extended release) and clonidine, and bupropion, an antidepressant. The fourth group includes medicines that are proven to be at least somewhat effective, but whose side effects prevent their regular use, such as the tricyclic antidepressants, and the medicines that have less research support for their use but are tried if all else fails, such as Modafinil. Let's review each of these groups of medicines.

## The Stimulants

The family of medicines known as the stimulants includes two related medicines, amphetamine (AMPH) and methylphenidate (MPH). The exact mechanisms of action of AMPH and MPH are slightly different, but their effects and side effects are essentially the same. Thus they are discussed together.

The effect of the stimulants on children was first reported in 1937, when benzedrine, a form of amphetamine originally developed for the treatment of asthma and allergies, was found to decrease the activity level and improve the compliance and classroom performance of children in a residential facility (Bradley, 1937). Bradley reported a "spectacular" improvement in school performance, with greater drive, comprehension, and accuracy of work. This response to stimulants was noted, but interest in it did not gather until the late 1950s and early 1960s.

Methylphenidate was originally synthesized in 1944 as a derivative of amphetamine and was marketed as a geriatric medicine in the early 1960s. Through the 1970s methylphenidate (as Ritalin) was used, if somewhat sparingly, to treat hyperactive children. By the later 1980s it was used more commonly. Because of its short duration of action, however, about 3-4 hours, a second dose had to be taken; hence the image of children lining up at the school nurse's office during lunch. In 1996 Adderall, an amphetamine product that had been marketed during the 1960s as an appetite suppressant named Obetrol, was introduced as a treatment for ADHD with a purported duration that would help the child throughout the school day without the child's having to take a second dose. It quickly became very popular, and through the 1990s the use of methylphenidate and amphetamine increased dramatically. (Pemoline, a medication with a similar mechanism of action, was used from the mid-1970s through 2005, when its production was discontinued because of slowing sales, possibly the result of an infrequent association with liver damage.) During the later 1990s and into the new millennium, drug companies introduced a variety of long-acting forms of methylphenidate and amphetamine, thus allowing patients to take their medicine once in the morning or in combinations that covered more of the day.

The effect of the stimulants is to decrease hyperactivity and improve attention. Scores of double-blind, placebo-controlled studies have proved this effect. Approximately 70% of children with ADHD respond to a trial with either methlyphenidate or amphetamine. Of those who do not respond, the majority will respond to a trial of the other stimulant family. The point is that if the patient does not respond to the first stimulant tried, it is helpful then to try the other type of stimulant.

It is also important to realize that, despite the myth that only those with ADHD respond to stimulants, even those without ADHD respond. In a classic study, Rapoport and colleagues (1980) gave amphetamine to children with and without ADHD and to adults without ADHD. (The concept of adult ADHD was still a few years away.) The research team found that all three groups had improved focus. Thus a positive response to treatment with a stimulant does not ensure the diagnosis of ADHD. Nevertheless, patients with borderline ADHD may well benefit from stimulants. Therefore justifying a stimulant trial by absolutely fitting the requisite number of ADHD criteria is not necessary.

### How the Stimulants Work

The stimulants increase the level of dopamine and norepinephrine in the synapses of the prefrontal cortex, which requires these neurotransmitters to be in a narrow range for it to function optimally (Gamo, Wang, & Arnsten, 2010). They probably also improve the symptoms of ADHD through their effect on other areas of the brain.

Methylphenidate and amphetamine work in different ways that are not fully understood. On the one hand, methylphenidate blocks the reuptake pump that would transport dopamine and norepinephrine into the presynaptic neuron. These pumps are labeled the dopamine transporter, commonly referred to as DAT, and the norepinephrine transporter, NET. Amphetamine, on the other hand, blocks the reuptake of dopamine and norepinephrine by competing with these substances for the DAT and NET. In that way amphetamine itself ends up transported into the neuron and then into the vesicles that store the dopamine and norepinephrine. Doing so displaces the neurotransmitters being stored in the intracellular vesicles and thereby causes a release of dopamine into the synapse.

Also of note, the d-isomer, that is, the right-handed form of methylphenidate molecules, more powerfully binds the DAT and NET. The d-isomer of amphetamine also more powerfully binds the DAT, but the binding of NET is done equally by both the d- and l-isomers of amphetamine. Therefore mixed salts containing both d- and l-amphetamine (namely, Adderall) affect both DAT and NET, whereas d-amphetamine (namely, Dexedrine) affects only DAT.

These effects are somewhat dependent on the dose of the medication taken and the rapidity with which it enters the neuron. Snorting, smoking, or injecting stimulants leads to a much more rapid influx of medicine into the brain than swallowing a stimulant in pill form. This rapid change has different effects on different parts of the brain. For example, when the DAT of a part of the brain called the nucleus accumbens is saturated, there is an increase in dopamine in the synapse and a concomitant increase in euphoria, which reinforces taking the medicine so that the abuser wants to take it again. This effect is not seen by those who use the medicine at reasonable doses taken orally, as prescribed by their clinician. (Cocaine also blocks the DAT, but unlike methylphenidate, it leaves the brain quickly. This rapid turnover is also theorized to lead to cocaine being more reinforcing, causing the user to want to take it again [Paykina & Greenhill, 2008]).

In addition, the once daily, slow-release forms of the stimulants developed over the past 10 years or so are not simply longer acting and more convenient than the immediate-release stimulants. Their different timing of release into the bloodstream might also cause a different effect. That is, because they start more slowly and are present at the DAT and NET for a longer duration, there is a greater chance of their affecting the transporters so as to decrease the symptoms of ADHD without affecting the nucleus accumbens in a way that causes euphoria (Stahl, 2008).

To be clear, however, in discussing these mechanisms of action, I am comparing appropriately dosed, slow-release medicines taken orally and high doses of stimulants snorted or taken intravenously, and thus very immediately released. The responsible use of stimulants, in the immediate-release or slow-release forms, does not lead to euphoria and does not effectively stimulate the parts of the brain that are reinforcing or that thereby lead to the desire for ongoing use.

How these synaptic effects of stimulants translate into diminishing the symptoms of ADHD is not fully understood. Although, during the 1970s, some thought that the stimulants had a paradoxical effect on children (otherwise, why would one give a stimulant to an already hyperactive youngster?), as we've seen from the experiment of Rapoport and colleagues above, the effect is pretty much the same in children and adults. When parents question how stimulants will help their child slow down, I often explain that they stimulate the inhibitory neurons that run from the frontal lobes of their brain, the way one would stimulate the car brake if one wanted to slow down. This is certainly a highly simplistic view of the mechanism of the stimulants but one that helps parents grasp the apparent paradox.

## Clinical Indications of the Stimulants

The most important indication for the use of stimulants in child psychiatry is the treatment of ADHD. In adults, the stimulants are used to treat ADHD and at times to treat refractory depression and narcolepsy and to enhance energy or combat apathy, particularly in patients with medical illnesses. In children, however, they are used almost exclusively to treat ADHD. An interesting question is whether some particularly sleep-deprived adolescents also benefit from the wakefulness-enhancing properties of the stimulants.

In treating ADHD, either MPH or AMPH will diminish hyperactivity and improve focus, the cardinal symptoms of ADHD, in about 70% of those treated, compared to about 20% or fewer of those given placebo. As already noted, the figure of 70% can be raised to over 90% by trying a second stimulant. This benefit, which is more powerful in lessening hyperactivity than inattention, is one of the most reliable pharmacologic responses in psychopharmacology (see Paykina, 2008 for a list of studies). It is important to note that these studies are on subjects with rigorously diagnosed ADHD, and the effects of the stimulants are more reliably reached in those with ADHD without comorbidities.

The effects of stimulants have been noted in a variety of spheres, including tests of attention, such as the continuous performance tests, and measures of achievement, such as of arithmetic and reading (Scheffler et al., 2009).

Clinically these changes manifest differently in different areas of the child's life. The diminished hyperactivity and impulsivity lead to the child's being less disruptive in class, with less calling out, less interrupting, less finger tapping, and less off-task behavior. On medicine, these children stay on task and show more initiative, so that occasionally parents will report with a sense of wonder that for the first time the child read a book to completion or, without prodding, sat down and finished her homework. Children taking stimulants are more cooperative with peers, evoking more social acceptance and fewer warnings from the teacher. They are also significantly less aggressive toward peers and demonstrate less antisocial behavior, such as stealing.

At home this change in behavior leads to more compliance and better interactions between child and parents. In sports, children on stimulants tend to be more focused and engaged. And, very significantly, long-acting MPH helps teenagers drive more attentively and therefore more safely (Cox et al., 2006).

Parents sometimes have their own expectations of medicine, for example, that it will help the child "cope" better. While the effect of stimulants can seem magical, it is better for parents to have reasonable, if modest, expectations, and then be surprised if a magical response occurs. It is also important for parents to appreciate the subtle difference between a target symptom and a symptom that medicine might not improve. For example, while medicine might be expected to decrease impulsivity, it might not improve the low self-esteem, difficulty reading social cues, and poor social judgment that are characteristic of many children with ADHD. In this sense, medicine should not be expected to change all facets of the difficulties that underlie a child's social problems.

Changes caused by medicine occur while the medicine is at adequate levels in the bloodstream and cease when the blood level of medicine diminishes. Interestingly, some parents do report a halo effect. That is, even though the medicine should have worn off by the end of the school day, a parent occasionally reports that the patient continues to do well, completing homework and being more compliant, for the remainder of the day. One could conjecture that this might be due to patients' feeling that they are capable of meeting expectations, or perhaps to the diminished evening stress experienced by the parents, no longer having to worry all day about their child's functioning. In any case, while some experience this late-day halo effect, children do not learn how to focus or control their impulsivity while on stimulants so that they can stop the stimulants, having learned these lessons. In short, it is best to think of the stimulants as working only while they are present in the body.

Most studies of these effects are short-term, showing benefit for up to three months, though some recent studies have been longer than one year. The best-known of these is the Multimodal Treatment Study of Children with Attention Deficit/Hyperactivity Disorder (MTA, 1999a, 1999b). This large, government-funded, multisite study compared four treatment approaches over 14 months of treatment. Almost 600 children with ADHD, combined type, were divided into four treatment groups. The first group was treated with medication, usually an immediate-release stimulant, prescribed by the research team physician, and an intense behavior management program. This program was multilayered and included 35 sessions of parent training in both an individual and group format, ongoing behavior therapy consultation for the teacher, a behaviorally trained aide who worked with the child in the class for 14 weeks, and attendance by the child at an 8-week, 45-hours-per-week summer camp specializing in ADHD and including social skills training and behavior modification. The second group was treated only with medication prescribed by the research team physician. These children were mostly treated with MPH, and sometimes AMPH, and followed with monthly visits. The third group received only the intense behavior treatment program. The fourth group, called the community care group, received care as usual from their local medical and mental health professionals. The treatment of about two thirds of this last group included stimulants. It is important to note that, because the benefit of stimulants has been so well established, this study did not include a placebo group initially. The goal of the study was not to prove that medicine is effective but rather to compare it to other treatments.

These four treatment groups were kept in place for 14 months, at which point the children were assessed. After that, patients were free to choose their own treatment. The entire group was reassessed at 24 months, 36 months, 6 years, and 8 years.

After 14 months the combined treatment group did best, with 68% "normalizing," that is, being without ADHD symptoms. This compares to 56% of the medication only group, 34% of the behavior treatment group, and 25% of the community care group. At this point a group of almost 300 children began to serve as classroom controls. That is, these were randomly selected children who were also assessed at this time for ADHD symptoms. Of this group, about 88% were without ADHD symptoms. This control group allowed the researchers to conclude that while the combination treatment group did best, they did not do as well as a random group of children in the long run.

In short, after 14 months of treatment, the two groups prescribed medication by the research team had significantly fewer symptoms of ADHD and ODD than the other two groups. The question arises as to why the community care group did not do well, despite two thirds' having being treated with medication. The answer seems to be that, while they were often treated with medicine, they were treated at lower doses than the medication only group (MPH at 20 mg/day versus 30 mg/day) and less frequently (twice versus three times daily dosing). In addition, they were seen less frequently by their clinician (twice per year versus monthly) and for shorter periods of time (17 minutes versus 30 minutes). The take-home message is that medicine is not a panacea but must be used at adequate doses and couched in a supportive clinical relationship.

That noted, the patient's compliance with taking medicine is never certain. Thiruchelvam, Charach, and Schachar (2001) found that approximately half of treated children continued their stimulant medication for three consecutive years, adherence being associated with younger age, higher teacher-rated ADHD symptoms, and fewer signs of oppositionality at school. And at the eight-year follow-up of the MTA (Molina et al., 2009), about 60% of those who had been medicated during the initial 14 months had stopped their medicine and were not taking medicine at follow-up. This serves as a sober reminder to clinicians that patients ultimately decide the actual treatment.

The MTA offers other insights as well. Comorbid diagnoses affect the response to treatment. For example, those with oppositional defiant disorder and conduct disorder improved significantly more frequently when receiving medication. Rigorous medication treatment seems necessary for the treatment of these children.

Yet children with comorbid anxiety did well when treated with behavior treatment alone, medicine adding little benefit. This suggests that behavioral interventions should be stressed to those with comorbid anxiety. One fascinating finding was that parents whose children received only behavioral intervention were more satisfied with the treatment than parents whose children received only medicine, although this second group clearly did better.

In addition, those with complicated situations—for example, a child with severe ADHD, a low IQ, and a depressed parent—do poorly despite being treated with combination therapy. So there seem to be some children with an unfortunate combination of risk factors who do poorly even though they have been treated with the most intense treatment possible, a reminder that medicine is not a panacea.

Last, children with manic-like symptoms, though not strictly diagnosed bipolar disorder, responded positively to stimulants, suggesting that, contrary to popular belief, these children can be treated with stimulants.

After the initial 14 months, the MTA became a naturalistic follow-up study, the families being free to choose whatever treatment they wanted. This gave researchers the opportunity to see what happens to children with ADHD over subsequent years. The benefits accrued to the combined treatment and MPH only groups during the first 14 months began to diminish over the following year. This seemed to result from those who had been treated with medicine beginning to stop their medicine and those who had been treated with behavioral intervention beginning trials of medicine. By three years, the initial differences between the groups were completely lost. This, again, might point to the need for the ongoing and rigorous use of stimulants if one is going to maintain the benefits of having taken medication.

Given the importance of the ongoing use of medicine, it is also interesting to note that at three-year follow-up, the subjects in all four treatment groups were improving. And after eight years (Molina et al., 2009), the child's initial presentation, not the initial treatment group, was more predictive of later improvement, with higher-functioning children from more stable families doing better. That is, children who began the study with more severe ADHD symptoms, more conduct problems, lower IQ, and less social advantage and those who had a weaker response to any initial treatment had worse outcomes. The initial 14 months of intense treatment did not have enduring effects on functioning. As a group, all the children with ADHD, now teens, were improved over their baseline functioning but were not doing as well as their non-ADHD peers. Instead they had more symptoms of ADHD and oppositional defiant disorder, lower grades, a higher rate of repeating a grade, and higher rates of arrest and of psychiatric hospitalization. In fact, even the minority who had continued their use of medicine into adolescence, albeit not according to the original treatment regimen, were doing no better than their unmedicated peers with ADHD, except on a measure of math achievement, thus calling into question the impact of ongoing medication treatment on long-term functioning.

Without an initial control group, it is difficult to draw firm conclusions. Among its many findings, however, the MTA seems to say that medicine as prescribed in the short run of about one year is effective, that most patients with ADHD slowly improve, but that, even with ongoing medicine, patients with ADHD do not fare as well as their peers without ADHD. They continue to have both academic and social difficulties.

In another, longer-term study, Klein and colleagues (2004) compared MPH alone to MPH combined with psychosocial management, including parent training, academic assistance, psychotherapy, and social skills training. The results were similar to that of the MTA. These researchers (Abikoff et al., 2004a) found that over two years, while all children improved, those receiving psychosocial interventions with medicine did no better than those taking MPH alone. Those children who received the psychosocial intervention could have their stimulant discontinued no more successfully than those in the MPH only group. In addition, the researchers found that in this group of children with ADHD but without learning disorders, if MPH was used optimally, weekly individual academic intervention did not add benefit (Hechtman et al., 2004a). Further, they (Abikoff et al., 2004b) found that social skills training did not improve social behavior. And they (Hechtman et al., 2004b) concluded that parent training improved parents' knowledge of parenting but not their actual parenting. In short, this study found that over two years, many usual interventions do not add to the benefits of a rigorously used stimulant.

In assessing the efficacy of the stimulants in treating ADHD, one must see the questions raised by these long-term studies in the context of other research revealing possible long-term biological benefits.

The possibility that stimulants change the neuroanatomical differences displayed by those with ADHD remains an open question. For example, Shaw and colleagues (2009), in comparing the MRIs of teens with ADHD who had been treated with stimulants with those of teens not treated, found that those treated with stimulants showed a slowed thinning of the cortex compared to those who were untreated. While the groups did not differ clinically, the MRIs of the treated groups were more similar to those of youths without ADHD. The clinical meaning of this kind of intriguing finding remains to be seen.

Clinically, other follow-up studies give credence to stimulant treatment being associated with better outcome. Charach, Ickowicz, and Schachar (2004), in a study lasting five years, showed the continued efficacy of MPH as measured by teacher-reported symptoms. That is not to say that these youngsters did as well as those without ADHD, although continued benefit was evident. And Biederman and colleagues (2009) followed children with ADHD and controls for 10 years. As young adults, those children with ADHD who had been treated with stimulants for an average of six years had a lower rate of repeating a grade and lower rates of disruptive behavior, as well as of depression and anxiety disorders, than those who had not.

In summary, the stimulants offer continuing benefit to many with ADHD and, it seems, more benefit than any other treatment. Many children with ADHD will improve as they age whether or not they take medicine. Many with significant comorbidities will do poorly despite taking stimulants, although the stimulant might significantly diminish traits such as oppositionality. Nevertheless, even with optimal treatment, as a group children with ADHD do not seem to do as well as their non-ADHD peers, with many being at significant risk for a number of problems in life. Finally, it bears recalling that these conclusions are reached from the study of those who fit rigorous criteria for ADHD, not the somewhat marginal cases many clinicians treat.

## Using the Stimulants

Let's examine the process of treating a patient with stimulants.

### Before starting

Before starting a patient on a stimulant, it is important for the treating clinician to have taken a careful history, ensuring that the ADHD diagnosis is correct and documenting comorbid conditions. Medical history, in particular about any potential cardiac conditions, must be obtained. Seizure history is also particularly important because, while some seizures are obvious, unmistakable, and already known to parents, others are subtle and easily missed, and can be mislabeled as the inattention of ADHD.

> Sophie is seen as a 7-year-old space cadet. She frequently misses directions and always seems one step behind. Her parents deny a history of seizures. But when the physician demonstrates three-second staring episodes and explains that these could be seizures, Sophie's parents are less certain. An electroencephalogram (EEG) reveals that Sophie has been having petit mal (or absence) seizures throughout the day, accounting for her frequent lapses. Sophie is referred to a pediatric neurologist for treatment of her seizures.

Family history must also be reviewed. This sheds light on the patient's genetic predisposition to psychiatric disorders, including ADHD. It also helps the clinician learn about the parenting style with which the patient is being raised. This might affect everything from discipline to homework support to the reliability with which medicine is given. Asking about the medical history of close family members is also important. In particular, knowledge about a history of tics, seizures, cardiac arrhythmias, or sudden death is especially valuable. It is important to be aware of the presence in the home of someone who abuses drugs or alcohol, since the stimulants can be abused or sold by someone for whom they have not been prescribed.

> *Six-year-old Peter is being effectively treated with Adderall. His physician notes, however, that his mother, who doles out the medicine as the doctor has instructed, requests prescriptions slightly earlier than expected every month. Either the pharmacy is not supplying the full month's supply, or someone else is depleting the bottle. After being confronted with this, Peter's mother monitors the pill supply more closely and discovers that her husband, who has a history of drug abuse, has been siphoning off a few pills every month.*

The clinician should also make sure that the patient has had a physical exam within the past year. Baseline pulse and blood pressure should be measured and monitored as the patient's dose is increased. Baseline height and weight should also be noted and followed about every three or four months. Weight might initially be monitored more frequently, especially if a young child is taking a relatively high dose of stimulants.

*Getting started*

If the decision has been made to begin a medicine, I start with an FDA-approved one. Usually I start by prescribing a stimulant, rather than atomoxetine or guanfacine. The stimulants have been used longer and are more reliably effective. Whether to begin with MPH or AMPH is often a matter of the clinician's experience. While many patients will respond to either of these medicines, some will respond to only one or the other. Unfortunately, which will be effective is unpredictable.

The other differences between MPH and AMPH are their duration, the delivery methods available, and the fact that AMPH might, on average, have a slightly higher rate of some side effects, such as appetite suppression. Sometimes patients will come in with their own anecdotal information about a neighbor whose child responded so well to or had a side effect on one or the other of these medicines. I warn parents about anecdotal information and assure them that for every person they find who responded well or poorly to either medicine, I can find others who did not.

In starting a stimulant, many clinicians begin with a long-acting form, using the sound reasoning that it will offer the most coverage for the school day and, sometimes, after school. I tend not to have a hard and fast rule about this. Instead, I individualize my decision, influenced by other factors such as the patient's age. For example, in younger children (roughly younger than about 8) I tend to start with an immediate-release form for a few reasons. First, my experience is that some younger children (especially preschool and early elementary school age) are more prone to develop irritability or moodiness on long-acting medicines. Although there is a greater chance of rebound moodiness on immediate-release medicines, this tends to be briefer and less noxious to parents than their child taking a medicine for the first time, then being miserable and crying for hours. After a long afternoon of tears and tantrums, parents are liable to give up prematurely on stimulants or put the offending medicine on the list of medicines never to be used again. This is sometimes unfortunate, because a few years later, when the child is older, the same medicine might offer benefit without the risk of repeating the moodiness.

My second reason for starting many children on an immediate-release stimulant is that the change in the child's behavior can be more obvious after use of a short-acting medicine. In particular, a teacher's observation that the child was uncharacteristically focused and well behaved before lunch, but not after lunch, is a powerful indication that the medicine is effective. After this is established, switching to a longer-acting medicine is considered. This change often adds a brief hassle for parents, but many find it worth the trouble.

Ultimately each patient finds a duration of medicine that is effective in meeting his or her needs. Some, who want to minimize the amount of medicine or who have a need for increasing their attention only during morning classes, take a short-acting medicine only on the mornings of school days. More commonly, a short-acting medicine is taken with breakfast and again with lunch, or a long-acting stimulant is taken in the morning for coverage throughout the school day or longer. At other times, one might use a long-acting medicine through the day and add a short-acting stimulant in the afternoon or evening on all or only some days.

It is important to note that on a milligram to milligram basis, AMPH is about twice as potent as MPH. That is, 10 mg of MPH is equivalent to about 5 mg of AMPH. These, however, are rough estimates, which do not hold for every patient. I recommend taking stimulants with breakfast, since this increases their absorption and lessens the possibility of gastric distress for some patients. It also ensures that patients have eaten breakfast, in case their appetite is suppressed for lunch. If stimulants are taken more than about 30 minutes before breakfast, the patient's appetite might be suppressed, or she might suffer some gastric distress and skip breakfast.

Having said that, I find that infrequently a parent will choose to give the stimulant, especially if the child is particularly rambunctious in the morning and does not suffer from appetite suppression, about an hour prior to the scheduled wakeup time. The parent wakes the child early, gives the medicine, then lets the child return to sleep, thus allowing the child to awaken already medicated, ensuring a much smoother morning routine before school.

The patient is started at the lowest dose (typically MPH 5 mg or AMPH 5 mg), which is then increased by 5 mg every three to five days until an effective dose is reached. (With AMPH, or MPH in young children, the dose is often increased by 2.5 mg). The patient's weight is not readily correlated with the dose used, so that each patient goes through roughly the same sequence of doses. Nevertheless, heavier patients (teens) sometimes require a higher dose.

On average, higher doses equate with greater response. Usually a patient will remain at a stable dose for years. Some patients occasionally require an increase in dose, but this amounts to finding a new plateau, not starting on a road of continuing increases. This tends to occur with MPH, particularly in the first year, more than AMPH. When a stimulant has become ineffective, which occasionally happens, a stimulant from the other family of stimulants is sometimes effective (that is, changing from MPH to AMPH or vice versa). Changing back to the original stimulant might eventually be possible, presumably because receptor sites on the postsynaptic neuron adapt to the first medicine and then readjust in its subsequent absence.

The stimulants are effective within about 30 minutes of having taken an effective dose. There is no need to build up a blood level, as with the antidepressants. It is also important to recall that the stimulants work for hours after they have been taken. A course of stimulants does not cure the person of his or her symptoms, like a course of penicillin. And one doesn't learn how to focus or control one's impulses by taking stimulants, although the experience of being behaviorally, socially, and academically successful is an important experience for the child.

After starting at the lowest dose, the dose is increased every three to five days. I find this time frame useful for two reasons. First, a three-day trial is sufficient to show the efficacy or lack of efficacy of a particular dose. I find one or two days insufficient because there are many random factors that influence whether a child does well or poorly for a day or two. Three days, however, is sufficient to consider it a pattern. Second, usually a five-day trial is the maximum because, if the trial is longer, parents tend to forget to observe or obtain information from the teacher at that dose. Parents then get into a rut of giving the same dose and forget to call with follow-up.

If one forgets to take a stimulant, the medicine is simply not in effect. One does not need to take the medicine later in the day. One can take the medicine later, but then is vulnerable to side effects, such as decreased appetite or insomnia, later that day.

Knowing when an effective dose has been reached is complicated because there is a linear relationship between dose and response for those with ADHD, combined type, but patients with ADHD, predominantly inattentive type, do better at lower doses (Stein et al., 2003). Deciding on the optimal dose to treat ADHD is controversial. Some clinicians increase the dose until side effects are reached and then back down to a dose lower than the one that results in side effects. Others will increase until an adequate response is seen, then stop. In either case the dose should be increased sufficiently for the clinician to know if any potential response was reached.

*Mrs. Thompson is not crazy about starting Tara on Adderall, although, on the basis of years of observations by many teachers, this treatment is strongly recommended by her psychiatrist. She reluctantly starts Tara on Adderall XR 5 mg, and thinks that there*

*might be some response. But fearing side effects, she decides not
to increase the dose. Tara's teacher says Tara may have responded,
but she is unsure. After three months the teacher is even less sure.
Mrs. Thompson, full of hesitation, agrees to increase the dose to
10 mg. She and Tara's teacher are amazed at Tara's clear response.*

Because some patients respond preferentially to MPH or AMPH,
if there is no response to the first stimulant, a medicine of the other
family should be tried. That is, if the patient does not respond to
methylphenidate, one of the amphetamines should be tried and vice
versa.

Although frequent dose increases are not expected, some patients
require a dose increase occasionally. Most often that means after a few
months or years, not weeks. This should not be confused with patients
who seem to do well immediately after starting the medicine, then a few
weeks later require an increased dose. This seems to reflect more of a
honeymoon reaction experienced by some patients. I am often unsure
whether this is an initial placebo response or whether there truly is a
need for an increased dose. It is of note, however, that one must beware
of parents accurately observing an improvement in behavior, but then
making that behavior the new baseline, which, a few months or even
years later, they want to improve further.

It is also important to see the patient's functioning in the context
of the time of the school year. I find that I receive more phone calls
from parents who feel the dose is insufficient around March–April than
in September–October. My guess is that by spring, factors other than
medicine are at play. Younger children are getting tired of having been
in school for eight months. And disorganized adolescents have had
sufficient time to fall well behind in their work, leaving their parents
frustrated and the teens defensive. Although tinkering with the dose of
medicine can be very helpful, it often misses the point. More important,
one must be sure that the apparent need for an increased dose does not
mark the onset of another disorder, such as depression or anxiety.

Patients take stimulants for varying numbers of days each week.
On the one hand, some require the use of the stimulant seven days a
week, throughout the entire year. The rationale is that the ADHD is

present not only during school hours and that these children are at risk all the time. On the other hand, for many patients ADHD is essentially a school-based disorder. That is, if they did not have to go to school, their parents would never have sought treatment. These children often take their medicine on school days only. Regardless of which group the patient is in, I recommend to all parents that they give their child medicine on the weekends, at least initially. My purpose is to educate the parent about the effects of the medicine. Too often parents call with questions or comments having given the medicine on school days only and therefore unaware of the effect the medicine has on their child.

Some patients, for reasons of behavior or social interaction, require the greatest possible coverage throughout the day. Others, who use the medicine only during school, sometimes try to increase coverage to include the evening, when the child is doing homework. After the stimulant has been shown to be effective, different forms of the stimulant can be mixed. For example, one might prescribe a long-acting MPH in the morning, then add an immediate-release MPH in the afternoon or evening. This second dose might be used some but not all days of the week. Sometimes the particular combination depends on the age and needs of the patient. Sometimes an extended-release form of the stimulant takes longer to absorb than the immediate-release tablet. In these cases, an immediate-release stimulant might be given simultaneously with an extended-release pill with breakfast.

High school students can present a challenge in that after a day at school, they like to do their homework at 10 P.M. Balancing the need for stimulant coverage in the evening with the adolescent's need for sleep is tricky. College students make their own idiosyncratic schedules and often prefer immediate-release forms that they can take for short spurts, thus minimizing the emotionally constricting feeling of the stimulant throughout the day. These needs must be balanced with the possibility that the college student will share medicine with a friend and that immediate-acting stimulants are more easily abused than long-acting stimulants.

There is insufficient information on combining different families of stimulants. Research is beginning to support combining a stimulant with atomoxetine. This combination is occasionally used by some clinicians, although patients on the combination are likely to experience more side effects than those taking only atomoxetine. Combining stimulants with guanfacine XR is also being studied.

Measuring the effects of stimulants is another challenge. This is easier in younger children, because the teacher, who spends the bulk of the school day with the patient, can offer observations about the child's decreased hyperactivity or improved focus. Elementary school and sometimes middle school teachers are also able to provide baseline and then follow-up rating scales (such as the SNAP-IV, Conners, or CAP) that demonstrate the medicine's efficacy.

Parents often ask if the teacher should be told that medicine is being started or that rating scales are being used to measure the efficacy of the medicine. I usually tell parents to inform the teacher beforehand that medicine is being considered but that the child's medication status is purposely being kept from the teacher. This prevents the teacher's observations from being biased by knowing whether the child is on medicine. I also tell parents to assure the teacher that once a decision is made, the teacher will be informed about whether the child is taking medicine. This respects the teacher's role in caring about the child without jeopardizing his or her objectivity. While teachers (and parents) often feel that their observations would be objective, research suggests that they, like all people, are influenced by their expectations (Waschbusch et al., 2009). Trials in which observers are "blind" to the child's medication status are therefore more reassuring that any change is truly pharmacological and not due to the placebo effect.

Measuring drug efficacy is much more difficult and frustrating with high school students. Often adolescents are uncertain about the medicine's efficacy, their teachers are unable to offer significant insights, and their parents are unable to offer observations of the patient while on the medicine, which has worn off at the end of the school day. Some parents use a psychologist to confirm the medicine's efficacy by giving the patient a brief test of attention span on and off medicine.

Sometimes parents, especially of high schoolers, use grades as a measure of the medicine's efficacy. While dramatic improvements are telling, the risk is in putting too much stock in the minor, random movements of grades and feeling the need to increase the dose because a few, or even all, of the child's grades went down. One has to remember that many factors influence an adolescent's grades. These range from the deleterious effect that social preoccupations often have on school performance to the benefit that occurs when the adolescent suddenly realizes that college applications are just around the corner.

Concomitant parent counseling, psychotherapy, family therapy, and the like, as well as frequency of follow-up, are always an individual decision. Recall that the complicating factors with which many children with ADHD must deal, such as comorbid diagnoses or parental psychiatric difficulties, all lower the probability that stimulants alone will be effective. In these cases the addition of some ancillary treatment can be helpful. These cases are also more likely to require more frequent follow-up from the physician, who will need to monitor the medication as well as continuously evaluate for comorbid disorders.

> Matt's parents want his ADHD treated, but it's Matt's defiance that is causing them sleepless nights. They hope that a stimulant will make Matt more compliant. Unfortunately, this happens only minimally. The nurse practitioner treating Matt strongly recommends ongoing parent counseling to help Matt's parents act as a team and suggests that Matt's mother be seen for treatment of her depression.

In other cases, some children with mild ADHD and other assets, such as good intellect, language skills, and social skills, and a compliant, resilient disposition without comorbid depression or anxiety, and living in stable, non-stressful homes, do well with medicine alone and do not require therapy. These children can be seen relatively infrequently.

*Stopping*

The duration for which to use stimulants must also be an individualized decision. Although in decades past, stimulants were discontinued during adolescence because doctors thought that ADHD was outgrown during those years, this turned out not to be the case for many. Therefore, many continue to use stimulants through the teen years. Patients, however, should be given an annual trial off medicine to ensure that medicine is still necessary. Sometimes this is a planned trial, but often it is inadvertent, such as when the parents forget to renew the prescription on time, thus living with an unmedicated patient for a few days.

> *Melissa's mother calls for a new methylphenidate prescription the first week in January. She tells her physician that the family just returned from a winter recess vacation in Florida. In all the pre- vacation hubbub, she forgot to pack Melissa's medicine. She reports that after one week with an unmedicated Melissa, it is very clear to her and her husband that Melissa continues to need methylphenidate.*

This case also points out that when one decides to discontinue a stimulant, the medicine can be abruptly stopped. It does not have to be tapered.

One difficulty in using the stimulants is that they are classified by the FDA as Class II substances. Class II medicines are classified as such because of their abuse potential and, in some states, require written, not phoned in, prescriptions that cannot be automatically refilled.

## Use in Special Groups

Let's look at the use of stimulants in very young children and for specific conditions and disorders.

### Preschoolers

The Preschool ADHD Treatment Study (PATS), the first major study of stimulants in this age group, treated children aged 3 to 5½ with methylphenidate at different doses (Greenhill, Kollins, et al., 2006). While all doses reduced the symptoms of ADHD, the optimal average dose was just under 5 mg three times daily. Overall, the young children responded best to either 2.5 mg or 5 mg three times daily.

The children tended to have a higher rate of side effects than older children, with more irritability, emotional outbursts, and repetitive thoughts. In addition, they had diminished appetite and more difficulty falling asleep, particularly at the higher doses of 5 mg and 7.5 mg, although even at these doses, fewer than 10% of the children were affected.

In short, methylphenidate is helpful in preschoolers with ADHD, albeit usually at lower doses and with a greater risk of side effects than in older children. This need for lower doses seems to contradict the point made in an earlier chapter that, because of their relatively larger liver, younger children might tolerate a higher dose of medicine. Methylphenidate, however, appears to be metabolized more slowly in young children, and the side effect of irritability seems to point to their being more sensitive to the stimulants. Again, this demonstrates that children are not small adults and that there are any number of factors that must be taken into account in prescribing medicine to children.

*Pervasive developmental disorders*

Methylphenidate has been found more effective than placebo in treating the hyperactivity associated with pervasive developmental disorder (Research Units on Pediatric Psychopharmacology [RUPP], 2005b). The response, however, was less than what one would find in children who have ADHD without PDD, and side effects were more frequent. Similarly, Ghuman and colleagues (2009) found that about half of a small group of preschool children with PDD or intellectual disability responded to methylphenidate with a decrease in ADHD symptoms. About half suffered side effects, however, including emotional lability and an increase in stereotypical behaviors. In summary, children with PDD might respond to stimulants, albeit at a lower rate than those without PDD and with a higher risk of side effects.

*Comorbid anxiety disorders*

ADHD and anxiety disorders are often comorbid in child patients. These children can be treated with a stimulant and an SSRI for anxiety, as there seems to be minimal interaction between these medicines. Nevertheless, one must be careful not to be fooled by the fidgety, distracted child who has an anxiety disorder and not ADHD. While a trial of a stimulant can be done quickly and seem immediately effective, sometimes one is lulled into its ongoing use, missing the anxiety that is the true problem. If one can delineate the underlying anxiety disorder, often a challenge, it should be treated first. Educating the parent and patient about anxiety and using cognitive behavioral techniques can often be helpful.

*Tourette's*

ADHD occurs in a substantial number of patients with Tourette's. Therefore, the question of treating these patients with a stimulant is of obvious significance. In general, the stimulants improve the ADHD symptoms of those with Tourette's and do not exacerbate tics. (See the section on side effects for a more complete discussion.)

*Bipolar disorder*

Although many assume that stimulants should not be given to those with bipolar disorder, a number of studies show that children with bipolar disorder do not suffer adverse effects when given stimulants and that they might in fact improve. Adding a stimulant to treatment with a mood stabilizer might also help the treatment response (Carlson, 2009). If a child is acutely manic, however, stabilization on a mood stabilizer should precede the addition of a stimulant (Practice Parameters on ADHD, JAACAP, July 2007).

## Side Effects of the Stimulants

For the overwhelming majority of patients, the side effects of the stimulants are mostly transient, reversible, or easy to manage.

*Headache*

Infrequently a child will complain of a headache upon initiating a stimulant. When headaches are present, they are usually transient, are manageable with or without over-the-counter pain medicine, and do not prevent the ongoing use of the stimulant.

*Stomachache*

Infrequently a child will complain of gastric upset when taking a stimulant. Usually this is minimized by taking the medicine with food.

*Pulse and blood pressure*

Slight increases in pulse rate and blood pressure are expected but are usually inconsequential. Infrequently these increases are greater than expected. Even in these situations they are generally not at a level beyond what a child experiences while playing sports. Nevertheless, the child's pulse and blood pressure should be monitored with dose increases and at follow-up visits so that, if a sustained increase is noted, a decision can be made about whether it should impact the use of medicine. For example, if a child's pulse rate increases to 120 beats per minute or higher when he is playing soccer for an hour, it is not medically problematic. If, however, the child's pulse is to be sustained at that level through the course of many hours every day by the use of a stimulant, the physician must decide whether that might be detrimental. In these situations, best clinical judgment and possibly a consultation with a pediatric cardiologist, not long-term data, might have to suffice.

## Cardiac arrhythmia and sudden death

This topic has garnered the most press in recent years. Death being the most significant of side effects, the potential for a fatal arrhythmia weighs very heavily in any evaluation of risks and benefits. For the same reason, however, it is the side effect most subject to needless fear. That being said, let's take an objective look at this topic.

In 1999 the American Heart Association (Gutgesell et al., 1999) did not recommend any specific cardiovascular monitoring for children treated with stimulants. Ten years later the possibility of sudden death from stimulants became headline news. What happened? In short, between 1999 and 2003, 19 cases of sudden death in children treated with stimulants was reported by the FDA (http://www.fda.gov/ohrms/dockets/ac/06/briefing/2006-4202B1_05_FDA-Tab05.pdf). These reports often consist of incomplete information supplied by physicians and sometimes supplied by the pharmacist, a sales rep, a newspaper, or a parent. Therefore the information about these cases is often sparse (for example, based on unknown doses taken for an undetermined length of time) about situations sometimes complicated by the patient's having taken other medicines concomitantly (e.g., insulin, olanzapine, cetirizine) or having other medical conditions (e.g. heart disease, diabetes, obesity). Such incomplete and complicated information is enough to cause fear but insufficient to lead to the conclusion that stimulants were the cause of death.

Putting all these questions aside, to assess risk we need to know if, given that about 2 million children per year take stimulants, are 19 deaths, while tragic, more than the expected rate of spontaneous sudden death in children who do not take stimulants? That rate is estimated at between 0.6 and 6 per 100,000 per year (see Biederman et al., JAACAP, 2006, for references). There are many difficulties in determining the risk of sudden death among those taking stimulants, including the rarity of this event and the difficulty of determining the number of children who actually take the stimulant prescribed for them.

Research is under way to try to answer these important questions, although this research is difficult and time-consuming. In the meantime, what should the clinician do? First, it is important to explain to parents that these events, even if they are caused by stimulants, are rare in the truest sense of the word. The risk of being struck by lightning in one's lifetime (1 in 5,000 according to the National Weather Service) is far greater than the risk of dying suddenly from taking a stimulant. Second, in addition to making sure that there has been a recent physical exam, clinicians should take a careful cardiac history, asking about congenital cardiac malformations, cardiac arrhythmias, unexplained fainting or other indications of an arrhythmia, shortness of breath, chest pain, or other symptoms of cardiac disease. In addition, because there might be a genetic component to cardiac defects, one should inquire about a family history of arrhythmias, unexplained faints, or sudden and unexpected death. (Adopted children, with their lack of family history, can present a challenge in this regard.)

Whether a baseline cardiogram (EKG) is necessary has been a source of controversy. Some clinicians will do one to rule out the possibility of an underlying arrhythmia, and others will not. If one does an EKG, one must realize that it ascertains only whether a patient might have a putative risk factor for the rare event. A normal EKG does not guarantee safety, as every parent would wish. In addition, cardiovascular diseases are not absolute contraindications to stimulant use. If a patient has a cardiac problem, the risk of stimulant use must still be weighed against the risk of leaving ADHD untreated.

*Appetite*

Decreased appetite is the most common side effect of stimulants and, in my experience, affects approximately 50% of children. Usually this amounts to a slight-to-moderate decrease in lunchtime appetite, although the decrease can be more significant. Sometimes appetite is suppressed until dinner. This problem is solved by moving dinner to a slightly later hour. When children do have a depressed appetite at lunch, they often have a rebound increase in appetite after the medicine wears off, so that by the end of the day, the child's intake is adequate. Although some feel this side effect might be more pronounced on AMPH, it is also a common side effect of MPH.

*Sleep*

If taken late in the day, stimulants tend to cause insomnia. When they are taken in the morning, this is rarely a problem. Occasionally patients taking long-acting stimulants, such as Concerta or Vyvanse, have difficulty falling asleep, so some patients refrain from using these medicines on the weekend, when children and adolescents might not awaken until late morning or even later. Paradoxically, some hyperactive children who cannot settle down for bedtime will actually fall asleep better if given a short-acting stimulant during the evening. This might help the patient settle down for bedtime without causing the expected insomnia.

*Mood*

The stimulants affect mood in a variety of different ways, although for many this effect is clinically insignificant. First, some children, especially young children and those with PDD or mental retardation, will become irritable or sad on a stimulant. This effect reverses when the medicine wears off but is often a reason not to use the stimulant. A child might also develop what is known as "rebound." This word is used in different ways. Some patients will become moody shortly after the medicine, especially a short-acting medicine such as immediate-release MPH, wears off. One must be careful to distinguish a true rebound from the child's simply returning to his or her baseline but seeming worse in contrast to how compliant he or she was while the medicine was working. Other patients become moody later in the afternoon. This is typically transient, often lasting less than a half hour, and is usually managed, or at least tolerated, by parents. It must be distinguished from the typical end-of-the-day "witching hour" misbehavior experienced by many families. In decades past, when only immediate-release medicines were available, adding a second dose about four hours after the first sometimes lessened the rebound. Today, with the increased use of long-acting medicines, it is less of a problem. Last, a child will occasionally experience increased anxiety on medicine. This is reversible but must be appreciated in deciding whether the benefit of the medicine outweighs the risk.

## *Loss of spontaneity*

Many parents are concerned that their fun-loving if impulsive child with ADHD will lose his or her spontaneity if treated with a stimulant. Some patients do become more affectively constricted. That is, they seem more serious and without the broad range of expressiveness their parents are used to seeing. Some adolescents also complain that they do not like the way the stimulant makes them feel, that they've lost their "creativity" or spontaneity. Lowering the dose of the stimulant sometimes alleviates this, although doing so sometimes also loses the benefit of the stimulant.

## *Growth*

The question whether stimulants inhibit height and weight growth has been discussed for decades. The concern stems from their obvious suppression of appetite and the fact that the increase in synaptic dopamine inhibits growth hormone (Faraone et al., 2008). In discussing this topic, one must be careful to distinguish between height and weight, as well as MPH and AMPH. It is also important to realize that children take different doses of stimulants for different lengths of time at different points in their development and that the effect of the stimulant might change over the course of treatment. All these might impact the extent of the stimulant's influence on growth. In addition, some have raised the question whether ADHD itself affects growth, another potentially confounding variable.

At this time, research has shown that both MPH and AMPH slow growth in height and weight to a small but statistically significant, degree, at least over the initial few years of treatment. Arguably, AMPH may have a slightly greater effect on weight than MPH. Of course, height cannot be lost, but patients can potentially lose weight. These effects are probably dose related, with higher doses of medicine causing greater slowing. On average, the MTA (Swanson et al., 2007) study demonstrated that after three years of stimulant treatment, children were approximately 2 cm (less than 1 inch) shorter than expected and 2 kg (about 4½ pounds) lighter than expected. This is similar to the findings of other studies. The PATS (Swanson et al., 2006), which looked at the treatment of preschoolers, is of particular note. This study found that heights were 20% less than expected and weight growth was 55% less than expected, stressing the need to follow these parameters closely in this age group.

This slowing in growth seems to be greater for taller and heavier children, greater in children than in adolescents, and greater for those who have taken a larger cumulative amount of stimulants. Over time these effects weaken, so that in the MTA study, the effects were greatest in the first year of treatment and lessened in subsequent years. Nevertheless, after three years, children treated with stimulants were still slightly lighter and shorter than expected. Pliszka and colleagues (2006) found, however, that despite an initial slowdown, after three years, treated patients were at their expected height and weight. Long-term studies of young adults who had taken stimulants during childhood for up to 5 years (Gittelman, Klein, & Mannuzza, 1988) and 10 years (Biederman et al., 2010) have shown that they are at their expected height. The perfect study, examining children who took a standard dose of stimulants from childhood through adulthood and comparing them to a placebo group, has not been, and probably cannot be, done.

The mechanism for this effect on growth is poorly understood. Although diminished appetite is the obvious suspect, the situation is more complex, and while appetite is obviously important, it is not necessarily true that loss of appetite alone leads to slowed growth or weight gain. Studies in humans and other mammals indicate some effect on growth hormone, prolactin, and cartilage growth. These findings are inconsistent, however, and there is some evidence that receptors adapt over time, possibly accounting for the eventual catch-up in growth.

Clinically, all patients should have a baseline measurement of height and weight, as well as follow-up measurement every three to four months, or more frequently if indicated. So while the effect of stimulants on height and weight is important, practically speaking, with frequent follow-up, a slowdown should be neither a surprise nor dangerous. There are no current guidelines for what level of growth deceleration constitutes grounds for lowering the dose of medicine or changing medicines, and if one changes from one stimulant to another, there is no guarantee that the effect will be any different. It is reassuring that most of the evidence indicates that if the stimulant is discontinued, height returns to what is expected. If height is consistently compromised, consultation with a pediatric endocrinologist is recommended.

Weight that is not increasing as expected can usually be followed while the patient is encouraged to eat foods of a higher caloric content. Some clinicians have used periactin as an appetite enhancer. Patients will often refrain from using stimulants on weekends or during the summer, reasoning that this will allow for growth catch-up. While this makes common sense, research data do not clearly support this. Also, if the medicine's effect on growth diminishes over time, these steps may not be necessary. The use of drug holidays must always be balanced, too, against the risk of untreated ADHD. For overweight children, sometimes slowing the increase in weight is a hidden, and welcome, benefit and pushes the clinician to rethink the balance of benefits and risks.

*Tics*

The listing of tics as a side effect of stimulants is based on case reports and small case series from the early 1960s (Bloch et al., 2009). The association seemed reasonable in that stimulants increase synaptic dopamine and the antipsychotics, which are the most effective treatments of tic disorders, block dopamine. The more recent research, however, does not strongly support the implication that stimulants cause or exacerbate tics.

As a backdrop for this discussion, consider that approximately 20% of all school-age children (with and without ADHD, with and without stimulant treatment) will experience a transient tic during the elementary school years. So tics are a fairly common event during childhood. In addition, in children with ADHD and a comorbid tic disorder, the ADHD usually precedes the tic disorder by a couple of years. Therefore, if a child with ADHD is treated with a stimulant and develops a tic within the next few months or years, it is very possible that the tic would have occurred anyway (Bloch et al., 2009).

The question of tics can be divided into two parts. Do the stimulants cause tics in those who have never had them? And do the stimulants exacerbate the tics of those who already have them—either transient tics or a chronic tic or Tourette's disorder? Law and Schachar (1999) gave MPH and placebo to a group of children with ADHD who had no history of tics and a group with a history of tics. Of those without a history of tics, about 20% of those treated with MPH and about 17% of those treated with placebo developed a "clinically significant" tic. This was a statistically nonsignificant difference indicating that MPH does not seem to cause tics. Of those with a history of tics, about one third of the children had a worsening of tics, whether they were given MPH or placebo, indicating that MPH does not seem to worsen tics. Gadow and colleagues (1995) treated children with ADHD and a tic disorder with MPH and placebo and found that MPH did not exacerbate tics. In fact, in their two-year follow-up of these children (Gadow et al., 1999), tics did not change in frequency or severity, despite ongoing treatment with MPH. Other studies (Castellanos et al., 1997) have pointed to relatively high doses of AMPH, but not MPH, having a possible slight effect on increasing tics.

The bottom line is that there is no evidence that stimulants, particularly MPH, cause tics in a child who has not had them or exacerbate tics in a child who has. Having said that, one must remember that these studies were relatively small and therefore might not catch the relatively rare event. Most clinicians have seen a child for whom tics seem to worsen on stimulants. So although this is infrequent, and while accurately linking the stimulant to a naturally vacillating condition like tics is vexing, the clinician should remain open to the possibility that for any particular patient, a stimulant might exacerbate a tic and need to be discontinued.

*Psychotic symptoms*

This is a very infrequent occurrence, with Ross (2006) making a very rough estimate that approximately 1 in 400 patients is affected. It is manifested by a variety of symptoms, including hallucinations, delusions, and manic symptoms. There are few guides to predict who will experience this, but fairly predictably psychosis is reversed within a few days of discontinuing the medicine. This side effect is not a problem for children with "uncomplicated" ADHD using typical doses of stimulants, but is most significantly a problem for children who seem predisposed to psychosis or those who take large doses of stimulants that are beyond typically prescribed doses. Although inattention is usually only one of many symptoms of these diagnostically challenging children, the possibility that a stimulant will precipitate psychosis is often a concern. If a child has a history of ongoing psychosis, stimulants should not be prescribed.

If a child begins to experience psychosis, the stimulant should be discontinued. Treatment with antipsychotic medicine is generally not necessary, as the symptoms should resolve within a few days. After the psychotic symptoms resolve, if there are no ongoing complicating clinical issues, the stimulant can be retried, albeit with careful monitoring of the patient.

## Addiction

Because the stimulants have been known as drugs of abuse, a common fear among parents is that their children will become dependent on or addicted to them. It is important to distinguish between abuse and dependence. The core of dependence is the compulsive use of the substance, usually with the need for increasing doses and a withdrawal accompanied by physical symptoms. The crux of abuse is a pattern of repeated use of a substance with "significant adverse consequences" (DSM-IV, p. 182), such as interfering with legal, medical, or social functioning. I would add, in my definition of "abuse," that the substance is being used for a purpose other than its medically intended purpose, namely to get a high or a rush.

Given these distinctions, let's first address the question of dependence. There are no data supporting the idea that children treated with stimulants in a medically responsible manner become dependent on the stimulants. Personally, I do not recall ever having seen this happen, although I have seen many adolescents discontinue stimulants despite the protests of their parents. This is not dependence. Occasionally an individual patient might require an increase in his or her dose of medicine. This infrequent adjustment to a new and lasting plateau differs, however, from a fairly continuous increase in the required dose.

Do children and adolescents abuse their stimulants? In general, they do not. Rapoport and colleagues (1980) reported that one difference between the use of AMPH by a group of adult men who did not have a history of childhood learning or behavior problems and a group of boys with and a group of boys without hyperactivity (i.e., ADHD) was that the adults reported some feeling of euphoria. The children did not. Children do not experience euphoria and do not abuse stimulants. Adolescents with ADHD do not experience euphoria at prescribed doses and generally do not abuse their stimulants, though some do. These teens take excessive doses orally, or they snort, smoke, or inject the medicine. Usually, tablets of MPH or AMPH are crushed and snorted. Long-acting capsules prevent this abuse.

Recall that the slow absorption of medicine through the GI tract differs from the abrupt and rapid increase when the medicine is snorted. The reinforcing effect of stimulants is thought to result from the rapid increase in dopamine in the nucleus accumbens of the brain. This rapid increase results from higher doses and a quicker route of entry, namely snorting, with smoking and injecting being even more rapid (Volkow, 2006). Long-acting capsules are difficult to crush. In addition, they increase synaptic dopamine at a slower and steadier pace than immediate-release tablets and then do not produce the rush sought by some.

Another concern is whether the use of stimulants during childhood increases the chances of later substance abuse during adolescence and young adulthood. This does not seem to be the case, although ADHD itself is a risk factor for later substance abuse. In a meta-analytic review of six studies, Wilens and colleagues (2003) found that treatment with stimulants lowered the risk for alcohol and drug use disorders. While one group of researchers (Lambert, McLeod, & Schenk, 2006) has found evidence to the contrary, most have found that stimulant treatment does not increase the possibility of later substance abuse and might decrease it (Biederman et al., 1999; Wilens et al., 2003).

*Diversion of stimulants*

While this is not a physical side effect, it is listed here because it is a public health issue. Over recent years, with the increased use of stimulants, more stimulants are being used by those who obtain them from their friends, not their physician. Wilens and colleagues (2006) found that approximately 11% of young adults, with an average age of 20 years, diverted their prescribed stimulant medicine to others, although all of those diverting their medicine had ADHD and either comorbid conduct disorder or substance abuse disorder. Those without these comorbidities were much less likely to divert their medicine. Of note, all the medicine diverted was of the immediate-release type.

The nonprescribed use of stimulants is largely a problem among college students, but it is also a problem among high school students and adults. Wilens and colleagues (2008), looking at 21 studies, estimated that 5–9% of grade school and high school youth and 5–35% of college-age individuals had used nonprescribed stimulants in the prior year. The most common reason given for the use of these medications is to help the student focus or stay alert, usually to aid studying and thereby raise grades. The desire to party and get high was a second reason. In Wilens's review "whites, members of fraternities and sororities, individuals with lower grade point averages . . . and individuals who report ADHD symptoms are at highest risk for misusing or diverting stimulants" (2008, p. 21). This seems to indicate that the stimulants are used more by "marginal" students trying to get by than by successful students trying to be more successful.

*Obsessions and compulsions*

Although obsessions and compulsions, such as hand washing, can be seen, this side effect tends to occur very infrequently and reverse with discontinuation of the medicine.

## Contraindications to Using Stimulants

There are a number of conditions that are concerns, and sometimes relative or absolute contraindications, to the use of stimulants.

*Psychosis*

Because stimulants can exacerbate psychosis, they should not be used in patients with active psychosis or a history of schizophrenia or manic psychosis. Some children who present with "complicated" ADHD might, in fact, be pre-psychotic, although with no crystal ball, this is difficult to predict. If these children are treated with a stimulant, they must be observed carefully.

*Cardiac disease or high blood pressure*

As I've discussed, most patients will experience a minor increase in blood pressure while taking stimulants, so already existent hypertension is a contraindication. In addition, because of the risk of negatively affecting the heart, those with cardiac symptoms or disorders should not take stimulants or should first consult a pediatric cardiologist.

*Glaucoma*

The stimulants carry the risk of increasing the pressure within the eye, although this is rarely, if ever, a problem in children.

*Drug abuse*

Those with a history of drug abuse or dependence, especially of stimulant abuse, should be given stimulants only very carefully. While this can be done in a controlled setting, treating these patients, some of whom have ADHD, on an outpatient basis requires careful monitoring of the medication supply and the patient's use of it.

*Allergy to a stimulant*

A patient who has had an allergic reaction to a stimulant should not be given that medicine again. Trying a different stimulant, however, or even the same stimulant produced by a different company, is reasonable. Also, when patients report a history of a drug allergy, it is important to ask for the details, as patients sometimes use the word "allergy" to characterize what was actually an adverse reaction.

*Seizures*

Although seizures can result from toxic doses of stimulants, this is not a side effect at the usual therapeutic doses. A history of seizures is almost always listed as a contraindication to stimulant use, although it is not clear what data support this contention. Nevertheless, children whose seizures are controlled can be treated with stimulants (Gonzalez-Heydrich, 2006). If seizures worsen, the stimulant should be discontinued. In treating these children one must be cognizant of the comorbidities of children with seizure disorders, the risks of uncontrolled ADHD and the potential for epilepsy or the child's antiepileptic medicine to cause the symptoms of

ADHD. This highlights the need for a thorough evaluation and good seizure control with antiepileptic medicine with minimal side effects.

*Anxiety*

As already noted, anxiety is not a contraindication to the use of a stimulant. Both Diamond and colleagues (1999) and the MTA study (1999) showed that children with and without anxiety improved when treated with stimulants. Interestingly, in the MTA study, children with ADHD and anxiety who were treated with behavior therapy alone improved more than those in community care, thus suggesting that optimal treatment for these children might include behavioral treatment or at least the monthly support given to the "medicine only" group. Clinically, the child who seems to have ADHD and comorbid anxiety can be difficult to treat, not because the stimulant increases the anxiety, but because symptoms such as fidgetiness and inattention might be due to the anxiety disorder and not ADHD. This is a problem of diagnosis, not treatment.

*Tics*

As noted above, a history of tics is not a contraindication of stimulant use. Such patients should nevertheless be monitored for an exacerbation of tics, a vexing task, given the natural waxing and waning of tics.

## Drug Interactions

Let's consider the known interactions between stimulants and other substances. In doing so, we should recognize that methylphenidate has a complex metabolism and is therefore not particularly influenced by other medicines. Amphetamine is similar. However, in contrast, one of amphetamine's metabolic pathways is via the CYP450 enzyme 2D6, so that medicines that inhibit 2D6 could, at least theoretically, increase amphetamine levels.

*MAOIs*

MAOIs are absolutely contraindicated for a person taking a stimulant because of the risk of a potentially lethal spike in blood pressure.

*Caffeine and decongestants*

These are not absolutely contraindicated. Nevertheless, any substance that can increase heart rate can, when added to a stimulant, at least theoretically add to the risk of too rapid heart rate or arrhythmia.

*SSRIs*

There does not seem to be a problem with using stimulants in patients being treated with an SSRI for depression or anxiety. Because one metabolic route of AMPH is through 2D6, inhibitors of 2D6, such as fluoxetine, paroxetine, and bupropion, will increase blood levels of AMPH. This effect has been noted in animal studies (Greenhill, AACAP Meeting, 2009).

*Atomoxetine*

Although research supporting the use of a stimulant with atomoxetine is in its early stages, some clinicians use this combination. In general, the dose of each medicine is minimized. Side effects, however, might be elevated.

*Illicit drugs*

College students will often have the foresight to refrain from taking their stimulants when they are planning to use alcohol or illicit substances, although sometimes those using the stimulants to get high will purposely take them with other illicit substances. It is important to warn young people about this practice, in particular about using stimulants with drugs such as cocaine and Ecstasy, both of which can predispose the person to a potentially fatal cardiac arrhythmia.

## Methods of Delivering the Stimulants

As we've seen, some patients require the effect of stimulants only during the school day and others require these effects for as long as possible every day of the week. Given the short duration of action of the immediate-release AMPH and MPH tablets, the drug companies have tried to provide alternative methods of delivery to maximize the effect of the stimulants with the addition of flexibility.

The stimulants are currently available in a variety of forms. The immediate-release tablet was the original form of methylphenidate and amphetamine. Each tablet contains one dose of medicine which, when swallowed, is promptly absorbed into the bloodstream. The duration of action of this type of pill is approximately three to four hours for methylphenidate and four to six hours for AMPH or mixed amphetamine salts.

The stimulants are also available as capsules containing beads of medicine. The beads are constructed so that some release one dose of medicine immediately and others release a dose of medicine a few hours later. Thus the beaded capsule lasts for approximately twice as long as the immediate-release tablet. This also improves compliance for the afternoon dose, since when the pill is taken in the morning, one is taking both the morning and afternoon doses. Another benefit of these beaded products is that the capsule can be opened and the beads sprinkled onto a spoonful of apple sauce, ice cream, or other food if the child has difficulty swallowing pills. The beads, however, should not be chewed, as that changes the timing of the medicine's release. Older forms of slow-release MPH and AMPH did not use beads but rather were in the form of a slow-release tablet that could not be sprinkled.

The stimulants are also available in other forms discussed below.

Of note, increasing the dose of methylphenidate does not increase the duration of the medicine. It only increases the effect of the medicine during the time it is effective. Increasing the dose of amphetamine, however, might increase the duration of the medicine.

A caveat is in order before we go forward. Take the durations of action with a grain of salt. First, they vary from person to person. Some people experience the average duration and others do not. My experience is that this variability is particularly true of the long-acting forms of either MPH or AMPH. Second, sometimes patients do not experience as long a duration as the manufacturer reports. That might be because, although the medicine is still more effective than if the patient took no medicine, as the medicine wears off, the patient does not have the same experience of its effect as when the medicine was at its peak blood level.

Also, when switching from an immediate-release to an extended-release preparation, I do not simply switch from the immediate-release pill to an "equivalent" dose in the extended-release form. Rather, I start the extended release capsule at a lower dose and then increase the dose as required. While this takes a few more days, it prevents patients from taking too high a dose of the extended-release capsule. (This principle is also true for changing from immediate release guanfacine to extended release guanfacine (Intuniv), an alpha agonist.)

## Specific Stimulants

Let's turn now to the forms in which various stimulants are available.

### *Methylphenidate products*

These come in a variety of forms.

#### *Methylphenidate*

MPH is sold as the generic, as Ritalin, and as Methylin. These immediate-release tablets contain d-MPH and l-MPH, the right- and left-handed isomers of MPH, although it is the d- isomer that is more pharmacologically active (Paykina & Greenhill, 2008). These immediate-release tablets last about three to four hours. For children who cannot swallow them, the tablets can be crushed into powder and put in a spoonful of water. They can also be cut in half in order to halve the dose. The Methylin brand of MPH is also available in chewable pills (2.5 mg, 5 mg, and 10 mg tablets) and an oral solution (as 5mg/5ml and 10mg/5ml).

#### *Focalin*

This is the brand name of dexmethylphenidate, or d-MPH, the right-handed isomer of MPH (or the same as MPH without the left-handed isomer). The thinking behind the development of this medicine was to use the more therapeutically active right-handed isomer, thus minimizing side effects. While some patients do very well on Focalin, many, in fact, have the usual side effects of MPH. It is important to note that because the pill contains only the d- isomer, the dose is about half the dose used for MPH.

#### *Ritalin SR and Metadate ER*

These are older forms of long-acting Ritalin, which do not use the beaded capsule method of delivery and therefore cannot be opened and sprinkled. They generally last about eight hours.

## Ritalin LA

This is the beaded capsule form of Ritalin and has a duration of about six to eight hours. Half the medicine is released immediately, and half is released about three to four hours later.

## Methylin ER

This is similar to Ritalin LA.

## Metadate CD

This is another beaded capsule form of methylphenidate. It differs from Ritalin LA in that it releases about 30% of the medicine immediately and 70% after a few hours. Thus the major effect is weighted toward the afternoon.

## Focalin XR

This is the beaded form of dexmethylphenidate. Interestingly, while one would expect these capsules to last about six to eight hours, which they often do, they are reported to work for up to 12 hours.

## Concerta

This is a long-acting form of MPH which looks like a capsule but does not use the beaded release mechanism. Instead it uses an osmotic-controlled release oral delivery system (OROS), which allows for three doses of medicine to be delivered over the course of the day. In essence, the first dose of medicine is painted onto the outside of the pill and releases immediately after being swallowed. The second and third doses are in compartments within the pill along with a mechanism that absorbs water. As water is absorbed, it applies pressure within the pill, so that after about four hours the medicine in one of the two compartments is released through a small hole in the tip of the pill. About four hours later, after more water has been absorbed, the other compartment releases the third dose of medicine. Thus the pill has a duration of about 12 hours, or three times the duration of the immediate-release tablet. Of note, sometimes the shell of the pill goes through the intestines intact, albeit having released its medicine, and can be seen in the toilet the following day. I tell this to younger children, who, after a bowel movement, can otherwise be startled to see their pill floating in the toilet. It is also important to tell families that opening or cutting Concerta will destroy its release mechanism. It must be swallowed as is. The smallest dose of Concerta is an 18 mg pill, which contains 4 mg on the outside and then two 7 mg compartments for later release inside. It is easiest to see this as roughly equivalent to taking 5 mg of methylphenidate three times daily.

### Daytrana

This is the patch form of MPH and is generally applied to the patient's hip in the morning. The medicine is slowly absorbed and sometimes does not start to work for about two hours. It then goes on to work until about three hours after the patch is removed. The patch should be removed after about nine hours, so the maximum duration of the medicine is about 12 hours. The dose of the medicine is adjusted by using different-sized patches, which contain different doses of medicine. The benefit of this delivery method is that it does not need to be swallowed and can be removed before nine hours, thus electively shortening the duration of its action and side effects. The downside of the patch is that it can cause local irritation to the skin and thus should be rotated from spot to spot. Of note, however, one study found that the medicine was better absorbed when the patch was applied to the hip than when it was applied over the shoulder blade. Thus, placement location matters. Also of note, when absorbed through the skin, both d- and l- isomers enter the brain, so the dose required through the patch might be lower than the dose needed when one takes MPH in pill form.

## Amphetamine products

These are also available in a variety of forms.

### Amphetamine

This d-amphetamine product is sold as a generic or as Dexedrine immediate-release tablets. Its duration is approximately four to six hours.

Patients often confuse Dexedrine with Dexatrim, the latter being an over-the-counter appetite suppressant to induce weight loss.

### Mixed amphetamine salts

This combination of four different salts of amphetamine is sold as a generic or as Adderall. During the 1960s it was marketed as Obetrol for weight reduction, albeit as a combination of different salts. Its duration of action is approximately four to six hours. This duration exceeded that of immediate-release MPH, which had been the popularly used stimulant until the 1990s. This duration became a marketing advantage, since it did not require children to get a second dose from the school nurse at lunchtime. Some children, however, experience a shorter duration of action.

### Methamphetamine

This is a long-acting form of amphetamine, marketed as Desoxyn, but not as widely used for ADHD because of its association with abuse.

### Dexedrine spansules

This is the long-acting capsule of Dexedrine. It does not use the beaded delivery system and cannot be sprinkled.

### Adderall XR

This is the long-acting capsule of Adderall. It uses the beaded release mechanism and so can be opened and sprinkled. As with Adderall, the capsules are available in a fairly large number of doses. Its duration is approximately nine hours.

### Vyvanse

This form of d-amphetamine is also known as lisdexamfetamine dimesylate. It is d-amphetamine bound to lysine, an amino acid. After the medicine is absorbed in the small intestine, the lysine is cleaved off the d-amphetamine, at which time the d-amphetamine becomes active. If one introduces the medicine through another route, namely snorting, smoking, or injecting, it is ineffective. This provides a means of preventing abuse. An added benefit of Vyvanse is its long duration, reportedly up to

13 hours, but again, not for everyone. Roughly speaking, Vyvanse 30 mg is equivalent to Adderall XR 10 mg.

# Atomoxetine

In 2003 atomoxetine became the first non-stimulant to be FDA approved for the treatment of ADHD. The initial enthusiasm for this medicine revolved around its not being a Schedule II (controlled substance) medicine, so prescribing was easier. Also for some patients one dose in the morning often lasts until the next day.

### How Atomoxetine Works

Atomoxetine is a selective norepinephrine reuptake inhibitor, blocking the norepinephrine transporter and thus the reuptake of norepinephrine into the presynaptic neuron. This effect increases both norepinephrine and dopamine in the prefrontal cortex but not in the nucleus accumbens. Therefore atomoxetine does not have abuse potential. Because it does not increase dopamine in the striatum, it is less likely to cause tics. In fact, in a placebo-controlled study of children and adolescents with ADHD and a tic disorder (Allen et al., 2005), atomoxetine diminished tics better than placebo. (Selective norepinephrine reuptake inhibitors are sometimes labeled SNRIs, but they should not be confused with serotonin/norepinephrine reuptake inhibitors, which are also labeled SNRIs. See Chapter 7.)

It is important to note, atomoxetine is metabolized by the cytochrome P450 enzyme 2D6. About 5–10% of the population have less 2D6 and are therefore so-called slow metabolizers of atomoxetine. In these patients the serum half-life might be four times longer (about 20 hours), the blood levels higher, and the side effects more pronounced than in so-called fast metabolizers. These fast metabolizers, having an excess of 2D6, might require higher doses of atomoxetine or twice-daily dosing because the medicine is metabolized so quickly, with a serum half-life of about five hours.

### Clinical Indications of Atomoxetine

Atomoxetine has been shown to be effective in the treatment of both the hyperactivity and inattention of ADHD. In a double-blind, placebo-controlled study of children and teens with ADHD, Michelson and colleagues (2002) showed that once-daily dosing of atomoxetine was effective in reducing the symptoms of ADHD. It has also been shown effective in twice-daily dosing (Michelson et al., 2001). When compared with a stimulant, atomoxetine is found to be less effective (Practice Parameters for ADHD, July 2007). Therefore, even though it is FDA approved for the treatment of ADHD, it is usually seen as a second-line treatment. Nevertheless, some patients respond very well to atomoxetine.

Because it inhibits the reuptake of norepinephrine, the possibility that atomoxetine had antidepressant effects was raised. In a double-blind, placebo-controlled study (Atomoxetine ADHD and Comorbid MDD Study Group, 2007), however, this was not found to be the case. Nevertheless, Geller and colleagues (2007) found that atomoxetine lowered the anxiety levels of patients treated for ADHD. This raises the possibility of treating those with ADHD and comorbid anxiety with one medicine instead of the often used combination of a stimulant and an SSRI.

Atomoxetine also offers some other advantages over the stimulants. These include its lack of desirability to drug-abusing patients and its potentially long duration of action, often allowing for dosing once in the morning.

## Using Atomoxetine

Unlike stimulant dosages, the dosage of atomoxetine is related to the patient's weight. Therefore, atomoxetine is generally started at a weight-adjusted dose of about 0.5 mg/kg. It is then increased after about four days to around 1.0–1.2 mg/kg. This can be done on a once-per-day dose, although side effects may be minimized by giving the medicine twice daily. This dose is often effective. Some patients will have a greater response if the dose is increased to 1.8 mg/kg (Michelson et al., 2001).

Although a response might be seen after the first week, the optimal response may not be found until as long as six weeks later. Therefore, the 1.0–1.2 mg/kg dose is maintained for about four weeks before increasing to the higher dose range. Newcorn and colleagues (2009) found that about half of patients begin to respond optimally within the first month of treatment, although they continue to improve more by taking the medicine longer. The researchers also found, however, that about 40% of patients do not respond within the first month and are less likely to respond even after taking the medicine longer. Only about one in five patients who did not respond within the first month went on to become a responder. Therefore, if no response is seen within the first month, consideration should be given to making sure the patient is receiving the maximal dose, if tolerated, or to changing to another medicine. The study also suggested that some patients respond to small doses of medicine and do not require the maximum doses.

Despite its short half-life, some patients find atomoxetine lasts all day when given in the morning. This response is not understood, but may occur because the effect at the synaptic level is longer than the duration of time the medicine stays in the blood. Some patients, however, require twice-daily dosing. Donnelly and colleagues (2009) report that treatment over three or four years was generally well tolerated.

When atomoxetine is discontinued, the medicine can be stopped without being tapered. I find it prudent, however, to taper the medicine slowly every few days.

If the patient does not respond to a stimulant or to atomoxetine, a trial of the other should be considered, as there is some indication that many patients respond selectively to one or the other (Newcorn et al., 2008).

## Side Effects of Atomoxetine

A number of side effects have been noted among patients taking atomoxetine.

### Tiredness

Tiredness occurs during the day in about 10–20% of patients. For many, this subsides after the first month, if the patient can tolerate it through that time. Night sleep is not adversely affected by atomoxetine, and in fact insomnia might be improved.

*Gastrointestinal*

Although atomoxetine might not have the same appetite suppressant effects of the stimulants, about one quarter to one half of patients complain of nausea, abdominal pain, and other GI symptoms, which can diminish food intake. Dividing the dose into twice-daily dosing or taking the medicine with food might help. These side effects might also decrease over time, if the patient can manage until then.

*Cardiac*

Because there are significant differences between the effect of atomoxetine on the pulse rates and blood pressures of slow and fast metabolizers (Michelson et al., 2007), prudence suggests a routine check of pulse and blood pressure in case the patient is a slow metabolizer.

*Liver*

Cases of hepatitis have been reported, but this seems to be the rare occurrence. Elevated liver enzymes are very infrequent and do not seem to be of clinical importance. Nevertheless, some clinicians test the blood for baseline liver enzyme levels and then repeat these after a few months.

*Growth*

There might be a slight and transient effect on height and weight growth (Yates, 2004). Donnelly and colleagues (2009) found no significant change in growth over three or four years. And Spencer and colleagues (2007) showed an initial change in height and weight at about one to two years, but no change for most children after five years. In short, height and weight should be monitored, but atomoxetine should not be avoided for this reason if it is otherwise clinically indicated.

*Suicidality*

Atomoxetine carries a black box warning from the FDA for causing suicidality. This is based on a review of over 1,300 patients, finding that the rate of suicidality in those taking atomoxetine was about 4 per 1,000, with 1 patient making a suicide attempt. No patients treated with placebo demonstrated suicidality. Thus there seems to be a risk, albeit one that is very small.

*Tics*

Atomoxetine does not seem to have an adverse effect on tics and might improve them (Allen et al., 2005).

### Drug Interactions

Because atomoxetine is metabolized by 2D6, care must be taken when it is given with drugs that inhibit 2D6. This inhibition can cause the blood level of atomoxetine to be higher than expected.

### *Fluoxetine, paroxetine, and bupropion*

These are all 2D6 inhibitors, though bupropion less so. Therefore the dose of atomoxetine must be lowered.

### *MAOIs*

Though rarely used, these should not be used within two weeks of stopping atomoxetine.

# Alpha Agonists: Guanfacine and Clonidine

The alpha agonists are medications used to treat adult hypertension that for many years have also been used to treat a variety of pediatric difficulties, albeit off-label. Their uses have included the treatment of ADHD, insomnia, and tics. During the 1980s clonidine became the first alpha agonist used to treat ADHD, being more effective at diminishing impulsivity and hyperactivity than improving attention span and therefore more often used to treat children with more disruptive, aggressive ADHD. Subsequently, guanfacine became more widely used because of its longer duration and tendency to cause less sedation than clonidine. Guanfacine extended release was then developed to further extend the duration without abrupt changes in blood levels and, in 2009, was the first alpha agonist to receive FDA approval for a pediatric use. Subsequently, long-acting clonidine was also approved.

### *How Alpha Agonists Work*

The alpha agonists are selective alpha 2A receptor agonists. These receptors are located throughout the brain. Affecting those in the prefrontal cortex via axons coming from the locus coeruleus is thought to lead to improved attention and diminished impulsivity. By reducing the firing of neurons in the locus coeruleus, the alpha agonists minimize arousal (Scahill, 2008).

## Clinical Indications of the Alpha Agonists

In a double-blind, placebo-controlled study, Sallee and colleagues (2009) have shown guanfacine extended release to be effective in treating ADHD. Interestingly, guanfacine improved both hyperactivity-impulsivity and inattention at least as well as atomoxetine, although this study did not obtain ratings by teachers. These positive effects began within the first week and increased as the dose was increased. At higher doses of 3 mg and 4 mg, these effects were noted to be as powerful as those of the stimulants. Unfortunately, this efficacy was proven in children but not adolescents. Furthermore, until it is proven in a direct comparison with the stimulants, including teacher ratings, I would continue to consider the stimulants the first-line treatment for ADHD.

The alpha agonists have also been used to treat tic disorders in children, albeit without FDA approval for this use (see Chapter 8 on antipsychotic medicines). Although they are not as effective as medicines such as haloperidol, they are generally seen as first-line medicines because of their generally mild side effect profile. Of particular note, the alpha agonists have been used to treat children with ADHD and comorbid tics and, if both these disorders require treatment, might be the first choice of medicine. The Tourette Syndrome Study Group (2002), however, found that a combination of MPH and clonidine was more effective than either MPH or clonidine alone.

Because of their strong sedating effect, the alpha agonists, particularly clonidine, have been used to induce sleep in children with insomnia (see Chapter 10 on sleep disorders). This popular use of the alpha agonists, especially in treating the insomnia often associated with ADHD, is off-label.

## Using the Alpha Agonists

Guanfacine extended release is started at 1 mg daily and increased by 1 mg increments approximately weekly. Sallee and colleagues (2009) showed an eight-hour duration for the 1 mg and 2 mg doses and a 12-hour duration for the 3 mg and 4 mg doses, thus finding the medicine to be fairly effective throughout the day. While some change in ADHD symptoms might be seen within the first week, a full trial of one month might be necessary in the treatment of ADHD. In treating tic disorders, an 8–12 week trial of an alpha agonist is sometimes necessary.

When used for ADHD, clonidine is usually started at 0.05 mg in the morning and then, after about three days, is increased to 0.05 mg twice daily. After a few more days, it is increased to three times daily. Then every few days, each dose is increased by 0.05 mg. When used for sleep, clonidine is started at 0.05 mg at bedtime, then slowly increased by 0.05 mg increments up to a total dose of about 0.3 mg. Clonidine does not have to build up. Rather, it works immediately to induce sleep.

## Side Effects of the Alpha Agonists

Let's consider some common side effects of the alpha agonists.

### Sedation

Tiredness is the most common side effect, probably affecting up to about 25% of patients. This tends to start early in treatment but resolve over subsequent weeks. Nevertheless, it is the most common cause of patients' deciding to discontinue medicine.

### Cardiac

Pulse and blood pressure tend to decrease as the dose of medicine increases. Sallee and colleagues (2009) found that these measures were not clinically significant. Nevertheless, particularly because of this medicine's history of use as a treatment of hypertension, blood pressure and pulse should certainly be monitored. While EKG changes seem infrequent, some clinicians do baseline and follow-up EKGs. Of particular note is the need to educate families about the potential for rebound blood pressure increase if clonidine, which is short acting, is stopped abruptly.

### Gastrointestinal

Stomachache and nausea affect approximately 5–10% of patients.

*Dry mouth*

This has been noted in some patients.

*Headache*

Headache affects about 20% of patients.

## Drug Interactions

The combination of an alpha agonist with a stimulant has been used for many years, in particular for children with ADHD and a tic disorder. The Tourette Syndrome Study Group (2002) found that the combination of stimulants and alpha agonists tended to diminish side effects of each. Nevertheless, given the lack of data on the use of this combination of medicines on large numbers of children and the theoretical possibility of their causing an adverse cardiac effect, the combination should be used cautiously, particularly in those with cardiac risk factors.

Table 6.1. reviews the doses typically used with medicines approved for treating ADHD.

# Bupropion

Bupropion is marketed as an antidepressant for adults and is covered in greater detail in Chapter 7 on antidepressants. Because of its effects on dopamine and norepinephrine, it has also been used as an alternative and off-label treatment of ADHD to be used if the patient fails trials with a stimulant, atomoxetine, or guanfacine extended release. In addition, bupropion might be considered for treating an adolescent with ADHD and depression.

In a double-blind, placebo-controlled study of children, Conners and colleagues (1996) showed immediate-release bupropion to treat effectively the symptoms of ADHD, albeit not as well as the stimulants. Doses were in the range of 3–6 mg/kg per day in divided doses, and positive effects were seen as early as the third day. And in a small study, which had no placebo control, using bupropion SR to treat adolescents with ADHD and comorbid depression, Daviss and colleagues (2001) found that slightly more than half showed improvement in both depression and ADHD, slightly more than one quarter showed improvement in depression only, and one patient showed improvement in ADHD but

| TABLE 6.1. Commonly Used FDA-Approved ADHD Medicines | | | |
|---|---|---|---|
| **Brand name** | **Generic name** | **Typical starting dose** | **FDA maximum/day\*** |
| *Amphetamine preparations* | | | |
| Adderall | mixed amphetamine salts | 3–5 year old: 2.5 mg/day 6 and older: 5 mg daily–twice daily | 40 mg |
| Dexedrine | d-amphetamine | | |
| Dextrostat | d-amphetamine | | |
| Adderall XR | mixed amphetamine salts | 6 and older: 10 mg/day | 30 mg |
| Dexedrine spansules | d-amphetamine | 6 and older: 5–10 mg/day | 40 mg |
| Vyvanse | lisdexamfetamine | 20–30 mg/day | 70 mg |
| *Methylphenidate preparations* | | | |
| Focalin | dexmethylphenidate | 2.5 mg daily–twice daily | 20 mg |
| Methylin | methylphenidate | 5 mg daily–twice daily | 60 mg |
| Ritalin | methylphenidate | | |
| Focalin XR | dexmethylphenidate | 5 mg daily | 30 mg |
| Metadate CD | methylphenidate | 10–20 mg daily | 60 mg |
| Ritalin LA | methylphenidate | | |
| Concerta | methylphenidate | 18 mg daily | 72 mg |
| Daytrana | methylphenidate | 10 mg patch | 30 mg patch |
| *Selective norepinephrine reuptake inhibitor* | | | |
| Strattera | atomoxetine | less than 155 lbs: 0.5mg/kg | lesser of 1.4 mg/kg or 100 mg |
| *Alpha agonist* | | | |
| Intuniv | guanfacine extended release | 1 mg/day | 4 mg |

Note: Based on Practice Parameters for ADHD, July 2007, p. 905.

\*FDA maximum doses for some medicines can be exceeded off-label, if cautiously. These doses are usually not greater than approximately 25–50% above the FDA maximum, depending on the medicine.

not depression. Of note, the improvement in ADHD in this study was observed by parents but not teachers.

## Tricyclic Antidepressants

The tricyclic antidepressants (TCAs) have been used for over 50 years to treat a variety of disorders, including depression, anxiety disorders, and enuresis. They have been largely replaced by other medicines and are reviewed more fully in Chapter 7 on antidepressants. Because of their effect on catecholamines, they have also been used to treat ADHD.

The TCAs have been shown to be effective in the treatment of ADHD. They must, however, be used cautiously in children and reserved for situations in which more proven and safer medicines have failed to treat effectively a child whose difficulties mandate treatment with medicine.

## Modafinil

Modafinil is a non-stimulant wakefulness-enhancing medication used to treat narcolepsy and sleep phase disorders in adults. It is equivalent to approximately six cups of coffee in promoting alertness in sleep-deprived adults (Paykina & Greenhill, 2008). Its mechanism of action is not well understood.

Modafinil has been used off-label to treat ADHD. In a double-blind, placebo-controlled trial treating children and adolescents with ADHD, Greenhill, Biederman, and colleagues (2006) found modafinil to treat ADHD effectively. Although side effects in this study did not cause patients to discontinue the medicine any more than placebo, those taking modafinil did report more insomnia, headache, appetite suppression, and weight loss.

Modafinil is generally started at 50–100 mg daily and increased to 200–400 mg daily (Scahill, 2008). It seems to have no cardiac side effects. In a large trial, however, one case of a child with Stevens-Johnson syndrome and a case of visual hallucinations were reported, after which the manufacturer withdrew its application to the FDA for approval for the treatment of ADHD (Paykina & Greenhill, 2008). At this time it must be considered an alternative treatment of ADHD to be used if more established and better understood treatments have failed.

# Case Examples

*Case 1: Arthur is a sweet, likable 7-year old who tries hard to do what he is told. He has been hyperactive since he started walking at 10 months. He cannot sit at the dinner table for more than half a minute, and his parents report that he is constantly annoying his siblings. He requires immediate follow-up when asked to do any task. His teacher reports that although he has no learning disabilities, Arthur cannot sit at his desk like his peers and that he misses instructions and leaves most of his work incomplete. Arthur is successfully treated with methylphenidate, on which he is less active, far more attentive, and more able to do what his parents and teacher ask of him. His skilled parents are then very capable of managing him behaviorally.*

*Comment:* Arthur represents the fairly straightforward case of ADHD, without comorbidity. He is treated successfully with a stimulant, and because his parents and teacher are quite adept at managing him behaviorally, he requires little else in the way of treatment beyond the monitoring of his medicine.

*Case 2: Allyn is 8 years old and has a long history of being fidgety, impulsive, and inattentive. In addition, however, she has always been demanding, defiant, highly irritable, and easily provoked. She is somewhat less squirmy on methylphenidate but continues to be oppositional and to experience temper outbursts.*

*Comment:* Allyn might have ADHD, but her more pressing diagnosis is probably oppositional defiant disorder (ODD). Although she requires a thorough evaluation, ruling out other diagnoses such as depression, the comorbid diagnoses of ADHD and ODD suggest that simple treatment with a stimulant will be insufficient. Other pharmacological interventions might be considered, but ongoing parent counseling and possibly individual psychotherapy are almost certainly required.

*Case 3: Fifteen-year-old Tawanda is doing well in life but struggles in school. She is intelligent but cannot focus on her reading, which seems torturous, and which she chronically resists. Thus*

*she has difficulty with homework and is doing poorly in many
of her academic classes. She is quite capable at and can focus
intently on her art assignments. Her parents want to know if she
has ADHD and whether stimulants would help her live up to the
academic potential predicted by her intellect. She does not fit clear
criteria for ADHD, predominantly inattentive type, but is started on
Adderall with some success. Both she and her parents are satisfied,
although she plans to discontinue the stimulant when she moves
into her field of interest.*

*Comment:* Youngsters like Tawanda highlight the important role of
educational achievement in our society. If Tawanda could forgo reading
literature and history and simply move into fashion design, which she
longs to do, she would probably show no significant signs of ADHD.
Stimulants, however, have helped her focus on reading and thus raise her
grades a notch. The medical risk has been minimal.

*Case 4: Brian is 10 and has experienced a series of tics over recent
years. First, Brian blinked continuously for a few months. One year
later, Brian began to scrunch his nose frequently. This lasted a few
months, after which he began to experience an ongoing shoulder
shrug. Brian's parents could live with the tics. But Brian's impulsivity was getting him tossed out of class and driving them crazy.
Ritalin was started. A few weeks later, Brian began clearing his
throat excessively. Brian's mother wondered if this was caused by
the Ritalin.*

*Comment:* Determining if a tic is due to a stimulant or simply the
natural waxing and waning of tics is a vexing task. Although research
has shown that children with a history of tics develop tics whether they
are on a stimulant or placebo, rarely one sees a child whose tics seem to
correspond perfectly with the use of stimulants. In these cases, if stimulant
use is mandatory, the tics might be treated with an alpha agonist.

## CHAPTER 7

# Antidepressant and Antianxiety Medicines

The antidepressants, misleadingly named, encompass a few different types of medicine. They include the monoamine oxidase inhibitors (MAOIs), the tricyclic antidepressants (TCAs), the selective serotonin reuptake inhibitors (SSRIs), the serotonin-norepinephrine reuptake inhibitors (SNRIs), and a random group of others, some of which are related to one another. (Note that the S in SNRI stands for "serotonin," not "selective," as the first S in SSRI does.) By far the most commonly used of these in child psychiatry are the SSRIs, the best known being Prozac (fluoxetine). But the other groups are of more than historical note in adult psychiatry and play an interesting role in understanding the development of psychopharmacology in child psychiatry.

The antidepressants are misleadingly labeled in that they are used to treat depression but also to treat adults with anxiety disorders, such as social anxiety disorder and panic disorder, obsessive-compulsive disorder (OCD), posttraumatic stress disorder (PTSD), eating disorders, and premenstrual dysphoric disorder (PMDD). They are also used to treat children with many of these disorders, although their use is often off-label. In fact, although none of the SSRIs is approved for the treatment of youth with anxiety disorders (other than OCD), and only two are approved for the treatment of those with depression, the SSRIs are actually more effective as antianxiety medicines than they are as antidepressants. The SSRIs provide a good example of a medicine that allows the diagnostician a little wiggle room in deciding whether the patient has more depression or more anxiety. At the end of the day, the SSRI (so-called) antidepressants treat them both.

As a group, the antidepressants were deeply ingrained in the psychopharmacology revolution of the 1950s. Iproniazid, a medicine that inhibited monoamine oxidase (an enzyme used to break down monoamines) and was used to treat tuberculosis in the early 1950s, was observed to improve the mood of some patients with tuberculosis. This helped lead to the theory that monoamines, such as norepinephrine and serotonin, were important in causing depression. Even though the use of iproniazid was discontinued, this finding led to the development of other MAOIs to treat depression. Unfortunately, they were associated with a significant difficulty, that is, the requirement of abstaining from certain foods and drinks or else risking a severe increase in blood pressure, possibly requiring emergency medical care (see the discussion below).

A few years later it was noted that imipramine, which was being tested in the treatment of schizophrenia, also elevated mood. Imipramine is a compound whose central molecule is composed of three rings, a similar structure to that of the antipsychotic phenothiazines. With a substitution of nitrogen for sulfur, the molecule went from being an antipsychotic to an antidepressant, and the three-ringed medicines that followed became known as the tricyclic (three-ring) antidepressants. The TCAs dominated the treatment of adult depression for the next 30 years.

By the 1980s, medicines were being developed to enhance selectively the effects of serotonin, and by 1988 the most famous of these, Prozac (fluoxetine), was being marketed as an antidepressant that did not cause many of the anticholinergic and cardiac side effects of the TCAs or require the significant dietary restrictions of the MAOIs. For this as well as other reasons I'll discuss, Prozac and the SSRIs that followed largely replaced the TCAs and MAOIs.

Because the antidepressants treat both depression and anxiety, I examine their use for both types of disorders in this chapter. At the end of this chapter I discuss those medications that are labeled the antianxiety medicines or anxiolytics. These include such medicines as the benzodiazepines and buspirone and are used to treat anxiety, not depression.

## How Antidepressants Work

In general, the three basic types of antidepressants increase the synaptic levels of monoamines, namely norepinephrine, serotonin, and to some extent dopamine. The way they accomplish this, and the combination of monoamines that are changed, are what differentiate the various families of antidepressants.

Monoamine oxidase is an enzyme that breaks down monoamines after they have crossed the synapse from the presynaptic neuron to the postsynaptic neuron. MAOIs inhibit monoamine oxidase, thus increasing the level of monoamines in the synapse. Presumably this increased level of monoamines is what treats depression. Of importance to note, the original MAOIs developed in the 1950s irreversibly inhibited monoamine oxidase. Recall that the nervous system is a complicated place and that monoamines do not simply transmit messages relating to mood. In particular, norepinephrine also plays a role in regulating blood pressure, and if its level is too high, blood pressure can soar. We'll see how the MAOIs can cause that to happen when I discuss their side effects.

There are two monoamine oxidases, MAO-A and MAO-B. These break down different monoamines and are found in different parts of the body. MAO-A has a greater effect on norepinephrine and serotonin, neurotransmitters thought to be involved in depression. MAO-B has a greater effect on dopamine and other amines.

The TCAs increase the level of monoamines in the synapse, not by preventing their breakdown but by inhibiting their reuptake back into the presynaptic neuron. Significantly, however, the TCAs, like the MAOIs, also affect many other neurotransmitters, for example, by blocking some receptors of acetylcholine and histamine. Interfering with these other neurotransmitters causes many side effects and is one of the reasons why drug companies developed the SSRIs, which have fewer effects on many different neurotransmitters.

The different TCAs affect these different neurotransmitters to different degrees and so present different side effect profiles. For example, amitriptyline is fairly anticholinergic (blocking acetylcholine). This causes it to have more anticholinergic side effects, such as dry mouth and constipation.

The SSRIs, such as Prozac and Zoloft, selectively block the reuptake of serotonin back into the presynaptic neuron, thus increasing the levels of serotonin in the synapse. In general, they have minimal effects on the other neurotransmitters. The SNRIs, namely Effexor (venlafaxine) and Cymbalta (duloxetine), are slightly different in that they block the reuptake of norepinephrine as well as serotonin. Remeron increases serotonin levels by causing the presynaptic neuron to release more serotonin, not by blocking the reuptake of serotonin back into the presynaptic neuron.

Wellbutrin stands somewhat apart from the others in that it affects levels of dopamine and norepinephrine, although its exact mechanism is not known.

## Clinical Indications of the Antidepressants

Before discussing the disorders treated by the antidepressants, I want to repeat a basic theme of this book. Developing children and adolescents are complicated, constantly changing beings who are impacted by numerous forces, including their families, their friends, their sexual relationships, their schools, their jobs, the substances they place in their body, and so many more. While the clinician searches for, and sometimes finds, a conglomerate of symptoms called a disorder, any childhood disorder exists in a still maturing person who is responding emotionally to a host of often invisible but usually powerful forces. Sometimes these forces create a clinical picture that resembles, but is not, a disorder. And if a disorder is diagnosed, the solution is not necessarily medicine.

For example, children are influenced by the functioning of their parents. Weissman and colleagues (2006) found a diminished rate of psychiatric disorders in the children of depressed mothers who responded to treatment and an increased rate of psychiatric disorders in the children of mothers who did not respond to treatment. For some children, the treatment of their disorder consists of treating their parent's disorder.

Adolescents can be exquisitely sensitive to the influence of their peers. This includes everything from clothing styles to suicidal behavior, making it prudent to consider environmental changes before rushing to medicine in some cases.

When one considers how difficult it can be for an adolescent to share with the clinician the various forces behind his or her behavior, one should take care not to jump too hastily to the conclusion that the adolescent has a depression that requires an antidepressant. Often guidance, support, or just the tincture of time is sufficient. More than once I have seen an adolescent's "depression" disappear with the advent of a boyfriend or girlfriend, albeit sometimes one who is depressed. I am also often amazed at the powerful effect a change of environment can have on many depressed adolescents. Whether this means hospitalization, residential placement, or simply a change of friends, the effect is often dramatic, obviating the need for medicine.

If an antidepressant is required, one must consider the role of therapy, whether supportive or more specific, such as cognitive behavioral or interpersonal therapy. Sometimes family therapy is required to deal with the family dynamics that played a role in causing or exacerbating the depression, and other times it is necessary to deal with the family dynamics that are caused by having a depressed youth in the home.

In short, treating children and adolescents is not simple; it can be tricky and should almost never be reduced to simply finding the right medicine.

That being said, let's examine the indications for using antidepressants, focusing on depression and anxiety disorders. After examining the role of antidepressants in treating depression, I discuss their role in the treatment of anxiety disorders. We'll look at the group of social anxiety disorder–separation anxiety disorder–generalized anxiety disorder separately from obsessive-compulsive disorder, panic disorder, and PMDD. I examine the use of these medicines to treat disorders such as trichotillomania, eating disorders, and PTSD in Chapter 11.

## Depression

Depression, which affects about 2% of children and 6% of adolescents (Birmaher et al., 1996), is a disorder consisting of excessive sadness accompanied by a group of symptoms enduring over time. It is not simply a matter of transient sadness or being demoralized, symptoms that are part of normal development. Patton and colleagues (2008), in a study of almost 6,000 adolescent girls, found that about half had some depressive symptoms, most of which resolved within the year. This is an important distinction because, while a moody, irritable young person, especially an adolescent, can cause parents and school staff to feel a compelling urge to treat, particularly with an antidepressant, medicine might not be necessary. And if the antidepressant is effective, there is a fairly good chance that it is the placebo response at work.

The data on treating depression is culled from studies of youth who fit the criteria for major depression. According to DSM-IV, these consist of a change of functioning represented by either depressed (or irritable) mood or marked "diminished interest or pleasure in all, or almost all, activities" (DSM-IV, p. 327), accompanied by at least four other symptoms, such as change in appetite, change in sleep pattern, fatigue, feelings of worthlessness, or suicidal thoughts. The depressed mood must occur "most of the day, nearly every day" (DSM-IV, p. 327) over at least two weeks and cause significant distress or impairment. These symptoms can occur as a single episode or as recurrent episodes.

That is a fairly high standard and is not usually met by many adolescents who are seen as "depressed" by those around them. That is also the standard by which we know that antidepressants are effective. We cannot extrapolate to assume that medicine will also diminish the demoralization of those who do not have major depression.

If an episode of major depression represents a dramatic change in the patient's presentation, a more subtle depressive disorder is dysthymic disorder. This disorder also consists of a depressed (or irritable) mood that occurs "most of the day, for more days than not" (DSM-IV, p. 349), and is accompanied by a minimum of two other symptoms, such as hopelessness, fatigue, or insomnia. Instead of requiring a two-week duration, however, these symptoms must occur for at least one year, such that the person has not been without the symptoms for more than two months at a time. Clinically, these are patients who are chronically sad or irritable, though more functional than the typical patient with major depression. Although they are functional, their functioning is impacted by their disorder, and they often seem perpetually grouchy and gloomy. One can imagine the difficulty of distinguishing a young child's dysthymic disorder from the child's prickly, irritable, lifelong, inborn temperament, if the two are in fact different. The line between temperament and disorder is a fuzzy one.

Although both major depression and dysthymic disorder are associated with a variety of risks, about 70% of children and adolescents with dysthymic disorder will develop major depression, called double depression. This usually occurs after about two or three years and is a particularly malignant combination, putting the patient at greater risk for functional impairment, substance abuse, suicidality, bipolar disorder, and other psychiatric disorders (Birmaher et al., 1996).

Of the many problems caused by depression, one of the most significant is its frequently chronic course. Birmaher and colleagues (1996) reported that although about 90% of depressed youth will improve over 24 months, about 70% will have another episode within the next five years. And Curry and colleagues (2010) found that 96% of adolescents had recovered from their initial depressive episode after five years. But, almost half had experienced another episode of depression. Lewinsohn and colleagues (2000) found that only about 25% of depressed adolescents were free of psychiatric disorder at approximately 24 years old. Another 50% of these young adults had depression, sometimes alone and sometimes comorbid with another disorder, and the last 25% were not depressed but did have another psychiatric disorder. Those with a history of depression were also at higher risk for substance abuse, more severe depressive episodes, and more stress and conflict. Another study, by Rao and colleagues (1993), showed that about 5–10% of teens with depression would commit suicide within the next 15 years. In short, depression, as defined by DSM-III and IV, is a serious, life-threatening illness for which proactive treatment must be considered.

Research is also providing a greater understanding of the disorders of preschool-age children. Although depression was previously not thought possible in this age group, Luby and colleagues (2003) found that DSM-IV criteria are effective in diagnosing preschoolers with more severe depression and that slightly modified criteria might be even more effective. In particular, while irritability is seen as a common symptom of depression, it casts too wide a net, as many non-depressed preschoolers are also irritable. When, however, irritability is seen in the context of excessive guilt, the inability to enjoy, and social withdrawal, depression should be more highly suspected (Luby, 2009).

As I've noted, medicine is almost never the only treatment for depressed children and adolescents. Some type of therapy, whether supportive or more specific, such as cognitive behavior therapy or inter-personal psychotherapy, should always be considered. At the very least, educating the patient and his or her family about depression is crucial. Medicine, however, can be life-saving. What is the evidence that it is helpful?

Most of the data regarding the efficacy of antidepressants to treat depression are based on short-term studies. These studies answer the question whether, relative to placebo, the symptoms of depression decrease substantially over about 6 to 12 weeks. This question must be distinguished from whether these medicines are effective over many months or a year or longer. The extent of improvement must also be kept in mind. Are the patients completely better and back to their usual selves? Or are they simply much better, albeit with ongoing symptoms? And if the latter, what are the consequences?

The first group of medicines studied in the depression of youth were the TCAs. From the 1960s through the 1980s, these medicines had been found effective in treating adult depression. During those years, the thinking of mental health professionals changed from seeing children as not cognitively mature enough to experience depression to seeing them as able to experience adult-like depression. In the wake of that realiza-tion, researchers began to study whether the TCAs, which were effec-tive for adults, would also be effective for childhood depression. In the meantime, clinicians, previously without any pharmacologic treatment for this disorder, extrapolated from adult psychiatry and used the TCAs to treat children and adolescents. The MAOIs were not widely used in children because of safety concerns relating to the need for severe dietary restrictions. Despite their efficacy in adults with depression, the pediatric studies of the 1970s and 1980s failed to show that the TCAs were more effective than placebo.

By the 1990s the SSRIs had arrived, and studies examining their efficacy were begun. Before I review these, a reminder is warranted. To prove itself effective, the medicine must be more effective than placebo. If placebo is ineffective, being more effective is relatively easy. But if placebo is very effective, medicine will have a harder time proving itself effective. In fact, in most of the SSRI studies the rate of response to placebo is greater than 30% and often higher than 40% or even 50%. Medicine would have to be quite effective to better those rates. Interestingly, one analysis of this phenomenon demonstrates that the placebo rate is higher in studies that use a greater number of study sites, thus suggesting a way to refine research so that the results are clearer (Bridge et al., 2009).

Another difficulty in evaluating the pharmacologic treatment of youth depression rises from the disclosure that, until recently, some studies with negative findings were not published. Having only some of the data available renders decision making a challenge at best. With that caveat, the positive findings can be reviewed.

In an early study, Emslie and colleagues (1997) found fluoxetine to be more effective than placebo in treating children and adolescents with depression. In this study, 56% of those treated with medicine improved significantly, while only 33% of those treated with placebo did so. In another study, Emslie and colleagues (2002) again found fluoxetine to be effective.

Keller and colleagues (2001) found paroxetine more effective than placebo in treating adolescent depression. In the same study, imipramine, a TCA, was not more effective than placebo. Interestingly, although the researchers found the patients to be improved, the rating scales of neither the patients nor their parents reflected this improvement. In addition, this is one example of positive findings being tainted because negative findings were withheld (Connor, 2004). Also, in a subsequent double-blind, placebo-controlled study of depressed children and adolescents, Emslie and colleagues (2006) found that paroxetine was no more effective than placebo.

After combining the data of two controlled studies, Wagner and colleagues (2003) reported that sertraline was more effective than placebo. While the rate of response of those taking sertraline was 69%, however, the response rate of those taking placebo was 59%. Although this is a statistically significant difference, it gives a sense of how high the placebo response rate can be.

In a study of adolescent depression, Emslie and colleagues (2009) found escitalopram, an isomer of citalopram, effective. With a placebo response of about 50%, however, the response to escitalopram, while significant, was not powerfully different. And in a study of children and adolescents with depression, Wagner, Jonas, and colleagues (2006) did not find escitalopram significant. Yet when children and adolescents were looked at separately, there was some indication that the response of adolescents might have been significant. Again this underscores the point that children and adolescents should be seen as two different populations. Wagner, Robb, and colleagues (2004) also found that citalopram was more effective than placebo in treating depression in children and adolescents.

The most significant study at this writing has been the large government-funded Treatment for Adolescent Depression Study (TADS) (March, 2004). This 12-week study compared three treatments with placebo in over 400 moderately to severely depressed teens. The three treatment groups consisted of one group treated with fluoxetine and cognitive behavioral therapy (CBT), one group treated with fluoxetine only, and one group treated with CBT only.

After three months, 71% of the group treated with medicine and CBT responded, while 60% of the fluoxetine group, 43% of the CBT group, and 35% of the placebo group responded. This leads to a few conclusions about the short-term treatment of adolescent depression. First, patients treated with fluoxetine alone responded better than those taking placebo, thus proving the efficacy of fluoxetine with roughly the same response rates as in the 1997 study by Emslie and colleagues.

Second, the group given both treatments showed the greatest rate of improvement, thus lending credence to the recommendation that, while depressed adolescents respond to fluoxetine, they respond even more when a therapy, in this case CBT, is added to the treatment regimen. Notably, however, other studies did not confirm that CBT added value to an SSRI alone in treating depression (Clarke et al., 2005;

Melvin et al., 2006; Goodyer et al., 2007), although possibly CBT is more valuable in treating the anxiety than the depressed component of these patients' disorder.

Third, once again, the number of depressed adolescents who responded to placebo was not insignificant. And last, almost 30% of the adolescents treated with both fluoxetine and CBT were not considered to be responders, and almost one third of those who significantly improved still had three or more symptoms of depression.

It is also interesting to note which patients did the best after 12 weeks. They included those who were younger than 16, those who were doing better before the onset of depression and were depressed for fewer than 40 weeks, those with no comorbid diagnoses or only one, those with fewer suicidal thoughts, and those without a history of hopelessness or a comorbid anxiety disorder (Curry et al., 2006). In short, younger teens with less complicated and briefer depressions were most responsive initially to pharmacologic treatment. Older teens with more protracted depressions and more complicated diagnoses tended to be less responsive.

The TADS (2007) has also provided follow-up of the treatment groups after 18 and 36 weeks. By 18 weeks, the fluoxetine-only group and the CBT-only group were approaching the response rate of the combined group, which at that time was 85%. And by 36 weeks, these two groups had the same response rate as the combined treatment group. So while combined treatment was initially best, and while medicine was initially superior to CBT, by about nine months all groups were equal. I discuss the practical implications in the following section. Before we feel too sanguine about the ultimate treatment possibilities of either medicine or CBT alone, however, let's remember that nine months is a long, painful, and potentially dangerous time to wait with a depressed adolescent.

In addition to these studies of the SSRIs, some of the other antidepressants have been studied, unfortunately revealing a lack of efficacy relative to placebo. For example, Emslie and colleagues (2007) showed that venlafaxine ER was ineffective in the treatment of children with depression but possibly effective in the treatment of adolescents—another reminder that one cannot simply extrapolate conclusions from one age group to another. In addition, mirtazapine and nefazodone have both failed to prove themselves better than placebo. Bupropion has not been studied in a controlled trial.

In summary, the evidence supports the use of at least fluoxetine and escitalopram for the treatment of pediatric depression, and these are in fact both FDA approved for the treatment of depression in youth. Some evidence also supports the use of some of the other SSRIs, such as sertraline and citalopram.

As already noted, however, some caveats are in order. First, all studies demonstrate a high (sometime very high) placebo response rate. Second, while the rates of improvement are at about the 60% level, that means that 40% of depressed youth do not respond, leaving the clinician with the difficult task of trying to help these youngsters. (Dealing with these non-responders will be covered in the next section). Third, although two medicines have proven their efficacy in at least two studies, it is unclear whether the others are also effective. This awaits further evidence. In fact, escitalopram, effective in two trials, was ineffective in another trial. Fourth, most studies showing, or not showing, a response to medicine lasted about 8 to 12 weeks. These studies may be too short to prove the efficacy of medicines that can take weeks or months to be effective. Last, it is unclear how to understand the negative studies revealed over recent years. In short, while the SSRIs are clearly a significant help to many, they are not perfect, and the clinician should not be drawn into seeing them as a panacea for the serious problem of youth depression.

In addition, controlled studies of treating preschoolers are lacking. The assumption that this age group can be treated like older children has led some to use SSRIs in treating preschoolers. Nevertheless, the lack of data supporting this practice, and the possibility that young children are more prone to activation (discussed below), has led others (Luby, 2009) to recommend against this treatment, unless absolutely necessary, and toward the use of certain types of psychotherapy instead.

### Anxiety Disorders

Besides depression, the anxiety disorders are the other major indication for treating a pediatric patient with an SSRI. Because they often coexist, I consider generalized anxiety disorder (GAD), social anxiety disorder, and separation anxiety disorder together. I then consider panic disorder and obsessive-compulsive disorder (OCD) separately.

The anxiety disorders are characterized by excessive anxiety in response to specific precipitants, although sometimes there is an increase in anxiety without a specific precipitant. The classic paradigm for an anxiety disorder is the well-known simple phobia, in which a common object or activity precipitates an out-of-proportion feeling of anxiety, which can be accompanied by a variety of somatic reactions such as sweating and shaking. Because many children experience phobias, and because most phobias are confined to well-circumscribed events, they are easily recognized and usually interfere little in the person's everyday life. In general, their treatment is behavioral, and so they will not be considered here.

Similarly, GAD, social anxiety disorder, and separation anxiety disorder reflect excess anxiety, though not in response to such a well-circumscribed precipitant. In addition, the anxiety can manifest as tantrums and defiance, which the child, and sometimes the parent, does not recognize as anxiety based.

GAD manifests as a globally excessive anxiety and apprehension, with frequent "What if . . . ?" questions reflecting concerns about virtually anything. This was amply demonstrated by an overly anxious patient of mine who was an excellent math student in the fourth grade, but worried about how he would perform on the SATs he would take in seven years. The worries can be about the future, the child's family, school, world events, or virtually anything else and can sometimes manifest as irritability. Often these worries are accompanied by physical symptoms, including sensations such as feeling wired, stomachaches, headaches, tiredness, and insomnia. Differentiating GAD from ADHD can sometimes be a difficult, but important, task.

Social anxiety disorder reflects excessive concern about being scrutinized by others. Children with social anxiety often have difficulty meeting other children, resist reading or speaking aloud in class, sit by themselves on the bus, and are generally seen as extremely, in fact painfully, shy. Children with selective mutism are sometimes thought of as having a variant of social anxiety disorder. These children refrain from speaking in public, although they speak freely at home, and can cling tenaciously to this pattern of behavior. They often rely on other children in their class to speak for them.

Separation anxiety disorder, typically occurring in younger children, is characterized by a fear of being away from the caregiver, which can lead to a reluctance to attend school or birthday parties, difficulty being alone at bedtime, shadowing the parent around the house, and excessive anxiety when parents leave the house, even if they're only going out briefly. Frequently these children fear that something terrible will occur to their parent. In recent years these children have become increasingly tied to their parents by cell phone.

Social anxiety, separation anxiety, and generalized anxiety disorder all interfere with normal expectations of children in ubiquitous activities. The ability to proceed through life without excess worry, to separate from caregivers at age-appropriate times, and to socialize with peers is almost assumed. A child who has difficulty attaining these abilities often slides by without anyone knowing, or with people ascribing the behavior to personal style. For example, the child who does well in school and has friends but is a chronic worrier is dismissed by others as "a good kid, but a worrywart," the child's GAD having been relegated to a matter of personal style rather than a disorder. Only those who know the child well will realize how difficult life can be for that child. The child with separation anxiety disorder is seen as "kind of clingy, but she'll get over it," unless her behavior demands attention because she adamantly refuses to attend school. Because of this, many of the roughly 10% of children who suffer from an anxiety disorder suffer silently, slipping through the cracks and rarely causing enough of a disturbance to be recognized.

The consequences of having an anxiety disorder can be quite significant, however. Through their childhood and adulthood, these children are at greater risk for physical symptoms, academic problems, depression, substance abuse, and suicide attempts. Not the least problem faced by these children is the increased risk of ongoing anxiety or of developing another psychiatric disorder. For example, Colman and colleagues (2007) did a 40-year follow-up of over 3,000 adolescents who had been evaluated at 13 and 15 years of age. They found that an adolescent who had anxiety or depression at both 13 and 15, when compared to either those who had anxiety or depression at only one of those ages or to a control group, had a much higher rate of anxiety or of having been treated for a psychiatric disorder. As with depression, a compelling question is whether early treatment can change that discouraging course.

The treatment of these anxiety disorders rests on the use of behavioral treatment, such as CBT, and the use of medication. Which of these should be initiated first, or whether they should be used simultaneously, has been the focus of some investigation. Although I will not review the studies showing the efficacy of behavioral therapy, a few comments about it are necessary.

First, behavioral therapy, particularly cognitive behavior therapy, is best done by a qualified therapist. Such therapists are not always available, and when they are, the family must be willing to invest the time and effort in learning and practicing behavioral therapy. This can be a challenging sell to some parents in the age of psychopharmacology, when taking a pill seems so simple. In addition, some children are unable or unwilling to engage in CBT, which takes a certain level of directedness.

Second, however, is that whatever benefit the patient accrues from behavioral therapy will last a lifetime. The initial course of treatment is typically a series of sessions and then a periodic booster session. Once a new cognitive approach is learned, the patient's ongoing use of CBT techniques effectively amounts to self-imposed booster sessions. This is a powerful self-perpetuating process that becomes a part of the way the patient thinks and obviates the need for medicine. Many feel that CBT should, ideally, be the first treatment for an anxiety disorder.

Severe dysfunction, comorbidities such as depression, and the inability to engage in CBT can create a compelling case that medicine should be initiated sooner rather than later. The medicine used in that circumstance is usually an SSRI. Sometimes a novel antidepressant is used. The TCAs are still prescribed occasionally, as are the benzodiazepines in selected situations. Buspirone also has a place in this group. It is important to note that none of these medicines is FDA approved to treat these anxiety disorders in youth. Nevertheless, as we'll see, the SSRIs are probably more effective for treating anxiety disorders than for treating other disorders, such as OCD and depression, for which some of them are FDA approved.

Rynn, Siqueland, and Rickels (2001), in a small double-blind, placebo-controlled study, found that sertraline at a small dose of 50 mg daily was effective in treating children and adolescents with generalized anxiety disorder. While anxiety improved, depression did not. So in this study, these two effects were independent of each other.

Birmaher and colleagues (2003), in a placebo-controlled study, found that over 60% of children and adolescents with these three anxiety disorders responded to 12 weeks of fluoxetine versus 35% of those given placebo. Interestingly, the response of those with social anxiety accounted for the high response rate of the anxiety group, and even in this group, patients were left with some symptoms of anxiety.

In a large double-blind, placebo-controlled study examining the effects of SSRIs on children and adolescents with these three anxiety disorders, the Research Units on Pediatric Psychopharmacology (RUPP) Anxiety Study Group (2001) found that after eight weeks, fluvoxamine at a maximum dose of 300 mg daily was effective in lowering anxiety. On one rating scale, 76% of those treated with medicine improved, while only 29% of those taking placebo improved.

In a still larger double-blind, placebo-controlled study of over 300 children and adolescents with social anxiety disorder, Wagner, Berard, and colleagues (2004) showed that about 77% of those treated with paroxetine responded, while only 38% of those treated with placebo did so. In addition, approximately three times the number of paroxetine-treated subjects were "very much" improved.

These four studies show growing evidence that different SSRIs are effective in treating these three anxiety disorders. In the largest study to date, Walkup and colleagues (2008) compared the effects of sertraline, CBT, a combination of sertraline and CBT, and placebo. In a 12-week study, almost 500 children and adolescents with these three anxiety disorders were randomly assigned to one of these four groups. CBT was delivered in 14 sessions, and sertraline was given at up to 200 mg daily. Approximately 81% of those treated with the combination therapy were rated as "very much" or "much" improved, compared to almost 60% of those treated with CBT, almost 55% of those treated with sertraline, and almost 24% of those given placebo. This study adds significant weight to the evidence that SSRIs are effective in anxiety disorders, but also that

CBT is equally effective. Most important, it shows that a combination of CBT and an SSRI is the most efficacious treatment, providing significant help to four of five patients.

Some groups of medicines besides the SSRIs have also been used to treat the anxiety disorders. Overall, either the evidence supporting their use is less convincing or safety concerns prevent their use as a first-line medicine. Venlafaxine, an SNRI, has been tested in treating anxiety disorders in children and adolescents. In a double-blind, placebo-controlled study of patients with social anxiety disorder, March and colleagues (2007) found venlafaxine ER to be an effective treatment, although the risk of suicidality was higher than in the placebo group. Venlafaxine ER has also been tested against placebo in generalized anxiety disorder, Rynn and colleagues (2007) finding that it bested placebo. In this study, however, those on venlafaxine, while not experiencing serious side effects, did experience a greater incidence of milder side effects such as loss of appetite, weight loss, somnolence, and increased pulse and blood pressure.

As we've seen in my discussion of depression, prior to the advent of the SSRIs, the tricyclic antidepressants dominated the treatment of depression and were also used in treating anxiety. Early placebo-controlled studies showed some efficacy of the TCAs, such as imipramine and clomipramine, in treating refusal to go to school (which probably correlates to the current separation anxiety disorder). Nevertheless, these studies, which date through the early 1990s, when the SSRIs were gaining popularity, have designs that confound our understanding of the results or do not conclusively show the medicine to be superior to placebo. Given the risks associated with the TCAs (see below), the medicines are not commonly used in the treatment of anxiety disorders at this time.

In addition, some research has looked at the benzodiazepines, such as alprazolam, and buspirone for the treatment of anxiety disorders. These will be examined at the end of the chapter.

### Obsessive-Compulsive Disorder

Obsessive-compulsive disorder (OCD) is categorized in DSM-IV as an anxiety disorder, but it is seen as distinct from the anxiety disorders discussed above. It affects about 1% of children and adolescents and must be distinguished from the developmentally normal rituals that are typical of many youngsters. Rather, those with OCD are plagued by intrusive thoughts or the compelling need to perform unwanted behaviors that seem pointless but feel like they must be done.

Common obsessions include intrusive thoughts of danger befalling loved ones, of aggression toward oneself or others, of repulsive sexual acts, of contamination by germs or toxins, of numbers and their mental manipulation, and so on. Compulsions include excessive washing, counting, straightening, repeating, checking, confessing, and hoarding.

Interestingly, recent research has shown that obsessions and compulsions coalesce into four different groups. Some patients suffer from contamination or cleaning rituals; others from aggressive, sexual, or religious obsessions; others from ordering and symmetry rituals; and still others from hoarding or checking (Mataix-Cols et al., 2009). While this categorization explains part of the difference among patients, the hope is that these types of distinctions will lead to better understanding of the causes and treatment of each type of OCD.

OCD can be an acutely debilitating disorder which prevents the person from going forward with his or her usual day-to-day activities. Over the long run, it is a disorder that has a waxing and waning course. In a fascinating follow-up study (Skoog & Skoog, 1999), the same physician who examined hospitalized adult patients with OCD in the 1950s examined these patients again 40 years later. Approximately half of these patients suffered from OCD for more than 30 years, while only about 20% had fully recovered over the 40 years.

The SSRIs and clomipramine have been proven effective in treating OCD, with four of them, namely the TCA clomipramine and the SSRIs sertraline, fluvoxamine, and fluoxetine, being FDA approved for the treatment of OCD in children (over a certain age) and adolescents. March and colleagues (1998) showed that sertraline was significantly more effective than placebo in treating OCD. In a double-blind, placebo-controlled study, Geller and colleagues (2001) evaluated the use of fluoxetine in children and adolescents with OCD and found that 49% of those treated with fluoxetine responded, compared to only 25% of the placebo group. In another double-blind, placebo-controlled 10-week study of fluvoxamine versus placebo in the treatment of OCD, Riddle and colleagues

(2001) showed that 42% of subjects responded, compared to 25% of those given placebo. In this study, the response to medicine began by week 1 of treatment with fluvoxamine. A study by Geller, Wagner, and colleagues (2004) has also shown the efficacy of paroxetine.

The most significant study of the SSRI treatment of OCD was the Pediatric OCD Treatment Study (POTS) (2004), a 12-week double-blind, placebo-controlled study comparing treatment with a combination of sertraline and CBT, sertraline alone, CBT alone, and placebo. In this study, as in others of the same format, those treated with an SSRI combined with CBT clearly improved the most. The sertraline-treated group and the CBT-treated group did not differ from each other.

Despite the clearly positive results for treatment with an SSRI, the most effective medicine for the treatment of OCD seems to be clomipramine, a TCA. In a small study of children and adolescents, Flament and colleagues (1985) showed clomipramine to be superior to placebo in the treatment of OCD. And DeVeaugh-Geiss and colleagues (1992) also found that clomipramine was superior to placebo in the treatment of OCD. This positive result seemed to continue over the course of a year. When compared to desipramine, another TCA, clomipramine, but not desipramine, was found to help diminish the symptoms of OCD (Leonard et al., 1989).

Given the efficacy of all the SSRIs in treating OCD, the clear difference between these two TCAs, clomipramine and desipramine, is explained by their different synaptic effects. Clomipramine strongly inhibits the reuptake of serotonin, and desipramine does not. Recall that the TCAs have many effects at the synapse, including on serotonin. Other than clomipramine, however, with its strong effect, the TCAs have only minimal effect on serotonin. Clomipramine, with its powerfully inhibiting effect on serotonin reuptake, became, in 1991, the first medicine approved for the treatment of OCD and still seems to be the most effective. Unfortunately, because of the side effects associated with the TCAs (see below), it is used only in cases of OCD in which the SSRIs have not been effective.

This differing efficacy of different tricyclics, with their different noradrenergic and serotonergic effects, in treating OCD and depression points to the different synaptic mechanism necessary to treat these two disorders.

Also of note from the POTS and other studies is that CBT is very effective in the treatment of OCD. Ideally, if a patient is capable, it is the first choice of treatment. Unfortunately, as noted above in my discussion of the other anxiety disorders, an adequate trial of CBT is time-consuming and can be expensive. In addition, trained therapists are not always available. For many patients I recommend one of a few books that the patient and parents can use to begin CBT on their own, with my periodic supervision. While this is not comparable to treatment by a trained CBT therapist, it at least helps to educate the patient and parents. This helps parents understand how their ongoing compliance with their child's compulsions, while understandable, reinforces and therefore prolongs them. Instead, the patient and parents should be encouraged to battle OCD, not simply cope with it.

### Panic Disorder

In adults, panic disorder is manifested by a series of panic attacks. Each attack is characterized by a fairly limited episode, typically about 20 or 30 minutes, of intense anxiety with no obvious precipitant. This anxiety is associated with a group of physical symptoms, most commonly palpitations and shortness of breath, but also symptoms such as dizziness, shaking, and sweating. Often the patient also has a sense of impending doom, as if he or she is going to die or go crazy. Sometimes the patient lands in the emergency room, certain that death is imminent, only to be sent home with the reassurance that it is not. Other times, she may feel as if she has to get out of what feels like a confined space. This may occur in an actual confining space, such as an elevator or a packed crowd, or simply a perceived confining space, such as the line at the supermarket. Some patients begin to avoid places where they have experienced panic attacks or felt confined. Agoraphobia, which in Greek means fear of the marketplace, is a powerful complication of panic disorder and refers to the patient's inability to leave the space in which he or she is comfortable. This might mean the inability to leave home or the area near home. The perennial fear is of experiencing a panic attack while being stuck someplace. This anticipatory anxiety, the anxiety of anticipating a panic attack, can be more debilitating than the actual panic attacks.

Children may not have such classically described panic attacks. Often they do not have the requisite number of symptoms for an event to be labeled a panic attack, or they do not describe their symptoms as clearly as an adult might. Nevertheless, their panic attacks can cause significant distress and dysfunction, including the inability to stay in class or even go to school. Other children might be unable to go to a friend's house or shopping. Some who fear the symptom of choking perpetually cling to a bottle of water.

While this disorder affects approximately 1% of youth, there is little in the way of double-blind, placebo-controlled studies supporting a specific treatment. Rather, clinicians must rely on case reports, small series of cases, the adult literature, and ultimately their own clinical wisdom in deciding a treatment plan.

The initial evaluation of panic disorder should include a medical history and physical exam. Panic attacks, which tend to run in families, can be caused, precipitated or mimicked by medical disorders such as hyperthyroidism and cardiac arrhythmias, and by the ingestion of substances such as caffeine. In addition, occasionally adolescents present, having used an illicit substance that caused a panic attack–like reaction.

The basic paradigm for the treatment of panic disorder is to use behavioral and, if needed, pharmacologic treatment. Educating the patient about the condition and how to use the techniques of CBT should be a standard part of any treatment, to the extent that the patient is capable of learning these. In short, my basic behavioral approach for dealing with panic attacks is to teach the patient that panic attacks are very uncomfortable but not dangerous, and that they are time-limited, like a bad stomachache or a thunderstorm. The patients' job is to use distraction techniques and relaxation techniques to endure the discomfort until it passes, so that panic attacks don't run their life. This is couched in a discussion of panic attacks as false alarms in the brain's anxiety center. The patient's job is to use the thinking parts of the brain to evaluate whether there is a danger, and if not, to shut off, or at least endure, the alarm.

Because panic attacks are such intense events, especially when unanticipated, many patients will expect, and some will require, medication. The basic paradigm for the pharmacologic treatment is to use a benzodiazepine to treat the acute anxiety of the panic attack and an antidepressant to prevent the recurrence of panic attacks. I'll review the use of benzodiazepines later in the chapter. Here I confine my discussion to the use of the antidepressants.

The antidepressants effective in the treatment of panic disorder include the SSRIs, the TCAs, and the MAOIs. In addition, some of the other antidepressants, such as trazodone, a postsynaptic serotonin antagonist, and reboxetine, a selective norepinephrine reuptake inhibitor, seem to have an anti-panic effect, but others, such as bupropion, seem to have less or no effect. The benefit of these medicines has been amply proven in adult patients and will not be reviewed here. Their benefit in children has been largely extrapolated from the adult research and proven by clinical experience and research done at a less rigorous level, not in double-blind, placebo-controlled studies.

The goal of these medicines is to prevent panic attacks. Their benefit seems to be mediated by their effect on the noradrenergic neurons of the locus coeruleus. Unlike the benzodiazepines, which affect the neurotransmitter GABA, they are not used on an as-needed basis for the immediate treatment of acute panic. A patient who presents with panic disorder might be started on an antidepressant early in treatment. This is to give the medicine a running start, because it will take a few weeks to be effective. Although all three groups of antidepressants are effective in treating panic disorder, in recent years the SSRIs have become the usual choice because of their ease of use and less bothersome side effect profile.

## Premenstrual Dysphoric Disorder

The symptoms of premenstrual dysphoric disorder (PMDD) occur during the week prior to the onset of a woman's monthly menstrual bleeding. It is manifested by marked depression, anxiety, anger, and rapidly changing moods. The woman might have other symptoms of depression, such as disturbed sleep and concentration, as well as physical symptoms such as breast tenderness and bloating. These symptoms cause marked dysfunction but tend to remit shortly after the onset of bleeding. The disorder affects about 4–7% of women, with a typical onset during the late 20s (Rapkin & Mikacich, 2008). Most women report that their symptoms began almost 10 years before their seeking treatment, suggesting that adolescents can also suffer from this disorder.

The SSRIs are used to treat PMDD with a response rate of 50–70% (Rapkin & Mikacich, 2008). The effective doses to treat PMDD tend to be modest relative to the use of these medicines for other disorders. For example, fluoxetine is generally effective at 10–20 mg daily, with studies showing that 60 mg daily was no more effective than 20 mg daily (Rapkin & Mikacich, 2008). While the SSRIs are FDA approved for use in adults, case studies and series support this approach in adolescents, particularly with fluoxetine at 20 mg daily (Nur, Romano, & Siqueira, 2007; Silber & Valadez-Meltzer, 2005).

The SSRIs tend to be rapidly effective, and symptoms tend to reappear soon after the medicine is stopped, thus raising speculation that the SSRIs have a different mechanism of action, whether being used to treat depression or PMDD. Some patients use the SSRI throughout the month, and others have used the SSRI only during the second half of the month, when symptoms are more likely to occur.

Rapkin and Mikacich (2008) review the importance of adolescent education and other nonpharmacologic treatments of the menstrual disorders of adolescence. The use of birth control pills to treat PMDD will be discussed briefly in Chapter 13.

## Using Antidepressants

Before medicine is used, every patient should have had a recent medical history and physical. This serves a few purposes. The first is to rule out a physical cause of the patient's disorder. While unlikely, physical problems, such as thyroid disease or systemic lupus, can cause depression. Other physical ailments, such as anemia, can cause symptoms, such as tiredness, that are mistaken for those of depression. While medical causes of OCD are less likely, the concept of pediatric autoimmune neuropsychiatric disorders associated with streptococcal infection (PANDAS) has become much researched and debated over recent years (see Chapter 11). And panic disorder is characterized by a host of physical symptoms, some of which could signal an underlying medical illness such as a cardiac arrhythmia, asthma, or thyroid disease.

The second reason for a medical history and physical is to know that there are no medical reasons that contraindicate an antidepressant. This is particularly true of the less often used TCAs, especially with their effects on cardiac rhythm and blood pressure. Fortunately this is usually less of a problem with the SSRIs.

The last reason for a careful medical history is that reviewing the patient's physical complaints gives the clinician a baseline from which to judge any complaints the patient has after starting medicine that could be misconstrued as having been caused by the medicine. Patients with anxiety disorders tend to be very sensitive to bodily sensations, which they then misidentify as side effects.

Although routine blood work is not required for the SSRIs, lab work, such as obtaining a measure of thyroid hormone, is often part of a routine physical exam for a depressed or anxious patient. Following a child's pulse, blood pressure, height, and weight is easily done and prudent while he or she is using medicine.

After one has made sure that the patient is medically stable, one must decide on a treatment plan. Because depression, the anxiety disorders, OCD, and panic disorder disrupt the patient's life in different ways and carry different risks, the choice of treatment sequence might differ. As we've seen, CBT can be a powerful treatment tool, and if the patient is willing, a trial of CBT is a reasonable first choice to treat all four of these difficulties.

## Depression

The onset of depression, especially in adolescents, frequently seems intertwined with the complicated social and emotional lives of young people. Family conflict, school stress, a breakup with a boyfriend or girl-friend, or similar circumstances frequently serve as the backdrop for the onset of depression. Those events are not necessarily causal. Sometimes, however, the patient will respond to supportive therapy. If the patient's safety is assured, a period of "watchful waiting" with supportive therapy and psychoeducation has been recommended before medicine is consid-ered for the depressed young person (Hughes et al., 2007). This includes teaching the patient and his or her family about depression. For example, the patient should understand that depression is not a moral or personal weakness. The patient's life stresses, which for teens can be considerable, should also be explored.

While respecting the patient's confidentiality and considering the particular family's dynamics, the clinician should involve the family in this process. This will, one hopes, help them appropriately modify their responses to the patient. Educating the family also teaches them that depression is a potentially recurrent disorder for which they and the patient will have to be on guard. Helping parents learn how to observe for future depression, without becoming overly intrusive on the teen's burgeoning independence, can be a challenge.

The decision to use medicine more immediately will be influenced by a few factors. Adolescents and children who are more severely depressed or anxious, particularly if there is significant suicide risk, merit more immediate consideration of pharmacotherapy, especially if a close family member has been very responsive to medicine. More immediate treatment should also be considered if the patient's depression is chronic or has been unresponsive to psychotherapy. Of course, before medicine is considered, the patient's safety must always be ensured.

In discussing the use of antidepressants, I focus on the use of the SSRIs because they are currently the most commonly used antidepressants and the only family of medicines, some of which are FDA approved.

Once one has decided to prescribe an SSRI, one needs to decide which medicine to use. In general, my preference is to start with one of the FDA-approved medicines, because this means that the medicine has proven to be effective in at least two double-blind, placebo-controlled studies and that the FDA considers the side effect profile to be outweighed by the potential benefits. Currently, for the treatment of depression, this means fluoxetine for children and adolescents or escitalopram for adolescents. The antidepressants are not FDA approved for the treatment of the anxiety disorders or panic disorder in children. Yet as we've seen, the SSRIs have proven beneficial for the anxiety disorders. Therefore, in the treatment of anxiety, FDA approval is not a consideration in deciding which SSRI to use.

Besides FDA approval, past success or failure with a particular SSRI strongly impacts the decision of which to choose. In addition, if a close family member, such as a parent or sibling, has had significant success with another antidepressant, I might forgo the FDA-approved medicines and start with the medicine that helped the family member.

In addition, sometimes one tries to use one medicine for two purposes. For example, in treating a depressed adolescent with ADHD, one might consider using bupropion as a single medicine to treat both conditions. In this case one is weighing the risks and benefits of polypharmacy with two well-proven medicines, namely a stimulant and an SSRI, against the risks and benefits of using one medicine, albeit one that is not as well tested for either condition. This is a matter for the physician's and patient's judgment.

While the SSRIs seem equally effective for the treatment of the anxiety disorders and OCD, the same cannot be said of the treatment of depression, where fluoxetine and escitalopram, and perhaps sertraline and citalopram, have bested placebo. Some clinicians will start with one of these medicines, and others will begin with a medicine that has either not separated itself from placebo or has not been tested. This is mostly a reflection of the clinician's experience and judgment.

In deciding which antidepressant to use, I consider half-life. I tend to avoid using paroxetine and venlafaxine as first-line medicines because of their relatively short half-lives and the paucity of data supporting their use, although these are also available in sustained-release forms. In addition, there is some question regarding whether the faster increase and decrease of blood levels of these medicines accounts for their questionably higher risk of suicidal ideation. Fluvoxamine has a shorter half-life but also more data supporting its use in certain disorders, such as OCD.

This is a good place to recall that children are not little adults. Sertraline, citalopram, and even (the non-SSRI) bupropion SR (sustained release) have all been reported to have shorter half-lives in children than in adults. This short half-life might make some children prone to withdrawal side effects when the morning dose wears off before expected (AACAP, 2007). Therefore, although adults can take most of these medicines once daily, children sometimes do better taking the medicine twice daily.

By contrast, fluoxetine has a longer half-life, which, when combined with the half-life of its most significant psychoactive metabolite, is about 10–14 days. This long half-life can be beneficial. If a patient forgets to take his or her medicine one day, there is less risk of withdrawal side effects and a greater assurance that the medicine will still be effective through that "forgotten" day. This can be useful for adolescents who "forget" to take their medicine. On the other hand, because of its long half-life, one has to wait longer for fluoxetine to leave the body. If one wants to start another medicine that is contraindicated with fluoxetine, this can be frustrating.

There are no specific dosing guidelines for any of the SSRIs. My preference is to initiate any SSRI at the lowest dose, which is maintained for about one week to a few weeks, depending on the clinical presentation. This is done to minimize initial side effects, in particular the activation (see below) that can occur after the first few days of medicine. Patients with anxiety disorders, particularly panic disorder, seem especially prone to this initial increase in anxiety, so I often start them on an especially low dose for the first week.

After the patient has been on the medicine for the first few weeks, the medicine is sometimes better tolerated, and one can begin to increase the dose a bit more aggressively. If the patient does not experience side effects, I raise the dose about every two to four weeks, while assessing the patient's progress. As has been noted, except for the initial low dose, the ultimate dose used by children and adolescents is no different from those used by adults (AACAP, 2007). Because the SSRIs can take weeks to work, however, one should not push the dose up too fast. This risks passing an effective dose and causing more side effects, although increasing the dose too slowly can waste precious time when one is treating a patient with a debilitating illness. The need to increase the dose more quickly might be more of an issue in treating depression than with the anxiety disorders.

To some extent, using the SSRIs is as much about duration as it is about dose. The medicine picks up momentum the longer it is taken. For example, as we've seen already in the TADS, the effect of medicine (as well as CBT) was greater at 16 and then at 36 weeks than at 12 weeks.

One can argue that because the SSRIs can take weeks, or even a few months, to gain momentum, one should wait eight weeks before increasing the dose. This protracted process would be impractical, as well as frustrating for patient and parents, and can leave the patient depressed or anxious for months.

The rate of increase is largely a function of how pressing the clinical problem is, the setting, and the doctor's comfort level. In general, hospital settings are more supervised, thus allowing a faster rate of increase. Unfortunately, sometimes doses of medicine are increased rapidly because of the need to spend only a limited number of days in the hospital. This does not necessarily make the medicine work faster, so, given an adequate dose, one might still need to wait three or four weeks before seeing the start of a response.

Yet there are some data supporting the fairly quick increase in dose. In an open-label study, Tao and colleagues (2009), showed that a significant positive response within the first month of treatment with fluoxetine, increased to 20 mg daily by the first week, predicted depressed youth having minimal or no symptoms of depression at the end of three months. In other words, if, after a fairly quick increase to 20 mg daily, the patient's symptoms do not diminish within one month, one should consider a treatment change such as increasing the dose, changing the medicine, or adding more of a psychosocial intervention.

The goal of treatment is remission of symptoms, not simply improving the patient's condition. Therefore, strong consideration must be given to increasing the dose of a patient who is already somewhat improved. Many clinical factors influence that decision to increase the dose, however, including the age of the patient, the severity of the depression, the presence of side effects, and so on.

One cannot predict which patient will respond to which SSRI; therefore, if the patient has no significant response within about one month at the highest dose I am comfortable prescribing, I consider switching to another SSRI. Certainly if no response is seen by eight weeks at a reasonable dose, the treatment should be reevaluated and probably changed. I generally prescribe a different SSRI and, if that fails, consider switching from the SSRIs to another medicine, such as venlafaxine (which has a slightly different synaptic effect) or bupropion (with a very different synaptic effect).

Brent and colleagues (2008) studied over 300 depressed adolescents who had not responded to a two-month initial treatment with an SSRI. They found that almost half the adolescents responded to a switch to either another SSRI or venlafaxine (although the venlafaxine group suffered more side effects). Adding CBT to this second medicine trial helped increase the response rate slightly. In short, if the first antidepressant is ineffective, there is a roughly 50% chance that a switch to another antidepressant will be effective.

If a patient with depression is not responding to an antidepressant, the clinician must first consider that the patient may not be taking the medicine. Adolescents, in particular, sometimes assert their independence or their dislike of side effects by abstaining from medicine. In addition, one must ensure that the dose of medicine used and the duration of the trial of medicine have both been sufficient.

Finally, if the patient is still not responsive, the clinician must make sure that the patient's diagnosis is correct. The initial diagnosis might have been incorrect, or the patient might suffer from an interfering comorbid diagnosis. In addition, adolescents and children can be influenced by social stressors. Adolescents are famously influenced by their peers. Unfortunately, teens with psychological difficulties often tend to have friends with difficulties, thus making the social impact potentially more devastating. Younger children are also very sensitive to the world around them, in particular, their parents. In short, when a child or adolescent is unresponsive to medicine, the impact of either an incorrect diagnosis or an overwhelming psychosocial stressor must also be questioned.

> *Lamar is being treated for depression. At age 16, Lamar's sense of psychological well-being is closely intertwined with his social life. Unfortunately, while some girlfriends can be pillars of support, Lamar's girlfriend is also depressed. Lamar is not responding to fluoxetine 40 mg daily. His physician is considering switching to another SSRI. She discovers, however, that Lamar's girlfriend has been frequently texting her suicidal thoughts to Lamar. Lamar has been in turmoil about whether to share this with a responsible adult or to keep it confidential as his girlfriend demands. It is unclear to Lamar's doctor whether changing antidepressants would be helpful.*

When all this has been done, the patient might still be unresponsive to medicines that have been well studied. In these cases, the clinician must consider whether to augment an antidepressant with another agent, such as lithium or thyroid hormone, or to add another antidepressant or other medicine, such as a stimulant. Although there are very few data to support this practice in youth, the severity and risks of depression must be weighed against the possible side effects of a combination of medicines.

Often, however, that level of pharmacological innovation is unnecessary, and the clinician can settle on the use of one medicine. Whichever medicine is effective, it is important to treat the patient as fully as possible. That is, one should not be content with a patient who is somewhat better, but should strive to get the patient more fully improved. Emslie and colleagues (2008) showed that depressed adolescents with continued symptoms after 12 weeks of fluoxetine were more likely to relapse over the next six months, despite ongoing medication treatment. And the TADS (Kennard et al., 2009) showed that those adolescents who continued to have a greater number of symptoms after 12 weeks of treatment did more poorly at 18 and 36 weeks, despite continued treatment. In short, maximal improvement in the first three months is an important goal, but the clinician must remember that some patients will not improve for a few more months.

Once the patient has responded to an SSRI, patients and their parents often want to know how long they should remain on medicine. No long-term data guide this decision. That medicine continues to be effective has been shown by Emslie and colleagues (2008), who assigned fluoxetine responders to continue their medicine or be switched to placebo for six months. During that time, about 40% of those taking medicine relapsed, while about 70% of those taking placebo did so. For this group, composed largely of adolescents with their first episode of depression, the continuation of medicine was clearly better than switching to placebo. Notably, however, even those who continued on medicine were vulnerable to a return of depression. In addition, the TADS has demonstrated that about one third of adolescents who went into remission with treatment did not maintain that remission over subsequent months (Kennard et al., 2009).

Nevertheless, in continuing medication, the rule gleaned from the adult literature is to continue for about one year from the time the medicine is most fully effective. This rule is based on knowing that most episodes of depression will have run their natural course during that time. Given our knowledge that episodes of childhood depression have usually run their course by about nine months, it makes sense to follow this rule.

In practice, this guideline is inexact for a few reasons. The first is that, despite this one-year rule, it is best to discontinue medicine at a time of minimal stress. Unfortunately, stress free blocks of time are difficult to find. The second difficulty with the one-year rule is that, while adolescents are often ready to discontinue the medicine, their parents are understandably petrified of the prospect of another round of depression. They therefore resist stopping the medicine. It is also important to remember that after the medicine has been discontinued, one might not see the resulting return of symptoms for a few months. So one should not be falsely reassured by a few symptom-free weeks.

The rule of continuing medicine for one year might also be modified because the patient has a history of recurrent depression whenever medicine has been discontinued or a history of double depression. Both of these situations might require the ongoing use of medicine for longer periods, although data supporting this plan are mostly lacking.

Nevertheless, when the time comes to discontinue medicine, it can be done in one of two ways. In either case, the medicine will be tapered over time to minimize the risk of discontinuation side effects, and so that, if the symptoms of depression recur, the medicine can be increased to a therapeutic level more quickly.

Tapering, however, can be done either quickly or slowly. If one wants to taper the medicine quickly, the dose can be lowered roughly every four days. With medicines such as sertraline or fluvoxamine, that might be done in 25 mg steps. With medicines such as escitalopram, that might be done in 5 or 10 mg steps. Only fluoxetine, with its very long half-life, can be discontinued abruptly, because it leaves the body very slowly, in essence tapering itself. In any case, after the medicine is tapered, the patient continues to be followed for the assessment of a return of symptoms.

Alternatively, the SSRI can be lowered by these amounts, then maintained at that dose for weeks or a few months before the next step down. This gradual decrease reassures parents and allows for the passing of transient adolescent stresses without causing one to conclude that they result from a lowered dose of medicine.

If the patient's symptoms return, the medicine is restarted. Again extrapolating from practice in adult psychiatry, this second course of treatment is generally a little longer than the first. With every failed attempt at stopping the medicine, the successive course of medicine is a bit longer than the one preceding. After about three failed attempts to discontinue the medicine (now accounting for 5 or 10 years), the patient is usually at least a young adult and should consider staying on the medicine for the foreseeable future. This prospect can seem scary and does not need to be initially discussed with children or even older adolescents.

In addition to depression, some patients will suffer from a comorbid disorder, which requires additional medication. The use of these drug combinations is based largely on clinical experience, not controlled studies. If the patient also has an anxiety disorder, typically the SSRI will treat both disorders. If, however, the patient is also psychotic, addition of an antipsychotic medication might be necessary. In that case, being aware of possible drug interactions is necessary. If the child also has ADHD, a stimulant can be added. Nevertheless, the addition of atomoxetine again requires an awareness of potential drug interactions. (For the treatment of bipolar disorder, see Chapter 9.)

A clinician will sometimes consider using another type of therapy, such as light therapy or, in cases of debilitating and refractory depression, electroconvulsive therapy (ECT). Light therapy consists of sitting in front of a 5,000–10,000 lux light each morning, with the light exposure shorter if the light is more powerful. Presumably the effect of light entering the eyes is to lower the brain's release of melatonin (see Chapter 10). This has been supported by a small amount of controlled research (Swedo et al., 1997). Recall our rule, however, that no therapy is without risk. Even seemingly innocuous light therapy carries the risk of headaches and even hypomania.

The far more controversial ECT consists of using electrodes to induce a seizure in a very controlled manner. While ECT is reserved for only the more extreme cases, the results can be dramatically effective. Although some side effects are possible, they have been overdramatized by many. The film *One Flew over the Cuckoo's Nest* continues to cast a long shadow. When ECT is considered, it must always be weighed against the risks of the patient's continuing to have the symptoms of a debilitating disorder.

Whatever the treatment, assessing the patient's progress is mandatory. This can be done with rating scales, such as the Beck Depression Inventory (Beck & Steer, 1987) or Children's Depression Rating Scale (Poznanski & Mokros, 1995), but should also include regular follow-up appointments with the clinician. This is necessary not only for ongoing therapy but also because even when treatments such as the SSRIs are effective, they are not fully effective, and the risk of relapse is significant. The TADS has shown that even among those depressed adolescents who have attained remission, one third do not maintain that remission. Ongoing monitoring is a must.

## Anxiety Disorders

In the short-term treatment of anxiety disorders, unlike depression, research supports the use of different SSRIs equally, so the choice of which medicine to use is the clinician's. The SSRIs are prescribed in the same way as for depression, except that, because of the tendency of the SSRIs to induce increased anxiety if the initial dose is too high, patients with anxiety are generally started on a lower dose. In addition, because of the efficacy of CBT and the clear evidence that an SSRI combined with a CBT is more effective than either alone, it is wise for the patient to learn the techniques of CBT, if possible.

If the patient does not respond to the first SSRI tried, it is advisable to try a second. Walkup and colleagues (2002) showed that about three quarters of children with an anxiety disorder who did not respond to fluvoxamine did respond to a subsequent trial of fluoxetine.

Although the anxiety disorders are less lethal then depression, because they are also less episodic than depression, the question of treatment duration can be more vexing. That is, in deciding when to stop the medicine, one generally can't wait for an episode of anxiety to pass, as one can for depression. While after a year or so consideration is given to discontinuing the medicine, there is also a likelihood that the patient will remain on medicine for a while longer.

Although they are without the same level of research support, medicines besides the SSRIs are also available for the treatment of the anxiety disorders and are considered if the patient has not responded to an SSRI. Venlafaxine is at the top of this list of second-tier medicines. The TCAs, because of their side effect profile, are lower on this list. Buspirone has a favorable side effect profile but is without clear evidence of efficacy.

Finally, the benzodiazepines (BZDs) are effective antianxiety medications in adults but do not have proven efficacy in children. Nevertheless, clinical experience suggests that they are effective in some children, though used on a short-term basis because of the risk, if small, of dependency. The BZDs might be used for a limited time in panic disorder (see below) or on a very limited basis to help the patient with certain phobias, such as a flying phobia, when behavioral treatments have failed.

### Obsessive-Compulsive Disorder

As we've already seen, research clearly supports the use of the SSRIs for treating OCD. FDA-approved medications include the SSRIs fluoxetine, sertraline, fluvoxamine, and, in SSRI- or CBT-resistant patients, the TCA clomipramine. Although clomipramine is the most effective, the other medicines seem to be equally effective among themselves and cause fewer side effects than clomipramine.

The SSRIs are initiated as they are in depression. The difference is that patients with OCD tend to require higher doses than other patients, so the process can take longer.

Although the SSRIs are effective in treating OCD, they are not a panacea. Many patients with OCD improve, some greatly, but the symptoms rarely disappear completely. Rather, they are greatly attenuated.

Sometimes the clinician is faced with the problem of medicine being only partially effective. Clinical experience suggests that a second medication can augment the response to the first. Medicines that have been used to augment include a low dose of clomipramine, a second SSRI, an antipsychotic such as risperidone, and buspirone. Benzodiazepines, such as clonazepam, might be helpful in decreasing acute anxiety.

In addition, d-cycloserine, a partial NMDA agonist, has been shown to promote learning during behavioral treatment of certain anxiety disorders. While it would still be considered experimental, d-cycloserine has been thought to augment the learning that takes place during CBT (Walkup, 2009).

Another interesting question regarding the use of SSRIs to treat OCD is how long the medicines need to be taken before benefit is seen. Some studies show benefit within the first few weeks, although as a rule, greater benefit is seen over the ensuing weeks or even months. Two intriguing, though uncontrolled, studies show that long-term treatment, namely over many months, may increase benefit. Cook and colleagues (2001) showed that many patients who did not respond to an SSRI in the first few months were responders after one year of treatment with sertraline. And Thomsen, Ebbesen, and Persson (2001) showed increasing benefit through the first year of treatment with citalopram that did not plateau until the second year.

Finally, in treating OCD, the benefits of CBT equal those of medication and, for those capable of doing it, should not be ignored. Unlike the effects of pharmacological treatment, these benefits stay with the patient long after the course of treatment ends.

## Panic Disorder

The SSRIs are often used in the treatment of children and adolescents with panic disorder, despite a lack of research supporting their use in youth. The goal is for the SSRI eventually to prevent the occurrence of panic attacks, not to treat the acute anxiety. In these cases it is common practice to start the patient on a low dose of an SSRI, then increase the dose slowly. My experience is that patients with panic disorder are particularly susceptible to having more anxiety precipitated if the initial dose is too high. Therefore a slow initiation at a low dose is prudent.

Some patients respond to the brief use of a benzodiazepine and do not require the initiation of an SSRI for longer-term prophylaxis. In these cases a benzodiazepine, taken when one feels the onset of a panic attack, helps lessen the intensity of an acute panic attack. Some clinicians will prescribe a brief course of benzodiazepines to be taken regularly on a once- to thrice-per-day routine in order to stay ahead of the anxiety. If, after a couple of weeks, the panic attacks do not abate or an underlying generalized anxiety becomes more apparent, an SSRI can be taken over the longer term.

While the SSRIs can take weeks to work, the benzodiazepines work within about a half hour. One can argue that many panic attacks have run their 20-minute course before the benzodiazepine takes effect. Yet many patients with panic disorder feel less anxious simply for having taken the medicine. After a few weeks, when they no longer require the benzodiazepine, whether or not they have been started on an SSRI, many patients feel more secure just knowing that they still have the benzodiazepine available. Some young adults have told me of pills that have disintegrated after being stored in their wallet or glove compartment for months. In the context of a treatment that includes patient education and CBT, this is not a problem.

An ironic problem, however, can result when the patient uses medicine to quell anxiety completely. Without any experience of anxiety, the patient is fearful of the return of anxiety, yet less motivated to learn CBT.

> *Clonazepam has successfully minimized twelve-year-old Katherine's symptoms of panic. When her physician tries to introduce cognitive behavioral therapy, Katherine becomes teary at any prospect of re-experiencing anxiety. Her anxious father automatically puts a comforting arm over her shoulder and gives the physician a look that halts him from proceeding. "The medicine's working, Doc. Can't we simply leave it at that?" This prevents Katherine from learning that she can tolerate small levels of anxiety. Katherine is started on citalopram, and her clonazepam is slowly discontinued. Her anxiety diminishes, but she remains fearful of experiencing a panic attack. A few months later Katherine is without panic and doesn't see the purpose of learning the cognitive behavioral techniques she might need when the medicine is discontinued.*

## Side Effects of the Antidepressants

### SSRIs and SNRIs

The SSRIs (and SNRIs) have a variety of side effects, some of which are the usual suspects found with most medicines (gastrointestinal distress, headaches, and so on) and others that are behavioral and unique to the SSRIs. Thankfully, most of these side effects are reversible when the medicine is stopped or the dose lowered.

*Gastrointestinal*

Some patients experience nausea, diarrhea, or upset stomach. These tend to be relatively infrequent and often go away over time.

*Sleep*

Some people become tired, while others become overly energized and unable to sleep. Some patients complain of nightmares or vivid and unusual dreams.

*Weight*

Although some adult patients experience an initial weight loss, about 25% will experience a generally small weight gain after months of taking medicine. In my experience this is not a significant side effect in children, although following a child's weight is prudent. Effexor XR, however, might affect a child's height and weight and therefore should be monitored (Rynn & Regan, 2008).

*Blood pressure and pulse*

The SSRIs tend not to have a significant effect on blood pressure and pulse, although cases of these have been reported. Effexor XR, which at higher doses is known to affect the blood pressure of adults, has been reported to affect these measures in children, and these should therefore be monitored (Rynn & Regan, 2008).

*Sweating*

Some patients complain about profuse sweating, a side effect that can be very disturbing, particularly to teens. Dermatologists sometimes suggest a possible remedy, such as Drysol (aluminum chloride hexahydrate), although my experience is that adolescence are often too emotionally sensitive to excessive perspiration to give the remedy a full trial.

*Activation*

This side effect is often cited, but usually not explicitly described. So, while definitions and therefore rates vary, probably about 10% of patients experience a side effect that might be labeled activation. These patients develop a restless, agitated, overenergized feeling, similar to that of having too much coffee. This reversible, but uncomfortable, side effect typically occurs within the first few days of using the SSRI, although it can occur a few months later. Patients with anxiety tend to be more prone to this side effect, especially if the initial dose is too high or increased too quickly. Although some patients incorrectly assume that the activation is anxiety, requiring an increase in the dose, activation is treated by lowering the dose or discontinuing the medicine. Sometimes, after the activation recedes, the patient can tolerate the medicine at a lower dose.

*Hypomania*

This relatively rare side effect consists of agitation, excessive silliness, grandiosity, sleeplessness, and other manic-like behaviors. This occurs weeks into treatment and must be distinguished from mania that presages the onset of bipolar disorder. Although bipolar disorder (as opposed to the symptoms of hypomania) does not appear to be a side effect associated with the SSRIs (Chang et al., 2010), one is obviously concerned about the symptoms of hypomania in a child or adolescent who is predisposed to bipolar disorder. Hypomania must also be distinguished from activation, which is dose-dependent and occurs within the first few days of treatment. Last, hypomania must be distinguished from the simple return to happiness that comes with the successful treatment of depression and the normal misbehavior that the anxious child might engage in when the anxiety disappears.

Studies in adults are inconclusive regarding whether the use of a mood stabilizer prevents this side effect, although these are frequently used in patients who would seem at risk for having an SSRI switch them into hypomania.

*Disinhibition*

Some patients develop a disinhibited quality, as if their anxiety has decreased to excess, leaving them without the usual inhibitory anxiety that helps people function. For example, one patient of mine, very uncharacteristically, began telling off the school bully. Another young adolescent girl, also uncharacteristically, told a classmate that she had a crush on him. This does not reflect personal growth but demonstrates an uncharacteristic lack of anxiety. In some cases, distinguishing this side effect from some of the others and from the child's usual behavior can be vexing.

## Apathy

Over time some patients develop a "who cares?" attitude. The usual concern for consequences diminishes. The patient might seem to lack motivation. These patients lose a sense of anxiety or emotional tension about circumstances that should provoke such tension. For example, one patient stopped doing schoolwork that she knew she should be doing. This can sometimes be confused with disinhibition, and I wonder if it is actually different.

## Serotonin syndrome

This potentially dangerous syndrome is the result of excess serotonin, usually caused by taking more than one medicine that affects serotonin levels. The syndrome consists of sweating, diarrhea, fever, tremors, blood pressure changes, and confusion. Other drugs that also affect serotonin include lithium, TCAs and MAOIs, the amino acid l-tryptophan, as well as illicit drugs such as LSD, Ecstasy, and cocaine.

## Decreased sex drive

Perhaps the most common complaint among adults taking SSRIs is a lowered interest in sex or a disturbance in some aspect of sexual ability. In females this can be a difficulty reaching orgasm, and in males this can be a difficulty maintaining an erection or in ejaculating. While this is not relevant to children, it can be very relevant to adolescents and highlights the need for an honest but sensitive relationship between patient and clinician. My experience has been that, when asked, most adolescents deny experiencing this side effect. Adolescents, however, will not typically offer this information without being asked and can privately worry about this important aspect of their lives if they are not asked. One adolescent was relieved to discover that his difficulty ejaculating when masturbating might have been caused by the medicine. Because hearing of any threat to their sexuality can cause many adolescents to recede into resistance without considering potential benefits, the clinician has a problem: when and how to inform patients about this side effect. While I sometimes share this side effect with adolescents from the beginning, knowing that they might go home and check out the proposed medicine on Google, other times I delicately ask the patient about these side effects only after he or she has been taking the medicine for a short while. The initial treatment of this side effect consists of waiting to see if it disappears on its own (difficult with an anxious teen), lowering the dose, or switching to a different medicine, although this side effect is present for all the SSRIs. Many prescription treatments, such as the addition of bupropion, sildenafil (Viagra), cyproheptadine (Periactin), or amantadine (Symmetrel), and over-the-counter remedies such as gingko biloba, have been tried. These are all, however, unproven and unreliable.

*Easy bruising*

Medicines that block the reuptake of serotonin (SSRIs and venlafaxine) might be more likely to interfere with platelet function, causing the patient to be more prone to bruising and bleeding. This seems to occur very infrequently, though the concomitant use of nonsteroidal anti-inflammatory drugs such as ibuprofen might increase the risk. In any case, the risk would still be small. De Abajo and Garcia-Rodriguez (2008) have shown that acid-suppressing agents might limit the risk of gastrointestinal bleeding in adults who use SSRIs and venlafaxine.

*Inhibited growth*

Weintrob and colleagues (2002) reported four cases of children who stopped growing while taking SSRIs. Nilsson and colleagues (2004), in a small study comparing fluoxetine with placebo, also found a difference in growth over 19 weeks. As always, care must be taken before extrapolating from case reports and small studies. Nevertheless, since this report, periodically measuring and weighing children who take SSRIs has become prudent. Definitive data are still lacking.

## Additional Considerations

Other issues should also be taken into account before prescribing antidepressants for children or adolescents.

*The suicide controversy*

The allegation that the SSRIs cause suicide has been the subject of numerous headlines and is arguably the main reason parents balk at allowing their child to take an SSRI. The side effect will be reviewed here, but its implications will be put into perspective in Chapter 15. The largest database examining whether SSRIs cause suicide looked at about 5,000 youth who were treated in a variety of studies (lasting a maximum of 16 weeks) for a variety of disorders (depression, OCD, anxiety disorders, even ADHD) by a variety of medicines, most but not all of them SSRIs. The researchers reviewing these studies classified "suicidality" in a number of ways, ranging from an actual suicide attempt to suicidal thoughts to self-injurious behavior. They found that there were no completed suicides in this group, and that, relative to those taking placebo, the pooled group taking medicines had an extra 1–2% chance of experiencing a suicidal thought or, less likely, performing a suicidal act. Some individual medicines (such as venlafaxine and Luvox) seemed to carry greater risk, while most of the others carried less risk. Other studies have similarly found no completed suicides. Some have found a similar slight association of SSRIs with "suicidality," (not completed suicides) although there are a host of difficulties in researching this. For example, one's conclusions depend on whether one looks at suicidal thoughts offered spontaneously by study subjects or only at those elicited by a study's rating scale. If suicidality is a side effect of medicine, its mechanism is not well understood. Some have hypothesized that some less inhibited patients who experience negative and disconcerting side effects are more likely to engage in suicidal behavior. Clinically, my bottom line is that I use the SSRIs but monitor the suicidal thoughts and behavior of all patients taking SSRIs. Because many of these patients are depressed, this would obviously be done anyway.

*Pregnancy*

In general, the SSRIs seem relatively safe during pregnancy. Their use during the first trimester did not increase the rate of most major malformations, in particular cardiac anomalies. And while there was a slight increase in some malformations, in an absolute sense this was seen as minimal (Alwan et al., 2007). Nor did SSRI use lead to minor malformations in the fetus (Wisner et al., 2009).

Nevertheless, reporting on malformations is a crucial but inadequate statement that does not do justice to the complicated topic of the other effects medicine can have on the fetus and then the infant. Serotonin plays many roles in the developing fetus, including the regulation of circadian rhythms, respiration, and the tone of arteries. Does the increase in serotonin caused by SSRIs, which then crosses the placenta, have an effect on the development of the brain or other crucial organs of the fetus? And if so, does this help or harm the child? Other issues are also of concern. Chambers and colleagues (2006) found an association between the use of SSRIs during the second, but not first, half of pregnancy and pulmonary hypertension in the newborn. Oberlander and colleagues (2006) also found that although the neonates of women who took SSRIs during pregnancy were in many ways no different from the neonates of untreated depressed women, the infants of treated women had a higher rate of low birth weight and respiratory distress. In addition, there is some concern that SSRI use is linked to a higher rate of preterm birth (Suri et al., 2007; Wisner et al., 2009) and withdrawal reactions in the newborn, such as jitteriness and feeding problems (cited in Gentile, 2010). (The difficult topic of weighing the risks and benefits of medicine use during pregnancy will be explored further in Chapter 11.)

*Laboratory tests*

Although the SSRIs do not require monitoring of lab tests, Effexor XR has been reported to affect serum cholesterol levels in children and therefore should be monitored (Rynn & Regan, 2008).

*Withdrawal*

Most of the SSRIs should be tapered slowly over about one or two weeks. A patient who stops them abruptly is liable to have withdrawal symptoms such as headache, stomachache, irritability, and dizziness. These symptoms tend to begin about two or three days after the medicine has been stopped and, though not dangerous, are uncomfortable, lasting a few days. Adolescents who unilaterally decide to stop taking their medicine are most prone to this experience. Fluoxetine, with its very long half-life, does not need to be tapered, since it tapers itself over the course of weeks.

*Overdose*

Arguably the most significant benefit of the SSRIs is that they are very safe in overdose attempts, particularly when used alone.

### Drug interactions

Some of the SSRIs significantly inhibit or induce some of the liver's cytochrome P450 enzymes. Each, however, affects these enzymes uniquely, and so one must know the particulars for any given SSRI. Because there are potential effects on many enzymes to many different degrees, one must generally rely on a printed or computer listing of them rather than on memory. Of note, sertraline and citalopram tend to affect these enzyme systems minimally. (See below for information regarding individual medicines.)

The FDA warns of using SSRIs or SNRIs concomitantly with the 5-hydroxytryptamine receptor agonists, or triptans (such as Imitrex), which are used to treat migraines. On the basis of about two dozen cases, the FDA concluded that the combination might put the patient at higher risk for serotonin syndrome, although this has been debated (see R. G. Wenzel, S. Tepper, et al., *The Annals of Pharmacotherapy*, November, 2008). In general, using an SSRI with another medicine that can increase serotonin levels must be done carefully.

The use of nonsteroidal anti-inflammatory medicines while taking SSRIs might increase the risk of bleeding, although the risk would still be small.

The SSRIs should not be used concomitantly with, or within two weeks of having discontinued, an MAOI.

# Specific SSRIs, SNRIs, and Novel Antidepressants

A caveat: Before I review these medicines, a few reminders are in order. First, recall that any particular medicine can have a range of durations, differing greatly from patient to patient. Second, remember that the effects of many medicines, but especially the SSRIs, on the different enzymes of the P450 system are plentiful and very varied. While this sounds confusing, some of the SSRIs affect the enzymes that metabolize them. So if an SSRI inhibits the enzyme that metabolizes itself, the longer one takes the medicine, the more the enzyme is inhibited, and the longer the half-life of the medicine. This is particularly true of fluoxetine and paroxetine. Current lists of drug interactions should be consulted when patients are taking more than one medicine. Third, the doses listed are approximate and can vary depending on the age of the child and clinical situation.

## SSRIs

Let's consider the benefits and disadvantages of the different SSRIs.

### *Fluoxetine*

The grandfather of SSRIs, fluoxetine is FDA approved for the treatment of OCD and depression in children and adolescents. It is unique among the SSRIs in that it has by far the longest half-life. Fluoxetine and its active metabolite have a half-life of about 10–14 days. This is both good and bad news. The bad news is that, after fluoxetine is discontinued, it takes weeks to taper itself. While this minimizes withdrawal side effects, waiting can be a bit frustrating if the clinician wants to increase the dose of another medicine. The good news is that patients who tend to forget to take their medicine still have a significant blood level. Also, with its long half-life, patients who are lowering the dose of their medicine can simply change from taking fluoxetine daily to taking it every other day, then every third day, and so on.

The effect of fluoxetine on the P450 system is also important in that, while it inhibits a number of enzymes, it is a strong inhibitor of 2D6 and 2C19. Thus a particularly relevant drug interaction in child psychiatry is with atomoxetine, which is metabolized by 2D6 and whose dose must be lowered if given with fluoxetine. Similarly, fluoxetine affects the metabolism of risperidone, whose dose must also therefore be lowered when given concomitantly with fluoxetine. Duggal & Kithas (2005) report a case suggesting that fluoxetine be used cautiously with aripiprazole.

Fluoxetine is generally started at 5 mg (children) to 10 mg (teens) daily, though sometimes lower, and increased slowly. It is available as pills and as liquid. Because of its long half-life, when trying to increase at a rate slower than the pills allow, one can use the liquid, or one can alternate a higher-dose pill with a lower-dose pill every other day. For example, when increasing the dose from 10 mg to 15 mg daily, one can give 10 mg every other day, alternating with 20 mg every other day, thus functionally attaining 15 mg daily. To simplify compliance, I have patients take one pill on the odd calendar days and two pills on the even days. On the 31st of the month and the first, the patient simply takes one pill each day to stay with the system.

### Sertraline

Sertraline is FDA approved for the treatment of OCD in childhood and adolescence but is also used to treat anxiety and sometimes depression. It has a half-life of about 24 hours and is therefore usually given once daily. In children and adolescents, however, it should probably initially be given twice daily, because at lower doses the half-life is only about 15 hours (Vitiello, 2008).

One benefit of sertraline is that it tends to affect the enzymes of the P450 system minimally, thus being easier to use with many other medicines. Nevertheless, at higher doses its inhibition of 2D6 can lead to an increase in desipramine levels, at least theoretically posing an increased cardiac risk. And its inhibition of 3A4 could inhibit the metabolism of pimozide, also raising a cardiac risk. Its inhibition of glucoronidation, another enzyme system, can inhibit the metabolism of lamotrigine.

Because sertraline is metabolized by many enzymes, inhibiting any one does not prevent sertraline from being metabolized. But medicines that increase the levels of many enzymes, such as carbamazepine and phenytoin (Dilantin), can lead to sertraline being metabolized faster, thereby lowering its blood levels.

In children, sertraline is usually started at 25 mg daily, although sometimes one starts at even 12.5 mg daily. In general, the dose is then increased in 25 mg increments. Sertraline is available in tablets and liquid.

### *Paroxetine*

Paroxetine has no FDA-approved indications in youth. It tends to be a relatively short acting medicine with a half-life of less than 20 hours. This has raised concerns about some patients' experiencing an uncomfortable withdrawal later in the day, which might arguably and theoretically predispose them to suicidal thoughts. For this reason I do not use paroxetine as my first choice of SSRIs.

Paroxetine tends to be a relatively "dirty" SSRI, affecting other receptors, such as cholinergic receptors. Therefore it tends to cause side effects relatively uniquely amongst the SSRIs, such as dry mouth and sedation. Paroxetine also inhibits the P450 enzymes 2D6 and 2B6, thereby causing some other medicines to last longer than expected. This is particularly important with medicines such as desipramine or, more commonly, atomoxetine.

Paroxetine is usually started at 5–10 mg daily and increased in 5–10 mg increments. Paroxetine is available in tablets and liquid. Paxil also is available as Paxil CR, an extended-release tablet.

### *Fluvoxamine*

Fluvoxamine is FDA approved for the treatment of OCD in children and adolescents and is perhaps the SSRI with the shortest half-life, about 15 hours. Therefore it is usually given on a twice-daily basis, starting at 25 mg daily.

Fluvoxamine significantly inhibits the P450 enzymes 2D6 and 1A2, although it inhibits other enzymes as well. Therefore it interferes with the metabolism of a host of medicines, so one should check a comprehensive list when prescribing fluvoxamine. Of particular interest, however, is its interference with the metabolism of caffeine at 1A2, making the morning cup of coffee last much longer than expected. In addition, because it is also metabolized by the 1A2 enzyme, cigarette smoke, which increases 1A2, can lead to lower levels of fluvoxamine.

Fluvoxamine is usually started at 25 mg daily and is available as tablets and as a once-a-day capsule, Luvox CR, which comes in 100 mg and 150 mg doses.

### Citalopram

Citalopram has no FDA-approved indications for children and adolescents. It has a half-life of about 35 hours. It tends to have relatively minimal effects on the P450 enzyme system and is metabolized by a number of medicines, thus being relatively unaffected by medicines that inhibit P450 enzymes. Like sertraline, however, medicines that increase the levels of many enzymes can decrease the level of citalopram.

Citalopram is available in tablets and liquid and is usually started at 10 mg daily.

### Escitalopram

Escitalopram is FDA approved for the treatment of depression in adolescents. Interestingly, it is the left-handed isomer of citalopram. That is, whereas citalopram is composed of citalopram molecules, which are mirror images of each other, escitalopram contains only the left-handed (and active) isomer.

For this reason, while it might not be completely accurate, the simplest way to think of the dosing of escitalopram is as half the dose of citalopram, since it has only half the molecules. Its interaction with P450 enzymes is similar to that of citalopram. It is also available in tablets and liquid.

### SNRIs

Now let's examine the SNRIs.

### Venlafaxine

Venlafaxine has no FDA-approved indications in children and adolescents. In fact it has not been shown to be better than placebo in the treatment of youth depression, although one study that found no response in children did find a response in adolescents (Emslie et al., 2007). It inhibits the reuptake of both serotonin and norepinephrine, although in adults its effect on norepinephrine occurs only at doses above 150 mg. It is metabolized by 2D6; therefore caution should be taken when venlafaxine is given with paroxetine, fluoxetine, and bupropion. While it is not a strong inhibitor of P450 enzymes, it has been shown to affect the levels of some medicines metabolized by 2D6.

It has a half-life of about five hours in adults and, interestingly, seems to have a greater risk of being associated with new suicidal thoughts, which is why I do not use it as a first-line medicine in pediatric patients. Its side effects tend to be similar to those of the SSRIs, although at higher doses it is associated with increased blood pressure. Also, as noted above, some (Rynn & Regan, 2008) recommend monitoring cholesterol. Venlafaxine might be more dangerous than the SSRIs in overdose. In addition, perhaps because of its short half-life, it is associated with more withdrawal side effects. It is available in tablets and capsules and in an extended-release (XR) form.

### Duloxetine

Duloxetine has no FDA-approved indications in children and adolescents and is infrequently used in this population.

### Desvenlafaxine

Desvenlafaxine is a metabolite of venlafaxine. It has no FDA approvals and no significant research on its use in a pediatric population.

## Other Antidepressants

Finally, we consider some antidepressants that do not fit neatly into a particular family.

### Bupropion

Bupropion does not affect synaptic serotonin levels but rather inhibits the reuptake of both norepinephrine and dopamine. It is probably for this reason that it has been reported to be effective as a treatment in ADHD too, albeit not as effective as the stimulants. Nevertheless, despite being prescribed to youth, it has no FDA-approved indications in this age group.

Bupropion is metabolized mainly by the 2B6 enzymes. It inhibits 2D6 and thus can interfere with the metabolism of venlafaxine.

Bupropion tends to be more activating than sedating and possibly to increase, rather than decrease, anxiety levels. Side effects include reduced appetite, headaches, rash, dry mouth, insomnia, and nausea. It might increase motor tics. Its advantage, however, is that it does not cause sexual side effects. At higher doses taken by adults, there is an increased risk of seizures, albeit probably at a maximum of 4 per 1,000. This side effect might be associated more with the immediate-release than the extended release formulations. Therefore, being at higher risk of seizures, such as having a history of seizures or an eating disorder, is a relative contrain-dication to bupropion. There does not seem to be an increased risk of suicidality. Although there seems to be less risk of inducing mania in bipolar adults, this has not been well studied in children.

Bupropion is available in an immediate-release, a sustained-release (SR), and also an extended-release (XL) once-daily form. It is also marketed, albeit not as Wellbutrin, as a treatment to help adults stop smoking.

### Trazodone

Trazodone is FDA approved as an antidepressant in adults but has no FDA indications in youth. Even in adults, it is more frequently used to induce sleep in those with insomnia. It has a half-life in adults of only about three to four hours, so when taken at bedtime it has minimal side effects the next day. It is metabolized by 3A4. The most notable side effect of trazodone is priapism, a prolonged and painful penile erection. This potentially requires surgery. While this is a rare side effect, families tend to balk at the use of trazodone as a sleep agent for the male pediatric population.

### Mirtazapine

Mirtazapine is FDA approved for the treatment of depression in adults and might have a more rapid onset of action than the SSRIs. There is a minimum of research on its use in children. It has a number of synaptic effects that lead to increasing the effect of norepinephrine and, thereby, serotonin. It also has antihistamine effects, which lead to the common side effects of sedation and somnolence. Interestingly, because the anti-histamine effects predominate at lower doses, these side effects are more common at lower than higher doses. Other common side effects include increased appetite, weight gain, and dry mouth, all of which occur in about 20% of adult patients. The possible consequence of increased cholesterol and triglycerides necessitates monitoring these blood levels. Mirtazapine does not cause sexual side effects.

Table 7.1 summarizes the dose range for various antidepressant and antianxiety medicines.

## Tricyclic Antidepressants

The tricyclic antidepressants (TCAs) are only infrequently used in child, and even adult, psychiatry today, having been largely replaced by the SSRIs. Nevertheless, they are considered in some situations and therefore merit mention.

Some of the TCAs block the reuptake of norepinephrine, and others block the reuptake of both norepinephrine and sertotonin. Most, however, affect a number of different neurotransmitters, and some block postsynaptic receptor sites as well as reuptake sites. In short, these are "dirty" drugs in that they affect many sites, thus also causing a variety of side effects.

The TCAs were the mainstay of the pharmacological treatment of depression and panic disorder in adult psychiatry from the early 1960s through the late 1980s. Testing of their use in separation anxiety and school avoidance in children was inconclusive, however, and their efficacy in the treatment of depression in children and adolescents was never proven to be better than placebo. In addition, many patients experienced a host of side effects. In fact, the only FDA-approved uses of the TCAs in youth are for bedwetting (imipramine) and OCD (clomipramine). Even for these conditions, the TCAs have been largely replaced by other medicines.

Although they are generally not used to treat depression, panic disorder, or other anxiety disorders in children and adolescents, their use is considered in those who have not responded to other medicines and for whom treatment is mandatory. During the era when stimulants were available only as short-acting medicines and were thought to exacerbate tic disorders, the TCAs were investigated as an alternative to the stimulants. They proved effective in the treatment of ADHD, though because of their side effects and other medicines that became available, they became a third-line treatment for ADHD. In addition, they are

## TABLE 7.1. Antidepressants and Antianxiety Medicines

| Brand name | Generic name | Starting dose | Max. dose range |
|---|---|---|---|
| **Selective serotonin reuptake inhibitors (SSRIs)** | | | |
| Prozac | fluoxetine | 5–10 mg/day | 20–60 mg/day |
| Zoloft | sertraline | 25 mg/day | 50–200 mg/day |
| Luvox | fluvoxamine | 25 mg/day | 50–300 mg/day |
| Paxil | paroxetine | 5–10 mg/day | 20–40 mg/day |
| Celexa | citalopram | 5–10 mg/day | 20–40 mg/day |
| Lexapro | escitalopram | 5–10 mg/day | 10–30 mg/day |
| Anafranil* | clomipramine | 25–50 mg/day | 2.0–5.0 mg/kg (by weight) |
| **Other antidepressants** | | | |
| Effexor XR | venlafaxine XR | 37.5 mg/day | 37–225 mg/day |
| Cymbalta | duloxetine | 20 mg/day | 40–120 mg/day |
| Wellbutrin SR | bupropion SR | 100 mg/day | 150–300 mg/day |
| Wellbutrin XL | bupropion XL | 150 mg/day | 150–300 mg/day |
| Remeron | mirtazapine | 7.5 mg/day | 30–45 mg/day |
| **Benzodiazepines** | | | |
| Klonopin | clonazepam | 0.25 mg | 0.25–2 mg/day |
| Xanax | alprazolam | 0.25 mg | 0.25–4 mg/day |
| Ativan | lorazepam | 0.25 mg | 0.25–6 mg/day |

Note: This table is intended only as a guideline. Most of these medicines are not FDA approved for youth. Therefore doses may be based on use in adults.

* Clomipramine affects neurotransmitters other than serotonin.

sometimes prescribed at low doses for the treatment of pain syndromes or insomnia.

The TCAs generally stay in the body for about 24 hours and therefore can be given once daily. Sometimes, however, they might be divided and given twice daily to minimize side effects. They are dosed from less than 2 mg/kg per day, according to the patient's body weight, with a maximum of 5 mg/kg per day. The dosing always begins on the low side and is raised cautiously, while blood levels, blood pressure, and electrocardiograms are monitored. In adults the TCAs usually take about three weeks before they are effective for depression and anxiety.

The side effects of the TCAs are many and depend on which neurotransmitters a particular TCA affects. Recall that the TCAs affect many neurotransmitters and therefore cause many side effects. Because each TCA has its own profile of neurotransmitters affected, each also has its own side effect profile.

In general, however, the TCAs tend to cause many anticholinergic side effects, such as dry mouth, constipation, and urinary hesitancy. In addition, they interfere with the ability of arteries to constrict when a person stands up, thus causing an orthostatic drop in blood pressure and brief dizziness. Tiredness is also a problem.

The most significant side effect, however, is the effect of the TCAs on cardiac conduction. This includes a slowing of the electrical conduction, and while this slowing can usually be monitored by obtaining a baseline and follow-up cardiograms, case reports of the deaths of children taking desipramine during the 1990s raised obvious concerns. Therefore, when TCAs are used, especially at higher doses, EKGs and medication blood levels should both be monitored. Overall, however, concern about this side effect and the lack of evidence of efficacy, except for OCD and bedwetting, make the risk-benefit ratio of the TCAs unfavorable as a first-line treatment approach.

Although they will not be reviewed in detail, the more commonly used TCAs are imipramine and amitriptyline and its metabolite, nortriptyline. The metabolite of imipramine, desipramine, is generally not used because of its association with the fatalities noted above.

## Monoamine Oxidase Inhibitors

The monoamine oxidase inhibitors (MAOIs) have been around since the psychopharmacology revolution of the 1950s. They have been found effective for the treatment of adults with depression, panic disorder, and anxiety. Some adult psychiatrists have found the MAOIs to be particularly helpful in atypical depression. In addition, selegiline, an MAOI that inhibits MAO B, is used to treat Parkinson's because of its effect on dopamine. Because of their side effect profile, the MAOIs are essentially untested and rarely used in child psychiatry.

The side effects of the MAOIs include sedation, insomnia, headache, and dizziness upon standing. The most significant problem with MAOIs, and the issue that prevents their widespread use, is their interaction with other medicines and certain foods. The essential problem is that MAO in the lining of the gut typically degrades the tyramine contained in certain foods. If the MAO is irreversibly inhibited (for example by an MAOI), the tyramine is not degraded and can cause an elevation of blood pressure. This hypertension can be life threatening and requires emergency medical care. Other substances, for example, some chemicals contained in cold remedies, can also cause an increase in blood pressure if taken with an MAOI. A list of tyramine-containing foods must be made available to the patient taking an MAOI so they can be avoided. Such foods include beer and certain wines and aged cheeses. One can readily see the difficulty in using the MAOIs with all but the most responsible adolescents, and even then, only when absolutely necessary.

## Benzodiazepines

The benzodiazepines, originally developed as muscle relaxants, were made famous in the 1960s by medicines such as diazepam (Valium) and remain an important class of medicines in the treatment of anxiety but not depression. In adults the BZDs are used by psychiatrists to treat anxiety and insomnia. Although, they can all be used to treat the acute anxiety of a panic attack, alprazolam and clonazepam have also been shown, like the SSRIs, TCAs, and MAOIs, to prevent panic attacks when taken on an ongoing basis and have an FDA indication for the treatment of panic disorder in adults. The BZDs are also used in anesthesia, as muscle relaxants, and to treat seizure disorders. Some of the BZDs have been marketed as hypnotics, to induce sleep, but this distinction is mostly a marketing tool, because all the BZDs could induce sleep if taken at bedtime.

The BZDs work by increasing the effect of GABA, the brain's inhibitory neurotransmitter, at the amygdala and prefrontal cortex. The BZDs are subgrouped into three types based on their chemical structure. This is important because, at least in adults, the medicines in each subgroup are metabolized differently and therefore have different durations of action. For example, the 2-ketobenzodiazepines (2-ketoBZDs), such as diazepam and clonazepam, are slowly metabolized in the liver, giving these medicines long durations of action. In addition, some of the metabolites of these medicines are also active anxiolytics, thus extending the functional duration of action even longer. The 3-hydroxybenzodiazepines, such as lorazepam, and the triazolobenzodiazepines (triazoloBZDs), such as alprazolam, are metabolized more quickly and therefore have shorter durations of action. In addition, those groups whose metabolism consists of being oxidized in the liver, namely the 2-ketoBZDs and triazoloBZDs, are affected by other medicines that affect the cytochrome P450 enzyme system. Thus care must be taken when using these BZDs with certain medicines, such as some of the SSRIs and birth control pills.

The BZDs are not FDA approved for use in the psychiatric disorders of children. They do, however, have a role to play in child psychiatry, in particular in the treatment of panic attacks and some types of acute anxiety. Children and adolescents with moderate or severe panic attacks benefit by having the acute panic anxiety diminished. During the onset of panic disorder, a BZD is often helpful when taken on an as-needed basis at the first feelings of panic. The onset of this disorder is associated with a feeling of generalized anxiety as one begins to live in anxious anticipation of the next panic attack. Taking a BZD regularly on a daily or twice-daily basis for a few days to weeks can help alleviate this anxiety. After the initial crisis has passed, one must be sure to encourage the patient to stop using the BZD regularly. At that point, many patients with panic disorder use the BZD on an as-needed basis if they feel the onset of panic. For many patients, this evolves into the feeling of calm they attain simply by knowing they have one pill available "just in case."

I purposely qualified the level of panic attacks for which BZDs should be used as moderate to severe to distinguish them from mild panic attacks. A mild panic attack is still an uncomfortable event and might merit medicine for acute anxiety. Nevertheless, I try to use the experience of this milder anxiety as a teaching moment, that is, as an opportunity for patients to see that they can endure the uncomfortable, but transient and not dangerous, panic. I encourage patients to see panic attacks as false alarms that consist of their body giving physical signals of danger (sweats, palpitations, shortness of breath) when in fact no danger is present. Their job is to learn to assess whether danger is present, and if not, to distract themselves (perhaps with a friend's or parent's help) until the attack passes. If the patient is able to do this, I defer the use of a BZD.

BZDs are also used in phobic anxiety when there is no reasonable alternative. For example, although most phobias should be treated behaviorally, this requires practice. Some phobias, such as the fear of flying in a plane, are difficult to practice. Programs exist to help people get past these phobias, but they are not always available, especially for children and adolescents. Therefore, on a very limited basis, BZDs can be useful in helping patients with flying phobia through their flights. When BZDs are used for this purpose, patients should "experiment" with the medicine once or twice before the day of the flight, thus minimizing the possibility of first-time side effects at 30,000 feet. In addition, I tell patients to take the medicine the night before the flight, or at least before they leave for the airport. This lowers their anxiety going into the feared situation, which makes treating the acute anxiety of flying easier.

The BZDs are also infrequently used to reduce the anxiety of complicated patients who have chronic anxiety. In these cases the BZD becomes one of the groups of medicines necessary to keep the patient functional.

In child psychiatry the most commonly used BZDs are probably clonazepam, alprazolam, and lorazepam. Each has its advantages, depending on the circumstance. Clonazepam, which is FDA approved in children only for the treatment of seizures, is used because it is relatively long acting. It therefore can help the patient without necessarily requiring a second or third daily dose. Alprazolam and lorazepam, by contrast, are used because they are short acting and therefore are less likely to interfere with one's mental acuity the following day. Clonazepam is also available in a pediatric-friendly wafer that disintegrates in one's mouth. The BZDs are metabolized by various enzymes that should be evaluated on an individual basis.

The most common and significant side effect of the BZDs is sedation, which is often dose-related and can be minimized by lowering the dose. Therefore, teens who drive should be cautioned to use the medicine initially in the evening when they can stay home. They should also be warned to avoid other sedating substances, in particular alcohol, when taking the benzodiazepines. Because of sedation, benzodiazepines are started at low doses and slowly increased. Another side effect experienced by a minority of young children is disinhibition, an agitated state. In addition, the ability to learn new information can also be impaired on the BZDs. While one should try to avoid the morning use of benzodiazepines because of their possible effect during the school day, sometimes that is exactly when the medicine is needed. In these situations, if used judiciously, benzodiazepines can lower the anxiety of some patients, thus making them available to learn.

The most significant long-term concern from using the BZDs is tolerance (the need for increasing doses) and addiction. Many clinicians feel that in treating adults with anxiety disorders, tolerance is the exception, not the rule, since many patients take a BZD for years without increasing the dose. BZDs are, however, abused by patients diagnosed with substance abuse and therefore should be avoided in the treatment of those patients.

After having been used on a chronic basis, the BZDs are discontinued by tapering slowly to minimize side effects and the possibility of precipitating a seizure. Fortunately this is not a major problem in using the BZDs for acute anxiety as I've described.

## Buspirone

Buspirone is a novel, non-benzodiazepine antianxiety agent that is not a GABA enhancer but rather is a serotonin agonist at both presynaptic and postsynaptic receptors. It also has some dopaminergic effects and was originally considered an antipsychotic. It is not an antidepressant, although some studies in adults suggest it might be (Schatzberg, Cole, & DeBattista, 2007). Although evidence for its efficacy has not been proven in controlled studies of children, some small studies have shown some efficacy in children with anxiety disorders. In addition, buspirone has been used to augment the SSRI treatment of OCD.

Buspirone is metabolized by 3A4, and thus its blood level can be increased by medicines that inhibit this enzyme. There are no dosing guidelines for buspirone in children and adolescents. In adults, buspirone is started at 5 mg twice daily and then increased slowly. Sometimes it needs to be used at doses of 30–60 mg daily. It can take a few weeks to become effective.

Side effects are usually mild and do not include the sedation, dependence, tolerance, and withdrawal sometimes associated with the benzodiazepines. Some will experience gastrointestinal symptoms, headache, and dizziness. Some patients will also experience agitation, impulsivity, and euphoria.

# Case Examples

*Case 1: Blaine, who is 9 years old, is brought for evaluation because he is fidgety and unfocused. His parents wonder if he has ADHD, a reasonable question. The evaluation reveals many symptoms of ADHD, and Blaine is started on a stimulant. Although the initial response is promising, after a couple of months it becomes less clear to Blaine's parents that the medicine is helpful. A closer evaluation leads to greater focus on Blaine's chronic anxiety. The stimulant is discontinued, and Blaine is started on fluoxetine, on which he gradually becomes less anxious and also less fidgety and more at ease.*

*Comment:* The distinction between ADHD and generalized anxiety disorder can be difficult in some children. Because the symptoms of ADHD are so well known, parents often present the child's symptoms as belonging to ADHD. In addition, the anxiety of some parents makes it more difficult for them to identify their child easily as suffering from an anxiety disorder.

*Case 2: Jon is 17 and has been markedly depressed for the past six months. When he comes to clinical attention, he is started on fluoxetine 20 mg daily. After two weeks he does not respond, and his parents try to push the physician to increase the dose. Jon's doctor assesses Jon's suicidal thoughts and determines that Jon's dose should not be increased, but that he should be hospitalized.*

*Comment:* The frustration experienced by Jon's parents is understandable. Increasing Jon's dose of fluoxetine after two weeks, however, will not make it work more quickly. And Jon's safety must be assured. Therefore, while waiting for the medicine to work, Jon is hospitalized.

> *Case 3: Fourteen-year-old Chip is being treated with fluvoxamine for OCD. His dose is being increased steadily, although as the dose approaches 250 mg daily, his parents become anxious. Their nephew is taking Lexapro 20 mg daily, and they are concerned because Chip's dose is much higher.*

*Comment:* Parents often fail to realize that medicine doses cannot necessarily be compared. One mg of Lexapro is not comparable to 1 mg of fluvoxamine.

> *Case 4: Jenny is 9 years old and has significant learning disabilities, including a language disorder. School work stresses Jenny to the max, a situation not helped by the personality of Jenny's rigid, demanding teacher. Jenny presents with extreme anxiety about school and is resisting attending. Her parents call requesting an antianxiety medicine.*

*Comment:* While Jenny has a learning disorder, her other diagnosis is probably adjustment disorder with anxiety, not an anxiety disorder, and is not helped by the SSRIs. Jenny needs a change of environments, namely, a class setting in which she feels competent, valued, and safe to acknowledge her learning disorders. Medicine should not be the first treatment tried.

## CHAPTER 8

# Antipsychotic Medicines

The antipsychotic medicines ushered in psychiatry's pharmacologic revolution when, in the 1950s, chlorpromazine, which was being developed as a medicine to be used during surgery, was discovered to diminish the hallucinations of patients with schizophrenia. Over the next 30 to 40 years, chlorpromazine and the other antipsychotics were the dominant treatment for psychosis. Then, in the early 1990s, a new type of antipsychotic medicines, such as clozapine and risperidone, was developed. The original antipsychotics came to be called the typical, or first-generation, antipsychotics (FGAs) to differentiate them from the newer atypical, or second-generation, antipsychotics (SGAs). Since then, an even newer generation of antipsychotics, such as aripiprazole, has been developed. For the purposes of simplicity, I'll consider these as part of the SGAs.

Over the past roughly 20 years, the SGAs have pushed their predecessors aside as the most commonly prescribed antipsychotics. While the older antipsychotics were known to be effective in diminishing the so-called positive symptoms of schizophrenia, such as hallucinations and delusions, the SGAs came on the scene touted as doing that and more. They also diminished the negative symptoms of schizophrenia, such as low energy and flat affect, and did so with a lower risk of the movement disorders caused by the typical antipsychotics.

Recent data have questioned whether the newer medicines are in fact better overall than the older medicines for the treatment of adult schizophrenia. I'll address that when I look at the data on the treatment of schizophrenia. For our purposes, in child and adolescent psychiatry, while the SGAs have been the more commonly prescribed antipsychotics over recent years, the primary reason for their being prescribed has generally not been psychosis. In fact, psychosis has not even been among the top three disorders for which antipsychotics have been prescribed to youth. This is an example of patient demand and (at least, perceived) successful clinical experience, not the family name of the medicine, determining its use. Instead, as we'll see, these medicines have been used to treat disruptive behavior disorders, bipolar disorder, tic disorders, and the extreme agitation of children with pervasive developmental disorders.

## How Antipsychotics Work

The best way to understand the antipsychotics is to recall the discussion of the neuronal pathways in Chapter 3, which stressed the importance of receptor sites and the location and function of the neuronal pathways in which they exist. Understanding the antipsychotics and their side effects is easier if one considers the neuronal pathways on which they work. Also, remember that medicines are not discriminating. They have synaptic effects on all pathways where they find receptors into which they fit. They do not go only where we choose. Therapeutic effects are caused by the changes at some synapses, and side effects are caused by changes at others. We will see, first, how antipsychotics cause benefits and side effects; then a more extended discussion of side effects appears later in the chapter.

The antipsychotics block dopamine at the four major dopaminergic pathways. The most important of these from a benefit standpoint is the mesolimbic pathway, which goes from the brainstem to the limbic system. On the one hand, all medicines that block the D2 of dopamine receptors in this pathway, including both FGAs and SGAs, decrease the symptoms of psychosis. On the other hand, all substances that increase dopamine at the D2 receptors in this pathway, such as high doses of amphetamines, increase psychotic symptoms.

The antipsychotics also block dopamine in the nigrostriatal pathway, which goes from the brainstem to the basal ganglia. This pathway controls involuntary motor movement. That includes maintaining the proper tension in our muscles, so we don't have to think continuously about keeping our leg muscles taut while we're waiting in line at the movies, and ensuring that our muscles work smoothly without undue rigidity or spasm. When the dopamine of this pathway is blocked, the patient can experience involuntary, or extrapyramidal, motor movements. The word *extrapyramidal* is simply a way of differentiating this involuntary motor system from the voluntary motor system, which is sometimes called the pyramidal system because of its anatomic appearance.

Dopaminergic neurons are also the means by which the hypothalamus controls the release of prolactin by the pituitary gland. Ordinarily, cells in the pituitary gland release prolactin, which stimulates the production of breast milk as well as other functions. The dopamine released by the hypothalamus tells the pituitary to inhibit milk production. When antipsychotics block dopamine receptors, they are removing this inhibition on milk production, potentially leading to breast enlargement and milk production.

Finally, dopamine is the neurotransmitter of the mesocortical pathway, which goes from the brainstem to the cerebral cortex and enables many higher cortical functions, such as spontaneity and motivation. When these are blocked by antipsychotic medicines, the patient can seem listless, uninvolved, and unmotivated.

While the FGAs block dopamine on these four pathways, the SGAs do the same and also block serotonin receptors. Because, among its many jobs, serotonin is also the neurotransmitter by which neurons tell themselves to release less dopamine, when serotonin is blocked, the neuron releases more dopamine. So the SGAs essentially lead to the release of more dopamine, but they also block dopamine receptors, rendering the extra dopamine less effective. If the balance of dopamine blocking and serotonin blocking is just right, then there is no functional increase in dopamine.

This system of balance between dopamine and serotonin exists in all of the dopaminergic pathways mentioned above, except the meso-limbic pathway, which determines psychosis. Therefore, by blocking dopamine and serotonin receptors, the SGAs effectively block dopamine to diminish psychosis but cause no effective change in dopamine in the other three pathways, thus minimizing side effects.

This is a good time for an important reminder. With these simple explanations, I am reducing the world's most complicated machine, and the lockbox of all our life experiences, to a one-paragraph explanation. As I've tried to stress, the brain is a vastly complex place with literally trillions of multiple types of synapses, all impacting one another. The medicines we use affect many receptors in many parts of the brain. As we'll see, each medicine affects a unique array of receptors, including those that are neither dopaminergic nor serotonergic, to varying degrees. In short, understanding the mechanisms of medicines is important, but what actually happens to real patients, whether it theoretically should or shouldn't, is far more important.

## First- versus Second-Generation Antipsychotics

As I've already noted, for a medicine to treat psychosis, it must block the D2 receptors for dopamine in the mesolimbic pathway of the brain. In fact, for it to be effective, approximately 60–80% of those receptors must be blocked. Both FGA and SGAs accomplish this, but the addition of serotonin blocking by the SGAs is a real change from the FGAs, causing a different profile of both benefits and side effects.

Both groups of medicines are effective in treating adult schizophrenia. While the FGAs proved to be effective in diminishing the positive symptoms of schizophrenia, such as hallucinations and delusions, the SGAs accomplished this as well as improving the debilitating negative side effects of this disorder, such as apathy, anhedonia (the inability to enjoy), and social withdrawal. Whether this benefit and the different side effect profile of SGAs is worth their higher financial cost in treating this disorder is still debated. The SGAs, however, have also proven beneficial in the treatment of bipolar disorder—both the manic and depressed phases. Sometimes an SGA is used alone for this purpose, and at other times it is effective when added to a medicine the patient is already taking.

In addition, the SGAs, like the FGAs, have been helpful in diminishing the agitation of patients with dementia, albeit with an FDA warning regarding side effects, or delirium. Although this is not a frequent use in child and adolescent psychiatry, child psychiatrists often try to decrease the agitation of children with pervasive developmental disorder (PDD) or sometimes extreme oppositional defiant disorder. The FGAs had been used successfully to treat children with autism and, less so, to treat agitation in children without PDD.

The rapid increase in use of SGAs in youth has been partially due to their increased use to treat children with PDDs, but more by their use to treat bipolar disorder and the extreme agitation of disruptive behavior disorders. Before they fell out of favor, the FGAs, particularly low-dose thioridazine (Mellaril), were used to treat children with extreme agitation, albeit not to the extent that the SGAs are currently used for that purpose. The reason for the increased use of the SGAs is unclear. It might be because they are truly more effective at treating agitation or because of their relative lack of side effects involving movement. The increase might also be due to their discovery during the age of psychopharmacology, when patients generally expect to receive a prescription, or simply because they are more aggressively marketed.

Certainly the side effect profiles of the SGAs have been a change from those of the FGAs that preceded them. The most feared side effect of the FGAs had always been their potential for causing a variety of motor movements, one of which (tardive dyskinesia) was often irreversible. On the one hand, the SGAs offered a vast improvement in lowering this risk, although how much the risk was lowered is unclear. On the other hand, the SGAs increased the risk for significant weight gain and with it the risk of diabetes mellitus and increased levels of cholesterol and triglycerides. As we'll see, some SGAs are more prone to causing this side effect than others. Whether the lower risk of movement disorders is worth the higher risk of weight gain is debated.

So far a few SGAs have been FDA approved for use in youth. These include risperidone, olanzapine, quetiapine, and aripiprazole for adolescents with schizophrenia and bipolar disorder, and risperidone and aripiprazole for extreme agitation in patients with autism. Pimozide and haloperidol, both FGAs, are FDA approved for the treatment of Tourette's disorder in youth, albeit with different age indications.

With that as background, let's look at the disorders for which the antipsychotics offer potential benefits and then at the side effect profiles of these medicines. Then we'll look at each of the medicines.

## Clinical Indications of the Antipsychotics

Antipsychotic medicines are prescribed for treating a number of disorders affecting children and adolescents. In this section I review the proof that they are beneficial.

### Schizophrenia

Before I start to discuss the potential benefits of using antipsychotics to treat childhood schizophrenia, we have to consider terminology. The word *psychotic* is not synonymous with *schizophrenia*. Schizophrenia is a disorder, which I describe below. The term *psychosis* has been defined in different ways. In general, it implies a break with reality testing, most often manifested by the experience of hallucinations, delusions, or a thought disorder. Hallucinations are most commonly auditory; the person hears voices when there is no outside source of the voice, yet thinks the voice is real. Not every experience of hallucinations represents psychosis, however. For example during bereavement, some hear the loved one's voice but know the person is not present. Delusions are fixed, false beliefs, such as the belief that one is Julius Caesar. A thought disorder is an illogical flow of thought often manifested by jumps from one topic to another without the person's being aware that the listener is completely lost. Psychosis is not a disorder per se but rather a state signifying an underlying disorder, the way fever signifies illness, but it could be caused by a bacterial infection, viral infection, or a host of other physical ailments. While psychosis is the *sine qua non* of schizophrenia, others, such as those with bipolar disorder, can also be psychotic.

Schizophrenia is a disorder affecting about 1% of the population, manifested by hallucinations, delusions, or a thought disorder. It typically begins in the late teens or early 20s. Historically, schizophrenia has been seen as having a downward-spiraling course, but this is currently being questioned.

Drawing the lines to define the exact age of childhood onset schizophrenia (COS) is somewhat subjective. Patients with schizophrenia having an onset before 18 years of age have generally been labeled as having COS or early onset schizophrenia. Those whose illness begins before age 13 are labeled as having very early onset schizophrenia. Both of these are seen as continuous with the adult form of schizophrenia. The very early onset cases are more malignant and, thankfully, very rare.

Over the years, many children diagnosed with schizophrenia have been mistakenly diagnosed. In the past, children with autism were misdiagnosed as having schizophrenia. Today some of these children are seen as having bipolar disorder and others as having a syndrome labeled "multidimensionally impaired" by researchers at the National Institute of Mental Health. These children have transient, often stress-related psychotic symptoms, impaired social skills, and emotional lability. Significantly, follow-up data reveal that these children do not develop schizophrenia. Finally, non-disordered preschool children can experience hallucinations as a normal response to stress and thus be mistakenly diagnosed as schizophrenic.

What is the evidence that medicine is effective in treating childhood schizophrenia? We'll look at the studies but must acknowledge that, whatever benefit patients receive, current treatment is relatively ineffective. Even with the best available therapy, many patients are left with continued psychotic symptoms and a low level of functioning.

The data supporting the use of antipsychotics in childhood schizophrenia must be divided into studies of the FGAs and studies of the SGAs. Studies on the use of the FGAs go back to the 1970s, and they do support their use, though not as robustly as some of the other medicines I've discussed, such as the stimulants for treating ADHD. For example, Spencer and colleagues (1992) showed that haloperidol, at an optimal dose of 0.5–3.5 mg daily, was more effective than placebo. This study, however, included only 12 children taking haloperidol and 12 taking placebo. In fact the total number of children on FGAs studied from the late 1960s through the late 1990s amounts to only about 200, the bulk of those studies being done before the 1980s. Nevertheless, the response rates were generally favorable and slightly better than we'll find with those of the SGAs.

The SGAs have also been studied in relatively few children and also tend to show efficacy in treating COS. For example, Zalsman and colleagues (2003), in a study of 11 adolescents with schizophrenia, showed that treatment with risperidone led to significant improvements in functioning as well as in positive, but not negative, symptoms. Other studies have echoed these findings. Findling, McNamara, Youngstrom, and colleagues (2003), albeit in an open-label trial, found that treatment with olanzapine led to improvements in both positive and negative symptoms in a small group of adolescents with schizophrenia. And in a large double-blind, placebo-controlled study, Findling and colleagues (2008) found aripiprazole to be effective in treating adolescents with schizophrenia. As Ross (2008) points out, however, the relative effect of FGAs and SGAs compared to placebo is relatively low, with fewer than half of patients responding.

The SGA for which there is the best evidence of efficacy in adult schizophrenia is clozapine. Although, because of its risk of serious side effects, this medicine has not been used as a first-line treatment, all studies, albeit not blind, have found it helpful. As we'll see, however, clozapine carries with it the dangerous side effect of agranulocytosis.

There has been significant debate regarding which is more effective, the FGAs or SGAs, in treating adult schizophrenia and, more recently, COS. Sikich and colleagues (2008) found that the SGAs olanzapine and risperidone were no more effective than the FGA molindone in treating children and adolescents with early onset schizophrenia. All three medicines led to a decrease in symptoms by less than half.

Approximately half the children in this study chose to be followed in a continuing double-blind extension of the study for about the next year (Findling et al., 2010). Interestingly, only slightly more than 10% of them completed the year on their original medicine, many patients choosing to stop the medicine, often because of side effects or inadequate response. The three medicines continued to be equivalent to one another in decreasing symptoms, with most children's improvement reaching a plateau by eight weeks of treatment. While the small number of children in this study limits the conclusions, one can appreciate the difficulty in treating these children and the limited usefulness of medicine for many of them.

There are a number of difficulties with these studies of the treatment of childhood schizophrenia, including whether they were done on inpatients or outpatients, younger children or older adolescents, and the dose and duration for which the medicine was used. In addition, whether the patient had been previously treated also seems to exert an effect on the patient's response. Studies using patients who have never before been treated tend to show more effect. This might mean that patients previously treated are a more treatment-resistant group. Given the rarity of this disorder and its devastating nature, finding ideal study subjects is also quite difficult.

## Bipolar Disorder

The characteristics of bipolar disorder will be reviewed in the chapter on mood stabilizers, so only the efficacy of antipsychotics in treating this disorder is discussed here. The discussion focuses on the SGAs because there has been no research on the use of FGAs to treat bipolar disorder in children and adolescents. In addition, as will be mentioned in the chapter on mood stabilizers, one must first distinguish between the treatment of the manic phase and of the depressed phase of bipolar illness. And one must also distinguish between the acute treatment and the maintenance treatment of each of these phases of the disorder. Acute treatment refers to the treatment used to solve the immediate problem, whether depression or mania. Maintenance treatment refers to the ongoing preventive treatment after the immediate problem has been resolved. Each of these phases and treatments might require different approaches. Treatment of the mixed states and rapid-cycling states of bipolar disorder further complicates the discussion.

The use of the SGAs to treat bipolar disorder has been well established in adults. Most of the SGAs have been proven effective in, and are FDA approved for, the treatment of acute mania in adults and the maintenance phase of bipolar disorder. In addition, some of the SGAs, namely olanzapine (albeit in combination with fluoxetine as Symbyax) and quetiapine, have also proven useful and are FDA approved for acute bipolar depression.

There is less research on the use of the SGAs in adolescent and, especially, childhood bipolar disorder. Nevertheless, the existing research shows their efficacy in treating acute mania, and risperidone, olanzapine, quetiapine and aripiprazole have been FDA approved for treating manic or mixed states in adolescents.

In a double-blind, placebo-controlled study of children and adolescents with mania, Findling and colleagues (2009) showed aripiprazole at 10 mg or 30 mg daily to be more effective than placebo starting in the first week of treatment. And in a double-blind, placebo-controlled study of children and adolescents, Haas and colleagues (2009) found that risperidone was also effective in treating mania. In this study, the authors felt that the lower dose of 0.5–2.5 mg daily had a better risk-benefit ratio than the higher dose of 3–6 mg daily.

Tohen and colleagues (2007), in a double-blind study lasting three weeks, showed that olanzapine, at doses ranging from 2.5–20 mg per day, was more effective than placebo in treating adolescents with mania. The group treated with medicine was doing better than the placebo-treated group after one week of treatment, but even more so after two weeks. Other studies have shown the efficacy of other SGAs, such as quetiapine and ziprasidone.

The SGAs can be particularly helpful in treating acutely manic adolescents who are also psychotic. In this situation, while mood stabilizers are useful, the addition of an SGA might add benefit in preventing relapse (Kantafaris, Coletti, & Dicker, 2001).

Even in treating non-psychotic manic adolescents, the use of two medicines concurrently is seen as a frequent necessity. In a double-blind, placebo-controlled study of adolescents with acute mania, DelBello and colleagues (2002) found quetiapine to be a useful addition to divalproex. And Pavuluri and colleagues (2004), albeit in an open-label study, found that risperidone, when added to divalproex or lithium, was a useful adjunct in treating child and adolescent bipolar disorder.

There is no notable research on the treatment of acute bipolar depression (as opposed to mania or mixed states) or on maintenance treatment (as opposed to acute treatment) of bipolar disorder with SGAs. (See Chapter 9 on mood stabilizers for a broader discussion of this topic.) And the research that has been done is not always hopeful. For example, DelBello and colleagues (2009), in a double-blind, placebo-controlled pilot study, found that after eight weeks, quetiapine was not effective in treating the depressive symptoms of adolescents with bipolar disorder. These results were different from those of adult studies.

## Pervasive Developmental Disorders

Autism was originally described by Leo Kanner in 1942. Describing 11 patients, Kanner reported problems in relating to others, language difficulties, the need for sameness, and stereotypies (or repetitive, purposeless movements). Initially, practicing according to the zeitgeist of those decades, many psychiatrists saw autism as caused by the child's having a cold, aloof mother. Fortunately, since then, much time and effort have been invested in exploring this disorder. Over recent decades autism has come to be seen as having a neurological cause. Also, the concept has been broadened, so that autism is considered one of the group of pervasive developmental disorders (PDD). Most notable among the others is Asperger's disorder (see Chapter 11).

Autistic disorder, as currently described, is manifested by an impairment of social interaction, such as poor eye contact and an inability to share interests with others; an impairment of communication, such as a delay or lack of spoken language; and a pattern of highly stereotyped behaviors, such as hand flapping, or restricted interests, such as an abnormally encompassing preoccupation. It is markedly impairing and often associated with mental retardation.

For many years autism was seen as a rare disorder, affecting about 3–5 per 10,000 children. Currently the prevalence of this disorder is seen as about 13 in 10,000, and with the expanded concept of PDD, the overall rate of all PDDs is approximately 30–60 per 10,000. The prevalence of Asperger's disorder is seen as 2.5 per 10,000 or a bit higher. I stress this fact because the frequency with which patients present with this diagnosis seems far higher than the research-based prevalence rates. My guess is that this represents the use of this diagnosis by many parents and clinicians to explain children with a variety of social difficulties.

The treatment of the PDDs is beyond the scope of this chapter. Confining this discussion to the pharmacological treatment, however, I must start by saying that currently there is no treatment for the underlying difficulty of the PDDs. There is only symptomatic treatment for some of the common and clinically significant difficulties facing these children.

The most immediately disruptive symptoms of children with PDDs revolve around the patient's frequent agitation, irritability, and aggression pointed at oneself or others. In addition, stereotypies and inattention or hyperactivity are symptoms that have merited study. Here I review the effect of antipsychotics on aggression and stereotypies. The use of stimulants to improve focus or the SSRIs to decrease compulsive behaviors is reviewed in those respective chapters.

Before the advent of the SGAs, haloperidol, an FGA, was used to treat what was then called autism. This was evidence based, Anderson and colleagues (1989) finding that haloperidol was more effective than placebo in treating young children with autism. Because of their side effect profile, however, the FGAs were largely replaced by the SGAs by the 1990s, except in treatment-resistant cases.

Risperidone and aripiprazole are currently the only FDA-approved medications for the treatment of a PDD-related behavior. They are approved for the treatment of the extreme irritability experienced by these children. The RUPP study (RUPP, 2002) was the first double-blind, placebo-controlled study examining the effect of risperidone in youth. After eight weeks, risperidone at an average dose of just under 2 mg daily was found to diminish irritability very powerfully. It also reduced the repetitive behaviors known as stereotypies.

Shea and colleagues (2004) published another double-blind, placebo-controlled study of children also demonstrating the efficacy of risperidone, at an average dose of just over 1 mg daily, in diminishing the irritability of PDD. Owen and colleagues (2009), in a double-blind, placebo-controlled study, found that aripiprazole was effective in lessening the irritability of children and adolescents with autistic disorder. Other studies, albeit open-label or using a smaller number of subjects, have shown the efficacy of other SGAs such as olanzapine and quetiapine. While the effects were sometimes impressive, the use of these, as with all medicines, must be weighed against their risks.

The benefit to treatment with risperidone in the RUPP study carried over the subsequent 16 weeks for most subjects who continued the next, open-label part of the trial. When medicine was gradually replaced by placebo over four weeks, however, many, but not all, of the subjects had a return of symptoms (RUPP, 2005a). In fact, enough subjects had a return of symptoms that the trial with placebo was discontinued.

## *Tic Disorders*

A tic is a sudden, repetitive, but not rhythmic motor movement. Common tics include the quick, repetitive eye blink or eye roll, shoulder shrugs, nose scrunches, and grimaces. Tics can also be vocal, including sniffling, throat clearing, quick subvocal hums, or, rarely, words. Tics can also be complex behaviors, such as jumping, touching, smelling, or repeating words. The infamous tic of spitting out forbidden words (coprolalia), whether racial insults or obscenities, is infrequently seen in everyday general practice. Often parents incorrectly label habits such as nail biting as tics. In addition, the compulsions of OCD can be confused with complex tics. In general, compulsions are "voluntary" behaviors associated with a specific anxiety, which is temporarily, if irrationally, relieved by performing the compulsion (for example, the fear that if I don't say, "I love you, Mom," my mother will have an accident). Although many will feel a premonitory urge before the tic, tics are involuntary and not driven by a specific concern.

Tics are common occurrences in childhood, affecting up to an estimated 20% of children. Tics begin at an average age of about 7 years, but most commonly within a range of about 6–12 years. Often when parents report a first tic during the latter half of that range, careful history taking will reveal an earlier overlooked tic. Tics tend to peak at 10–11 years of age and decrease during adolescence. Even among those with more chronic tic disorders, only a minority report tics persisting by young adulthood.

Tics tend to be exacerbated by the child's being stressed or tired, and they can be diminished by activities the child finds absorbing. The child can also voluntarily suppress the tic for short periods of time. Oftentimes, when a child suppresses a tic for long periods, for example, during the school day, the urge to tic intensifies, and tics increase in frequency after the suppression has stopped, that is, after the child returns home. During the weeks to months when they are present, tics occur regularly through the day, usually many times each minute. A behavior that happens every few days is not a tic, and a behavior that occurs a few times per day is probably not a tic.

Tics have a variety of patterns over time, though a consistent characteristic is that they tend to wax and wane. As we'll see, this characteristic of waxing and waning is vexing for the clinician trying to establish whether treatment is effective. For the overwhelming majority of children who experience a tic, the tics are transient. That is, most children experience a phase of ticcing that lasts from weeks to a few months. Some of these children will tic for a few months and then the tic disappears, only to be replaced by another tic a few weeks or months later. But within about a year the child's phase of ticcing has ended.

A minority of patients experience tics that last longer than one year and are diagnosed with a chronic motor or vocal tic disorder. Though estimates vary, roughly 1% or fewer of children have Tourette's disorder, which by definition includes the experience of motor and vocal tics. Family studies have shown that Tourette's and chronic tic disorder are related phenomena. Even in these less frequent but more severe disorders, the tics often wax and wane over time, even during treatment with medicine.

Children with a transient tic disorder, and many with chronic tic disorder or Tourette's, do not require pharmacologic treatment. Parents are often best advised to learn about the disorder and possibly explain it to their child, if appropriate. Watching one's child tic can be extremely frustrating for the parent who only wants to step in and help the child regain control of these involuntary actions. Educating school staff is very important because teachers are key to setting the classroom environment and to explaining these phenomena to the child's classmates, if necessary. Recently, habit reversal therapy, a behavioral therapy, has been used to help patients control their tics.

While transient tic disorder usually requires only parental education, the treatment of chronic tic disorder and Tourette's first requires an appreciation that these are often accompanied by other comorbid disorders, such as ADHD or ODD, and anxiety disorders, such as OCD. For that reason, Tourette's is the classic example of the need for a comprehensive evaluation that considers more than the patient's presenting complaint.

Treatment of these comorbid disorders is usually the most pressing therapeutic need and generally requires the same approach they would receive if they were not comorbid with Tourette's. The treatments for these comorbid disorders are covered in the chapters on the stimulants (for ADHD) and the SSRIs (for anxiety and OCD). In addition to these comorbid disorders, children with Tourette's often have a rigid and intense temperament that can lead to debilitating explosiveness. This is frequently diagnosed as ODD, leading to treatment with medicines such as the SGAs.

As mentioned above, while the comorbid conditions might require treatment, most tics do not. If, however, the tics themselves are seriously impacting the child's functioning, medicine should be considered.

Tourette's is the one disorder in child psychiatry in which the FGAs are still a proven and accepted mainstay of treatment. The SGAs are relatively recent entries in treating the tics of this disorder. The alpha agonists, such as clonidine, though not FDA approved for tic disorders, have also been used for many years and are discussed in more detail in Chapter 6.

The alpha agonists are often the first line of treatment for mild Tourette's. While they are generally not as effective as the antipsychotics, their low level of side effects makes them a better first choice. Although they require an 8–12 week trial, they may also be useful in diminishing any impulsive or hyperactive symptoms of associated ADHD. If the alpha agonists are not effective and the tics are moderate to severe, the decision must be made whether the side effects of the FGAs or SGAs are worth the possible benefit of diminishing tic frequency. Given the side effects, which I discuss below, these are not medicines to be used casually for a relatively mild tic disorder.

Starting in the late 1960s, haloperidol and pimozide, both FGAs with strong D2 receptor antagonism, were shown to be more effective than placebo in diminishing tics. They are the two FDA-approved treatments for Tourette's. They are arguably equivalent in effectiveness, but the potential cardiac side effects of pimozide make haloperidol the first choice of the two.

The lack of efficacy of clozapine, an SGA with relatively weak D2 antagonism, makes the case that strong D2 antagonism is required for effective tic suppression. In fact, SGAs with strong D2 antagonism have been shown to be effective in treating Tourette's. Risperidone was found to be more effective than placebo in two studies. In a double-blind, placebo-controlled study of adolescents and adults, Dion and colleagues (2002) found risperidone, at an average dose of 2.5 mg daily, to be effective. And in another double-blind, placebo-controlled study, Scahill and colleagues (2003) found risperidone to be effective in reducing tics by about 30% after eight weeks, which was significantly better than placebo. Risperidone was also found, albeit in a small study, to be superior to pimozide (Gilbert et al., 2004).

Other SGAs have also been used to treat Tourette's. In a pilot study, ziprasidone was found to be superior to placebo (Sallee et al., 2000). Aripiprazole was shown to be effective in an open-label study (Lyon, 2009). At the time of this writing, because of its tolerability, some experts (Coffey, 2010) recommend it as a treatment to be used if the alpha agonists have failed.

## Special Groups: Young Children

Young children who are considered for treatment with an SGA tend to be complicated youngsters with many diagnoses who live in chaotic households (Egger, 2010). They are often taking more than one medication. Research supporting the use of SGAs in 3- to 5-year-olds is lacking, however, consisting essentially of case reports and open studies. Despite the lack of supporting research, the use of SGAs has increased over the past 10 to 20 years, being used typically for severe irritability and aggression, often in children with a PDD or mental retardation.

While this might be clinically justified, the non-FDA-approved use of SGAs must be carried out cautiously in this group and only after a complete evaluation and adequate trial of psychosocial intervention. Often these patients are diagnosed with ODD and ADHD. In this situation, one should initially treat the ADHD directly with a stimulant, since this treatment is better substantiated by research (Gleason, Egger, & Emslie, 2007) and has a more benign side effect profile. When ADHD is not present and an SGA is considered, Gleason and colleagues (2007) recommended starting with risperidone rather than a mood stabilizer. This should be used at the lowest possible dose. In addition, because of the significant risks involved, the practitioner should avoid the continuous and ongoing use of the SGAs. Instead, after about six months the medicine should be tapered to ensure that it is still necessary.

## Using Antipsychotics

Whether the FGAs or the SGAs, the antipsychotics must be used cautiously. The side effects of increased weight gain associated with many of the SGAs and increased movement disorders with the FGAs should cause one to consider carefully whether the potential benefit merits the medical risk. When the decision is made to proceed, over recent years the SGAs have become the medication group of choice. While this has been debated for the treatment of adult schizophrenia, for the more common uses in child psychiatry, such as severe aggression, irritability, and bipolar disorder, I see the SGAs as generally preferable because one can more easily monitor weight gain, which is usually reversible.

Before starting an antipsychotic medicine, the patient should have had a recent physical exam. In addition, before starting an SGA, baseline pulse, blood pressure, weight, and lipid profile should be obtained and then followed regularly (see below). Some practitioners also obtain a baseline cardiogram.

Choosing which SGA to start is largely based on the disorder treated and on the clinician's preference in consultation with the patient and family. Risperidone has the largest body of evidence, although many prefer to base the decision on side effect profile. For that reason some prefer aripiprazole, with its lower impact on weight. Still others prefer quetiapine if insomnia is an issue.

Whichever medicine is used, the dose is minimized and only slowly increased, a good example of the maxim "start low and go slow." In general, a clinical effect should be observed within two weeks. If not, one should consider changing to a different SGA. The SGAs are generally used for a few months before their discontinuation is considered. Many parents, however, despite their concern about potential side effects, will balk at decreasing the dose for fear of a return of symptoms. Obvious side effects, such as weight gain or extrapyramidal side effects (EPS), can change their decision fairly quickly. When side effects are not present and the effective dose is minimal, parents, often recalling the extreme irritability that caused the initiation of the SGA, are reluctant to relinquish the medicine. When the medicine is discontinued, this is done slowly over a few weeks.

The SGAs are usually used alone initially, although (as we'll see in Chapter 9) in the treatment of bipolar disorder, polypharmacy is often the rule. In addition, if SGAs repeatedly fail, they might be used with another medicine.

The SGAs are also used on an "as needed" or prn basis, particularly for extremely agitated hospitalized patients. Pappadopulos and colleagues (2003) recommended that nonpharmacological crisis techniques be used before medicine and that the use of medicine for this purpose be minimized, since intramuscular injections of medicine are more likely to cause side effects, while intramuscular injections of placebo also reduce aggression. They recommend that changing the standing dose of the SGA be considered if the patient requires emergency doses too frequently. For patients who "cheek" their medicine (that is, hide it in their cheek and then spit it out), they recommend liquid risperidone or quickly dissolving olanzapine instead of injections.

## Side Effects of Antipsychotics

As we've seen, a modest body of evidence supports the use of the antipsychotics for treating children with a variety of disorders. Nevertheless, their use has outstripped the evidence that they are effective. While clinicians find these medicines very helpful, their side effects are potentially very significant and force the practitioner to consider carefully whether the potential benefit outweighs the risk.

The side effects of the antipsychotics, like their clinical effects, are based on their effect on receptor sites. For example, side effects caused by dopamine receptor blockade are different from those caused by histamine receptor blockade. Therefore, the unique array of effects each medicine has on receptors impacts the side effect profile of that medicine.

All the antipsychotics cause what I have referred to as "the usual suspects," that is, the side effects that you find in the list of side effects for almost any group of psychiatric medicines. They are generally not dangerous in the short run, but they must be recognized. Sometimes adjustments must be made because of them. Although they are common to many medicines, the percentage of people who experience them is generally low. (For the percentage of patients experiencing any of these side effects on a particular medicine, one must research that particular medicine). These "common" side effects usually occur in approximately 10% of patients, although that number might be higher or lower for any particular medicine. They include headaches, dizziness, rashes, dry mouth, gastrointestinal discomfort, nausea, and vomiting. They also include side effects that seem contradictory, for example, drowsiness and lethargy in some patients and insomnia in others. Although they do not present a direct danger to the patient, certainly teens who drive must be warned about the possibility of sedation.

The following are specific side effects caused by either the FGAs or SGAs, although some are more likely with one or the other.

## Extrapyramidal Side Effects

The extrapyramidal side effects (EPS) are the original most troubling and most discussed side effects of antipsychotic medicines. During the 1960s through 1980s, this was the group of side effects that deservedly captured most of the attention. The EPS are a result of dopamine blockade at the nigrostriatal tract and manifest in a number of different ways. Different FGAs were more or less likely to be associated with some of the EPS, but now that the FGAs have largely been supplanted by the SGAs, particularly in child psychiatry, those differences seem less important.

Unfortunately, children and adolescents are more sensitive than adults to these side effects. And, although the EPS are more commonly associated with the FGAs, they can occur in patients using SGAs as well. For example, in a group of short-term studies of risperidone, 8–26% of children experienced EPS. Meanwhile, clozapine and quetiapine seem less associated with these side effects (Correll, 2008). Correll (2008) also points out that using an SSRI concomitantly with an SGA might increase the risk of an EPS.

*Dystonia*

The most acutely dramatic of the EPS is dystonia, or a dystonic reaction. This is a sudden spasm of a single muscle or muscle group. This might manifest as one's head being stuck in position, turned painfully to the side, or one's eyes being stuck looking in one direction. Dystonic reactions typically occur very early in treatment or after a dose increase. While very dramatic and uncomfortable, thankfully this side effect is equally dramatically and immediately reversed by an intramuscular injection of an anticholinergic medicine such as benztropine (Cogentin) 1–2 mg or diphenhydramine (Benadryl) 25 mg. Oral benztropine is effective but takes longer to work.

*Pseudo-parkinsonism*

Pseudo-parkinsonism is manifested by a rigidity that leaves the face looking expressionless and the patient walking in a slow-moving shuffle without normal arm swing. It is called pseudo-parkinsonism because it resembles the symptoms of patients with Parkinson's and is caused by the same lack of dopamine transmission. These "parkinsonian" side effects usually begin a few weeks after starting the medicine but seem rare with the SGAs. They are sometimes diminished by an anticholinergic medicine taken orally every day and some clinicians will start an anticholinergic medicine simultaneously with the antipsychotic in an attempt to prevent this side effect.

*Akathisia*

Akathisia is a very uncomfortable feeling of restlessness, which sometimes manifests as fidgetiness but is more notable as a subjective feeling of the need to move. This is potentially difficult to diagnose because many children with psychiatric disorders who are being treated with antipsychotic medicine are fidgety and restless at baseline. Differentiating the side effect of akathisia from the underlying disorder is obviously an important distinction because it determines whether the dose should be increased or decreased. Although, like the rest of the EPS, akathisia is more likely with the FGAs, some of the SGAs, especially aripiprazole, also carry significant risk. As with the other EPS, titrating the medicine more slowly or lowering the dose might diminish the risk of akathisia. Otherwise, starting a benzodiazepine such as clonazepam, a beta blocker such as propanolol, or possibly an anticholinergic medicine might be helpful.

## Tardive dyskinesia (TD)

This is the most feared of the EPS. It is an involuntary movement disorder manifested by any number of body movements. Most commonly TD appears as a movement of the lips and tongue, akin to the way an older person constantly adjusts his or her dentures. It is labeled tardive dyskinesia because it is a dyskinesia, or maladaptive motor movement, and tardive because it often starts after a long period, namely months or years, of taking the medicine. Studies in adults have shown that the cumulative dose of antipsychotic is important in causing TD, which seems to affect about 20–40% of adult patients taking FGAs. This risk is lower with the SGAs, but exactly how much lower is unknown. In addition, the risk might be lower in children.

The mechanism causing TD is unknown. It might be due to receptors becoming supersensitive to dopamine after having been chronically blocked. The SGAs might result in fewer EPS because their added serotonergic blockade may lead to increased dopamine release, resulting in fewer EPS (Rapoport, Gogtay and Shaw, 2008).

Because TD is potentially irreversible, its treatment consists first of prevention. That means carefully assessing whether the potential benefit of taking medicine is worth the risk, then minimizing the risk by using the medicine at as low a dose and for as short a time as possible. Because cumulative dose seems to be significant in increasing the risk of TD, keeping the dose as low as possible makes sense. The anticholinergics that are used to treat the other EPS seem to exacerbate TD, as do caffeine and anxiety.

Of particular note, a small minority of patients can experience a withdrawal dyskinesia, that is, the same movement as TD but beginning soon after the medicine is discontinued. This is a function of the previously blocked receptor sites no longer being blocked but being supersensitive to dopamine. Withdrawal dyskinesias are less common with SGAs than with FGAs and are frequently transient. They can be seen however, when a patient switches from an SGA with strong D2 blockade, such as risperidone or aripiprazole, to one with weaker D2 blockade. Slowly decreasing the high-blockade SGA while slowly increasing the dose of the low-blockade SGA might minimize the risk of this dyskinesia.

*Neuroleptic malignant syndrome (NMS)*

This dangerous syndrome consists of a group of symptoms, including high fever, muscle rigidity, confusion, sweating, and high blood pressure, which usually occur within a few weeks of starting an FGA. It is more frequently seen with the FGAs, although it has been reported in adolescents who have taken SGAs. Laboratory test findings include a high white blood cell count, albeit with no infection, and an elevated level of creatine phosphokinase (CPK), an enzyme that originates in muscle. The cause of NMS is unknown, although excessive blockade of dopamine has been theorized. There is no way to predict who will suffer from this infrequent side effect, although a rapid increase in dose, the use of concomitant medicines, and dehydration may increase its likelihood. Because it is potentially fatal, it requires immediate medical attention.

## Weight gain and metabolic side effects

The most troubling, and unfortunately too common, side effect caused by the SGAs is weight gain. While it can occur with both FGAs and SGAs, this side effect occurs in as many as half of those using SGAs (Fedorowicz & Fombonne, 2005). It can be difficult to distinguish from the weight gain to which children and adolescents with psychiatric disorders are prone. This weight gain has a number of negative consequences ranging from the social consequence of being teased, to the psychological consequence of feeling different and unattractive, to the medical consequence of being at increased risk for elevated cholesterol and blood sugar. The long-term medical consequences of obesity are many, including higher risk of cardiovascular disease, sleep difficulties, and metabolic disorders such as diabetes. Thus this side effect can be both insidious and dangerous.

The SGAs have become notorious for this side effect, the risk varying with the medicine. The highest risk is associated with clozapine and olanzapine, followed by risperidone and quetiapine, followed by paliperidone. The least risk appears to come from aripiprazole and ziprasidone, which have a risk about equal to that of haloperidol, an FGA (Correll, 2008). Children seem to be at greater risk than adults. Parents sometimes ask if taking a stimulant, with its propensity to decrease appetite, can lower the risk of weight gain on an SGA, but unfortunately it does not. Combining an SGA with a mood stabilizer, with its own propensity to cause weight gain, can lead to increased weight gain (Correll, 2007).

The extent of the weight gain is not insignificant. Sometimes, when told of this side effect, parents respond that their skinny child could stand to gain a few pounds, so let's try the medicine. A few weeks later, however, when their child's face begins to round, they have second thoughts. The weight gain can be formidable. For example, Ratzoni and colleagues (2002) found that after 12 weeks of treatment, adolescents on olanzapine increased their body weight by about 11% and those on risperidone by about 6%. For a 150-pound adolescent, that translates to about 16 pounds. And in a larger study of SGAs, Correll and colleagues (2009) found that after 10 weeks, olanzapine was associated with the greatest weight gain, 8.5 kg (or about 18 pounds). One longer-term study (Ross et al., 2003) suggested that after the initial increase, weight plateaus. Nevertheless, the weight gain can be considerable.

Medically, the most significant risk stemming from weight gain is the possibility of causing the metabolic syndrome. About 5–10% of adolescents in the general population suffer from this syndrome.

The metabolic syndrome consists of abdominal obesity, high levels of cholesterol and triglycerides, glucose intolerance, and high blood pressure. This leads to an increased risk of cardiovascular disease and insulin resistance, which in turn leads to diabetes. While weight gain seems to play a role in the development of the metabolic syndrome, the SGAs might have a direct effect on the action of insulin.

Henderson and colleagues (2000), in a five-year study of adults with schizophrenia taking clozapine, showed that, on average, over 7% of the population developed diabetes with each additional year of exposure to the medicine. Put another way, after five years, a little over one third of the patients had developed diabetes. In a three-week study of adolescents with bipolar disorder taking olanzapine versus placebo, Tohen and colleagues (2007) found that over 40% of those adolescents taking olanzapine had a greater than 7% weight gain compared to only 2% of those patients taking placebo. In addition, patients taking olanzapine had significantly higher increases in blood sugar, cholesterol, and triglycerides.

Because of the potential for developing the metabolic syndrome, patients who are to be started on an SGA should have their baseline blood pressure measured, as well as blood levels of cholesterol, triglycerides, and glucose. Some clinicians will also ascertain the patient's waist circumference. In addition, height and weight should be measured and body mass index (BMI) calculated. BMI, as well as blood levels of cholesterol, trigycerides, and glucose, should be monitored about every 6–12 months, but every 3 months if the patient is at high risk. This category includes those who are obese or have a high BMI, those with a family history of these kinds of medical problems, and those patients taking clozapine or olanzapine, the two highest-risk medicines.

The metabolic syndrome is a good reason to minimize the dose and duration of taking an SGA, although this must be weighed against the substantial benefit of these medicines for some patients. In addition, patients should be advised on ways to manage their weight, including the importance of exercise, avoiding sugary drinks and second helpings, and eating slowly. Correll and Carlson (2006) also advise minimizing intake by serving meals in small portions (not family style) on small plates. They also suggest restricting fast food to no more than once each week and avoiding activities linked to excess eating, such as watching TV or playing video games for more than two hours each day. Addressing eating style as a family matter helps take some of the embarrassing pressure off the patient.

If the patient's weight gain is substantial, a change of antipsychotic medicine should be considered. Over recent years, some clinicians have used other medicines to induce weight loss in patients who must remain on the SGA. These include orlistat, amantadine, metformin, and topiramate (Correll & Carlson, 2006). Metformin has been tested and found effective in children and adolescents (Klein, Cottingham, & Sorter, 2006).

### Elevated prolactin

The hypothalamus, which signals the pituitary gland to release many of the body's hormones, works in an opposite fashion with regard to prolactin. That is, the chemical by which the hypothalamus stimulates the pituitary gland, prolactin-inhibiting factor (PIF), is an inhibitory substance that tells the pituitary not to release the hormone prolactin. Prolactin-inhibiting factor does this by stimulating D2 receptors in the pituitary gland. In other words, through PIF, the hypothalamus tells the pituitary not to release prolactin.

As D2 blockers, the antipsychotics block these PIF receptor sites and thereby increase the amount of prolactin released into the body. Of course, the most common reason for a woman to have an elevated prolactin level is pregnancy, not the use of an antipsychotic. Birth control pills, kidney failure, and excess thyroid hormone can also elevate prolactin levels.

Since prolactin stimulates milk release, the side effects associated with D2 blockade by the antipsychotics include breast enlargement (in pubescent boys and girls) and milk letdown (in pubescent girls). Prolactin also inhibits the release of some sex hormones. Thus, other effects caused by increased prolactin include inhibiting menstruation and diminishing sex drive, as well as erectile difficulties, osteoporosis, and excess hair growth.

The ability of the antipsychotics to cause these symptoms varies with their affinity for the D2 receptor. Risperidone and paliperidone are most potent, followed (in order) by haloperidol, olanzapine, ziprasidone, quetiapine, and clozapine. In general, the ability of antipsychotics to have this effect is dose dependent, so there is greater risk at higher doses. Over time this prolactin elevation tends to disappear, and it is reversible after the medicine is discontinued. Whether the high levels of prolactin are associated with changes in bone density, sexual maturation, or the risk of breast cancer is unknown. Aripiprazole, because of its partial D2 agonism, might actually increase the effect of PIF, thus lowering prolactin levels.

There is no evidence suggesting that subclinical elevations of prolactin are associated with medical risks. Since some of the general population have elevated prolactin levels but are without symptoms, prolactin levels are not generally monitored in patients on antipsychotics unless symptoms are present. Prolactin levels tend to vary throughout the day and are elevated by food, exercise, stress, and some medications. Therefore a blood sample for prolactin, when necessary, should be obtained first thing in the morning before other medications are taken.

If one discovers an elevated prolactin level in an asymptomatic individual, this might simply need to be followed, although a pregnancy test should be obtained. If symptoms are present, however, the dose of the antipsychotic should be lowered or the medicine changed to one with a lower risk of prolactin elevation. If the clinician is concerned about possible prolactin effects, consultation with the pediatrician or pediatric endocrinologist is recommended.

### Cardiac side effects

As we've seen with other classes of medicines, the cardiac side effects of greatest concern are those that affect the heart's conduction system. These changes in conduction can be sudden, leading to a potentially fatal heart rhythm. Fortunately, this happens infrequently. In one study of adults, the rate of sudden death was about 18 per 10,000 patient years. Nevertheless, it has been associated with the adult use of both FGAs and SGAs, with higher doses carrying greater risk (Ray et al., 2009).

Some antipsychotics have been more clearly associated with this potential problem. In particular, ziprasidone, an SGA, has been associated with a potentially dangerous prolongation of heart conduction in a minority of a small sample of children. Because of the potentially dire consequences, this effect must be monitored.

In addition, thioridazine, an FGA, was also more strongly associated with this conduction prolongation than other FGAs and thus is rarely used today. And clozapine has been reported to have an association, albeit low, with possible myocarditis, an inflammation of the heart.

Last, because of their blockade of alpha receptor sites that help regulate blood pressure, antipsychotics such as clozapine and quetiapine have been associated with dizziness.

In general, the pulse and blood pressure of patients taking antipsychotics should be monitored after a few months and then annually. Those taking ziprasidone or clozapine should have a baseline EKG, which is followed as the dose is increased.

### Agranulocytosis

Agranuloctyosis refers to a significant decrease in the number of white blood cells, which are used to fight infection. This potentially fatal side effect seems uniquely associated with clozapine and tends to occur in the first three months of use. The number of adult patients experiencing this side effect is less than 1%, with a significantly lower number dying because of it (Alvir et al., 1993). Nevertheless, because of the potential danger, clozapine is used less than the other SGAs and is reserved for cases in which it alone is helpful.

In one study of this side effect, about 16% of youth who were given clozapine had a decrease in white blood cell count, although the majority of them experienced only a mild decrease (i.e., not to the low level considered agranulocytosis). Interestingly, about half of the children who were given clozapine again were able to take it successfully.

Because of the possibility of this side effect, those taking clozapine must monitor their white blood cell counts regularly, particularly during the first three months of use. This is done by a simple blood test.

### Liver toxicity

Although an elevation of liver enzymes can be observed in adolescents taking antipsychotic medicine, the extent of actual liver toxicity is unclear. Therefore a prudent approach is to measure liver enzymes by doing a blood test after three months on the antipsychotic and then every 12 months.

### Anticholinergic side effects

The anticholinergic side effects, such as dry mouth, blurry vision, and urinary hesitancy, are rare with the SGAs, except clozapine, which has more anticholinergic activity. This anticholinergic effect can also influence heat control leading to heat stroke. Some of the FGAs are more prone to causing these side effects, but currently their use is minimal in children and adolescents.

### Eye problems

Side effects of vision are rare with the SGAs, although cataracts have been associated with quetiapine use in dogs. This is of dubious relevance to humans. In addition, thioridazine, an FGA, has been associated with problems of the retina at doses greater than 800 mg daily.

## Seizures

While seizures are rare in patients taking antipsychotics, these medicines are thought to lower the seizure threshold, making seizures more likely. Given this concern, more caution is advised when the antipsychotics are prescribed to someone with a history of seizures.

# The First- and Second-Generation Antipsychotics

Let's take a more detailed look at individual antipsychotic medications.

## Specific Second-Generation Antipsychotics

There are currently about a half dozen SGAs, including clozapine, risperidone, olanzapine, quetiapine, aripiprazole, and ziprasidone, the last two really being members of the third generation of antipsychotics.

### *Clozapine*

Clozapine was the first marketed SGA. It works by blocking dopamine at a number of different dopamine and serotonin receptors. It binds D2 relatively weakly and is strongly anticholinergic. It is not FDA approved for use in children and adolescents.

When clozapine was introduced in the late 1980s as the first SGA, its ability to improve the negative symptoms of schizophrenia gave hope that the SGAs would be a major improvement over the FGAs, which had been used for the previous 30 years. And in fact, clozapine has proven uniquely effective in adult schizophrenia.

A few early studies in children with schizophrenia showed it to be superior to haloperidol (Kumra, 1996), an FGA, and very effective in children with schizophrenia who did not respond to other medication. In particular, one study showed it to be more effective than olanzapine in improving the negative symptoms of childhood schizophrenia (Rapoport, Gogtay and Shaw, 2008).

The unique efficacy of clozapine, however, must be measured against its significant side effects. These have led to its diminished use in both adults and children. The most important of these is agranulocytosis (see above). This requires that white blood cell (WBC) levels in the blood be monitored on a regular basis.

In addition, clozapine can lower the seizure threshold, making seizures more likely. This is particularly worrisome in children with PDDs, who are already more prone to seizures. Because clozapine is strongly anticholinergic, side effects such as dry mouth and orthostatic blood pressure changes must be monitored. Clozapine is also one of the SGAs most strongly associated with weight gain. Therefore the patient must be followed for changes in weight and blood levels of cholesterol, lipids, and sugar. Clozapine is also relatively sedating.

Clozapine is metabolized by a few different enzymes. Of particular importance are its potential interactions with fluvoxamine, fluoxetine, and paroxetine, all of which inhibit some of the enzymes that metabolize clozapine. These therefore have the potential to increase clozapine levels, although individuals might vary greatly. Other substances that increase the level of various enzymes, such as cigarettes and some antiseizure medicines, can decrease clozapine levels. If, however, these substances are stopped, enzyme levels drop, and clozapine levels might increase.

Overall, the use of clozapine is hampered by its side effects. It nevertheless remains a treatment of choice for children with schizophrenia who have not responded to other treatments.

### Risperidone

Risperidone is FDA approved for use in adults with schizophrenia and with mania. It was also the first SGA to gain FDA approval in children, being approved for the extreme irritability and agitation of children with autistic disorder. Subsequently it was approved for the treatment of adolescents with schizophrenia and 10- to 17-year-olds with bipolar disorder mania or mixed states. Risperidone has also been shown to be as effective as pimozide and clonidine in treating the tics of Tourette's disorder.

Risperidone strongly binds many dopamine and serotonin receptors, as well as those of histamine and the alpha1 receptors of norepinephrine. It does not significantly bind the muscarinic receptors of acetylcholine.

Risperidone is moderately associated with weight gain, sedation, and headache. In addition, among the SGAs it is relatively strongly associated with parkinsonian side effects, such as stiffness. This seems more common if the medicine is increased rapidly or to moderately high doses, that is, greater than about 3–4 mg per day (Schur et al., 2003). In these studies, however, the rate of EPS was still less than that of the FGAs, and in other studies no EPS were found.

Risperidone is relatively strongly associated with increases in prolactin levels. These increases tend to peak early, then moderate over the course of the first year of continued treatment (Findling, 2003). Clinical symptoms, however, affect a minority of patients. About 30% of girls will have a new onset of skipping one menstrual period during a three-month period of taking risperidone. And about 5% of already pubescent youth will experience nipple discharge. Some but not all clinicians obtain a baseline prolactin level prior to initiating treatment with risperidone. This course does not need to be followed, however, unless clinical signs and symptoms appear.

Risperidone is metabolized by 2D6, so medicines such as fluoxetine and paroxetine can slow its metabolism. Medicines that increase liver enzymes can lead to risperidone being metabolized faster, thus lowering its blood levels. Also of note is that risperidone can increase the blood level of carbamazepine.

The typical starting dose of risperidone is 0.25–0.5 mg daily. I have found, however, that starting as low as 0.125 mg daily can be effective in extremely irritable children, especially younger children or children with PDDs. If higher doses are ultimately necessary, sometimes these can eventually be decreased to doses as low as 0.125–0.25 mg daily.

### *Olanzapine*

Olanzapine was first introduced in 1996 and is FDA approved for the treatment of adults with schizophrenia and mania. It is also approved for the treatment of adolescents with schizophrenia and 10- to 17-year-olds with bipolar mania or mixed states. Olanzapine binds to the receptors of dopamine, serotonin, and histamine. It also binds alpha1 adrenergic receptors of norepinephrine and the muscarinic receptors of acetylcholine.

Olanzapine is moderately sedating and moderately anticholinergic. It is not as potent as risperidone in causing EPS. Its most significant side effect is weight gain. With clozapine, it is the SGA most noted for this side effect. In a study by Tohen and colleagues (2007) of bipolar adolescents, patients given olanzapine gained an average of about 8 pounds within the first three weeks. Sikich and colleagues (2008) found an average weight gain of about 13 pounds over eight weeks in psychotic children. Given these considerable increases, body weight, cholesterol, lipids, and blood sugar must all be carefully monitored.

Although the metabolism of olanzapine does not appear to have significant interactions with other medicines, care must be taken. In addition, fluvoxamine, caffeine, and cigarette smoking can all decrease levels of olanzapine.

## Quetiapine

Quetiapine, first released in 1997, stands out among the SGAs as being a relatively weak binder of the D2 receptors. It also does not seem to have significant anticholinergic or antihistamininic effects. It does have some blocking effect at the alpha1 adrenergic receptor.

Quetiapine is FDA approved for treating schizophrenia, mania, and bipolar depression in adults and has also been found helpful when added to lithium and valproate for the treatment of bipolar disorder. It is also approved for the treatment of adolescents with schizophrenia and 10- to 17-year-olds with bipolar mania or mixed states.

Quetiapine is very short acting, with a half-life of about three hours, and must be taken at least twice daily. It is also available as a long-acting form, quetiapine XR, which can be taken once daily. It is long acting, however, only if taken on an empty stomach.

Quetiapine is sedating, especially when first used or if the dose is increased rapidly. While this can present as a side effect, for a patient who has insomnia, the sedating effect can be beneficial if the medicine is taken at night. Like clozapine, quetiapine seems to have a lesser effect on the D2 receptors of the nigrostriatal tract and therefore a low rate of EPS such as akathisia. As with many of the SGAs, weight gain can be considerable. Quetiapine causes less weight gain than clozapine and olanzapine but more than risperidone. Quetiapine can also produce orthostatic hypotension, a drop in blood pressure upon rising, in a small percentage of patients. This can lead to dizziness. A small number of patients have a transient increase in liver enzymes. Quetiapine has also been associated in a small number of cases with hypothyroidism, although this might improve despite ongoing treatment with quetiapine (Kontaxakis et al., 2009).

A unique side effect of quetiapine is that it has been reported to cause cataracts in dogs. The FDA therefore recommends baseline and follow-up eye exams every six months. Nevertheless, an increase in cataracts has not been found in humans (Shatzberg, Cole, DeBattista, 2007), and therefore the clinical relevance, especially in children, is open to question.

Quetiapine is metabolized by 3A4, and therefore its blood levels can increase if given with 3A4 inhibitors.

### *Aripiprazole*

Aripiprazole is FDA approved for use in adolescent schizophrenia and bipolar mania and mixed states. It is also approved to treat the irritability associated with autistic disorder. In adults, aripiprazole is FDA approved for treating schizophrenia and bipolar disorder and to augment an anti-depressant in treatment-resistant depression.

Although aripiprazole is being discussed as an SGA, it has a particular profile of receptor antagonism and is therefore a third-generation antipsychotic. Aripiprazole tightly binds D2 receptors as well as some serotonin receptors. It also, however, is a partial dopamine agonist. So it both blocks and partially stimulates dopamine receptors. The dopamine-blocking effect is more powerful than the dopamine-stimulating effect. It has a long half-life of about 70 hours and therefore can be given once daily or even every other day. This long half-life means that it should be increased slowly, since it can take about two weeks for a particular dose to reach a steady level in the bloodstream, so quickly increasing the dose might lead one to bypass a reasonable dose.

Aripiprazole has a relatively benign side effect profile among the SGAs in that it does not seem to cause significant weight gain, sedation, or cardiac difficulties. It does, however, tend to cause more motor restlessness than the other SGAs and is similar in that regard to the FGAs. This can be minimized by starting at a low dose and increasing slowly. Also, unlike the other SGAs, aripiprazole may lower prolactin levels in some patients.

Aripiprazole is metabolized by 3A4 and 2D6. Therefore substances that inhibit these enzymes increase its blood levels.

### *Ziprasidone*

Ziprasidone was first introduced in the United States in 2000. It binds relatively tightly to D2 receptors. It is an antagonist of some serotonin receptors and an agonist of others. It has a short half-life in adults and therefore is given twice daily.

Ziprasidone has no FDA approvals for children and adolescents but is approved for the treatment of adult schizophrenia and bipolar disorder. It has also been shown to diminish depressive symptoms in adults with schizophrenia.

While it has a relatively benign side effect profile, causing only mild EPS and weight gain, it is unique in that it has been found to cause cardiac conduction slowing in about 5% of adults. There is a paucity of information regarding this side effect in children.

While the metabolism of ziprasidone does not seem to cause significant problems, its use with other medicines that can affect cardiac conduction is problematic. In child psychiatry, pimozide and thioridazine are among the most notable.

### *Paliperidone*

Paliperidone is an active metabolite of risperidone and is approved for the treatment of schizophrenia in adults. At the time of this writing there is no information on its use in children.

### *Specific First-Generation Antipsychotics*

In child psychiatry, the FGAs have largely been replaced by the SGAs. Two FGAs, however, haloperidol and pimozide, are still FDA approved for use in Tourette's and are among the better-studied medicines for this disorder. As such, they will be the only FGAs discussed individually.

The FGAs are all phenothiazines and have a much higher ratio of dopamine blockade relative to serotonin blockade than the SGAs. The phenothiazines are sometimes classified by their molecular structure, for example, the aliphatics and the piperazines. More simply, they have been divided into those labeled "high potency" and those labeled "low potency." The high-potency antipsychotics include haloperidol, thiothixene, pimozide, and fluphenazine. The low-potency antipsychotics include chlorpromazine and thioridazine.

There are two basic practical differences between the high- and low-potency FGAs. First, the low-potency medicines tend to be prescribed in larger doses, typically in the 50s to 100s of milligrams. In years past, lower doses, such as 10 or 25 mg of thioridazine, were sometimes used for behavior control in children, but this was the exception, not the rule. The high-potency medicines are prescribed in lower doses, typically less than 20 mg daily, and often less than 10 mg.

The other major practical difference between these two groups of medicines is side effects. Because of their many synaptic effects, all antipsychotics can cause a variety of side effects. These include weight gain, increased skin sensitivity to sunlight, a lowered seizure threshold, and a number of other side effects. The low-potency medicines tend to cause more sedation, weight gain, and anticholinergic effects, such as dry mouth, constipation, and urinary hesitancy. The high-potency medicines tend to cause more EPS, such as dystonia and pseudo-parkinsonism. These EPS are treated with anticholinergic medicines such as benztropine, or dopaminergic medicines such as amantadine. Some clinicians give these medicines when beginning a high-potency antipsychotic, and others wait to see if the patient develops one of these side effects before adding a second medicine.

The slowing of cardiac conduction has been noted with all FGAs, but it is particularly prominent with thioridazine and its metabolite mesoridazine. Although such consequences are rare, these medicines have been associated with a few deaths, leading to an FDA-mandated black box warning. Currently they are rarely used.

### Haloperidol

Haloperidol continues to be used in moderate to severe cases of Tourette's disorder, particularly if medicines such as the alpha agonists have proven ineffective. While doses up to 20 mg daily were used in early studies, more recently doses less than about 4 mg daily are often used. The most important side effects of haloperidol are the EPS, such as parkinsonism, dystonia, akathisia, and tardive dyskinesia. Haloperidol also causes moderate increases in prolactin.

### Pimozide

Pimozide is as effective as haloperidol in the treatment of Tourette's disorder. As with haloperidol, higher doses were used in early studies, but more recently lower doses, less than 6 mg daily, are used. Pimozide, however, has been linked to a rare prolongation of cardiac conduction. Vulnerability to this side effect increases if one simultaneously takes a medicine, such as clarithromycin, that inhibits the enzyme 2D6, leading to an increased blood level of pimozide. This significant concern has led to a decrease in the use of pimozide. Nevertheless, when it is used, an EKG is recommended, done at baseline, during dosage adjustment, and then annually (Scahill, 2008) to monitor heart function.

| TABLE 8.1 Antipsychotic Medicines | | | | | |
|---|---|---|---|---|---|
| Brand name | Generic name | Starting dose | Disruptive behavior disorders | Psychosis (including bipolar) | Tic disorders |
| *Second-generation antipsychotics (SGAs ) (atypical antipsychotics)* | | | | | |
| Risperdal | risperidone | .25 mg/day | .5-3 mg/day | 0.5-4 mg/day | 1-3 mg/day |
| Zyprexa | olanzapine | 2.5 mg/day | 2.5-15 mg/day | 7.5-15 mg/day | 2.5-12.5 mg/day |
| Seroquel | quetiapine | 12.5-25 mg to twice daily | 100-600 mg/day | 300-600 mg/day | 75-150 mg/day |
| Clozaril | clozapine | 6.25-25 mg/day | nr | 150-600 mg/day | nr |
| Abilify | aripiprazole | 2 mg/day | 2-10 mg/day | 10-20 mg/day | 10-20 mg/day |
| Geodon | ziprasidone | 10 mg/day | 40-160 mg/day | 80-160 mg/day | 10-80 mg/day |
| *First-generation antipsychotics (FGAs) (typical antipsychotics)* | | | | | |
| Orap | pimozide | .5 mg/day | nr | nr | 2-6 mg/day |
| Haldol | haloperidol | .25-.5 mg/day | nr | 1-10 mg/day | 1-4 mg/day |
| Note: nr = not recommended. | | | | | |

Table 8.1 presents the typical dose ranges of antipsychotic medicines for children and adolescents. These are intended as general guidelines. Children will usually take doses at or below the lower end, and adolescents might take doses at or above the higher end. Some medicines are not FDA approved for those specific disorders and their dose ranges may be based on adult dosage, minimal data for children, and may differ from the FDA approved dose ranges. Most FGAs are not listed because there are insufficient data regarding their use in children and adolescents.

# Case Examples

*Case 1: Seven-year-old Maurice has been blinking numerous times each minute every day for the past month. His mother has tried everything to get him to stop his "nervous habit," including yelling, demanding, and bribing. Maurice can stop for a minute or two, but his mother feels that as soon as he forgets her threats, he starts again. She wants to know what he can be given.*

*Comment:* At this time Maurice does not require medicine. Rather, his mother needs to understand that this is probably a transient tic that will disappear on its own within a few months. In the meantime, she needs to hold her tongue. In addition, she needs to understand that Maurice's tics are not a reflection of underlying anxiety. Stress, however, such as from being constantly yelled at, can certainly cause anxiety, which would exacerbate his tics.

*Case 2: Twelve-year-old Derek's parents walk on eggshells. His frequent tantrums rule their house. Derek is always irritable and has a 15-minute tantrum daily, after which he simmers for another 45 minutes. He frequently worries, and because he is fidgety and unfocused in class, his teacher thinks he has ADHD. On Adderall, Derek is more focused but still irritable, and on sertraline, given for anxiety, he seems to become more irritable. On aripiprazole, Derek has fewer tantrums and is less irritable.*

*Comment:* Although Derek has been diagnosed with ADHD, with an anxiety disorder, and with oppositional defiant disorder, he is more complicated than the usual case of any of these. He has also been diagnosed with bipolar disorder. The one diagnosis that best captures Derek's condition is severe mood dysregulation disorder, a disorder being considered for inclusion in DSM-V, perhaps to be called temper dysregulation disorder. No treatment for this disorder has been well researched. The SGAs, however, are increasingly being used.

## CHAPTER 9

# Mood Stabilizers

The family of medicines known as the mood stabilizers includes lithium and a group of antiscizure medicines, such as valproic acid, carbamazepine, and lamotrigine. What binds these medicines is their efficacy, albeit sometimes unproven in children, in treating bipolar disorder. The label mood stabilizer originated with the finding that lithium stabilized the manic pole of bipolar disorder. Since then, other medicines with this effect have become known as mood stabilizers.

It is a common misconception that mood stabilizers are used simply to treat children and adolescents whose moods are seen by their parents as "unstable," an ill-defined, vague term that can apply to the moodiness of many children or the normal ups and downs experienced by adolescents. I have received any number of phone calls from parents requesting a mood stabilizer for their child for this reason. This represents an understandable misperception. I want to make it clear, however, that mood stabilizers treat bipolar disorder, not simply unstable moods.

Apart from lithium, mood stabilizers are often antiseizure medicines, or anticonvulsants. Over recent years, as we've seen, some of the antipsychotics, such as risperidone and aripiprazole, have also proven effective for treating bipolar disorder. Thus, although these medicines are always classified as antipsychotics, they are also used to treat bipolar disorder, albeit just the manic or mixed states in adults, and are therefore considered mood stabilizers by some. This is a good example of how names can be deceiving in psychopharmacology.

It is also a reminder that just because a medicine is classified as a mood stabilizer, we should not assume that it treats the acute phase and also prevents the mania and depression of bipolar disorder. Research studies, not the names of categories, need to prove that. As we'll see, different mood stabilizers might treat different phases of bipolar disorder.

## Clarifying Terms

Before I discuss the mood stabilizers, we must first address bipolar disorder, a confusing disorder that, over recent years, has found itself in the middle of tremendous controversy in child psychiatry.

Historically, bipolar disorder was first noted in adults who suffered from both depressive episodes and manic episodes. Each of these episodes typically lasts many months, although shorter episodes are now recognized. Depressive episodes are characterized by sadness, hopelessness, suicidal thoughts or behaviors, lack of energy, excessive sleeping or insomnia, and frequently the inability to carry out normal daily functions.

These episodes are in stark contrast to manic episodes, during which the person is chock-full of energy, talking rapidly and thinking too quickly to keep up with his own thoughts, acting impulsively, using poor judgment, and getting by on just a few hours of sleep without any diminution of his energy level. When manic, the person is either euphoric or very irritable and can be highly grandiose. Sometimes the very engaging and entertaining euphoria is a thin veneer for a biting and aggressive irritability. During a manic episode, these patients drink more than they should, have sexual liaisons with people with whom they would otherwise know they should not, or spend money they can ill afford to spare. In extreme cases the manic patient can be psychotic, experiencing hallucinations or delusions. There are many risks to bipolar disorder, including those obvious consequences that emanate from drinking alcohol, spending money unwisely, and engaging in sexual relationships in a wanton, ill-planned manner. Bipolar disorder also carries a high risk of suicidal behavior.

Adult patients with classic bipolar disorder have months-long episodes of depression, long episodes of mania, and periods during which they are their usual non-depressed, non-manic self. The condition used to be called manic depression, but the name was eventually changed to bipolar disorder to distinguish it from unipolar depression, or depression without manic episodes.

Sometimes these patients cycle more rapidly. If they have four or more episodes per year, they are said to be rapid cyclers. This is an important distinction, because rapid cyclers might not respond to the same medicines as non–rapid cyclers. Patients also sometimes have manic and depressive symptoms simultaneously. This is known as a mixed state and, like rapid cycling, might require a different treatment.

While the classic case of bipolar disorder is characterized by episodes lasting weeks to months, DSM-IV reflects the recognition that some patients have much shorter episodes of illness. It therefore requires that the manic episode be only one week in duration and that the depressed episode last only two weeks. This condition is currently known as bipolar I disorder. Sometimes a patient will have mania, but to a degree that falls short of meeting the full criteria or lasting only a few days. In that case the patient is said to have hypomania. When the episodes of hypomania are accompanied by episodes of depression, the patient is said to have bipolar II disorder. Patients find mania a very distressing and painful experience. It is associated with a high rate of suicide.

Many patients, however, find hypomania enjoyable and productive. During hypomania, patients are often more confident, outgoing, engaging, and energetic. During my training, I treated a middle-aged antique dealer with bipolar disorder who, as is fairly common, refused to stay on his medication. He reported enjoying the hypomanic experience and said that while hypomanic he wined and dined many wealthy widows to whom he sold lots of expensive antiques. The boredom of a normal mood was a tough sell.

This dichotomy of depressive and manic episodes is further complicated by the great difficulty predicting which patients with depression will later develop mania, thus changing their diagnosis from depression to bipolar disorder. In a study of adults, Fiedorowicz and colleagues (2011) found that almost 20% of patients made such a switch. At this time researchers are tackling the difficult task of determining ways to predict which patients will do so.

## Child and Adolescent Bipolar Disorder

The preceding is the basic template for bipolar disorder in adults. Applying that template to adolescents has been reasonably straightforward. Up to 60% of adult patients with bipolar disorder report that their symptoms began before they were 21 years old. So it is no surprise to find adolescents who present with the classic symptoms of adult bipolar disorder. For teens this can be a dangerous illness, placing them at an elevated risk for suicide, unprotected sex, drug and alcohol abuse, and other poor judgments.

The prevalence of bipolar disorder in youth is unclear. A study of high school students suggested a prevalence of approximately 1% (Lewinsohn, Klein, & Seeley, 1995). Bipolar disorder was thought to be extremely rare in children. For example, in the Great Smoky Mountains Study of psychiatric disorders in over 1,000 youth aged 9, 11, and 13, no cases of classic bipolar disorder were found (Costello et al., 1996).

If one applied the adult model of bipolar disorder to children, bipolar disorder in children was seen as rare. Then the following question was asked: Could bipolar disorder in children present not with the classic periodic manic and depressive episodes of adulthood but rather with chronic hyperactivity, impulsivity, and severe irritability and mood swings, including frequent, ferocious, extended tantrums? The suggestion by some researchers that this might be bipolar disorder, and the response by other researchers and, more important, the public, set a controversy in motion.

Clinicians had long known many child patients with a number of the symptoms of ADHD, but with an additional chronic irritability, ongoing defiance, and fierce temper. Sometimes this was thought of as malignant ADHD. Sometimes it was diagnosed as oppositional defiant disorder with a component of a mood disorder. The possibility of diagnosing such children with bipolar disorder was, in some ways, a welcome relief because it applied a unifying concept which would lead to treatment that was proven, at least in adults. The question of the accuracy of this diagnosis led to scientific research and much debate among mental health professionals.

For a while, the various viewpoints coalesced into the following basic presentations of bipolar disorder in children: the so-called broad phenotype, the so-called narrow phenotype, and the intermediate phenotypes (Liebenluft et al., 2003). Although some clinicians used the broad phenotype model of bipolar disorder in children, as we'll see, research has caused many to see these children as not having bipolar disorder at all. This model was applied to children who were chronically irritable and impulsive and had affective storms, more commonly known to parents as meltdowns. These were not the common childhood meltdowns experienced by many parents. Rather, they represented the extreme reactivity that leads to rages lasting an hour or two, occurring almost daily, and often many times per day, and that cause massive disruption to the child's life and home. These children were also often impulsive, unfocused, and hyperactive, with an abnormally sad, angry, or anxious mood between rages. Care had to be taken to distinguish these symptoms from the more usual and normal tantrums, silliness, and poor judgment of childhood.

The narrow phenotype model of childhood bipolar disorder is currently seen as a more accurate representation than the broad phenotype. This model tries to set a higher threshold for diagnosing bipolar disorder by requiring that the patient experience the symptoms of bipolar disorder for the durations required by DSM-IV and that they experience the specific mood changes of bipolar disorder, particularly euphoria or grandiosity. Manic euphoria in children is difficult to capture. It is often seen as excessive silliness or inappropriate cheerfulness. Unlike the normal silliness of children, this silliness goes on and on and begins to seem weird to parents. Grandiosity is different from normal childhood bragging or wishful thinking (for example, saying, "I know I'm going to hit a home run"). Rather, it is an expansive, inflated view of the self, different from the patient's usual persona, and seen in the context of other symptoms.

In addition, this narrow phenotype model tries to see the illness as periodic rather than constant, in keeping with the classic adult model.

This is very difficult, since a child with bipolar disorder might very well have preexisting anger problems or comorbidities that are hard to distinguish from the mood dysregulation of a manic episode.

Geller, Tillman, and colleagues (2004), researchers who have tried to use this narrow model, followed children over four years. They found that these children, with episodes starting from 4 to 11 years of age, had numerous cycles per day. These phases of bipolar cycling lasted, on average, a few years.

In short, clinically it is very difficult to tease apart the complicated presentations of these children. This is particularly true when one considers the high rates of comorbid ADHD, oppositional defiant disorder, conduct disorder, and anxiety disorders, whose symptoms often do not improve even when mania is resolved (Carlson, 2005). Determining whether mood fluctuations constitute very rapid cycles or are simply fluctuations within an episode presents another challenge.

Diagnosing bipolar disorder in children is also made difficult by the need to interpret the criteria of adult bipolar disorder in terms of child behavior and thinking. For example, asking an adult whether his thoughts are racing is different from asking the same of a 7-year-old. And determining when elation becomes abnormal or fantasies become grandiose is tricky. These present good examples of the need for the clinician who works with children to rely on the signs of a disorder more than the symptoms.

> *Eleven-year-old Isaac has always been an irritable, easily provoked, explosive youngster. He is difficult to get along with and defies his parents daily. Over the past year, on any given day, Isaac has had distinct episodes of extreme giddiness, laughing in an infectious manner at situations others wouldn't find particularly funny. During these times he is full of energy and talks quickly, sometimes making lewd comments to his mother and her friends that baffle and embarrass her. When brought to the school principal for misbehavior, he tells her that his father knows the superintendent and can easily get her fired. Other times, Isaac has episodes of being sullen and morose and expresses suicidal thoughts. During the course of any day, Isaac has periods of being silly and of being depressed. When asked, Isaac insists, "There's nothing wrong with*

*me." Isaac's grandfather had a bipolar disorder for many years before committing suicide in his 40s.*

Some have tried to differentiate childhood bipolar disorder from what has been called severe mood dysregulation (Liebenluft et al., 2003). This syndrome is not yet recognized as a disorder, but in my experience it provides a more useful way of seeing these patients than the diagnosis of bipolar disorder, a diagnosis that is easy to make but that might be inaccurate. The conglomeration of signs and symptoms labeled severe mood dysregulation includes an abnormal mood, such as anger or sadness, that is experienced for more than half of most days, marked emotional reactivity to negative stimuli on at least three days each week, and symptoms of high arousal such as inattention, restlessness, pressured speech, and insomnia (Leibenluft et al., 2003). Whether severe mood dysregulation represents its own disorder or is a group of common symptoms experienced by many with a variety of disorders remains to be seen.

Some studies have shown, however, that children with this syndrome are distinguishable from children with bipolar disorder, both on tests of brain function during a frustrating task (Rich et al., 2007) as well as on family histories of bipolar disorder (Brotman et al., 2007). On the one hand, this could be an important practical distinction, because children with mood dysregulation might not respond to the same medicines as children with bipolar disorder. On the other hand, sometimes patients with severe mood fluctuations and volcanic outbursts respond to some of the same medicines used for bipolar disorder. This response to medicine does not prove the diagnosis of bipolar disorder, a consequential diagnosis one should be hesitant to apply prematurely to a child.

As childhood bipolar disorder is being better defined, the evidence that it is a biologically based disorder is mounting. Genetic studies have found the concordance rate of bipolar disorder in identical twins to be 67%, while that of non-identical twins is 19% (McGuffin et al., 2003). In addition, there is evidence that brain circuits from the prefrontal lobes to the basal ganglia are affected. Research has also shown that it takes children with bipolar disorder a longer time to learn from newly rewarded behavior. In addition, these children might misinterpret faces showing extreme emotion as showing only mild or moderate emotion. These kinds of findings might have treatment implications, as the behavioral programs used to treat these children might need to be tailored to their neurological abilities and disabilities (Pavuluri & Sweeney, 2008).

It is also becoming clear that children with bipolar disorder have significant difficulties that are likely to continue. Birmaher and colleagues (2006) found that when these children were seen at follow-up, about 60% of the time they still had some symptoms of bipolar disorder. And at an eight-year follow-up, Geller and colleagues (2008) found that, while 88% of these children had recovered from mania, about 73% of them would have manic symptoms again. In short, while diagnostic criteria are being debated, these are children with significant and ongoing difficulties.

## Treatment Model of Bipolar Disorder

With that background, we can now examine the treatment of child and adolescent bipolar disorder. While I do not focus on the environmental or behavioral interventions that help these children, they must first be mentioned.

Children with this disorder often find themselves in chaotic family environments. Sometimes this reflects the family's higher genetic risk of bipolar disorder and other biologically based psychiatric illness. Other times it reflects family discord caused by a child with chronic and substantial irritability and tantrums. These children are very difficult for the best of parents to live with and frequently cause major disagreements and conflict for parents with an otherwise stable marriage. Siblings must also struggle to stay afloat in this sea of chaos. Attempts to manage family turbulence, whether by treating family members who have a psychiatric illness or providing parent and sibling counseling, is an important part of the treatment program.

In addition to trying to keep a calm, stable family environment, patients are encouraged to maintain regular sleep-wake cycles. Patients with bipolar disorder are prone to experiencing varying sleep patterns as part of their illness. Although the connection between sleep and bipolar disorder is not well understood, it is thought that maintaining sleep routines, such as keeping regular bedtimes and waking times, is important in managing bipolar disorder. Recent research also supports the use of family-focused therapy, cognitive behavioral therapy, and group therapy (see the work of David Miklowitz, Mani Pavuluri, and Mary Fristad).

The pharmacological treatment of bipolar disorder requires some orientation. As I've shown, bipolar disorder consists of episodes of mania and episodes of depression, albeit depression that is probably distinct from what has been called unipolar or major depression. The pharmacological treatment of each of these consists of their acute treatment during an active episode as well as maintenance, or preventive, treatment between episodes. The acute and preventive treatments of both manic and depressive episodes should be seen as four distinct treatment possibilities, which can differ considerably from one another. In addition, different treatment might be required for patients with mixed episodes or rapid cycling. If the patient is also psychotic—for example, hallucinating—another dimension is added to treatment. Last, we must remember that the treatment of children cannot simply be extrapolated from that of adults.

## How Mood Stabilizers Work

There are basically three types of medicine used to treat the different phases of bipolar disorder: lithium, certain antiseizure medicines, and certain antipsychotics. Although lithium was one of the first proven treatments for a psychiatric disorder, its mechanism of action is still unclear. There are a number of theories as to how lithium works. Unlike almost all the other medicines I've discussed, the mechanism may not be at the level of neurotransmitters crossing the synapse. Instead, it might affect the manner in which electricity is sent down the neuron. The way in which other medicines work as mood stabilizers also remains unclear (Nurnberger, 2009).

## Clinical Indications of Mood Stabilizers

As noted above, the treatment of bipolar disorder must be broken down into separate sections with the understanding that the evidence supporting many treatments for child and adolescent bipolar disorder is sometimes sparse. We'll look at the acute treatment of mania and of depression and then at the maintenance treatment of bipolar disorder, not distinguishing mania from depression, since this more specific information regarding maintenance is not available in youth.

## The Acute Treatment of Mania

The FDA-approved medicines for the treatment of acute mania in youth are lithium, which is approved for use in adolescents, and risperidone, olanzapine, quetiapine, and aripiprazole, which are approved for those over 10 years old. Interestingly, the FDA approval of lithium was grandfathered, more on the basis of its long-term use in adults than on its having been proven effective by the usual research criteria. The others are SGAs, which were discussed in detail in Chapter 8. Another SGA, ziprasidone, has been proven effective in at least one study but at this writing awaits approval by the FDA. Although divalproex has proven effective in treating adult mania, the data supporting its use in children and adolescents, as we'll see, are less certain.

Evidence of the efficacy of lithium in the acute treatment of mania in youth rests on a slowly growing body of research in children and adolescents. In an open-label trial of lithium, Kantafaris, Coletti, & Dicker (2003) found that 63% of adolescents with mania responded after four weeks. About 26% remitted, a stronger response, during that time. In a placebo-controlled trial, Geller and associates (1998) showed lithium to be effective in reducing substance abuse and improving overall functioning in adolescents diagnosed with mania and substance abuse.

Because many children do not respond to a single medicine, lithium has been studied in combination with other medicines. In an open-label study, Kantafaris, Coletti, & Dicker (2001) found that after four weeks of treatment with lithium in combination with an antipsychotic (either an FGA or an SGA), almost two thirds of adolescents with acute mania and psychotic features improved. Many patients did poorly, however, within the first week of discontinuing the antipsychotic, when the patient was left only on lithium. This study found that only half of those taking both medicines were stable enough to tolerate the attempt to discontinue the antipsychotic, and of those, only about half tolerated taking only lithium over the next four weeks. Findling, McNamara, Gracious, and colleagues (2003) found that lithium combined with divalproex was effective in reducing the manic symptoms of children and adolescents within eight weeks and that almost half did very well. In short, while research supports the use of lithium to treat acute mania, there is a lack of strong data proving the efficacy of lithium used alone as an acute treatment of mania in youth. Many of these young people are psychiatrically fragile, requiring two medicines, and even with these, many continue to have significant difficulties.

Of the antiseizure medicines, none is FDA approved for the acute treatment of child or adolescent mania. Although carbamazepine was the first studied of this group of medicines, the data supporting its efficacy are limited to case studies and a small open-label trial. Because of this lack of data and the difficulties in using carbamazepine, this medicine is not widely prescribed.

By contrast, divalproex sodium was approved for the treatment of adult mania in 1994 and has been used more widely in treating children. Nevertheless, the data proving its efficacy in children are essentially open-label. Papatheodorou and colleagues (1995) treated 15 adolescents with divalproex for seven weeks and found that more than half improved. And Wagner and colleagues (2002) treated 40 children and adolescents who had mania, hypomania, or a mixed state with divalproex, with about 60% responding, beginning during the first week of treatment, with continuing improvement over the next eight weeks. Pavuluri and colleagues (2005) also showed the efficacy of divalproex in a six-month, open-label trial in which almost three quarters of children and adolescents responded.

Like lithium, divalproex has been studied in combination with other medicines. DelBello and colleagues (2002) treated 30 adolescents with mania or mixed state with divalproex, then added either quetiapine or placebo. They found that those patients treated with divalproex and quetiapine did significantly better. In addition, Findling and colleagues (2006), in an open-label study, found that 90% of bipolar children and adolescents who relapsed when taking either lithium or divalproex alone improved when they were started on a combination of lithium and divalproex. The remaining children in this study required the addition of an antipsychotic medicine to the lithium-divalproex combination.

Of note, some medicines are used, but without proof of efficacy or despite the fact that research has failed to find them better than placebo. Oxcarbazepine had been found useful in case reports. In a large double-blind, placebo-controlled study, however, it was no more effective than placebo (Wagner, Kowatch, et al., 2006). This is a useful reminder of the limits of case reports and the need for more rigorous research.

Topiramate, another antiseizure medicine, was being studied in a double-blind, placebo-controlled trial when the trial was ended because of lack of efficacy in an adult trial, thus leading to inconclusive results (DelBello et al., 2005).

As we've seen, although the body of evidence for the efficacy of medicines in children and adolescents is building, it is far from satisfactory. For now, lithium, divalproex, or an SGA or some combination of these is the first-line choice, and unfortunately even they are only partially effective, when they are effective at all.

## The Acute Treatment of Bipolar Depression

Bipolar depression is a malignant part of the bipolar cycle and has been associated with the highest risk of suicide for those with bipolar disorder (Dilsaver et al., 1997). Nevertheless, the treatment of the depression of bipolar disorder is uncertain and is not necessarily the same as the treatment of unipolar, or major, depressive disorder. Some have found an unfavorable risk-benefit ratio when using SSRIs to treat adults with bipolar depression (Ghaemi et al., 2004). Nevertheless, the combination of fluoxetine and olanzapine (marketed as Symbyax) is FDA approved for the treatment of bipolar depression in adults. and it is still possible that SSRIs are effective.

The research basis for treating bipolar depression in youth is also wanting. Lamotrigine, an antiseizure medicine, has been shown in case reports and a small open-label study to be effective. For example, Chang, Saxena, and Howe (2006) treated 20 adolescents with bipolar depression with lamotrigine for eight weeks, and although some patients were also taking other medicines concomitantly, most responded to the medicine. Carandang and colleagues (2003) also reported that eight of nine adolescents, many with bipolar disorder, responded to lamotrigine, although again some had different diagnoses and were on other medicines.

Lithium has also been used to treat bipolar depression in adults. Its use in youth, however, is still not adequately proven. Approximately half of the 27 adolescents with bipolar depression responded when treated with lithium in an open-label trial (Patel et al., 2006).

Overall, however, clear evidence regarding the treatment of bipolar depression in youth is lacking. A confounding variable of research done on hospitalized adolescents is that, in addition to the high placebo response noted in studies of adolescents with unipolar depression, the structure added to the adolescent's life by virtue of the hospitalization might itself help minimize the symptoms of bipolar disorder, thus making the response to medicine seem greater.

### The Maintenance Treatment of Bipolar Disorder

Again, there is a decided lack of data to guide us in trying to prevent the recurrent episodes of this usually chronic and debilitating disorder in children and adolescents. The literature on adult bipolar disorder finds that lithium is very effective at preventing the relapses of mania and somewhat effective at preventing the relapses of depression. The general rule for treating adults is also to assume that lithium will need to be taken indefinitely, since bipolar recurrences can be frequent and dangerous. In addition, when lithium is discontinued, doing so slowly might lower the risk of recurrence.

Olanzapine and lamotrigine are also used in adults to prevent mania and depression, although lamotrigine is more effective in preventing bipolar depression.

There is a compelling need to understand the prevention of bipolar recurrences in children. Unfortunately, the data on effective treatments and the duration for which they should be used in children and adolescents are sparse. Findling and colleagues (2005) compared lithium and divalproex in the maintenance treatment of children and adolescents with bipolar disorder over 18 months, finding them equally effective.

### The Treatment of Mixed States and Rapid Cycling

Again, we must rely on the adult literature, which finds that patients with rapid cycling and mixed states might respond to lithium, but generally do not do as well on lithium as patients with less frequent cycling. Divalproex and carbamazepine are felt to be more effective than lithium in the treatment of rapid cycling and mixed states in adults.

In children and adolescents, the treatment of mixed states has often been grouped with the treatment of mania.

## Treating Bipolar Disorder

The first task in treating bipolar disorder is that of making an accurate diagnosis. As we've seen, this can be a confusing task, especially in children, and one must be careful not to diagnose this disorder prematurely to justify a particular treatment. This can start the process down the wrong road and commit the patient to years of incorrect, and possibly harmful, treatment.

If the diagnosis is made, however, one then chooses a treatment to fit the phase of the disorder diagnosed. If acute mania is diagnosed, one likely starts treatment with an SGA, lithium, or divalproex. If these are ineffective, research supports the trial of a combination of these.

As we've seen, the question whether to use an SSRI for bipolar depression has not been answered, although at least some data and clinical experience suggest that SSRIs should not be used, at least not alone. If the patient clearly has bipolar disorder, an SSRI should not be used initially for fear of switching the patient into mania. An SSRI can, however, be considered after the patient's mood is stable. If they wish to begin an SSRI, many clinicians first start the patient on a mood stabilizer to try to prevent a switch into mania. Unfortunately, there are no data to support the efficacy of this approach. If an SSRI is used, it should be started at a low dose with the patient carefully observed.

If the patient does not clearly have bipolar disorder, but the patient has a family history of bipolar disorder, or one is unsure whether the depression will develop into bipolar disorder as the child matures, then the risks and benefits of different treatment approaches or withholding treatment must be carefully reviewed with the family. In these difficult situations, the significant risks of continuing depression must be appreciated.

Another question without a clear answer is whether stimulant medication should be discontinued in a patient with bipolar disorder. Some feel that stimulants might exacerbate mania, although the evidence seems weighted against this possibility. When patients first present with inattention and impulsivity associated with severe irritability, the diagnosis is often difficult to discern, and stimulants are easy to use, with a readily apparent answer as to whether they will be effective. If the stimulant is clearly effective but other mood symptoms continue, the stimulant is sometimes continued while another mood-stabilizing medicine is added. We can see how easily one can progress to polypharmacy, so one must stay clearly focused on which symptoms are being helped by which medicine. If, however, one knows or strongly suspects that the patient has bipolar disorder, that diagnosis should be treated first. Then, if necessary, stimulants can be used to treat the unresolved ADHD symptoms. A few small studies have shown that adding stimulants to antimanic medicines does not worsen the patient's symptoms and may improve them (Carlson, 2009).

Although prescribing one medicine is the first choice, because many patients with bipolar disorder do not respond to a single medicine, the clinician must consider using more than one medicine, such as lithium plus divalproex, especially in severe cases. This also applies to the treatment of a patient with mania and psychosis, in which case an SGA would be added to lithium or divalproex to treat the psychosis. As we've seen, sometimes this means using lithium with divalproex or either of these with an SGA. Sometimes, however, an SGA alone is beneficial. In general, SGAs work more quickly when a quick response is necessary.

The treatment of bipolar disorder, including in patients with confusing and complex presentations that only suggest a diagnosis of bipolar disorder, can be a slow process. Doses are generally not raised quickly, and medicines must be given time to work. If this is not possible on an outpatient basis, then in-patient hospitalization must be considered. Sometimes a correct combination of medicines is found only after trial and error. Educating patients and their confused and frustrated parents about this process helps minimize their anxiety.

Last, as already mentioned, sleep difficulties are a cardinal feature of bipolar disorder. While the management of this problem is initially behavioral, the urge to medicate is often not far behind. The choice of treatment is based on clinical judgment more than controlled data, so it is important to remember that some antidepressants used as sleep agents, such as trazodone, might "switch" the person into mania and therefore should, if possible, be avoided.

If the diagnosis and treatment of bipolar disorder in children is confusing and lacking in evidence to direct the clinician, then the diagnosis and treatment of preschoolers with bipolar disorder is even more so. Diagnosing bipolar disorder in preschoolers is challenging in part because of the difficulty of distinguishing characteristics such as grandiosity and hypersexuality in this age group. Delineating symptomatic episodes from a baseline of irritability is equally trying. The treatment of children who are diagnosed with bipolar disorder consists of the same medicines used in older children, namely the mood stabilizers and SGAs. The research support of these treatments, however, consists only of open-label studies.

## The Mood Stabilizers

We turn now to an examination of the various kinds of mood stabilizers used to treat bipolar disorder.

### Lithium

Lithium is an element found in the periodic table of elements, which we remember from high school chemistry class. It is a metal found in the earth. It is made usable in salt form by combining it with different groups of molecules, so the lithium taken by patients as medicine is usually lithium carbonate or lithium citrate.

Its use in psychiatry was discovered in 1949 in Australia. While lithium was adopted more quickly by psychiatrists in the rest of the world, practitioners in the United States were relatively slow to use lithium because of the fear of toxic side effects that had been noted when lithium had been used freely as a salt substitute. By the1970s, its effect of preventing the mood swings of bipolar disorder was documented, safety precautions were understood, and the group of medicines that would become the mood stabilizers was off and running.

Over the decades since then, lithium has been used for many disorders, especially those that have a recurrent quality. In child and adolescent psychiatry it has been used to treat bipolar disorder, severe violent aggressive episodes, and, taking a lead from adult psychiatry, to boost the effect of antidepressants in unresponsive depression.

### *Mechanism of action*

Unlike with many of the other medicines I've discussed, which seem to increase or decrease the number of neurotransmitters at the synapse, the mechanism of action for lithium is unclear and complex. Probably it affects different parts of the brain in different ways and in different conditions. It seems to balance the effects of different neurotransmitters, including serotonin, norepinephrine, dopamine, and GABA; to have effects on important enzymes that impact brain plasticity, such as protein kinase C; and to affect neuronal signaling by its second-messenger effects.

### *Indications*

As noted above, the primary use of lithium is in the acute treatment of mania, and possibly bipolar depression, and in the prevention of bipolar mania and depression. It is FDA approved in adults for the treatment of acute mania and the prevention of bipolar cycling. It tends to be less effective in patients with rapid cycling, mixed states, more severe mania, or substance abuse, those with more episodes prior to starting lithium, and those whose bipolar sequence goes from depression to mania rather than from mania to depression (DeLeon, 2000; Mendlewicz, Souery, & Riveli, 2000).

Lithium is also FDA approved to treat acute mania in adolescents, although this use is based on its effectiveness in adults more than on research findings in adolescents. It has also been used to treat the explosiveness of hospitalized children with conduct disorder (Campbell et al., 1984; Campbell et al., 1995).

### *Use of lithium*

An important advance was made in the use of lithium when it was discovered that the amount of lithium in the blood could be monitored through testing. This allows the clinician to keep the blood level of lithium in a range associated with clinical improvement. If not carefully monitored, the blood level of lithium can exceed this range fairly easily and enter a toxic range. For this reason lithium is said to have a narrow therapeutic index, meaning that the toxic blood level is only slightly higher than the therapeutic blood level. Monitoring lithium blood levels is therefore an important feature of using lithium safely. So while the dose of lithium is important, its blood level is more important, since some patients will have a low blood level despite being on a high dose of lithium or vice versa.

This need for monitoring blood levels and the narrow therapeutic index of lithium also makes lithium difficult, but not impossible, to use in children and adolescents.

Although researchers have arrived at different formulas to determine the initial dose of lithium, it is usually started at a dose of 15–20 mg/kg per day. For a 40 kg (approximately 88 pound) child, this is about 300 mg twice daily. The dose is then increased gradually every four to five days while blood levels are taken a few days after each dose increase. Lithium is increased first by giving 300 mg three or four times daily, then by increasing one dose at a time to 600 mg. Single doses of 900 mg are avoided because of potential side effects. Sustained-release pills allow lithium to be given twice daily. Usually the total daily dose does not exceed about 1800 mg daily in youth, though again, following blood levels is crucial.

Blood levels are obtained through a blood sample taken at any standard medical laboratory. Because the target blood levels have been standardized by drawing blood about 12 hours after the last dose, it is important that the patient have blood drawn in the same manner approximately 10–12 hours after the last dose of lithium. Usually this means first thing in the morning, before the first dose of lithium is taken. Patients who forget and accidentally take their morning lithium should not have their blood drawn that morning, since this would lead to an inordinately high blood level that will be of no help to the clinician. They should simply wait for the next suitable morning.

The clinician usually aims for a lithium level of about 0.6–1.2 mEq/l, although when a patient is acutely manic, one might aim for the higher side. When a patient is stable and simply being maintained on lithium, the blood level is sometimes lower. An even lower level might be adequate if lithium is being used to augment another antidepressant or to diminish anger or irritability. In the treatment of acute mania, a response to lithium can be expected within about 7–14 days.

Before a patient starts lithium, a medical history, physical exam, and laboratory tests are required to ensure that there are no baseline medical difficulties. In particular, these should include, at minimum, blood levels of electrolytes, such as sodium, chloride, and potassium; a complete blood count (white blood cells, red blood cells, and platelets); creatinine and blood urea nitrogen (BUN), which measure kidney function; and thyroid hormone and thyroid-stimulating hormone. Many, but not all, clinicians will also do a baseline electrocardiogram (EKG). In addition, because of the association of lithium with cardiac anomalies in the developing fetus, a baseline pregnancy test should be done to ensure that a female patient is not pregnant. This also underscores the need for the female patient to have a clear understanding of the risks of pregnancy while taking lithium and sufficient impulse control to take appropriate precautions.

After the patient is stable on a given dose of lithium, blood levels of lithium should be checked approximately every three months. In addition, about every three to six months, blood tests of thyroid function and kidney function should be repeated.

Deciding when to discontinue lithium is a difficult clinical decision that weighs the significant risk of relapse of bipolar disorder against the risk of continuing lithium use. At that time, lithium is generally tapered slowly over a few months while the clinician watches carefully for the return of symptoms of mania.

### Side effects

Because of the many side effects associated with lithium, combined with the relative lack of information regarding the side effects in children, the following discussion includes the side effects seen in adults.

#### Gastrointestinal

Some patients will complain of stomachache, nausea, vomiting, and diarrhea due to local irritation of lithium on the GI tract. Taking lithium with food or dividing the dose might be helpful, as might switching to the liquid or long-acting forms of lithium. Because lithium toxicity can present with these symptoms, if these side effects persist, the patient should be checked for toxicity. In addition, persistent vomiting can affect the balance of electrolytes, which can in turn affect the blood level of lithium. Finally, some people experience a metallic taste after taking a dose of lithium.

### Renal (kidney)

Frequent drinking of liquids (polydipsia) and subsequent frequent urination (polyuria) are relatively common side effects. Sometimes this results in diabetes insipidus, the inability of the kidneys to concentrate urine. This can be reversed within a few days or weeks by lowering the dose or stopping lithium. (Psychiatrists treating adult patients will sometimes add hydrochlorthiazide, a diuretic, which paradoxically decreases severe polyuria, but this requires careful monitoring of an increasing lithium level and is not recommended in youth.) The possibility of lithium causing irreversible kidney damage has been much discussed in the adult literature, although this seems to be a rare event. Nevertheless, monitoring renal function on a regular basis is important. There is a lack of information on the long-term effect of lithium on the kidneys of children and adolescents.

### Neurological

A fine tremor in the hands is a frequent side effect in adults. This can affect handwriting. It is treated either by lowering the dose of lithium or by using propanolol, a beta blocker, which has been used to decrease tremor in adults. A more significant tremor and difficulty walking (ataxia) are signs of lithium toxicity. The tremor can sometimes be heard in the person's inability to articulate words (dysarthria). At more toxic levels, confusion and seizures can occur.

In addition to tremor, some patients will complain about slowed thinking, decreased creativity, and increased forgetfulness. These respond to lowering the dose.

### Cardiovascular

EKG changes have been reported but are generally benign. Nevertheless, some cases of significant cardiac rhythm changes have been reported.

## Dermatologic

A variety of rashes can occur from lithium use, but acne is the most frequent skin change. This has particular importance to adolescents. In addition, the aggravation of psoriasis has been reported, as has reversible hair loss.

## Endocrine

Although the cause is unknown, weight gain is the second most common reason for adults to discontinue lithium and is also noted in children. Increased appetite seems to be partly to blame, but increased drinking, especially of high-calorie fluids, also adds to the problem. About 20% of women develop low thyroid function (hypothyroidism). Routine follow-up of thyroid function is important in both males and females.

## Hematological

Lithium is known to increase the white blood cell count.

## Pregnancy

The use of lithium in pregnant women has been associated with an increased risk of Ebstein's anomaly, a heart defect in the infant. While the rate of this defect seems to be between 1 and 7 per 1,000, this is much higher than the rate of this defect in the infants of women who are not taking lithium. The defect seems to be associated more with use during the first trimester. In addition, the general rate of birth defects is higher among the offspring of women taking lithium than among those of women who do not. Therefore the risk of pregnancy must always be weighed carefully before treating adolescent females with lithium.

## Toxic levels

Most patients will not begin to experience toxic side effects at levels less than 1.5 mEq/l. Above that, many patients will experience mild symptoms such as tremulousness or gastrointestinal symptoms such as diarrhea and vomiting. As toxic levels of approximately 2.0–2.5 mEq/l are reached, the patient might experience extreme tremulousness, an unsteady gait, muscle weakness, and slurred speech. At still higher levels, cardiac arrhythmias, confusion, seizures, and coma can occur.

These requires urgent medical attention, possibly including the need for renal dialysis to lower the blood level of lithium quickly so that damage to the kidneys and brain is not sustained and, at higher levels, to prevent death.

### *Drug interactions*

It is important to be aware of substances that affect the level of lithium because they can readily elevate a therapeutic blood level of lithium to a toxic level.

Unlike many of the medicines I have discussed, which are metabolized in the liver, lithium is simply excreted by the kidneys, which balance the output of lithium with the output of other electrolytes, such as sodium. Therefore depleting or adding to the body's level of salt (sodium chloride) affects the blood level of lithium. For example, on the one hand, eating an excessive amount of a salty food (such as salted potato chips) can decrease the blood level of lithium, since more lithium is excreted. On the other hand, losing an excessive amount of body salt (for instance, through excessive sweating on a hot summer day) can increase the blood level of lithium, since the body will hold on to lithium. These processes can shift the blood level below the therapeutic range or into the toxic range. Therefore maintaining a reasonably stable ingestion and depletion of salt is important. Patients must be aware of excessive salt intake and of situations that deplete body salt, such as excessive sweating, diarrhea, and vomiting.

Other medicines can also affect the lithium level, which needs to be monitored more closely if these medicines are taken. Nonsteroidal anti-inflammatory drugs, such as indomethacin and ibuprofen, increase lithium levels. Lithium levels might also be increased by fluoxetine, fluvoxamine, thiazide diuretics, tetracycline, metronidazole (Flagyl), and marijuana. Theophylline and caffeine can decrease lithium levels, as might chlorpromazine. Carbamazepine used in combination with lithium has been reported to cause neurotoxic effects, such as disorientation. This should be considered a partial list. Individuals taking lithium who require other medicines should always check for possible lithium-medicine interactions with their physician.

## Divalproex

Divalproex sodium is a combination of valproate and valproic acid. Either of these names is often used to refer to divalproex sodium. The brand medicine Depakote consists of the combination, while Depakene consists only of valproic acid. All forms of divalproex sodium convert to valproic acid in the bloodstream. Divalproex was originally developed as an antiseizure medicine, though it has also been used since 1994 as a treatment for mania in adults. Its mechanism of action is not well understood.

### *Indications*

Divalproex is FDA approved for the acute treatment of mania in adults. On the basis of adult studies, it is also thought to be the medicine of choice for mixed states and, possibly, rapid cycling. It is not known to be beneficial in the treatment of bipolar depression. Divalproex is also approved for the treatment of migraine headaches, and there are some who use it for controlling aggression in adults with brain injury. It has no FDA approvals for psychiatric use in children, but is approved for the treatment of epilepsy in children older than 10 years.

Open-label trials have suggested that divalproex might be useful in the acute treatment of mania in youth. And Findling and colleagues (2005) have shown divalproex to be as effective as lithium in an 18-month double-blind trial in children and adolescents. In a double-blind, placebo-controlled study, however, Wagner and colleagues (2009) did not find divalproex extended release to be more effective than placebo.

Some research supports the use of divalproex in combination with lithium or an antipsychotic in the treatment of those who have not responded sufficiently to either medicine. For example, DelBello and colleagues (2002) found a combination of divalproex and quetiapine to be effective, and Pavuluri and colleagues (2004), albeit in an open-label trial, found divalproex in combination with risperidone to be effective.

While the role of divalproex in the treatment of youngsters with bipolar disorder in still uncertain, other studies are suggesting it has a role to play in the treatment of irritability and aggression. In a small double-blind, placebo-controlled study, Blader and colleagues (2009) showed that adding divalproex to a stimulant significantly decreased the aggression in a group of children with ADHD whose aggression did not respond to a stimulant alone or to psychosocial intervention. And in another small double-blind, placebo-controlled study, Hollander and colleagues (2010) showed that divalproex was effective in decreasing the irritability and aggression of children and adolescents with autism after 12 weeks.

### Use of divalproex

Taking a careful medical history is important prior to starting treatment with divalproex. In particular, information should be obtained regarding a history of liver dysfunction or hematological (blood) disorders. In addition, the patient should have baseline blood tests, including a complete blood count (CBC), and liver enzymes. It should also be ascertained that the patient is not pregnant and has been educated about the risks of pregnancy while taking divalproex. Because divalproex can cause weight gain, baseline weight should also be obtained.

Divalproex is generally started at about 10–15 mg/kg daily, divided throughout the day. The dose is then increased in 250 or 500 mg increments according to the patient's clinical response and his or her blood level of valproic acid. The total daily dose of divalproex generally does not exceed 60 mg/kg. Because the therapeutic index is higher for divalproex than for lithium, levels do not have to be followed quite as closely as they do for lithium. Generally, however, a blood level is obtained shortly after the medicine is started and then again as the dose is increased. After the patient is on a stable dose, levels can be checked about every six months. In addition, follow-up blood tests of CBC and liver enzymes should be obtained.

Blood levels should be drawn about 12 hours after the last dose and are generally kept between 50 and 125 ug/ml. These are the levels associated with seizure control, and though there is less information on the levels needed for mood control, they are used for this purpose also.

### Side effects

A number of side effects have been noted with the use of divalproex.

*Weight gain*

Increased weight is reported in about 50% of patients and is a frequent cause of discontinuing the medicine. This side effect might be dose related. Patients should be encouraged to take dietary precautions and exercise regularly.

*Neurological*

Divalproex has been associated with headache and tremor. In addition, sedation is a common side effect.

*Gastrointestinal*

GI upset is a common side effect and is usually experienced as stomach pain, nausea, vomiting, and diarrhea. These symptoms are dose related and are diminished by using the enteric-coated tablets.

*Hair loss*

Hair loss can occur as a result of divalproex interfering with the body's use of selenium and zinc. Some clinicians encourage patients to take selenium and zinc mineral supplements.

*Hematological*

Diminished platelet count can occur, so patients should be told to seek medical consultation if they note frequent or easy bruising or bleeding. In addition, platelet count is obtained with the CBC about every six months.

*Liver*

Fatal cases of liver toxicity have been reported in neonates. The risk seems to be lower for those older than 2 years. While the risk seems very low, patients must be aware of this possibility and the need to seek medical attention if signs of liver dysfunction occur, including nausea, loss of appetite, lethargy, or jaundice. Of course, other than jaundice, these not uncommon symptoms can be due to other causes and are not necessarily an indication of medicine-induced liver toxicity. Checking liver enzymes every six months is prudent.

*Hyperammonemia*

Ammonia levels are reportedly higher in those taking valproic acid and still higher in those taking valproic acid with another antiseizure medicine or with risperidone (Carlson, Reynolds, & Caplan, 2007). This side effect potentially causes a host of serious neurological consequences. Ammonia levels should be checked in patients taking valproic acid who develop unusual presentations.

*Pancreatitis*

Inflammation of the pancreas is another dangerous, if rare, side effect of divalproex and can occur after the patient has been taking it for a while. Patients should be warned to be aware of extreme abdominal pain and told that if this occurs, medical consultation should be sought.

*Polycystic ovary syndrome*

Polycystic ovary syndrome (PCOS) consists of acne, obesity, growth of excess hair, and loss of menses caused by excess androgens (male hormones). Despite the name, patients do not necessarily develop polycystic ovaries. PCOS has been associated with the use of divalproex in adults, but the link is not well understood. It is important for adolescent females to understand the possibility of PCOS and for the clinician to inquire about potential symptoms, so that endocrine or gynecologic consultation can be obtained if needed. The syndrome may be reversible.

*Pregnancy*

Divalproex has been associated with an increased risk of birth defects, especially neural tube defects, such as spina bifida, when taken during the first trimester. For this reason, pregnancy should be avoided while a patient is taking divalproex. Some suggest that folic acid be taken to help decrease the risk of birth defects.

## Drug interactions

Although problems of interaction between divalproex and other medicines are relatively unusual, because divalproex is highly protein-bound, it tends to displace other medicines from the proteins they are bound to, thus leaving more of those medicines free and able to interact. In addition, valproate is partially metabolized by the P450 enzyme system, so caution must be exercised when drugs that affect that enzyme system are used with divalproex. On the one hand, carbamazepine, oxcarbazepine, phenobarbital, and phenytoin can increase the enzymes that metabolize divalproex, thus lowering valproate levels. On the other hand, erythromycin, clarithromycin, fluoxetine, fluvoxamine, topiramate, aspirin, and ibuprofen can inhibit the enzymes that metabolize valproate and thus increase valproate levels. Divalproex can inhibit the metabolism of carbamazepine, phenobarbital, phenytoin, lamotrigine, tricyclic antidepressants, and some benzodiazepines. Therefore particular care must be taken when one is using divalproex and lamotrigine, since higher lamotrigine levels can increase the risk of a dangerous rash (see the discussion of lamotrigine below). In short, as more information about drug interactions becomes known, it becomes increasingly important for the prescribing clinician to check possible drug interactions to ensure safety.

## Carbamazepine

Carbamazepine was originally developed in the 1950s and used in the 1960s as a treatment for epilepsy. In the 1970s and 1980s evidence grew that it was effective in the acute treatment of mania and the prevention of bipolar disorder in adults. Because of drug interactions, it is more difficult to use than other medicines. Given this difficulty and a lack of data supporting its use, it is not widely prescribed and has no FDA approvals for use as a psychiatric medicine in children.

### Indications

While carbamazepine has been used with some success for adults with some forms of bipolar disorder, such as rapid cycling, the evidence for many uses is only suggestive. The only FDA-approved psychiatric use is of the extended-release form for the acute treatment of mania. The medicine is FDA approved for the treatment of epilepsy in children and adults and for the treatment of trigeminal neuralgia, a pain disorder.

The only data supporting the use of carbamazepine in children with a psychiatric disorder come from a small open-label study by Kowatch and colleagues (2000) in which medicine was effective in some children. In addition, some case studies have supported its use.

### Use of carbamazepine

Like divalproex, carbamazepine can cause significant changes in blood and liver function. Therefore a baseline medical history and lab tests, including CBC, liver enzymes, and pregnancy test, is crucial.

The dosing of carbamazepine is based on its use as an antiseizure medicine. While in children younger than 6 years carbamazepine is started at 10–20 mg/kg per day in two or three doses daily, the medicine is generally started at 100 mg twice daily in older children and 200 mg twice daily in adolescents. The dose is then increased by 100 mg or 200 mg increments every week until a clinical response or side effects are reached. In addition, blood levels of carbamazepine, taken about 12 hours after the last dose, are obtained with a target range of 4–12 ug/ml. The total daily dose of carbamazepine should not exceed 1 gram per day.

### Side effects

Let's look at the side effects associated with the use of carbamazepine.

*Hematological*

About 10% of patients have a modest decrease in their levels of white blood cells and platelets. More rarely seen, however, are significant drops in the number of platelets, white blood cells and red blood cells. Estimates of the risk of this type of event among adults vary widely from about 1 in 10,000 to 1 in 500,000, depending in part on the blood component. Following CBCs during the first few months of treatment is crucial, and significant decreases in any blood component becomes a medical emergency. Patients should be advised to inform their physician immediately about easy bruising and bleeding, which can signify a drop in platelets; signs of infection, such as sore throat, which can signify a drop in white blood cell count; or tiredness and lethargy, which can signify a drop in red blood cell count.

*Liver*

Liver enzymes might increase and therefore need to be followed.

*Dermatological*

Transient skin rashes occur in about 10–15% of patients and can rarely progress to the more medically dangerous Stevens-Johnson syndrome.

*Neurological*

Sedation is relatively common. Fatigue, dizziness, blurred vision, and unstable gait also occur.

*Gastrointestinal*

Nausea is relatively common and can be treated by taking the medicine with food, dividing the dose through the day, or changing the form of carbamazepine taken.

*Pregnancy*

Carbamazepine has been associated with fetal abnormalities, such as neural tube defects and craniofacial defects, when used in the first trimester. Folate supplements during pregnancy may be of help in reducing the risk.

### Drug interactions

Carbamazepine both affects the P450 enzyme system and is metabolized by it. Interestingly, because carbamazepine increases the enzymes that metabolize it, the longer carbamazepine is taken, the more enzymes there are to metabolize it. Therefore over time, the same dose of medicine will lead to lower blood levels of medicine. Blood levels must be obtained every two weeks for the first two months and then every three months thereafter.

Carbamazepine increases a fairly large number of enzymes, thus lowering the blood levels of many medicines, including aripiprazole, benzodiazepines, theophylline, sertraline, and antipsychotics. Carbamazepine can also lower the blood levels of caffeine and of oral contraceptives, thus causing them to fail (Cozza, Armstrong, & Oesterheld, 2003). Concomitant use of medicines that inhibit the enzymes that metabolize carbamazepine can increase carbamazepine levels. These medicines include fluoxetine, fluvoxamine, divalproex, and erythromycin.

## Lamotrigine

Lamotrigine is another medicine that is FDA approved for the treatment of seizures and has also been used to treat bipolar disorder.

Lamotrigine has a number of synaptic effects, including decreasing glutamate release, possibly blocking calcium channels, modulating the reuptake of serotonin, and blocking the reuptake of monoamines such as dopamine.

### Indications

Lamotrigine was the second medicine (after lithium) to be FDA approved in adults for the maintenance treatment of bipolar disorder. It has not been shown to be effective in the acute treatment of mania but may be effective in the treatment of bipolar depression in adults. In addition, case studies have raised the possibility of its use in rapid cycling and mixed bipolar disorder.

While lamotrigine has no FDA-approved psychiatric indications for children and adolescents, case reports, small retrospective studies, and an open-label study have found it effective in the treatment of adolescents with bipolar depression (Chang, Saxena, & Howe, 2006). Some (Carandang, 2006) have suggested a possible role for lamotrigine as being, like lithium, a medicine used to augment the response of better-studied antidepressants taken by depressed patients who are unresponsive to a single antidepressant.

### Use of lamotrigine

Because of the potential for causing Stevens-Johnson syndrome, lamotrigine must be started slowly and cautiously. While there are no clear guidelines, in adolescents lamotrigine can be started at 12.5 mg daily, then after one to two weeks increased to 25 mg daily for another one or two weeks. Thereafter the dose is increased by 25 or 50 mg increments every two weeks. In the open-label study by Chang, Saxena, and Howe (2006), the average final dose was about 130 mg daily, although daily doses can go up to 200 mg or higher.

### Side effects

A few side effects are associated with the use of lamotrigine.

## Dermatological

The most significant side effect is Stevens-Johnson syndrome, which includes a potentially fatal skin rash. This is a rare phenomenon and seems more likely when the medicine is started at high dose and increased rapidly, especially in younger children. Among the small number of pediatric patients in research studies, about 3% of youth develop a more common benign rash.

## Neurological

Some patients experience headaches, dizziness, and sleepiness.

## Gastrointestinal

Some patients experience nausea.

### Drug interactions

Valproic acid and sertraline increase blood level of lamotrigine and therefore need to be used cautiously, so that a toxic level of lamotrigine is not reached. Carbamazepine, phenytoin, phenobarbital, and oral contraceptives decrease the blood level of lamotrigine. Thus, if the oral contraceptive is started or stopped abruptly, lamotrigine levels can decrease or increase quickly. An abrupt increase in blood level might increase the risk for rash.

### Topiramate

Topiramate is an anticonvulsant chemically different from the other anticonvulsants. Its mechanisms of action include decreasing glutamate and aspartate levels and increasing dopamine and GABA transmission.

### Indications

Topiramate is FDA approved for the treatment of seizures in children and adults and in the prevention of migraine headaches in adults.

There are no FDA-approved psychiatric indications for topiramate. Kushner and colleagues (2006) reported that none of four double-blind, placebo-controlled studies showed topiramate, when given alone, to be effective in bipolar mania or mixed states in adults. Case reports indicate it could augment other mood stabilizers in the treatment of rapid cycling. One double-blind, placebo-controlled study (DelBello et al., 2005) of its use in youth with bipolar disorder was discontinued prematurely because studies were finding the medicine to be ineffective in adult bipolar disorder.

### Use of topiramate

Although there are no clear recommendations about the dosing of topiramate in youth bipolar disorder, topiramate is usually started at a dose of about 12.5–25 mg daily and increased by 25 mg each week to a maximum of 300 to 400 mg daily. In children it is usually given twice daily. It is not extensively metabolized and is excreted in the urine, mostly unchanged.

### Side effects

A few side effects of topiramate should be noted.

#### Neurological

Patients might experience decreased concentration, sleepiness, fatigue, dizziness, and memory problems.

#### Gastrointestinal

Patients sometimes experience decreased appetite, and topiramate is associated with weight loss in almost half of adults. Topiramate has been used in adult patients to battle the weight gain caused by other medicines, such as the SGAs (Schatzberg, Cole, & DeBattista, 2007).

#### Renal

About 1–2% of patients develop kidney stones while taking topiramate. Therefore patients should be encouraged to drink water.

### Drug interactions

Phenobarbital, carbamazepine, and phenytoin all decrease blood levels of topiramate by about half. Valproate and topiramate each modestly lowers blood levels of the other. Topiramate may lower the level of the estrogen component in oral contraceptives, thus reducing their efficacy.

## Oxcarbazepine

Oxcarbazepine is structurally similar to carbamazepine but was developed to avoid some of the effects of carbamazepine on liver enzymes. It is metabolized differently from carbamazepine and is less likely to cause the same serious side effects.

### *Indications*

Oxcarbazepine is FDA approved for the treatment of epilepsy in adults and children. It has no psychiatric approvals. It has been used to treat mania in adults with some success, although controlled studies proving its efficacy are lacking in children. While case reports of oxcarbazepine described possible benefits, in a large double-blind, placebo-controlled study, Wagner, Kowatch, and colleagues (2006) found oxcarbazepine to be no better than placebo in the treatment of children and adolescents with bipolar disorder.

### *Use of oxcarbazepine*

Some clinicians use oxcarbazepine to treat bipolar disorder, although, as noted above, this is not supported by controlled research. In a pilot study (Juruena et al., 2009) it was shown to be effective as an adjunct to lithium in the treatment of bipolar disorder in adults. When used, it is started at about 150 mg twice daily and increased approximately weekly.

### *Side effects*

Several side effects have been observed in patients using oxcarbazepine.

*Tiredness*
This is generally transient.

*Headache*
This is generally transient.

*Gastrointestinal*
Some patients will complain of vomiting or abdominal pain on a transient basis.

*Hyponatremia*

A decrease in serum sodium levels, hyponatremia is an infrequent, but not rare, side effect. It is potentially dangerous. Therefore a baseline sodium level should be done, and one should be alert for risk factors that might also influence sodium levels, such as the use of diuretics by teens trying to lose weight.

## Drug interactions

Oxcarbazepine only slightly increases some liver enzymes. Even this slight effect, however, can lower the blood level and therefore the efficacy of oral contraceptives. It also may inhibit the enzyme 2C19 and thus might increase blood levels of medicines metabolized by 2C19, such as phenytoin. In general, however, oxcarbazepine does not seem to interfere with the metabolism of most other medicines. In addition, its own metabolism is not greatly affected by other medicines.

## Gabapentin

Gabapentin is another antiepileptic which has been used by psychiatrists for a variety of conditions because it seems to cause few side effects. It works by increasing GABA levels in the brain.

## Indications

Gabapentin is FDA approved as a seizure medicine. It has no psychiatric indications in adults or children. Some double-blind studies have failed to find it effective in the treatment of adults whose bipolar mania or depression has not responded to more standard treatments (DeLeon, 2000). It has also been tried as a treatment for anxiety.

## Use of gabapentin

Gabapentin is used in doses given about three times daily, up to about 4800 mg daily. There are no standard treatment protocols for its use, particularly in children with bipolar disorder or anxiety.

## Side effects

Two categories of side effects are notable.

*Neurological*

Some patients experience sedation, tremor, and unsteady gait.

*Psychiatric*

About 4–7% of patients are reported to have experienced increased mood cycling.

### *Drug interactions*

Gabapentin is not highly bound to proteins. It is not metabolized but simply excreted from the body unchanged. In addition, it does not seem to increase or decrease liver enzymes. Therefore it does not tend to have significant interactions with other medicines.

## Case Examples

*Case 1: Eleven-year-old Hanna has always been known as having a sour mood. She insults easily, responding with teary pouts and slammed doors on an almost daily basis. Hanna briefly enjoys herself, but never for long, and never with more than a shade of happiness that gives her parents hope that she's maturing out of her perpetual funk. Hanna is never full of energy, grandiose, or excessively silly. Her moods are essentially unwavering and chronic, not changing and episodic. After a series of particularly virulent outbursts, her parents take her to the pediatrician, who thinks she might have bipolar disorder.*

*Comment:* Hanna might have dysthymic disorder or another type of depression or she might have oppositional defiant disorder. She does not, however, have bipolar disorder. Her disorder cannot be characterized as episodic, and she demonstrates no evidence of grandiosity, euphoria, or other signs of bipolar disorder. Whether she will at some point develop manic episodes remains to be seen. The pediatrician was fooled by the chronicity of Hanna's disorder and her extreme outbursts.

*Case 2: Hiro, 9 years old, has always had an edge. He is typically belligerent and defiant. In addition, he is being treated with methylphenidate for ADHD. Over the past six months Hiro has been increasingly aggressive, his hair-trigger temper landing him in numerous physical altercations with peers. His psychiatrist adds Depakote to his pharmacologic regimen, and Hiro's aggressive impulses lessen, even if they do not cease.*

*Comment:* Stimulants help improve the inattention and hyperactivity of many children with ADHD. In addition, stimulants often help these children become less defiant. Depakote, which has been used to treat bipolar disorder, has recently been used to minimize the aggression and defiance of children with ADHD.

*Case 3: Chiara is 14 and depressed. She has been sad and unable to enjoy the sports that usually excite her. Recently she has been suicidal. Her psychiatrist wants to start Chiara on Lexapro but is concerned that her mother has a history of bipolar disorder. She is unsure if Chiara's depression represents the onset of bipolar disorder, the mania to begin in the next few years, and she doesn't want the SSRI to precipitate the mania. She considers starting Chiara on a mood stabilizer before starting an SSRI or perhaps starting her on lamotrigine.*

*Comment:* The treatment of adolescent bipolar depression is without significant research and it thus fraught with apprehension. The treatment approach is largely based on each clinician's experience and judgment. Some clinicians find it prudent to begin a mood stabilizer to attempt to prevent possible mania and others do not.

*Chapter 10*

# Sleep Disorders and Medicines

O f the many difficulties faced by parents, few are as vexing to so many as bedtime. The child's need to function the following day makes bedtime a crucial part of the day. Parents' complaints, which seem to outnumber those of children and adolescents, range from the young child's refusal to sleep alone to the adolescent's refusal to go to bed at a reasonable hour.

Although sleep issues can seem to parents like simple acts of defiance, about 20–25% of children and the majority of youth with various psychiatric disorders, such as PDD, depression, and ADHD, suffer from sleep disturbances, many of which significantly affect and are affected by their functioning. The effect of sleep disturbance on mood, cognition, and attention impact the patient's school functioning, family functioning, and health status.

Because the medicines reviewed in the other chapters often affect sleep, and because understanding the nature of sleep is important in understanding sleep disorders, the basics of sleep architecture is reviewed first. An overview of sleep disorders is then presented. Last, treatment is examined—first the basics of good sleep hygiene and behavioral intervention and then the commonly used sleep medicines. It should be noted, however, that there are currently no FDA-approved medications for treating the sleep disorders of children. Thus the use of all the drugs discussed in this chapter is off-label.

## Sleep Architecture

The state that we refer to as sleep is actually divided into two distinct states, rapid eye movement or REM sleep, and non-REM sleep. REM sleep, which is known as the time during which we do most of our dreaming, occurs periodically through the night, generally for longer periods as the night progresses. Non-REM sleep is divided into stages 1 through 3, stage 1 being light sleep and stage 3 being deep sleep or slow-wave sleep. (Previously non-REM sleep was divided into stages 1 through 4. Stages 3 and 4 were combined, however, and called stage 3.) As REM sleep increases through the night, stage 3 sleep decreases in duration. Interestingly, stage 3 increases in duration when one is sleep-deprived, as if one has to make up for lost deep sleep.

When one falls asleep, one typically starts for a brief period in stage 1, what we commonly refer to as sleeping lightly, during which time breathing and the heart rate both begin to slow. One then advances into stage 2, which overall occupies about 50% of sleep time in young adults, and then into stage 3, often referred to as deep sleep. After stage 3 sleep, one goes back up through stage 2 and then stage 1. One then typically finishes the cycle with a short period of REM sleep. This "ultradian" cycle of stages 1 through 3 and then back up to REM sleep typically takes about 90 minutes in adults (60 minutes in children). The cycle is then repeated, so that a night's sleep consists of about four or five cycles of stages 1–3, then stage 2, then stage 1, and a period of REM. At the end of each sleep cycle the person has a brief arousal before returning to sleep.

There are characteristic changes in the brainwaves during different stages of sleep, which are easily measured on an electroencephalogram (EEG). For example, stage 2 sleep is characterized by the presence of sleep spindles and K complexes, and stage 3 is often known as slow-wave sleep because of the presence of large, slow delta waves on the EEG.

The proportion of time spent in the different stages varies through development. Infants typically spend about 50% of sleep in REM. By the preschool years, this decreases to about 20%, where it remains until late in life. Similarly, stage 3 sleep is greatest in early childhood, then decreases in adolescence and further during adulthood.

Different stages of sleep are associated with different sleep disorders, as we'll see. In addition, different medicines, both those used to induce sleep as well as those used in the rest of psychiatry, affect the brain during different stages of sleep, with a variety of consequences.

# Sleep Disorders

A simple way of approaching the sleep disorders is to divide them into disorders of initiating and maintaining or timing of sleep, roughly capturing what DSM-IV calls the dyssomnias, and the disorders that occur during sleep, what DSM-IV calls the parasomnias. I also discuss enuresis (bedwetting) and the sleep difficulties associated with psychiatric disorders such as depression or ADHD. I do not discuss the sleep disorders caused by various medical disorders and substance abuse. I use DSM-IV categories as general orienting points, with the understanding that DSM-IV differs from the International Classification of Sleep Disorders–Revised Manual (ICSD-2). DSM-V will probably evolve closer to ICSD-2. (For an excellent review of all the pediatric sleep disorders and their treatments, see Mindell and Owens, *A Clinical Guide to Pediatric Sleep*.)

As a point of clarification, while many complain of insomnia, the subjective sense of having difficulty falling or staying asleep or waking early in the morning, this is a symptom, with a variety of possible causes, and not a disorder itself. This symptom must be distinguished from the bedtime problems about which many parents complain.

## Dyssomnias

The dyssomnias, or disorders of falling and remaining asleep, take a number of forms.

## *Primary insomnia*

Primary insomnia, the difficulty initiating or maintaining sleep, is a term that is falling into disuse. ICSD-2 uses the term "psychophysiologic insomnia," which is characterized by anxiety and excessive arousal around falling asleep. This disorder, which typically starts in young adulthood, not childhood, is manifested by excessive concern and tension over not being able to fall asleep. Behaviors such as tooth brushing, associated with the frustrating struggle of bedtime, begin to signal a learned physical tension. The more the person expects to have difficulty falling asleep, the more difficulty that person has.

In addition, ICSD-2 uses the term "behavioral insomnia of childhood" to refer to bedtime resistance with the delay of sleep onset or prolonged night awakenings. One type of behavioral insomnia is limit-setting sleep disorder, a disorder affecting about 5–10% of children and manifested by the inadequate enforcement of bedtime by the child's caregiver, which leads to the child's stalling or refusing to go to bed at an appropriate time or refusing to return to bed after a nighttime awakening. Fears described by the child are not the anxieties of a child with an anxiety disorder but are typically mild or nonexistent. The caregiver's difficulty setting limits might be due to his or her own psychological issues, including depression or alcohol abuse. Once the problem is solved, the child's actual sleep is normal. Aging tends to solve this problem, as teens tend to take charge of their own bedtimes.

Sleep-onset association disorder is another behavioral insomnia. The term refers to the onset of sleep being impaired by the absence of a particular object or set of circumstances. Children with this disorder might need to fall asleep with the television on or with the parent present. But paradoxically, when these needs are met, watching television or having a stimulating bedtime discussion with a caregiver might keep the child awake. Sleep-onset association disorder sometimes begins when a parent needs to be involved at bedtime, such as by carrying around an infant with colic or comforting the child with chronic ear infections.

With all the disorders of sleep onset, one must make sure that the parents have chosen a reasonable bedtime, as some parents try to cling to the early bedtime of toddlerhood for too long.

Another cause of insomnia is the voluntary sleep restriction of teens who purposely keep themselves awake to play computer games, check out Facebook, or do homework. This is often identified as a difficulty by parents more than by teens, who frequently deny the effect that minimal sleep has on them or state that they make up for lost nighttime sleep by napping in the afternoon or sleeping late on weekends.

Part of the issue is that adolescents' natural shift of their sleep-wake cycle to go to sleep later clashes with their need to be up early to be in school before 8 A.M. Another issue of course is that the adolescent's desire to socialize has been aided by modern technology which allows this to happen at any hour and from any distance. Now that phones are no longer tethered to the wall and are capable of being silenced or used as texting devices without anyone knowing, parents' control has waned considerably. The solution to this problem is not pharmacological.

### Primary hypersomnia

Primary hypersomnia is the experience of excessive sleepiness despite having had adequate nighttime sleep. I have not found this to be a frequent complaint by parents or children. In children, this complaint must be distinguished from the behavior of those children who are simply slow moving and lack endurance but are not truly sleepy during the day. Particularly in adolescents, hypersomnia must be differentiated from the developmentally normal daytime tiredness of some young people and, even more commonly, as we've seen, the daytime tiredness associated with the sleep deprivation that plagues most teens who go to bed too late and wake too early in the morning. These patients cure themselves, at least partially, by taking long naps after school or sleeping very late on the weekends.

### Narcolepsy

Narcolepsy is also seen infrequently by the general practitioner. It is characterized by daily "irresistible attacks of refreshing sleep" (DSM-IV, p. 567). These attacks are accompanied by either cataplexy, brief episodes of the loss of muscle tone, or by hallucinations or sleep paralysis at the beginning or end of sleep episodes (DSM-IV). This is often treated with stimulant medicines, such as methylphenidate, or with modafinil (see Chapter 6).

### Breathing-related sleep disorder

This is commonly referred to as sleep apnea, characterized by frequent snoring, which indicates a blockage in the flow of air during sleep. Children with sleep apnea are also noted to be restless sleepers who are tired during the day. A common cause of this blockage in children is enlarged tonsils and adenoids, which are treated by adenotonsillectomy. Obesity and other conditions that contribute to upper airway obstruction or decreased airway patency, such as craniofacial abnormalities, allergies ,and hypotonia, are also risk factors. Whatever the cause, the airway obstruction leads to frequent brief arousals during the night, many of which go unrecognized as such by the patient, who is not attaining a sufficient amount of deep sleep. This leaves the person tired and prone to falling asleep during the day. Understandably, the tired child might also seem unfocused during the day. For this reason, sleep apnea should be considered in children being evaluated for ADHD. If sleep apnea is suspected, the child should have a physical examination by the pediatrician, and evaluation by an otolaryngologist or sleep specialist should be considered.

### Circadian rhythm sleep disorder

This is characterized by a mismatch between the person's sleep-wake cycle and the demands of the environment, such as when one frequently changes time zones. Those who work with adolescents often see teens whose natural shift to going to sleep later conflicts with their need to awaken for school the next morning. This is not a dyssomnia. Some of these patients, however, have an exaggerated sleep phase delay (in ICSD-2, circadian rhythm sleep disorder, delayed sleep phase type), making it difficult to fall asleep before 2 or 3 A.M. and causing extreme difficulty in waking in the morning. As a result, some adolescents, particularly those who have an underlying psychiatric disturbance, may fall into an ongoing pattern of not attending school. This leads to a true shift of their sleep-wake cycle as they sleep during the day and stay awake at night, thus perpetuating their absence from school. Melatonin is sometimes used to shift the onset of sleep earlier. Treatment, however, can also include a plan to shift, and maintain, the patient's sleep-wake schedule to an earlier time.

## Parasomnias

The specific parasomnias of DSM-IV are nightmares, night terrors, and sleepwalking.

### *Nightmares*

Nightmares are a frequent experience of childhood. A minority of children, however, have persistent terrifying nightmares that interrupt sleep. Because dreams occur mostly during REM sleep, which is more prevalent late in the night, nightmares tend to occur during the second half of the night. There is no evidence-based treatment for nightmares. Some have tried psychotherapy to understand the meaning of these frightening dreams. Others have tried having children write down their own optimistic conclusion to a recurrent nightmare before bedtime as a way of encouraging a form of control. Still others have tried medicines, such as clonidine, to try to suppress REM sleep.

### *Night terrors*

Nightmares are frequently confused with night terrors. The latter occur during stage 3 sleep and therefore are more frequent during the early part of the night. Night terrors are characterized by screaming and thrashing, associated with a racing heart, sweating, or other signs of the activation of the autonomic nervous system. The person seems terrified but is essentially unresponsive to others and therefore inconsolable. A major difference between night terrors and nightmares is that the patient does not remember night terrors the next morning, but can often recall the nightmare. Night terrors often come in bouts lasting a few weeks, then stop until the next round.

Some have tried treating night terrors with medicine that suppresses stage 3 sleep, such as diazepam or a tricyclic antidepressant. Most often, however, night terrors are treated behaviorally. For example, if a child's night terrors occur at a predictable time, then about 30 minutes before that time the child is awakened to the point at which he or she can mumble. Doing this nightly for a few weeks seems to end that round of night terrors.

### *Sleepwalking*

Sleepwalking, or somnambulism, is characterized by episodes in which a person rises from bed and walks about, with a blank look, unresponsive to others. This occurs during stage 3 sleep. The person can be awakened only with difficulty and, as with night terrors, does not recall the incident. Many children have an episode of sleepwalking, but fewer have an ongoing problem with it. The most important treatment concern is ensuring that the person is safe. Thus, bolting doors in a manner that would make them difficult to open and guarding the person from stairways are obvious initial approaches. Again, some have tried treating sleepwalking with medicines that suppress stage 3 sleep and with waking the child 30 minutes prior to the predicted sleepwalking (as with night terrors).

### *Enuresis*

Enuresis is the medical term for bedwetting. It is common during the first three or four years of childhood. By about age 5, however, most children usually stay dry at night. Children who have an ongoing and frequent inability to control their urinating are diagnosed with primary enuresis. While this is not technically a sleep disorder, most children with enuresis void during nighttime sleep only, not during the day. Wetting occurs randomly at all times of the night.

Because with every year after 4 years old about 15% of bedwetting children will gain control of nighttime voiding, and because only about 2–3% of children experience wetting at 12 years old, the most common treatment approach is simply to wait it out. During this time, many parents will reassure the child that the situation will improve and remind the child that (because there is an inherited component) good old Uncle Joe had the same issue until he was 10 years old. They will not make a fuss over the wetting but simply develop a nonpunitive system, often involving the child, of cleaning up and going back to sleep.

Some children are treated with the bell-and-pad behavioral system, which is typically more successful in children aged 8 and older. While there are different ways of doing this, the essential component is a pad placed on the bed or in the pajama pants that, when wet, sets off a bell or buzzer to awaken the child. With practice over the course of about four to six weeks, children learn to awaken themselves when they feel a need to void. This system takes some time and effort but has been shown to be as effective as medicine.

The medicines used to treat enuresis have been the tricyclic antidepressant imipramine and DDAVP (desmopressin). Imipramine, which was discussed in Chapter 7 on antidepressants, can have significant side effects. When used for enuresis, however, it is taken at minimal doses (1–2.5 mg/kg in one bedtime dose or about 25 mg) and tends not to cause many side effects. While its mechanism of action in treating enuresis is unknown, imipramine is generally used for about four to six months and is effective approximately 50% of the time. Nevertheless, up to 50% of children will relapse (Practice Parameter on Enuresis, 2004). Even though imipramine has had FDA approval for the treatment of enuresis for decades, because of its known cardiac effects and toxicity in accidental overdose and the availability of DDAVP, it is not often used for enuresis anymore.

DDAVP is a synthetic analogue of the antidiuretic hormone (ADH) vasopressin, a naturally occurring hormone that helps the kidneys hold on to water during urine production. There is some evidence that children with enuresis have lower levels of ADH at night. It had been available as a nasal spray and a pill but is now used only in pill form. DDAVP comes in a 0.2 mg pill. Children are started on one pill and can be increased to three pills at bedtime. The drug is effective for about 10 to 12 hours, but the next day there is a compensatory increase in urine production. There have been very few significant difficulties using DDAVP, although theoretically water intoxication and an ensuing seizure is of concern. Monitoring the child's electrolytes is not felt to be necessary, but if other medical difficulties are present, this might be recommended (Practice Parameter on Enuresis, 2004).

Success rates on DDAVP range from 10% to 65%, but as with imipramine, there is a high relapse rate when the medicine is discontinued. Some children use DDAVP nightly, but many use it only on sleepovers or when away from home, to save them the embarrassment of bedwetting.

## Psychiatric Disorders

Most clinicians working with children with psychiatric disorders probably spend a fair amount of time treating children who have sleep difficulties attributable to their disorder. This includes children with mood disorders, pervasive developmental disorders, ADHD, and others. There is very little research to guide us in the best approach, however. And while child psychiatrists use some medicines more than others, a host of medicines, ranging from over-the-counter products to prescription medicines, are prescribed to treat insomnia.

About two thirds of children on the pervasive developmental disorder spectrum experience sleep difficulties. These might include difficulty falling asleep, difficulty staying asleep, or irregular sleep-wake cycles.

Sleep difficulties are a key feature and one of the diagnostic criteria of depression; about two thirds of depressed children also have difficulty initiating or remaining asleep. The typical story is of a depressed teen who gets into bed at 11 P.M. but doesn't fall asleep until 2 or 3 A.M. A smaller but still significant number will wake early in the morning or be excessively lethargic and nap during the day. Some might have persistent insomnia, which might predict a relapse into depression.

The key element in treating the insomnia of the depressed youngster is to treat the underlying depression. It is sometimes necessary, however, to treat persistent insomnia separately from the depression. Sedating antidepressants treat the insomnia directly as well as the depression. But the most sedating of antidepressants were some of the tricyclic antidepressants, which have not been shown to be effective in youth depression. As a group, the SSRIs, which are used to treat youth depression, are sedating to a minority of patients. Some, namely paroxetine, are said to be more sedating but have not shown themselves to be effective in treating youngsters with depression, so to prescribe paroxetine to a child who is receiving another SSRI for depression raises the risk of the child's experiencing the serotonin syndrome. Child psychiatrists have tried a host of different medicines to treat the insomnia of depression, particularly trazodone, but also most of the medicines listed in the section on medicines later in this chapter.

A cardinal feature of bipolar disorder is diminished need for sleep during an episode of mania. Such patients often get by on about four hours of sleep, but more important, they don't feel the need for more. While high energy levels and lack of sleep are classic symptoms of bipolar disorder in adults, there is not an abundance of information about the sleep schedules of children with bipolar disorder, and what information does exist indicates that many children with bipolar disorder do not have a decreased need for sleep. Again, treatment of the underlying bipolar disorder is the most important treatment for the insomnia.

Because of their penchant for hyperactivity, children with ADHD are often assumed to be prone to needing less sleep or to insomnia. While parental reports of sleep problems are significantly more common in children with ADHD than in typically developing children, objective measures of sleep (actigraphy, polysomnography) in these children have not supported a significant difference in sleep architecture or sleep parameters. The exception is an increase in body movements during sleep and in night-to-night variability in sleep patterns.

Sleep issues in children with ADHD may be related to the presence of a comorbid primary sleep disorder, such as restless legs syndrome; the use of certain medications, such as the stimulants, which may delay sleep onset; or the presence of psychiatric comorbidities, such as anxiety, which in themselves may increase the risk of sleep problems. An increase in ADHD symptoms in the evening, as daytime ADHD medications wear off, may also interfere with sleep onset. Some children with ADHD appear to have a relative delay in circadian sleep-wake cycles, which may respond to an evening dose of melatonin. In addition, children with ADHD who are not sleeping might simply bring more parental attention to themselves than do their non-ADHD counterparts. Finally, many children with ADHD have never established sleep-promoting sleep habits (or sleep hygiene), such as a consistent bedtime and wake time, bedtime routine, and the avoidance of caffeinated beverages.

In any case, these children are frequently prescribed medicine to help them fall asleep. While antihistamines and melatonin are commonly used, the alpha agonists, such as clonidine, are used even more often. Many other medicines are also used.

## Sleep Evaluation

An evaluation of sleep should always precede determining a treatment plan. An evaluation includes an assessment of what the person is doing before bedtime. For younger children this includes determining when the parents come home from work and who participates in the nightly bedtime routine. For adolescents, it is important to determine after-school schedules, when homework is done, and how much time the teen spends interacting on Facebook, watching TV, and playing computer or video games. In addition, knowing whether the person takes caffeine or medicine that can interfere with sleep is crucial.

The following questions asked routinely will help the clinician screen for most major sleep issues. It should be noted, however, that parents are not always aware of what their child, especially their adolescent, experiences during the night.

Who is present at bedtime?

When is bedtime, and when are lights turned off with the expectation of falling asleep?

How much time elapses between lights off and actually falling asleep?

Once asleep, how often does the person wake during the night for more than a few minutes?

What time does the person finally awaken for the day? Are weekends different?

How much does the person snore?

What is the person's energy level during the day? How often and for how long does the person nap?

Is there evidence of other psychiatric disorders that might be interfering with sleep, such as depression, bipolar disorder, ADHD, an anxiety disorder, alcohol or drug use? Or is there a significant psychosocial stressor that might be interfering with feeling calm at bedtime?

What nonprescription remedies, including over-the-counter medicines and others, has the person tried or is the person using? In addition to asking parents, older children and adolescents should be asked directly about this.

## Sleep Hygiene and Behavioral Interventions

The overwhelming majority of sleep difficulties in childhood and adolescence should, after the evaluation and treatment of any underlying disorder, be treated with good sleep-promoting practices and behavioral intervention before sleep-inducing medicine is considered. These interventions, while not as immediately effective as medicine, have longer-lasting effects. Medicine is rarely the first choice of treatment.

In general, a good sleep routine and reasonable expectations are the essence of ensuring a good night's sleep. Understanding that one cannot try harder to fall asleep, as one can try harder to lift a heavy object, is crucial. To try harder to fall asleep only causes greater frustration and greater difficulty. Instead, one's goal is to put oneself in the mode in which one is most likely to fall asleep, namely a relaxed state in a comfortable bed in a dark, quiet room at a comfortable ambient temperature.

If one is sufficiently tired, one can fall asleep in the midst of a tornado of stimulation. In the long run, however, it is in the child's best interest to learn to fall asleep by using a routine that emphasizes being relatively unstimulated and feeling generally relaxed. For a child in our society, this usually means feeling at ease when alone, no small task for some children.

In addition to being comfortable and relaxed, the essence of good sleep habits, especially for children, includes setting a bedtime routine. The consistency of a routine helps diminish children's anxiety. Relaxing routines, such as listening to music or reading, are better than routines that are stimulating. Today, stimulating activities abound, ranging from watching TV to playing computer games to interacting on the Internet. The difficulty with these is not simply that they are emotionally stimulating. The light from the screen enters the eye and may suppress the normal nocturnal secretion of melatonin, thus delaying the onset of sleep. Although anyone who has fallen asleep with the TV on can attest that it is possible to override the changes in brain chemistry, light entering the eyes makes falling asleep more challenging. So in addition to the room being comfortable, it is better for it to be dark. Light exposure in the morning helps to suppress melatonin and increase wakefulness.

Exercise just before bedtime may raise body temperature, making the onset of sleep more difficult. Certain foods and medicines containing stimulating substances, such as caffeine and stimulant medicines, should also be avoided.

Besides good sleep hygiene, behavioral interventions are sometimes necessary to solve some of the difficulties of bedtime, such as limit-setting sleep disorder or sleep onset association disorder, disorders in which the child often does not want to sleep alone. Usually such children fall asleep easily if they are next to a parent, or even a sibling or friend. The solution to this problem is not medicine but behavior intervention. Parents need to work on a behavior plan to help the child feel secure yet capable of being alone.

The following summarizes one effective, if initially energy-intensive, manner of achieving this. After the usual bedtime routine, the parent puts the child to bed, then leaves for a brief period that the child can easily tolerate, perhaps a minute, reassuring the child that she will be back in one minute. The parent then returns in one minute, being sure not to become distracted by other tasks. If the child remains in bed until the parent returns, he receives another quick kiss goodnight and a sticker on a sticker chart. They should not engage in protracted conversation. The parent then repeats this, but returns after two minutes. Following the same procedure, the duration for which the child is left alone is very gradually increased. The time spent by the parent out of the child's room before returning plateaus at about 10 or 15 minutes. As the time alone increases, the child eventually falls asleep. The same procedure is used for a few days in row. The child usually becomes comfortable skipping the short-duration separation and settles into being left for 15 minutes. This is gradually discontinued.

## Sleep Medicines

While some specific medicines are used to treat some specific disorders of sleep, such as methylphenidate for narcolepsy, there are no FDA-approved sleep-inducing medicines for children. As we've seen, the first intervention is always environmental-behavioral. Sometimes, however, usually after behavioral intervention fails, a child with primary insomnia merits a trial of medicine.

When medicine is used, a few simple rules should be followed. Medicine should be used for the briefest period possible, usually a few weeks to a month. This is sometimes challenging because patients and parents are fearful of returning to a struggle with insomnia. Although the lowest dose should be used, because children metabolize medicine more efficiently, sometimes using a low dose leads to effectively underdosing, which can lead in turn to behavioral disinhibition in children. To avoid medication interactions, one should also always be aware of the other medicines taken by the patient. This obviously includes the possible interaction with illicit drugs, especially alcohol, sometimes used by teens. Last, as with all medicines, one should consider who is dispensing the medicine. Sometimes a child or, more likely, an adolescent, whose parents have already fallen asleep, medicates himself or herself and can be more likely to overmedicate, using the philosophy of "if some is good, more is better."

The following is a description of the medicines often used to treat insomnia in youth. Again, it should be stressed that none of these is FDA approved for use in children and adolescents, and many of these medicines have not been rigorously tested in the treatment of child or adolescent insomnia.

### Antihistamines

The antihistamines are the most commonly used medicines for inducing sleep in children and the ones most commonly recommended by pediatricians. Antihistamines are available both over-the-counter, most commonly diphenhydramine (but also chlorpheniramine), and by prescription, for example, hydoxyzine. Diphenhydramine, whose antihistamine effect also enables it to dry runny noses, is the substance in cold remedies that often helps patients fall asleep. In this instance, sleepiness is a side effect rather than a clinical effect. Yet this effect is what often leads people to take antihistamine-containing cold medicines, such as Tylenol PM, to help them fall asleep. The antihistamines are rapidly absorbed, bind to H1 receptors in the brain, and cause sedation. Newer antihistamines (such as loratidine) which do not cross the blood-brain barrier and therefore do not bind the brain's H1 receptors are not sedating.

The antihistamines are soporific but have minimal effect on sleep architecture. While they are effective at inducing sleep and decreasing nighttime awakenings in children (Russo, Gururaj, & Allen, 1976), a study of infants and toddlers, aged 6–15 months, found that diphenhydramine was no more effective than placebo in preventing nighttime awakenings (Merenstein et al., 2006). This provides an example of using a solution that looks good on paper but, when put to the test of a placebo-controlled study, does not work and only exposes infants to the (minimal) risk associated with diphenhydramine.

The side effects of antihistamines include sleepiness that can extend into the next day, a behavioral disinhibition that occurs in a minority of children, and anticholinergic effects, such as a dry mouth and nose. If used in an ongoing manner, tolerance can develop, necessitating the use of higher doses.

### Melatonin

Melatonin, another commonly used over-the-counter (OTC) sleep inducer, is actually a naturally occurring hormone normally secreted by the pineal gland in the brain. It has a natural cycle of ebbing and flowing during the course of the 24-hour day. Darkness stimulates the release of melatonin by the pineal gland. Melatonin goes to the suprachiasmatic nucleus of the anterior hypothalamus, a specialized part of the brain involved in regulating many of the body's hormones. At the hypothalamus, melatonin stimulates melatonin receptors (MT1 and MT2), which signal the body to prepare for the sleep that will be coming in a few hours. It does not significantly alter sleep architecture.

One can readily understand the mechanism of melatonin in the world of our prehistoric ancestors, when sleep was determined by the darkness, which followed the setting of the sun. Today people take melatonin pills, which essentially supplement their natural levels of melatonin. There is some evidence that those with insomnia have lower levels of melatonin.

Melatonin has two mechanisms of action. The first and more significant to normal biology is that, as noted above, it signals the coming of sleep, beginning its increase by mid-afternoon. (Therefore, supplementing one's naturally occurring melatonin is useful in people who need to readjust their circadian rhythm, for example, those who do shift work, travel to different time zones, or have delayed sleep phase syndrome.) The second mechanism is actually a useful side effect. Namely, because melatonin is slightly sedating, when given at bedtime it helps the person fall asleep.

Melatonin is not a medicine but a "supplement" sold at health food stores, and as such it is not subject to FDA approval as a medicine. Nevertheless, it has been studied and found effective in groups of patients, such as those with ADHD, although which mechanism is at work is unclear.

The widespread use of melatonin has given many a sense that the side effects are minimal. There are, however, some effects that need to be recognized. Theoretically, the extra melatonin one takes in a pill might suppress some of the other functions of the hypothalamus. Therefore, if one stops taking melatonin abruptly, the hypothalamus might suddenly be kicked back into action. This might lead to a sudden increase in the other hormones regulated by the hypothalamus, in particular those that regulate the sexual changes of puberty, causing the onset of these changes before they are expected. Again, this is a theoretical side effect, but it reminds us that even OTC substances may have unintended biological effects.

In addition, because the substance is not regulated by the FDA and therefore not held to the same standards as medicines, commercially available melatonin pills might vary in strength from one company to the next. The most commonly reported side effects are sedation (although that might be a benefit) and headache. Melatonin has been reported to increase seizures in the developmentally disabled but also to help the sleep of children with seizures, so its effect on the seizure threshold is unclear.

Because there are two mechanisms of action, there are two ways of using melatonin. The first, and the one that is consistent with its natural role in the body, is to take approximately 0.5 mg about five hours before bedtime, thus helping the naturally occurring increase in endogenous melatonin signal the brain to prepare for sleep. This is the way melatonin is used to help advance the sleep phases of adults. The second way melatonin is administered, and the more common way I have seen parents administer it to their children, is to give it at bedtime, since it is sedating. The doses used for this purpose range from about 2 mg to 5 mg, with higher doses if needed (Kratochvil & Owens, 2009).

Ramelteon is a prescription synthetic melatonin receptor agonist that acts selectively at two subtypes of melatonin receptors. Although it has been approved for the treatment of insomnia in adults, there have been no trials of this medicine in children, beyond case reports.

### Benzodiazepines

As we've seen in my discussion of the treatment of anxiety, the benzodiazepines effect a change at the GABA type A receptors in the brain, GABA being a significantly inhibiting neurotransmitter. There are a number of different benzodiazepines, some of which are approved for inducing sleep in adults. The most commonly discussed difference among the benzodiazepines is their duration of action, which ranges from short acting through intermediate acting to long acting. This is an important distinction because the longer-acting medicines are more likely to cause sedation the following day and also tend to build up more if used for many days in a row.

The benzodiazepines help people fall asleep faster and stay asleep. They also disrupt slow-wave, or stage 3, sleep. This suppressant effect on slow-wave sleep has led to trials of benzodiazepines in children with stage 3 parasomnias, such as sleep terrors or sleepwalking. Although benzodiazepines are rarely indicated for insomnia in children, their antianxiety and antiseizure effects are a benefit to a highly select group of children.

The duration of action of different benzodiazepines affects the patient in different ways. The longer-acting benzodiazepines help the person through the night, but they can lead to daytime sleepiness and impaired functioning. This might affect school performance but would be particularly dangerous in teens who drive. The shorter-acting benzodiazepines help the patient fall asleep, but they sometimes wear off during the night, leading to rebound awakening in the middle of the night.

Although the use of benzodiazepines is rarely indicated in children, when they are used, lorazepam is often a first choice because it is FDA approved for sedation, if not sleep induction, in children. Usually lorazepam is started at 0.25–0.5 mg at bedtime. The absorption time, duration of action, and time the medicine takes to begin to work are all important considerations in choosing a sleep medicine. The various benzodiazepines take varying amounts of time to reach their maximal blood level.

There are a number of side effects of which one should be mindful when using the benzodiazepines. Most obviously, they are sedating, and so must be used cautiously at times when alertness is important, such as when driving. It is especially important to caution patients about mixing benzodiazepines with other sedating substances, such as some medicines and alcohol, which could lead to excessive sedation or depress important vital functions such as breathing. Cognitively, as mentioned above, the benzodiazepines can have a blunting effect. In particular, this can manifest as an anterograde amnesia, or difficulty forming new memories. In addition, a small group of children can become behaviorally disinhibited on benzodiazepines. This might manifest as agitation and crying.

Last, the potential for tolerance (the need for higher doses), abuse, and dependence must always be considered. This side effect severely limits the use of benzodiazepines in youth and must be carefully weighed, especially before they are used to treat drug- or alcohol-abusing adolescents. For those who do use benzodiazepines for a protracted time, their abrupt discontinuation raises the risk of rebound seizures.

## Other Benzodiazepine Receptor Agonists

This group of relatively recently developed medicines, including short-acting zolpidem (Ambien) and zaleplon (Sonata), which are approved for sleep initiation insomnia, and longer-duration eszopiclone (Lunesta) and controlled-release zolpidem (Ambien CR), which are approved for sleep maintenance in adults, has become very commonly used by adults. They attach to GABA type A receptors, but unlike the benzodiazepines, they very selectively attach to GABA type A receptor complexes containing alpha1 subunits. Therefore, not only are these medicines sleep inducing, but also, because they do not bind to other receptors, they are without some of the other effects of the benzodiazepines, such as muscle relaxation and seizure prevention. Their use also does not seem to affect sleep architecture significantly.

These medicines have been studied minimally in children. In a double-blind, placebo-controlled study, Blumer and colleagues (2009) found zolpidem to be no better than placebo at helping children and adolescents with ADHD get to sleep. Because of the lack of data, the pediatric use of these medicines must be guided by the adult literature. As I have previously noted, this is potentially risky. Kratochvil and Owens (2009) note that some children have experienced disinhibition, including hallucinations, particularly if these medicines are used at too low a dose. I have received a few calls from parents whose children have acted in a bizarre manner after taking these medicines, sometimes administered by well-meaning parents who have shared their own sleep medicines with their child.

These medicines differ from one another by their duration of action. For example, eszopiclone (Lunesta) has an elimination half-life of five to six hours, yet that of zaleplon (Sonata) is only one hour. That means that zaleplon is helpful for inducing sleep but not for helping one stay asleep through the night.

While these medicines have side effects, addiction and the need for increasing doses of medicine, as with the benzodiazepines, do not appear to be significant side effects.

## Alpha Agonists

These medications (clonidine and guanfacine) are among the most commonly prescribed sleep-inducing medicines by child psychiatrists and pediatricians and are used particularly in the treatment of insomnia in children with ADHD, although they have not been rigorously studied for this purpose and are not approved for the treatment of insomnia in either adults or children. Rather, as we saw in Chapter 6, they are used to treat high blood pressure in adults. Nevertheless, retrospective chart review and case report studies have suggested that they may be effective for treating insomnia in children.

Clonidine is the more sedating of the two, but also the shorter acting, so one is more likely to experience rebound awakening during the night. Thus clonidine is primarily used to shorten sleep onset.

While many use clonidine without unwanted side effects, it has a narrow therapeutic index, which means that there is a small difference between a beneficial dose and a toxic one. It can also potentially cause low blood pressure, so one should monitor pulse and blood pressure. Some clinicians will obtain an EKG before prescribing the alpha agonists. Because of the short half-life, the abrupt discontinuation of these medicines, particularly clonidine, can lead to rebound hypertension. Theoretically this might be an issue when clonidine is used with stimulants that can increase blood pressure. The short half-life can also cause awakening during the middle of the night.

During the 1990s clonidine was reported to be associated with the sudden death of a handful of children who were also taking methylphenidate. Ultimately, however, these cases were complex enough that a link between the medicines and sudden death could not be made.

The effect of the alpha agonists on sleep architecture are minimal, although they can reduce REM and slow-wave sleep. Both of these medicines have been reported to decrease nightmares in children with PTSD (Horrigan, 1996).

### Tricyclic Antidepressants

As we've seen in Chapter 7, there are a number of different tricyclic antidepressants, each of which affects different neurotransmitters to different extents. Therefore each causes a different set of effects, including side effects. The tricyclics have not been well studied as hypnotics in childhood. Although some of them (amitryptiline, doxepin) are quite sedating in adults, only doxepin is FDA approved for the treatment of insomnia. Because of their multiple side effects, including dry mouth, low blood pressure, potential cardiac arrhythmia (particularly at higher doses), and the risk of cardiotoxicity in accidental overdose, these medicines are not used as often as they once were. They also have significant effects on sleep architecture, suppressing REM and stage 3 sleep. The REM suppression can lead to REM rebound and nightmares if the medicines are abruptly discontinued. The tricyclics might exacerbate restless legs syndrome (Kratochvil & Owens, 2009).

### Trazodone

This is a sedating antidepressant, which has been used frequently to treat insomnia in adults without being FDA approved for this indication. It works by blocking histamine receptors and inhibiting the binding of serotonin. It suppresses REM sleep and possibly increases stage 3 sleep. It is metabolized by the enzyme CYP 2D6, which must be considered if the patient is taking other drugs that influence this enzyme.

There is no controlled research of trazodone as a soporific in children. In adults, the dosing usually starts at 50 mg at bedtime (about half the typical antidepressant dose), which can be increased in 50 mg increments to 200 mg at bedtime. In children, without the benefit of research supporting or even guiding its use, trazodone should be started at 25 mg, probably not to exceed 150 mg.

Side effects in adults include sedation the following morning and lowered blood pressure, which could lead to dizziness. A rare but very serious side effect of trazodone is priapism, or a sustained penile erection. This is considered an emergency that requires immediate medical attention.

### Mirtazapine

Mirtazapine is another sedating antidepressant used off-label for insomnia in adults. It is an antagonist at the serotonin 2 receptor and an antihistamine. There are no controlled data supporting its use in children. In adults it is used at 7.5–15 mg at bedtime.

### Quetiapine

While the SGAs have generally not been used to treat insomnia, because it is short-acting and sedating, quetiapine has been used for this purpose. Because of the side effects associated with most SGAs, however (see Chapter 8), one must be prudent in the use of quetiapine for this purpose. In general, I limit my use of quetiapine for sleep to patients who I believe would otherwise benefit from it, in which case solving insomnia is simply an added benefit. In these cases, starting doses of quetiapine, about 50 mg at night, is sometimes beneficial.

See Table 10.1 for dosage recommendations for the various sleep medicines discussed in this chapter.

### Other Medicines

Although many other medicines have been used by practitioners treating children, either there is no significant research supporting their use or they are used only infrequently in children. Barbiturates, which had been used in adults, are no longer used because of side effects. And chloral hydrate, which had been used in children, is used only short-term because of possible liver damage. Some herbal preparations, such as valerian root, St. John's wort, and *Humulus lupulus* (hops), have shown some efficacy in adult or pediatric studies, or both, while there are safety concerns with others, such as kava and tryptophan.

**TABLE 10.1 Sleep Medicines**

| Brand name | Generic name | Dose range |
|---|---|---|
| **Over the oounter** | | |
| | melatonin | 0.5–5 mg/day |
| Benadryl | diphenhydramine | 25–100 mg/day |
| | chlorpheniramine | 4 mg/day |
| **By prescription** | | |
| *Antihistamines* | | |
| Atarax | hydroxyzine | 25–100 mg/day |
| *Alpha agonists* | | |
| Catapres | clonidine | 0.025–.30 mg/day |
| Tenex | guanfacine | 0.25–4 mg/day |
| *Antidepressants* | | |
| Desyrel | trazodone | 25–150 mg/day |
| Remeron | mirtazapine | 7.5–15 mg/day |
| Elavil | amitriplypline | 25–50 mg/day |
| *Antianxiety medicines* | | |
| Ativan | lorazepam | 0.25–2 mg/day |
| Klonopin | clonazepam | 0.25–1.0 mg/day |
| *Benzodiazepine receptor agonists* | | |
| Ambien | zolpidem | 5–10 mg/day |
| Sonata | zaleplon | 5–10 mg/day |
| Lunesta | eszopiclone | 1–3 mg/day |
| *Melatonin receptor agonist* | | |
| Rozerem | ramelteon | 8 mg/day |
| *Antipsychotics* | | |
| Seroquel | quetiapine | 25–100 mg/day |

Note: This table is intended only as a guideline as there is minimal, if any, research on using some of these medicines to induce sleep in children. None of these medicines is FDA approved for treating sleep disorders in youth. Therefore doses are based on use in adults, which is sometimes off-label.

# Case Examples

*Case 1: Scott is a perfectionistic eighth-grader. His mother complains that Scott does not get into bed until 1 A.M. and then has difficulty falling asleep. A careful history reveals that Scott is excessively concerned about his school performance and doesn't start his homework until after ice hockey practice every evening. So he's doing homework from about 8 P.M. until 12:30 A.M. Scott then needs a half hour to check his e-mail before he goes to sleep.*

*Comment:* Scott has sleep initiation insomnia, which might be linked to an anxiety disorder that lies beneath his perfectionism. This might be exacerbated by the normal circadian-based shift to a later sleep onset time occurring as he enters puberty. Scott presents a good example of the importance of taking a careful history. Medicine is not the answer to Scott's problem. His initial treatment should include advice regarding sleep hygiene and cognitive-behavioral measures targeted toward reducing anxiety and promoting relaxation. The intervention should focus on teaching Scott to manage his schedule and the demands made on him by school.

*Case 2: Drew is 8 and chock-full of ADHD symptoms. During the day he tries to be compliant but is all over the place. He can't settle down in the evening, so his frustrated parents finally made a rule that he doesn't have to go to bed, he only has to stay in his room. Drew finally falls asleep at about midnight. Then he's awake at 6:30 every morning. Drew's hyperactivity responds to a stimulant during the day. His pediatrician adds clonidine at bedtime to his medication regimen.*

*Comment:* Many children with ADHD have difficulty settling down at bedtime. Several possible contributing factors should be considered, including a direct effect on sleep of the stimulant medication and a possible return of or even rebound increase in ADHD symptoms after the stimulant has worn off in the evening. A sleep disorder such as restless legs syndrome, which has been linked to ADHD symptoms, should also be considered. Drew's pediatrician took a fairly common approach of using an alpha agonist at bedtime. When standard sleep-inducing medicines are not effective, some clinicians will try giving a small dose of the stimulant before bedtime. Although insomnia is a side effect of stimulants, paradoxically a stimulant in the evening helps settle some children at bedtime.

> Case 3: Tara is 17 years old and stays awake until about 12:30 every night checking out Facebook. Sometimes her friends will text her after she's gone to sleep. She's up at 6 A.M. for school every morning, although she does "catch up" on some weekend mornings. She has a long history of inattention and is given a trial of amphetamine, which, she says, helps her focus in class, though she also reports that she feels awake only on the days when she takes amphetamine. Her psychiatrist, who has been urging her toward better sleep habits, wonders what the amphetamine is actually treating.

*Comment:* The age of electronics ushered in the 24-hour day, with its almost addictive use of everything from TV to computers to cell phones. While this sometimes causes obvious difficulties, such as sleepy drivers, the impact of chronic sleep deprivation can be subtler. Sleep deprivation does not cause ADHD. Insufficient sleep does, however, have a negative impact on anyone's attempts to pay attention.

> Case 4: Maria is 16 and a junior in high school. Her mother notes that Maria has been napping most afternoons for about three hours and not going to sleep until 1 A.M. Getting Maria out of bed at 6 A.M. for school is a daily struggle. Maria has also been avoiding her friends. Her grades have plummeted, and she seems not to enjoy dancing as she has in the past. Maria is diagnosed with depression and started on fluoxetine. Three months later her mood is improved, she has stopped napping, and she is going to bed between 11 P.M. and midnight, like many of her friends.

*Comment:* The sleep difficulties of some patients represent a primary underlying psychiatric disorder, in this case depression, associated with a secondary insomnia. Given the bidirectional relationship between psychiatric disorders and insomnia, however, this nomenclature implying causality is gradually being replaced. Nevertheless, many psychiatric disorders, such as bipolar disorder, anxiety disorders, and psychosis, can cause a disrupted sleep schedule. This underscores the need for a careful history and examination of those for whom sleep is the initial complaint.

## Chapter 11

# Pharmacotherapy of Miscellaneous Disorders and Conditions

In this chapter we consider a number of conditions and disorders in children and adolescents that fall outside the categories discussed in previous chapters.

## Trichotillomania

Trichotillomania is a disorder characterized by the repeated pulling out of hair. This often leads to noticeable hair loss such as bald patches on the scalp or missing eyelashes or eyebrows. Pulling out pubic and leg hair can also be involved. This hair loss can lead to teasing by peers and frustrated parental efforts to bring a cessation to the hair pulling. Patients are often embarrassed about discussing this behavior, so history taking must be done gently, lest the child withdraw and deny. Bloch (2009) reports that the condition affects about 1–3% of the population, with a waxing and waning course often beginning at 11–13 years old. Like patients with tics and compulsions, some patients report an urge to pull that precedes the actual hair pulling or relief after pulling. These features have led some to wonder whether trichotillomania is similar to tic disorders and OCD. Many consider hair pulling by preschoolers to be distinct from trichotillomania in older children and adults (Bloch, 2009).

The assessment of hair pulling requires the clinician to evaluate carefully the circumstances in which the behavior most commonly occurs, any instruments used to pull hairs, and the feelings and thoughts that precede and follow the actual pulling, such as whether there is a conscious urge to pull. In addition, a dermatologic evaluation might be necessary to rule out any skin disorders.

The treatment of trichotillomania in children, especially the pharmacologic treatment, is based on case reports and uncontrolled trials. Before medicine is prescribed, however, habit reversal therapy (HRT) should be considered. This is a behavioral therapy in which the patient learns to become aware of the times when and places where pulling is more likely to occur and of the urges that precede hair pulling. Competing behaviors, those that cannot be performed while pulling, are then substituted. HRT has been proven more effective than fluoxetine and clomipramine in adults (Bloch et al., 2007).

If HRT fails to help the child with trichotillomania, families often want to turn to medicine. Because of the anxiety associated with trichotillomania, the SSRIs are often considered. It should be noted, however, that there are no controlled studies proving the efficacy of the SSRIs in children with this disorder. And although initial case reports and uncontrolled trials suggested that the SSRIs might be effective, three double-blind, placebo-controlled studies failed to find efficacy of the SSRIs (Bloch, 2009). As with tics, the waxing and waning of hair pulling can make proving efficacy of any treatment a challenge. At this time, given the lack of efficacy in adult trichotillomania, the SSRIs should not be used to treat this disorder in children, unless one is treating a comorbid diagnosis of anxiety or depression.

Bloch and colleagues (2007) do note that HRT was more effective than clomipramine, and clomipramine was more effective than placebo in treating adults. Whether this potential benefit outweighs the risks of using clomipramine in a child is a clinical judgment. There is also some concern that the effectiveness of clomipramine might diminish over time.

The effectiveness of naltrexone, an opioid antagonist that is FDA approved for the treatment of alcohol dependence and opiate dependence, has been suggested by positive case reports. As we've seen throughout this book, however, it's a long way from case reports to successful controlled studies.

Finally, N-acetylcysteine, an amino acid that modulates glutamate, has been shown in a 12-week double-blind, placebo-controlled study to be effective in treating adults with trichotillomania, with a positive effect occurring by six weeks of treatment (Grant, Odlaug, & Kim, 2009). While it must be remembered that this has not been proven in children, N-acetylcysteine has been used safely in the treatment of acetaminophen overdose in children (Bloch, 2009). Side effects include nausea and flatulence, and it must be used with caution in children with asthma. N-acetylcysteine can be bought as a dietary supplement, but it requires twice-daily dosing.

# Selective Mutism

Like trichotillomania, selective mutism is a disorder that resembles another, better understood disorder, in this case social anxiety disorder. For selective mutism, however, unlike trichotillomania, the similarities help decide on treatment.

Selective mutism is characterized by the child's refusal to speak in public, despite speaking normally at home. The classic presentation of this disorder is a child who speaks fully within his or her family but does not speak to teachers or peers in school. Although the prevalence of selective mutism is just under 1%, if one includes children who speak at a very low volume or very minimally, the prevalence is probably higher. The silence of children with selective mutism is not caused by a language disorder or an inability to speak the required language. My experience has been that the child with selective mutism is often highly persistent, so that, despite the many and varied attempts of parents to coax verbalizations, the child stubbornly clings to silence. Some evidence suggests that many children with selective mutism outgrow this disorder. For those who do not, it can be increasingly debilitating, as these children can be extremely shy and self-conscious in front of others.

Although the difficulties of many children remit, Steinhausen and colleagues (2006) have reported that many have ongoing psychiatric symptoms, such as social anxiety. Dummit and colleagues (1997) found that all 50 of the children with selective mutism they studied also had social phobia, and about half had another anxiety disorder as well. In addition, the parents of children with selective mutism have an elevated rate of social phobia (Chavira, 2007).

The treatment of selective mutism is primarily behavioral, especially since many young children outgrow the disorder. This behavioral treatment revolves around reinforcing the child for slowly increasing vocalizations, while being careful not to reinforce the patient's silence. This means, for example, not allowing other children in the class to speak for the child. If, however, the patient is not responding to this treatment, consideration should be given to starting the patient on an SSRI. In a small double-blind, placebo-controlled study, Black and Uhde (1994) showed some signs that fluoxetine was effective in helping these children. To the extent that selective mutism is an anxiety disorder, particularly a form of social anxiety, a trial of an SSRI is justified if behavioral intervention is ineffective.

## Eating Disorders

In this section I review two eating disorders: anorexia nervosa (AN) and bulimia nervosa (BN). AN is characterized by excessive attempts at weight loss, such as by overly restrictive dieting and overexercising, and a distorted body image, that is, seeing oneself as obese despite being severely underweight. AN typically begins during early adolescence. It requires a comprehensive medical exam at the outset. BN is characterized by binging episodes, consisting of excessive food intake, followed by purging behaviors such as vomiting and laxative use.

The treatment of AN is complex, involving behavioral therapy and family therapy, and will not be reviewed here. It should be noted, however, that weight restoration is a key to treatment, as the weight loss itself can cause changes in mood and other symptoms.

The pharmacological treatment of both adults and adolescents with AN is essentially unsupported, although medicines might be used for comorbid disorders. Treatment with SSRIs during the initial stages of AN has not been shown to be effective in the treatment of adults (Attia et al., 1998). Treatment after weight restoration was shown to be effective in one small study of adults (Kaye et al., 2001) but ineffective in another larger study (Walsh, Kaplan, & Attia, 2006). There are no randomized trials of medicine to treat adolescents with AN (Lock, 2009). As a result, there is no support for the use of medicines in the direct treatment of AN in adolescents at this writing. The use of medication, even for comorbid conditions, might be deferred until the patient has gained sufficient weight to establish the extent to which weight loss was causing the psychiatric symptoms.

The treatment of bulimia nervosa is also multidimensional, especially since patients with BN often have a multitude of cormorbid conditions. The treatment is usually based in family therapy or a variety of individual therapies, such as CBT. Unlike in the case of treating AN, pharmacotherapy does have a role in the treatment of BN. It should not, however, supplant cognitive-behavioral therapy and other nonpharmacological therapies.

Research supports the use of a variety of medicines to lower the rate of bingeing and purging. In a study of adults with BN (Fluoxetine Bulimia Nervosa Collaborative Study Group, 1992), fluoxetine effectively decreased bingeing and vomiting. Treatment with 60 mg daily was more effective than with 20 mg, and both were superior to placebo. And in a small open study of adolescents (Kotler, 2003), fluoxetine at 60 mg daily, combined with supportive psychotherapy, was found to be effective in reducing the symptoms of BN.

Walsh and colleagues (1988) found MAOIs to be effective in treating women with BN. Given the impulsivity of many of these patients, however, treating adolescents with BN with an MAOI should be restricted to extreme situations. Similarly, the TCAs have been found to be effective but are generally reserved for situations in which other medicines, such as the SSRIs, have failed. In addition, Horne and colleagues (1988) found bupropion to be effective in treating BN. Nevertheless, 4 of 55 patients experienced seizures, leading the authors to advise against using bupropion for BN. Overall, SSRIs, and arguably other medicines in select situations, might be a part of the treatment of adolescent BN, particularly for comorbid conditions. It should not, however, supplant family or various individual therapies as the first or only treatment.

# PANDAS

PANDAS is the acronym for pediatric autoimmune neuropsychiatric disorders associated with strep. This debated condition is characterized by tics or obsessions and compulsions in a child who has had a history of a streptococcal infection. The proposed mechanism of this disorder is that the antibodies the child produces to fight a strep infection are then turned against the basal ganglia of the child's brain, leading to symptoms. Given the large number of children infected with strep and the large number of children with transient tics, one can readily imagine that the coexistence of tics and a strep infection leads to great diagnostic confusion among parents and professionals alike.

The group of researchers at the National Institute of Mental Health (NIMH) who made the association between strep and OCD that led to the description of PANDAS laid out fairly exact criteria to be met before the child is given the PANDAS label (Swedo et al., 1998). These include the presence of OCD or a tic disorder with a prepubescent onset; an episodic course of these symptoms, including neurological abnormalities, such that, on more than one occasion, these symptoms occur in association with a group A beta-hemolytic streptococcal infection documented by a positive throat culture, or elevated anti-streptococcal antibodies. The tics and obsessions and compulsions seen in PANDAS are indistinguishable from those of a child with a tic disorder or OCD (Swedo & Grant, 2004).

The researchers at NIMH describe a course of dramatic increases and decreases in the symptoms of those with PANDAS, not the ongoing, fairly consistent, if waxing and waning, symptoms of those with a tic disorder or OCD. Often there is an explosive and sudden onset of symptoms, unlike the typical gradual onset of those with a tic disorder or OCD. They describe a slow improvement followed by a symptom-free period, during which throat cultures are negative or strep antibodies are not increasing, until the symptoms return during a subsequent strep infection. Because strep infections are ubiquitous in children, one episode that seems to associate an infection with symptoms is insufficient to diagnose PANDAS.

It is beyond the scope of this book to explore the controversy about PANDAS. Its presumptive treatment is worth noting, however. It is recommended that tics and obsessions and compulsions be treated as they would ordinarily be treated. That is, obsessions and compulsions can be treated with CBT or an SSRI, and tics can be treated with an appropriate medication, if necessary. While all agree that acute strep infections should be treated with antibiotics, the use of ongoing antibiotics to prevent a recurrence of strep is debated. In extreme unremitting cases, plasmapheresis or intravenous immunoglobulin is used. Generally this is done only at locations that have a particular expertise in researching and treating PANDAS.

## Disruptive Behavior Disorders: Oppositional Defiant Disorder and Conduct Disorder

The disruptive behavior disorders include oppositional defiant disorder (ODD) and conduct disorder (CD). They are often comorbid with ADHD, such that about 60% of children with ADHD also suffer with ODD. Fewer children with ADHD have CD.

ODD is characterized by a persistent level of defiance, anger, and argumentativeness. Often these are children with a "difficult" temperament, including a high degree of rigidity, persistence, and reactivity, characteristics often resulting in explosive tantrums that persist longer than the transient "summer storms" of other children. They are seen as irritable and easily provoked.

Some parents incorrectly identify their child as suffering with ODD because they see the child as oppositional or defiant. Children who merit a diagnosis of ODD, however, present with a level of defiance that leads to significant clinical dysfunction and is well beyond the average child's age-appropriate defiance. These are children who regularly bring their mothers to tears or their fathers to trying to outmuscle them in a fruitless attempt to control their misbehavior, an approach that leads to more problems than it solves. Considerable strain is put on relationships with siblings. Previously stable marriages are rubbed raw by the parents' frustration and discord over what to do with their child. Boys with ODD are at greater risk for progressing to conduct disorder (Rowe et al., 2002).

Conduct disorder differs from ODD in that the diagnostic emphasis is placed on the child's or adolescent's pattern of breaking societal rules. This includes aggression toward other people and animals, destroying property, stealing, cutting school, or running away from home. Young people with conduct disorder tend to have a poor prognosis.

A host of factors increase the risk for the disruptive behavioral disorders. These include medical factors (such as the mother's smoking during pregnancy), social factors (such as spending time with peers who engage in deviant behaviors), family factors (such as parents' use of alcohol and drugs), and cognitive factors (such as low intelligence). The extent to which ODD and CD share risk factors remains to be seen.

Although knowledge of risk factors might lead to better means of prevention, and while behavioral treatments are being investigated, there is no clear treatment approach to the disruptive behavior disorders. We will focus simply on the role of medication with the understanding that these patients probably represent a heterogeneous group with a variety of symptoms and comorbidities.

In using medicine to treat those with disruptive behavior disorders, the clinician must decide on the target symptoms. There are no medicines to stop stealing, cutting school, or breaking curfew. Usually, medicines are aimed at the symptoms of irritability, explosive tantrums, and aggression. It is important to note that this explosive aggression is often effectively treated by hospitalization when this is indicated. In fact, the symptoms of about half of these patients will be significantly reduced by hospitalization without the use of medication (Schur et al., 2003). While not implicating environmental circumstances as the cause of the aggression, this finding does highlight the importance of the environment in fanning the flames of any predisposition to volatility.

Unfortunately, aggression is not a simple concept. Rather it is a hornet's nest of confusion and debate. One common way of characterizing aggression is to see it as either predatory or reactive. On the one hand, predatory aggression is planned, unprovoked, and done with the intent to hurt, and usually leaves the predator without guilt. On the other hand, reactive aggression is impulsive, unplanned, and often done at a moment's notice when the person's emotions are provoked. Reactive aggression often leaves the aggressor feeling guilty and contrite. Predatory aggression is the aggression associated with classic CD that frequently develops into antisocial personality disorder. Reactive aggression is associated with a number of disorders, including ODD but also ADHD, PDD, and bipolar disorder.

The medical literature often does not take note of the nature of the aggression of the subjects being studied. Nevertheless, the type of aggression should be taken into account in deciding how to treat it. Most clinicians do not consider medicine to be very effective for treating predatory aggression, although, given the negative consequences of predatory aggression for the predator and the victim, medicine has some research support and might be tried. Of note, however, patients treated in studies of conduct disorder also often suffer from extreme irritability, mood lability, and explosiveness. In other words, it may be reactivity, not simple premeditated predatory aggression, that is being treated.

In a double-blind, placebo-controlled trial, Campbell and colleagues (1995) have shown that lithium is effective in reducing aggression in hospitalized children with conduct disorder who had not responded to other treatments, such as stimulants and FGAs. And Donovan and colleagues (2000) have shown divalproex to decrease aggression in youth with conduct disorder. In addition, in a pilot study, Findling and colleagues (2000) have shown that risperidone is effective in treating youth with conduct disorder. Notably, in a large and longer-term study, Reyes and colleagues (2006) found that risperidone prevented a relapse of aggression over a period of two years, although part of this study was open-label.

Though done on a wide variety of patients, research more strongly supports the use of some medicines rather than others for reactive aggression. Studies examining the use of SGAs to treat aggression have shown at least risperidone to be very effective. Unfortunately, these studies have tended to limit their focus on patients with low-normal intelligence or those with autism. For example, in an eight-week double-blind, placebo-controlled trial, McCracken and colleagues (2002) found that risperidone was helpful in reducing aggression in 101 autistic youth. In this study, aggression continued to diminish throughout the entire eight weeks of the study. In a double-blind, placebo-controlled study, Snyder and colleagues (2002) showed risperidone to be effective in decreasing aggression in a group of children with subaverage IQs. And Aman and colleagues (2002) found that risperidone was helpful in reducing the aggression of 118 children with subaverage intelligence. Positive effects were also noted in studies examining other SGAs, such as olanzapine. These, however, have usually involved a small number of subjects or were chart reviews or open-label studies.

The frequent comorbidities of children with ODD can lead to significant diagnostic and therapeutic confusion. The dysfunction on which the clinician focuses will affect the choice of treatment. Interestingly, recent research points to both emotional and motoric antecedents of ODD, albeit perhaps different types of ODD. Stingaris, Maughan, and Goodman (2010) found that high emotionality and high levels of activity at 3 years old each predicted ODD at about 7 years old, although the different antecedents were associated with different comorbidities with the ODD. Specifically, internalizing disorders were more often comorbid with the ODD when the child was previously seen as highly emotional, and ADHD (albeit not inattentive type) was more often comorbid when the child was previously seen as having high activity. This suggests that these different pathways to ODD might lead to different comorbidities and, possibily, different treatment approaches. This is demonstrated clinically by the clinician's frequent decision whether to treat the child with ODD by treating the underlying anxiety with an SSRI or treating the symptoms that represent ADHD with a stimulant.

While a trial of stimulants might lead to decreased impulsivity and improved attention span, research supports the efficacy of the stimulants in also improving compliance and decreasing disruptiveness, defiance, and aggression (MTA, 1999a; Klein et al., 2004). When ODD is associated with underlying anxiety, SSRIs are often considered. On still other occasions, the child's explosive temper and irritability dominate the presentation, and bipolar disorder might be diagnosed and a mood stabilizer or SGA prescribed. Although the diagnosis of bipolar disorder might be incorrect, these medicines might help anyway.

The beta blockers are a family of medicines used by some to control aggression, albeit off-label. The beta blockers are so named because they block the beta receptors of adrenergic neurons. There are a few subtypes of these receptors, which are located throughout the body, such as in the heart, muscles, lungs, and brain. Not all beta blockers are able to cross the blood-brain barrier into the brain, so only some have been used to treat aggression. More commonly, the beta blockers have been used in adults to treat high blood pressure and certain cardiac problems. Nevertheless, propanolol, in particular, has been shown in some case reports and open trials to decrease aggression.

The side effects of the beta blockers include slowed heart rate, mildly diminished blood pressure, and increased difficulty dilating the lung's bronchi. Therefore, blood pressure and pulse must be monitored, and children with asthma should avoid these medicines. Additional side effects include sedation, decreased blood sugar in diabetics, dizziness, and sleep disruption (Riddle, et al, 1999).

While there is minimal research on polypharmacy, many children with severe aggression are treated with, and the clinical situation sometimes demands, more than one medicine. In a small double-blind, placebo-controlled study of children with ADHD and aggression, Blader and colleagues (2009) have shown that children with ADHD and a disruptive behavior disorder whose aggression did not respond to a stimulant medicine, over eight weeks responded more frequently to the addition of valproic acid to the stimulant than to the addition of placebo.

In addition, the alpha agonists have been used to treat aggression. Clonidine and guanfacine, which have been used to treat the impulsive and hyperactive symptoms of ADHD, have been effective in diminishing the aggressive symptoms of these children (Raishevich, Pappadopulos, & Jensen, 2008). Although in a placebo-controlled study of children with ADHD and a comorbid disruptive behavior disorder Hazell and Stuart (2003) demonstrated decreased aggression using clonidine, more data is certainly needed.

Despite evidence of their efficacy, and because of their side effect profile, the FGAs, such as haloperidol and thioridazine, have largely fallen out of favor in treating aggression.

In short, without firm guidelines, the comorbid diagnosis and the extent and type of the aggression often help the clinician decide whether to use medicine and which medication should be used first. Trials of groups such as the stimulants or alpha agonists are fairly safe and easy. Many will save groups such as the SGAs and mood stabilizers for more intense aggression.

## Posttraumatic Stress Disorder

Posttraumatic stress disorder (PTSD) is a pathological response to having experienced an extreme traumatic event, such as involving a serious injury or being threatened with death. It is characterized by the reexperiencing of the traumatic event, for example, through intrusive recollections, nightmares, or the feeling that one is reliving the event. The person avoids reminders of the event and might feel detached or as if the future will be foreshortened. In addition, there are symptoms of hyperarousal, such as insomnia or irritability (DSM-IV, 1994).

PTSD is a complex disorder that is made more complex in children because their symptoms might differ according to their developmental level. For example, young children might relive the traumatic events through play, while older children might have more of a sense of how such trauma might affect their future. In addition, while some children experience single, well-circumscribed traumatic events, others experience chronic, ongoing, if sometimes subtle trauma. For example, being beaten up once is different from being hit on a daily basis.

Trauma affects the child in a variety of ways. Trauma, especially chronic trauma, impacts the developing brain. In addition, trauma affects the child's caregivers and entire family. Because children are highly sensitive to the mental state of their caretakers, they respond to their caretakers' response to the trauma. And because children are affected by their family's cohesion, the family's ability to stay together after the traumatic event also affects the child.

The most important interventions in treating, or preferably preventing, PTSD in children are psychosocial. Interventions such as keeping the child with his or her caretakers, trying to ensure that the caretaker maintains his or her best possible mental health, preventing further exposure to trauma, and giving the child a sense of control are all important in helping the child with PTSD. These are accomplished through a variety of therapies, such as trauma-focused CBT, and educational initiatives. The research on the treatment of children with PTSD will not be reviewed here.

Medicine has some role in this treatment, although pharmacologic treatment is generally not supported by significant research. In two placebo-controlled trials of sertraline (Robb et al, 2010; Cohen et al, 2007) medicine failed to best placebo treatment of PTSD in youth. Case studies have found the alpha agonists useful in decreasing the hyperarousal of these children. SGAs and mood stabilizers have been reported in case studies and open-label studies to be possibly effective in treating youth with PTSD. Interestingly, propanolol has also been studied with mixed results.

In short, research does not support the use of medicine to treat PTSD directly. Nevertheless, medicines are used in the treatment of isolated symptoms, with the knowledge that the underlying PTSD is probably better treated through CBT or another type of psychotherapy. For example, children with PTSD and sleep difficulties, whether insomnia or nightmares, are sometimes treated with medication, such as the alpha agonists, but this does not obviate the need for a broader therapeutic approach.

## Asperger's Disorder

Grouped with the pervasive developmental disorders, such as autistic disorder, Asperger's disorder is essentially a disorder of social relatedness. As such, it shares with autism some of the difficulties in social interactions, such as poor eye contact. Patients with Asperger's disorder, like those with autism, are also often preoccupied with a well-circumscribed interest or behavior. Nevertheless, Asperger's disorder is distinct from autism, lacking its language delays.

That said, while those with Asperger's have no language impairment and might even have expansive vocabularies, their use of language as a social tool can be lacking. Instead, those with Asperger's typically use language to lecture others about their narrow interest without heeding the, frequently waning, interest level of the listener.

Patients with Asperger's also tend to cling rigidly to certain routines. In addition, they often have low sensory thresholds, thus being very sensitive to the fit of their socks or to loud sounds or sudden noises. Patients with Asperger's also often have difficulty with visuospatial-oriented tasks and graphomotor skills, as well as other motor and cognitive abilities.

Asperger's is a relatively rare disorder with a prevalence of about 2 per 10,000, making it less common than autism. Nevertheless, it is a diagnosis that is commonly used. My impression is that this disorder is relatively easy for the untrained to misinterpret and consequently arrive at an incorrect diagnosis. In fact, children with Asperger's are not simply socially behind their peers but tend to have odd ways that can be off-putting to peers.

There is no medicine to treat the core dysfunction of those with Asperger's. Nevertheless, they are often brought to the attention of clinicians for one or more of several issues. These include inattention, irritable outbursts, and anxiety or sadness. Most of these difficulties should initially be dealt with at an environmental level. For example, if one understands the source of the child's outbursts as frustration caused by an inability to manage particular social relations, the first answer should be to help the patient manage socially, not to give medicine for irritability. The patient might be taught to use a rehearsed script to get through a certain social interaction.

When symptoms arise that require medicine, however, the symptoms should be treated as they otherwise would be, albeit with the realization that those with Aperger's (and other PDDs) sometimes respond differently to some medicines. When inattention is problematic, stimulants can be used, although as a group, patients with PDDs are more sensitive to certain side effects, such as irritability, and therefore more likely to discontinue the medicine. A small open-label study by Posey and colleagues (2006) did find atomoxetine useful in treating the ADHD symptoms of youth with PDD. Low doses of an SGA, such as risperidone, can be used to modulate extreme irritability, as they would be in treating someone with autistic disorder. Guanfacine, an alpha agonist, was found useful in decreasing hyperactivity in a small open-label study (Scahill, 2006).

An SSRI can be used to attempt to treat anxiety. However, while the SSRIs are effective in treating OCD and therefore are often used to try to diminish the compulsive behaviors of those with Asperger's, in a placebo-controlled study of 149 children and adolescents, King and colleagues (2009) have shown that the repetitive behaviors of patients with a variety of pervasive developmental disorders did not respond to citalopram, an SSRI. These children did demonstrate more side effects, such as impulsivity and insomnia.

All in all, my experience has been that the SGAs effectively decrease agitation, but that the SSRIs and stimulants, while sometimes effective, can often be disappointing.

# Drug and Alcohol Abuse

The treatment of adolescents for drug and alcohol abuse is multifaceted, requiring a team approach, and is therefore a topic unto itself. It will not be reviewed here. Medicine, however, can be involved in two ways. The first is to lessen symptoms during detoxification. This relatively new field has not been well studied in adolescents. The other is to treat the comorbid psychiatric disorders that frequently plague these adolescents. While the distinctions are clinically important, I will not distinguish here between types or combinations of substances abused. What is important is that I am talking about teens who merit a diagnosis of substance abuse, not normal adolescent experimentation.

In general, adolescents diagnosed with substance abuse are a complex lot, manifesting a host of difficulties ranging from comorbid psychiatric diagnoses, such as depression, anxiety, and ADHD, to highly conflicted psychosocial stresses, such as fights with parents and histories of being abused. No medicine resolves all these difficulties, and therefore medicine is never the sole treatment, despite everyone's hopes that simply finding the right medicine will make the problem go away. Instead, these patients are the poster children for the need to have a comprehensive treatment plan implemented by an integrated team. This plan might include everything from family therapy to CBT to residential treatment. That said, medicine might be helpful in treating comorbid psychiatric disorders, an important function, given the fact that substance abusing teens with comorbid psychiatric conditions are at an increased risk for alcohol and drug dependence and a variety of psychosocial problems (Grella et al., 2001).

Those with substance abuse often have a history of ADHD. Sometimes the teen has a long history of known and previously treated ADHD. Other times, when ADHD has not been previously diagnosed, some will try to find the signs of ADHD in the behaviors of the substance-abusing adolescent, hoping that the diagnosis justifies a stimulant trial that will cure the substance abuse. Although a properly diagnosed adolescent can benefit from stimulants, such hopes can go unrealized.

In treating ADHD, the clinician must be wary of putting stimulants that can be abused into the hands of substance-abusing teens. For this reason, using long-acting stimulants such as Focalin XR or Concerta, which cannot be easily crushed and snorted, is advisable. Vyvanse is another stimulant that is designed to prevent abuse. Finally, atomoxetine, guanfacine XR, and bupropion are non-stimulant alternatives.

Depression, which is also commonly found in substance-abusing teens, is associated with a higher rate and earlier onset of substance abuse and negatively affects the treatment outcomes of these teens. Those with depression and substance abuse have a higher risk of completed suicide (Practice Parameter on Depression, 2007). While there are few controlled studies of antidepressant treatment of teens with depression and substance abuse, treating depressed substance-abusing adolescents with SSRIs or other antidepressants might improve a sometimes bleak long-term prognosis.

Similarly, drug-abusing adolescents should be screened for anxiety disorders, which can also be treated with an SSRI. As with stimulant medicines, care must be taken in treating these adolescents with benzodiazepines, which, while potentially helpful, often need to be avoided because of their abuse or addiction potential. While adolescents with bipolar disorder are prone to abuse drugs and alcohol when manic, the underlying bipolar disorder is the treatment priority.

## Pregnancy and Breast-Feeding

While certainly not a disorder, pregnancy and breast-feeding require the most careful consideration of medicine, since while treating one individual, namely the mother, the clinician is also concerned about harming the other, namely the fetus or infant. Although it may seem counterintuitive to most people's automatic concern about harming the fetus, scientific research has complicated the issue by illustrating the ways in which treatment of the pregnant woman can later help, rather than harm, her child. For example, maternal depression increases the effect of genetic risk for schizophrenia. This raises the possibility that treating a depressed pregnant woman will affect the fetus's brain development and thereby lower her child's risk of suffering from schizophrenia (Freedman, 2010).

Obviously this issue spawns myriad concerns, taxing the clinician's use of the risk-benefit ratio as does no other decision and mandating a discussion between the pregnant woman and her physician. I review some of the basic principles that guide the decision-making process. Nevertheless, this topic demands that the patient and her physician look carefully at the most current data and consider all sides before making a decision.

First, the most important principle is the complicated nature of the risk-benefit ratio. When measuring benefit, the clinician is usually assessing benefits to the mother. Yet one must also consider the potential benefit to the fetus. That includes the benefit of developing in the womb of a non-depressed woman. Children born of mothers with depression are more often born prematurely, at lower birth weight, and with lower Apgar scores. They have higher levels of cortisol and catecholamines, cry more often, are more inconsolable, and have more irregular sleep patterns (cited in Marcus & Heringhausen, 2009). Although the answer is unknown, we must also ask whether being bathed for nine months in higher-than-normal levels of stress-related hormones, such as cortisol, increases the possibility of depression in the child. Might the mother's use of an SSRI during pregnancy make the child less prone to depression?

The benefit to the infant also includes the postpartum benefit of being cared for by a mentally healthy mother. It is in the child's best interest for the mother not to be depressed or overwhelmed by anxiety. If keeping the pregnant woman mentally healthy during the pregnancy improves the possibility that she will be mentally healthy after the child is born, that is a significant benefit to the child.

In assessing risk, one must assess the risk of side effects to the pregnant woman. Obviously one must also assess the risks to the fetus. These, however, can be many, and each deserves consideration. Fetuses, like children, as I stress in the rest of this book, are constantly developing, so a first consideration is at what stage of pregnancy the medicine is being given. The concern in using medicine early in the pregnancy is about affecting the early formation of organs and thus creating the potential for malformations. The concerns later in pregnancy revolve more around the viability of the infant after birth.

In short, one must consider the impact on the fetus during the different phases of pregnancy, then during labor and delivery and immediately postpartum, then during the first few years of life, then later in childhood, and finally in adulthood. One must consider how all this affects a variety of organ systems. (For a more specific discussion about the antidepressants, see Chapter 7.) The patient should always request and discuss up-to-date information on this topic from her health care provider.

In addition, for many women, the effect on the infant via breast-feeding must be weighed. Unfortunately, there is a lack of research on this topic. Fortinguerra, Clavenna, and Bonati (2009) found that fewer than one third of psychiatric medicines had published evidence supporting their use during breast-feeding. A few medicines were contraindicated during breast-feeding, but many had no available data to inform patients and physicians. Long-term data were particularly sparse.

Fortinguerra and colleagues (2009) caution against evaluating groups of medicines, recommending that each medicine be seen separately. For example, rather than make a blanket statement about SSRIs, they advise against the use of fluoxetine, escitalopram, and citalopram, and recommend the use of sertraline, paroxetine, and fluvoxamine, which have shorter half-lives and a lower excretion rate in breast milk. Similarly, olanzapine, chlorpromazine, valproate, and carbamazepine have relatively low excretion into breast milk, whereas lithium and clozapine have a greater rate of excretion into breast milk and are therefore contraindicated.

In short, the use of medications during breast-feeding is not contra-indicated, and a woman should not forgo the benefits of breast-feeding because she is taking medicine. Rather, the mother and physician must weigh the benefits and risks of breast-feeding while taking medicine against those of not breast-feeding or of stopping one's medicine in order to breast-feed. The risks to mother and child of a mother suffering a return to psychiatric symptoms should not be minimized. A woman considering breast-feeding should be cognizant that the medicines she takes can enter her breast milk, albeit in low amounts for some medicines, and that her child should be monitored for any signs of toxicity. In any case, the general rule should be to use the minimally effective dose.

# Case Examples

*Case 1: Caren is 4 years old and will not talk to her lovely nursery school teacher. She is absolutely and completely silent in school. The other children in class learn to respond to Caren's hand motions. At home, Caren speaks volumes. Her parents report that Caren is very self-conscious and as stubborn as a mule. Caren is diagnosed with selective mutism. Her psychologist tries to work with the teacher to reinforce any vocalization Caren utters. After a few months, everyone is becoming very frustrated. Caren is started on a low dose of fluoxetine and within a month is beginning to speak in school.*

*Comment:* Some have seen selective mutism as a form of social anxiety disorder. Such children display an extreme self-consciousness outside of their families, and they cling tenaciously to their silent stance. While many children will outgrow this condition, predicting who will do so is difficult. Some, therefore, choose to treat the child with an SSRI, which is sometimes effective.

*Case 2: At 11 years old, Alex is bringing down the house. He is defiant to his parents, whose marriage is rupturing over how to handle Alex, and he is obnoxious to his sisters, who refuse to have friends over. The guidance counselor is in constant contact with Alex's parents over his lack of attention in class and his arguments with peers in the halls. Alex is diagnosed with ADHD and ODD. At some point, bipolar disorder is considered. Because of the strong evidence of anxiety, a diagnosis of an anxiety disorder is also considered. Methylphenidate helps Alex focus but is insufficient for treating his outbursts and irritable defiance. Alex is therefore given trials of risperidone, aripiprazole, and valproate. None of this is effective. The possibility of an anxiety disorder leads to a trial of sertraline and fluvoxamine, which help minimally. Five years later, Alex is in high school. He no longer refuses to take methylphenidate, but he takes no other medicines. He has matured considerably and is a sensitive person and a diligent student. He is still highly persistent, but gets along well with his parents and friends.*

*Comment:* Children like Alex can be the focus of considerable family turmoil and endless attempts at pharmacologic control. While sometimes these attempts are successful, the clinician must be careful to appreciate that many of the difficulties of some children, even those that cause considerable turmoil, diminish as they mature. The endless search for the "right" medicine is sometimes fruitless. In these cases, far greater importance must be placed on patience, and on helping the family manage the chaos precipitated by the patient.

*Case 3: Fourteen-year-old Bradley has Asperger's. He relates in an awkward manner and speaks in a monotone with a telegraphic cadence. He hyperfocuses on learning the minute details of the workings of trains but is unfocused in class. He also feels compelled to touch yellow objects, which annoys his father. His clinician starts Bradley on Adderall to help him focus in class, and this seems to be of moderate help. A year later his parents request medicine to help Bradley stop touching yellow objects. A trial of sertraline is unsuccessful.*

*Comment:* Children with Asperger's present the perfect example of a disorder whose core issues do not respond to medicine but whose associated symptoms might. There is no medicine for Asperger's. Although these patients are more vulnerable to side effects, sometimes their inattention responds to a stimulant. Their compulsive symptoms, however, while appearing to be similar to those of OCD, tend not to respond to SSRIs.

## Chapter 12

# Alternative Medicines and Treatments

Alternative medicines include herbal remedies, dietary supplements, and other "natural" substances used by patients to treat a wide variety of ailments or to enhance a wide variety of traits. These medicines are used to treat disorders such as depression, bipolar disorder, anxiety, autism, and more. And they are used to enhance physical appearance, improve athletic performance, induce sleep, and promote wakefulness. Although one usually thinks of these substances as treatments, such as omega-3 fatty acids and St. John's wort, it is reasonable, at least for the sake of argument, to put the morning cup of coffee many need to get going into this group of substances.

If patients see a difference between prescription medicines and over-the-counter medicines, most see an even larger difference between both of these and alternative medicines. In fact, while many patients use these substances, frequently they do not mention them when the clinician asks them what medicines they give their child. Some patients seem embarrassed, as if to say, "I know it's not traditional, but what's the worst that could happen?" This comment often hides an underlying worry about the side effects of more traditional medicine or a desperate need to try anything to solve the problem. Others hope the alternative medicine works but simply don't see it as "real" medicine about which the doctor needs to know.

The assumption is often that these medicines are "natural" and therefore can only offer benefit without potential risk. This is simply incorrect. It is wise to remember that tobacco, alcohol, and poison ivy are all natural substances. Any substance that can offer benefit, whether originating in the lab or in the garden, can bring side effects. Molecules are like adolescents: they do not go only where you want them to. This means that the molecules of any medicine, whether prescription or alternative, go to both the parts of the body we want them to go to and the parts we'd prefer they avoid. In short, alternative medicines can have side effects and can interact with other traditional medicines taken by the patient.

Many of these substances have not been rigorously tested, especially in children, so their proof of benefit might be anecdotal and their risks unquantified. In addition, because these substances are often considered food supplements and are therefore not monitored as closely as prescription drugs, they are more likely to be subject to contaminants, mislabeling, and variable dosing per pill. In addition, those substances that are derived from plants are subject to the normal variations in different batches of plants grown in different parts of the world.

Nevertheless, some of these medicines have been tested and offer either an alternative treatment or at least hope as a future treatment. While traditional medications have more often been tested, it is as well for traditionalists to remember that physicians, particularly child psychiatrists, have often treated patients' complaints with medications whose effects have not been proven. To do otherwise would often mean sitting by and watching a person struggle as we wait for science to offer sufficient proof of efficacy.

This chapter offers a brief review of the more common alternative medicines used in child psychiatry and the level of evidence that informs their use.

# Omega-3 Essential Fatty Acids

Fatty acids are a part of the triglyceride molecule, the chief component of fat. While humans can produce most fatty acids, the "essential" fatty acids (EFAs) must be taken in the diet, for example, through certain types of fish and oils. Omega-3 is simply a designation of the location of a double bond in the EFA molecule. There are three types of EFAs, namely alpha linolenic acid, eicosapentaenoic acid, and docosahexaenoic acid. The membranes of neurons are full of these EFAs, which might impact the way neurons transmit electric current. It is hypothesized that the reduced amount of EFAs in the Western diet has contributed to increased rates of depression, ADHD, and other conditions (Rey, Walter, & Soh, 2008).

Research in adults suggests that the EFAs might be effective in treating or augmenting the treatment of depression and bipolar disorder. One small study of prepubescent children with depression of recent onset (Nemets et al., 2006) showed that treatment with omega-3 was more effective than with placebo. Notably, while 70% of those taking omega-3s improved, none of those taking placebo improved, a surprising lack of placebo response. A double-blind, placebo-controlled study (Amminger et al., 2010) of adolescents and young adults who were at very high risk of psychosis showed that 12 weeks of treatment with omega-3 polyunsaturated fatty acids decreased the risk of progressing into psychosis. Interestingly, these results continued over the next 12 months, although the treatment with omega-3s did not. In this study, the omega-3 consisted of eicosapentaenoic acid, docosahexaenoic acid, and vitamin E.

Thus far, research findings of the effects of the EFAs on ADHD are inconsistent and certainly not robust. Research is also under way regarding the use of omega-3s to treat tic disorders. It is important to remember that which of the three EFAs is used in any study might effect the outcome of the study.

Side effects of EFAs include gastrointestinal distress, belching, and a fishy odor to one's breath. There is also concern that at higher doses, the EFAs might interfere with blood clotting, especially if combined with other anticlotting medicines.

## Evening Primrose Oil

Evening primrose oil is a source of essential fatty acids. One of the fatty acids contained in commercially prepared evening primrose oil is gamma-linolenic acid, which is converted to other fatty acids theorized by some to be diminished in children with ADHD. Taking evening primrose oil increases the level of these fatty acids and theoretically improves the symptoms of ADHD.

Two studies (Aman, Mitchell, & Turbott, 1987; Arnold et al., 1989) did not find a significant difference between placebo and evening primrose oil (given as Efamol) in improving ADHD symptoms. In the small study by Arnold and colleagues (1989), d-amphetamine was significantly better than evening primrose oil and placebo in treating ADHD, although there was some indication that teachers saw a significant decrease in hyperactivity in those taking evening primrose oil.

On the basis of these two studies, when used, evening primrose oil is given at doses of 3–4 grams daily. Although it is reported to be generally well tolerated, side effects include mild gastrointestinal symptoms and headache. A question whether evening primrose oil causes people to be more prone to seizures remains, and therefore it should probably be avoided in those who are already seizure prone or who take medicines that might make them seizure prone, such as bupropion.

## St. John's Wort

St. John's wort is derived from an herb grown around the world and is probably named for Saint John the Baptist, since it blooms around his birthday. Also known as rose of Sharon, it has been used for centuries to treat a variety of ailments and even to prevent evil from befalling soldiers (Schatzberg, Cole, & DeBattista, 2007).

St. John's wort is commonly used to treat adults with mild depression in Germany, from where most of the research on this substance derives. Unfortunately, the research on adults is inconsistent, so definitive conclusions are difficult to reach.

St. John's wort has many components with a variety of effects on different receptors, so it is unclear which one has any particular effect. Hypericum and pseudohypericum are thought to be two of these active components.

Nevertheless, the most common assumption is that the mechanism of action is as a serotonin reuptake blocker, similar to the SSRIs.

The most common side effects of St. John's wort tend to be mild and infrequent. They include gastrointestinal upset, dry mouth, fatigue, anxiety, headaches, and sensitivity to sunlight, especially among fair-skinned people, although these are not commonly reported at therapeutic doses. In addition, it has been associated with hypomania and case reports of problems affecting other organ systems.

There is also a concern that if St. John's wort is given with an SSRI, the patient is vulnerable to developing a serotonin syndrome (see Chapter 7). Some clinicians therefore recommend that the patient stop taking St. John's wort for a few days prior to taking an SSRI (Schatzberg, Cole, & DeBattista, 2007). Of particular concern, there is evidence that St. John's wort increases the P450 3A3/4 enzyme, thereby affecting the metabolism of many other medicines, including medicines used by children, such as some antiasthma and anticonvulsant medicines.

While there is no significant research on the use of St. John's wort in children, in adults it is started at about 300–600 mg daily. This is equivalent to about 0.9–1.8 mg of hypericum. The dose is hard to calibrate, however, given the variability in the herb, the part of the plant used, and the way it is prepared. As with standard antidepressants, a response is generally not seen for about four weeks.

## Kava

Kava is derived from the plant *Piper methysticum Forster*, which is grown in the South Pacific. It is crushed, placed in water, and served as a drink whose purpose is to lessen tension and increase relaxation. It has also been used to reduce pain and decrease seizures. Theories of its mechanism of action include its having an effect on GABA, NMDA, and serotonin receptors, as well as possibly inhibiting MAO or blocking the reuptake of norepinephrine.

Research on adults indicates a possible anxiety-lessening effect relative to placebo after eight weeks of taking kava.

Few side effects are reported at low doses. At higher doses, some experience dizziness, gastrointestinal symptoms, and visual disturbances.

When kava is used chronically, some develop a reversible yellow discoloration of the skin. Kava has been shown to decrease the tone of the uterus and therefore should not be used during pregnancy. It has also been associated with serious liver damage.

In addition, the chronic overuse of kava is associated with breathing problems and diminished levels of platelets and certain white blood cells. There are also a host of other physical difficulties associated with very high chronic kava use, although these might not be due to kava only. Kava is also thought to cause intoxication that can impair motor coordination, including driving, and might add to the effects of alcohol and benzodiazepines.

## Gingko Biloba

The leaf extract of the *Gingko biloba* tree has been used to treat many medical problems but is especially used to improve memory deficits associated with dementia in the elderly. In children and adolescents, gingko has been studied as a treatment for ADHD and found to be less effective than methylphenidate (Salehi et al., 2009). The use of gingko to treat dyslexia and the sexual side effects of SSRIs has also been investigated.

Mild side effects have included headaches, rashes, and gastrointestinal upset. The most significant side effect is the increased risk of bleeding in patients using anticoagulants.

## Caffeine

Because it is a staple of every kitchen, some parents have a low threshold for giving their child a little coffee in the morning. Many have heard that it is chemically related to the stimulants used to treat ADHD, and giving a food product certainly seems safer than giving your child a prescribed medicine. Treating ADHD with caffeine therefore serves as a wonderful demonstration of the different ways of approaching the question of what constitutes a medicine.

One way of seeing the use of caffeine is that the child is simply drinking an innocuous, commonplace food substance, and if his symptoms improve, we have benefit without risk. The other way of seeing the use of caffeine is that the molecules that would make it effective are no different than if they were delivered in a measured-out capsule manufactured in the lab. From this viewpoint, these molecules, whatever their source, are seen as needing to prove their benefit and capable of causing side effects. I include a short discussion of caffeine because some parents continue to see it as "only a food" and use it to treat ADHD, and because it is a substance found in everything from some sodas to coffee ice cream to Excedrin which can affect daily activities, such as sleep.

Caffeine promotes the actions of dopamine at the synapse. It thereby promotes wakefulness and improves vigilance. Does this similarity to stimulants indicate that caffeine would also diminish the symptoms of ADHD? It seems not. In a small study comparing caffeine to methylphenidate in the treatment of ADHD, Garfinkel, Webster, and Sloman (1975) found methylphenidate superior. Arnold and colleagues (1978) compared treatment of ADHD with caffeine to treatment with methylphenidate and with d-amphetamine and found that caffeine was inferior to both medicines and comparable to placebo. Elkins and colleagues (1981) did find that high doses of caffeine led to increased vigilance in boys without ADHD. But those doses also led to increased motor activity.

So it is possible that at some doses caffeine might improve at least the vigilance of children with ADHD. If this were proven to be true, however, the practical difficulty with using caffeine as a medicine would be that the amount of caffeine in a cup of coffee varies depending on how much caffeine is in that batch of coffee and exactly how much coffee is in the cup. In short, even if it were effective, using coffee as a medicine would be imprecise at best.

In addition, as I've said before, caffeine, like all potentially beneficial substances, is prone to cause side effects such as jitteriness and stomachaches.

# EEG Biofeedback

EEG biofeedback is an often publicized way to treat ADHD. Electric current, which can be measured by an electroencephalogram (EEG), normally flows through the brain at different frequencies. Biofeedback attempts to change the electrical activity of different frequencies and thereby the manifestations of ADHD. One type of biofeedback attempts to decrease the impulsive and hyperactive symptoms of ADHD by increasing brainwaves in the faster frequency range. The other type of biofeedback attempts to decrease slower brainwave activity and thus diminish inattention. Unfortunately, the conclusions of most studies assessing this form of treatment are limited because of flaws in the study design. So at this time, EEG biofeedback is not accepted as a proven treatment of ADHD.

## Placebo

Placebo is not an alternative treatment, as are St. John's wort or the omega-3s. Nevertheless, as we've seen throughout this book, placebos play a crucial role in child psychiatry and, in fact, in all of medicine. Every effective treatment has a placebo component, the effect beyond the action of the "active" part of treatment. This can be a large part of the effectiveness of any treatment. A treatment must prove itself superior to placebo to prove that it is itself effective.

Neurocientists search for increasingly specfic ways to change the neuron. But helpful changes also occur because the treating doctor wears a white coat or speaks with authority or practices in a fancy office. These changes might also occur because the pills are blue and not red or because they are tablets and not capsules or because the name of the medicine starts with an *X* and not a *D*. Pharmaceutical companies are very interested in all these other characteristics of medicine that might improve its efficacy, even if they do not know what neuronal changes increase the efficacy. But they are most interested in finding the active molecule that causes change.

In research, the role of placebo is to imitate the real medicine in every way, thus causing the same synaptic changes as the real medicine, except for the changes made by the molecule thought to be the active part of the medicine. Whatever synaptic changes are caused by the pill being blue will be negated by the placebo pill also being blue. Whatever synaptic changes are caused by the pill being triangular will be negated by the placebo pill also being triangular. By ensuring that the placebo imitates everything about the real medicine except its active molecule, we can surmise that any increase in benefit when the active medicine is given is due to the active molecule and not all the other characteristics of the medicine.

How the placebo effect works is unclear. But it does work. Change is caused not by the active treatment but by the powerful force of expectation of change caused by all the other components of treatment. Expectation changes the subjective experience of the individual. It also causes measurable physical changes. For example, dopamine release increased in some areas of the brain of those with Parkinson disease when they were told there was a strong possibility that they'd be given medicine, but in fact were given placebo (Lidstone et al., 2010). The expectation of benefit is thought to stimulate neurons involved in receiving rewards.

The power of expectation is also demonstrated in an experiment in which researchers deceived people, who were told they had been given different doses of caffeine but were actually given placebo. Both their subjective observations and objectively measured pulse rates varied depending on the dose of caffeine they thought they had received (Kirsch & Weixel, 1988). Similarly, the power of expectation was shown in a study of boys whose mothers thought their children's behavior was unduly influenced by sugar. Those mothers who believed their child had been given sugar saw the child as more active, even though the child was actually given a non-sugar substance (Hoover & Milich, 1994).

Expectation affects the observations of those treated and those observing. Placebo is used to control this factor by providing expectation without the actual biological intervention being tested. As we've seen throughout this book, the placebo response rate of different treatments in child and adolescent psychiatry can be quite high, typically about 20% in the use of stimulants to treat ADHD and about 40% or higher in the use of antidepressants to treat adolescent depression.

Why is this so important? If the patient improves, who cares how it happened?

In one way, it doesn't matter. If the patient improves, the goal has been reached. The patient might not care whether the improvement was caused by the introduction of a specific medicine or the color of the medicine or the reassuring and convincing manner of the physician.

Over recent centuries, however, science has come to value proving that an intervention is effective. This expectation puts the responsibility on the provider to prove that the solution offered is effective and protects the patient from the proverbial snake oil salesman who touts his treatment as effective but without proof. Not that all treatments are proven. Still, the clinician should be able to offer an honest assessment of the degree to which he or she thinks the offered treatment will be effective. Nevertheless, many physicians will knowingly use the placebo effect because he or she thinks it to be in the patient's best interest. Others believe that patients could be given placebo, but only with their informed consent. This consent might be for the possibility of receiving placebo. This leads to a discussion of ethics and demonstrates the evolving nature of the doctor-patient relationship.

This chapter has not reviewed definitive conclusions about the use of herbal and other alternative remedies in the treatment of childhood psychiatric disorders. Such clear recommendations are not possible, as research on this topic is still in its infancy. The major point of the chapter has been to encourage the reader to see these alternative treatments as medicines and to treat them as one would prescription medicines, namely, demanding proof of their efficacy and being duly cautious about their potential for side effects and interactions with other substances.

## Chapter 13

# Nonpsychiatric Medicines
# with Psychiatric Effects

Throughout this book I have focused on the medicines used to treat psychiatric disorders. But children and adolescents also use nonpsychiatric medicines, some of which have, or are thought by some to have, psychiatric effects. In this chapter I review some of the medicines that raise the greatest concern. This is certainly not an exhaustive list of the many side effects of the many medicines prescribed to children and adolescents. In particular, I have omitted discussion of the FDA warning about suicide to those taking antiepileptic medicines because of the lack of data regarding youth at this time. Rather, I have chosen to discuss medicines about which those who work with adolescents often have questions.

## Isotretinoin (Accutane)

Acne is one of the most common scourges of adolescence. About half of adolescents experience acne, and about 10% suffer from moderate to severe acne. Acne adds to the social awkwardness of many young adolescents, causing embarrassment at a time of life already primed for self-consciousness. The importance of appearance in a media-driven society exacerbates the problem.

Studies report that acne is associated with psychiatric symptoms, such as of depression and anxiety. One large study of Norwegian teenagers (Halvorsen et al., 2010) found that those with severe acne had rates of suicidal ideation of about 25%, or two to three times the rate in those with no acne or mild acne. In addition, these young people had greater social impairment than their peers. Many adolescents do not seek treatment for their acne. Those who do come to clinical attention with severe acne often consider the use of isotretinoin (Accutane). Yet they are often inhibited by their fears of medicine-caused depression and suicidality.

Isotretinoin is a retinoid, a synthetic relative of vitamin A. The retinoids have been used to treat severe nodulocystic acne. Isotretinoin was introduced as Accutane in 1982 as an alternative to vitamin A, and while it can be highly effective, it has been associated with a variety of significant side effects. Perhaps the best known of these is its extreme teratogenicity, as it has been estimated to cause birth defects in almost 30% of pregnancies, far higher than the population base rate for malformations of 3–5%. Despite being contraindicated during pregnancy, a small number of women will become pregnant while taking isotretinoin (Berard et al., 2007).

Isotretinoin has also been associated with a number of psychiatric side effects, chiefly depression, psychosis, and suicidal ideation. As I've stressed, however, an association is not the same as causality. The important questions are whether there is an association, and if so, is isotretinoin causal. Studying this problem is complicated by the association of acne with psychological symptoms such as depression, anxiety, and suicidality.

There have been a number of case reports and case series that report psychiatric symptoms, beginning from one day to a few months after the patient starts taking isotretinoin. Some larger studies, such as those comparing those who take isotretinoin with those who take other medicines, have not shown an increase in depression. For example, in comparing adolescents with acne treated by isotretinoin to those treated with a conservative therapy, Chia and colleagues (2005) found no increase in depressive symptoms and a decrease in depressive symptoms in both groups. And, in a study of Swedish adolescents and adults, Sundstrom and colleagues (2010) found that, although there was an increased risk of attempted suicide for the months during and after treatment, that risk was already increasing before treatment began. The authors note that suicide attempts were uncommon. In addition, they found that those who had made a suicide attempt prior to starting isotretinoin made fewer suicide attempts after treatment than those who made a first attempt after starting treatment. This led the authors to suggest that a history of suicide attempts should not be a contraindication to treatment with isotretinoin.

As we've seen with other medicines discussed throughout this book, the use of isotretinoin challenges the clinician and patient to weigh benefits against risks. Reversing an adolescent's severe case of acne can free the teenager from significant social insecurity. This must be weighed against, among other side effects, the possible, if unproven, psychiatric effects of depression and psychosis. Nevertheless, if isotretinoin is used prudence suggests monitoring the patient for depression and suicidal thoughts during and after isotretinoin use, although the same monitoring could be recommended for those with severe acne who do not take isotretinoin.

## Steroids

When one mentions steroids, people immediately think of bodybuilders, muscles ripping through their T-shirts, like the Incredible Hulk, or baseball players reaching for prodigious numbers of home runs. The steroids, however, are a complex group of medicines with numerous therapeutic uses. To understand the effects of steroids, it helps to understand the different types of steroids.

Cholesterol is the molecule from which all steroids are derived. Through a complex series of chemical reactions, cholesterol is transformed into the corticosteroids and sex steroids. The corticosteroids include the glucocorticoids, such as cortisol, prednisone, and others, and the adrenocorticoids, such as aldosterone. The sex hormones include progesterone, testosterone, and estrogen.

Each of these hormones has a different function. Aldosterone is important in maintaining electrolyte balance. Progesterone and estrogen are crucial in the development of female sexual characteristics and sexual functioning, as testosterone is critical in the male. Cortisol is essential in the metabolism of carbohydrates, proteins, and fats, and it increases in response to stress. In short, the steroids represent a number of different molecules, each having a host of functions throughout the body and each used therapeutically for different purposes.

The corticosteroid cortisol is the steroid probably best known to patients and, along with its synthetic forms, the one most commonly used by physicians, except perhaps gynecologists. Among its many, many effects, cortisol prevents inflammation and is therefore used to minimize the negative effects of arthritis, asthma, Crohn's disease, and many other ailments.

When used therapeutically, the corticosteroids must be used prudently. One significant effect of using corticosteroids is that their presence at high levels can suppress a variety of hormones whose production is controlled by the hypothalamus and pituitary gland. Prolonged use of corticosteroids can also leave the patient prone to infection, peptic ulcers, high sugar levels, mood disturbances such as mania and depression, and a variety of other problems.

As important as the corticosteroids are, they do not garner many headlines. The steroids in the news are anabolic androgenic steroids (AASs), which are synthetic derivatives of testosterone. In other words, these steroids come from a different branch of the metabolic tree whose trunk is cholesterol and are the substances most people refer to as "steroids." The AAS are anabolic, meaning they build tissue, most important, muscle. And they are androgenic, meaning they are related to testosterone, an androgen, or male hormone. Like cortisol, the AAS have a host of different effects, including on protein metabolism, the development of sexual characteristics, and cognitive functioning. Therapeutically they are used to build tissue, such as for patients who suffer from wasting due to AIDS, cancer, or severe burns.

Because the AAS allow more frequent and intense workouts, leading to the development of larger muscle mass, athletes use AAS to enhance their athletic performance. This performance enhancement was first noted in 1889 by the noted physiologist Charles Brown-Sequard. In an unusual example of putting science above concern for himself, at the age of 72 Dr. Brown-Sequard injected himself with a mixture of the semen, blood, and juice from the crushed testicles of a dog and a guinea pig. Over a series of subcutaneous injections, he noted his strength and energy to be enhanced, his constipation to be decreased, and the arc of his urine to be improved (Brown-Sequard, 1889). The use of AAS was off, if not yet running.

The use of substances such as herbs and animal extracts to enhance athletic performance dates back to ancient Greece. Brown-Sequard's discovery eventually put testosterone on the list of candidates used to foster enhancement. After more research, the AAS began to be used by athletes to enhance strength and performance. This began in the 1950s with the use of steroids by Soviet weightlifters and then returned to the world stage when female German Olympic athletes used them during the following decades. Since then, the use of AAS and a host of other substances has been a worldwide phenomenon.

The use of AAS has expanded from enhancing athletic performance to enhancing appearance. They have been used by those who want to bulk up to look buff, as well as those with body dysmorphic disorder (Rashid, Ormerod, & Day, 2007), a disorder of extreme preoccupation with a physical characteristic which impacts one's ability to function. In this case the preoccupation is with looking overly weak and frail, and the AAS are used to build muscle mass.

The number of adolescents using AAS is not minimal. In a large nationwide survey of twelfth-grade boys, Buckley and colleagues (1988) found that about 6% of them used or had used steroids, the majority starting before they were 16 years old. In a large survey of high school students in Denver, Tanner, Miller, and Alongi (1995) found that just under 3% of students, and 4% of the boys, used steroids. In short, the use of AAS among adolescents is not rare, although those who use AAS are often secretive, not sharing their use of steroids with their physician.

AAS are taken by mouth, injected intramuscularly, or applied as a cream or ointment in amounts ranging from 10 to 100 times the therapeutic dose when used to enhance performance or appearance. They are generally used in one of three ways. These are stacking, which refers to the use of more than one AAS simultaneously; cycling, the use of 4- to 12-week cycles of taking AAS, followed by about 8 weeks off the AAS, followed by another round of taking AAS; and pyramiding, or building up to a peak dose and then tapering.

There are a multitude of side effects from using AAS, both medical and psychiatric. The most common side effects are mild and reversible. These include acne and testicular atrophy, each of which occurs in about half the users. Gynecomastia, or increased breast tissue in males, occurs in about 25% of users and can be irreversible. This is caused by some of the androgens being metabolized to estrogen, causing an increase in breast tissue.

More infrequent but serious side effects include high blood pressure, cardiac arrhythmias, liver tumors, abnormal sperm count and sterility, premature closure of growth plates, changes in sugar metabolism, lowered high-density lipoprotein cholesterol (so-called good cholesterol), and increased low-density lipoprotein cholesterol (so-called bad cholesterol). In addition, the increase in muscle size can overwhelm tendons and ligaments, raising the risk of injuries (Rashid et al., 2007).

Female users of AAS are also at risk for breast atrophy, irregular menses, hirsutism (excessive hair growth), male pattern baldness, and hoarseness. AAS users will often use other medicines to try to prevent some of these side effects, leading to their own form of polypharmacy.

The AAS also cause a number of very significant psychiatric side effects, with a higher prevalence occurring with higher doses of AAS. These include increased mood swings, irritability, and aggression. 'Roid rage is the term used for the violent rage that can occur during a cycle of AAS. The aggression of those on AAS is both physical and verbal and often aimed at wives and girlfriends. Pope and Katz (1994) found that almost 25% of AAS users experienced significant mood problems, including depression, mania, and hypomania. Mania manifests with racing thoughts, euphoria, hyperactivity, and grandiosity. About 10% of users become depressed after steroids are withdrawn. These symptoms typically resolve within a few weeks of discontinuing the steroids. Psychotic symptoms occurred in 3–12% of users.

Additional risk of using AAS comes from the sharing of needles among AAS users and ensuing infection. There is also some concern that the AAS are gateway drugs, since many AAS users end up using opioids, sometimes given to them by the same dealer who sold them the AAS.

# Birth Control Pills

Birth control pills (BCPs), or oral contraceptives, have been available in the United States for about 50 years, having reached the status of being known as simply "the Pill." BCPs work by giving a woman a higher than usual amount of estrogen and progestogen and thereby inhibiting the hormones that usually stimulate the monthly cycle of ovulation. Taking the BCP for three weeks during the month inhibits ovulation. When the BCP is then stopped for one week, the woman experiences bleeding.

Although there are a variety of BCPs using different combinations of different hormones taken for different numbers of days, there are essentially two types of BCPs. Most contain a combination of a progestogen and estrogen, though some contain just a progestogen. A monthly cycle of BCPs consists of about 21 active pills and about 7 inactive pills. The latter are not physiologically necessary but are used instead of stopping the pills for a week, thus allowing the woman to continue the daily routine of taking one pill. This increases the chance that she'll remember to restart the new 21-day cycle at the appropriate time.

Like all medicines, BCPs carry a list of side effects, although because different BCPs contain different combinations of hormones, generalizing about side effects is tricky. For example, weight gain is a side effect on some but not all combinations. Similarly, an increased risk of breast cancer might be related to a particular BCP formulation. Deep vein thrombosis has also been reported. BCPs are associated with such benefits as decreased acne and improvement of dysmenorrhea.

Approximately 55% of sexually active teenage girls in the United States take BCPs (Abma, Martinez, & Copen, 2010) as a means of birth control. When one considers that 42% of teens have had sexual intercourse (Abma et al., 2010), that is a substantial number. Still other teens use BCPs as a treatment for an underlying gynecologic problem.

The relevant questions include whether BCPs cause increased moodiness in non-depressed females, whether BCPs exacerbate preexisting depression, and whether BCPs improve the moodiness of those with premenstrual dysphoric disorder. Most of the research on these topics has been done on premenopausal women (including late teens). As we've seen throughout this book, the conclusions cannot simply be extrapolated, in this case downward, to all adolescents.

The first question is whether BCPs cause increased moodiness. In a large study of almost 1,000 women, Joffe, Cohen, and Harlow (2003) found that most women tolerated BCPs without any worsening of premenstrual mood. More relevant to our concern about adolescents, in a placebo-controlled study of 76 adolescent girls, O'Connell, Davis, and Kerns (2007) found that the treatment group and the placebo group had similar numbers of depressed symptoms, thus pointing to a lack of negative effect of BCPs.

The second question is whether BCPs exacerbate preexisting depression. In their study, Joffe and colleagues (2003) found that about 75% of women with a history of depression tolerated BCPs without a problem. About 25%, however, did have a premenstrual worsening of their depressive symptoms. In a group of premenopausal women with a history of depression, Young and colleagues (2007) showed that those taking a combination BCP had less depression and anxiety and better physical functioning than those not taking hormone treatment. Overall, BCPs were seen as having a small effect on mood and did not increase depressive symptoms.

The last question is whether BCPs, rather than worsening symptoms, can improve the symptoms of those with premenstrual dysphoric disorder (PMDD). PMDD is manifested by irritability, anger, anxiety, depression, and a host of other symptoms causing dysfunction during the luteal phase of the menstrual cycle, or the last five days prior to menstrual bleeding. It occurs in 2–8% of women. Women with PMDD have normal levels of reproductive hormones. Symptoms might be due to the increased sensitivity of their mood to the fluctuations of estrogen and progesterone.

In a small study, though not placebo controlled or blinded, Joffe and colleagues (2007) found that a 21-day cycle of BCPs helped decrease the premenstrual symptoms of depression in women whose depression was already successfully being treated by an antidepressant. In a double-blind continuation of the study, an estrogen taken during the last seven days of the month helped no more than placebo taken during that time. It should be emphasized that these women were already being treated with antidepressants. Interestingly, Joffe and colleagues (2003) found that women with premenstrual mood syndrome (PMS), best thought of as a mild form of PMDD and affecting many more women, benefited from BCPs, suggesting that women will respond differently to BCP's, perhaps dependent on their mood history.

In a survey of a variety of studies, Oinonen and Mazmanian (2002) concluded that overall the use of BCPs did not negatively impact mood. They did, however, find a subgroup of women whose moods were negatively affected. This negative effect might be greater in those with such difficulties as a history of depression, psychiatric symptoms, and pregnancy-related mood symptoms. Masse and colleagues (1998) also found that the psychological status of first-time users of BCPs was not affected during a six-month trial of BCPs.

In short, much needs to be learned about this confusing topic, which is made more complex by the different ages of patients, the different combinations of hormones used, and the different types of mood changes. For now, the take-home message seems to be that most females with depression tolerate BCPs well, but a substantial minority do not. In addition, most females do not have significant mood changes when taking BCPs, some with mild moodiness might improve, and those with PMDD should not rely on BCPs alone to treat their problem.

Finally, from a functional perspective, the use, misuse, or lack of use of BCPs by adolescents is plagued by the misconceptions this age group has about BCPs (Hamani, Sciaki-Tamir, & Deri-Hasid, 2007). Of the many medicines discussed in this book, perhaps none illustrates the teenage patient's burgeoning independence as well as the decision to use BCPs. This topic therefore stresses the importance of the adolescent's relationship with the clinician and the need for that relationship to be built on trust and openness.

*Chapter 14*

# Talking with . . .

As we near the end of this book, it is important to put all the pharmacologic information into perspective. The disorders of child psychiatry are a function of brain chemistry. Sometimes the neuronal dysfunction is caused by genetic factors. Sometimes it is caused by environmental factors. Recent research has focused on the importance of the interactions between the two. This book has concentrated on the medicines that change the neurochemistry of children with psychiatric symptoms and disorders, independent of cause.

By focusing on medicines, as we have, one could misconstrue our understanding of children's psychological difficulties and their treatment as being simply a matter of using medicine to change the patient's faulty neurochemistry. This would be incorrect. A broader and more complete understanding of the dysfunction and treatment of children would use what adult psychiatrist, George Engel, has called the biopsychosocial model (1977), thus also acknowledging the role of psychological and social factors in influencing behavior and its dysfunction. For example, the biopsychosocial model would not reduce the anxious child's anxiety to resulting from "anxious genes" passed down from an anxious father. Rather, this system's model also acknowledges the role of the father's constant reminders to be careful as a social influence and the child's identification with the anxious father as a psychological influence.

As a child psychiatrist, I would include the impact of the child's school within the biopsychosocial model. The demands of school play a fundamental role in highlighting, if not causing, the weaknesses of some children. And dysfunction in school can play a major role in determining whether some children are diagnosed with a disorder. School provides the social environment in which children live for at least 30 hours each week and brings to the fore another group of adults who have a vested interest in the child's functioning.

This demonstrates a key way in which child psychiatry is different from adult psychiatry. In short, it involves more people. The classic relationship between psychiatrist and adult patient involves two people, doctor and patient. The many systems (family, community, work) in which the adult lives are certainly important. But when others, such as a spouse, become involved in the treatment, everybody's warning lights begin to flash lest a boundary violation occur.

In child psychiatry, while confidentiality remains an important principle, people other than the patient are involved from the beginning. Most important are the parents, who likely initiated the consultation and who authorized the treatment, particularly if it includes medicine. In addition, with the increasing trend toward split treatment—that is, one clinician, often a psychologist or social worker, seeing the patient in therapy and another, often the child psychiatrist, writing the prescription—other professionals are intimately involved in treatment. There are also often teachers, school psychologists, school social workers, school nurses, guidance counselors, occupational therapists, speech therapists, pediatricians, parent coaches, parents' therapists, and more who are involved in the child's treatment. Truly, the treatment of a child with a psychiatric disorder is often a team effort.

The clinician's decision to prescribe medicine and determination of whether it is effective is often aided by the observations of many of these people. Thus communication between the child psychiatrist and the child's parents (or other caretakers), the child's therapist, the child's teacher, and often the school psychologist, who coordinates the school effort, is routinely important. A busy pediatrician is also often involved, sometimes peripherally, yet sometimes at the hub, and school nurses are frequently on the front line through the school day, doling out medicine, fielding physical complaints, and offering support. The communication among these parties, but specifically that involving the prescribing clinician, often determines whether and how medicine is prescribed and then the patient's compliance with taking medicine.

A caveat: crucial to communication is a standard language. The different ways people use the same or similar words often present a challenge. Parents who describe their adolescent as "depressed" often mean demoralized, if sometimes chronically. The psychiatrist who describes the adolescent patient as "depressed" often means that the patient fits all or most of the DSM-IV criteria for depression. A parent whose child is on a stimulant might also describe the child as "depressed," but meaning withdrawn, flat, or zombie-like. These distinctions have major implications for treatment. When professionals and parents talk with one another, knowing how someone is using certain terms is crucial to understanding that person's concerns.

A second caveat: effective communication depends on trusting relationships. Without trust, communication is suspect. This is true when parents don't believe that the physician is informing them about all of a medicine's possible side effects. And it is true when the teacher doesn't believe a parent's account of how homework was completed. A multitude of factors erode trust, thus interfering with communication.

## The Parents

The parents are obviously integral to the relationship between prescriber and child patient, usually being the parties who initiate the consultation. Through their observations, the clinician first learns the nature of the presenting problem. Only after communicating with the parents can the clinician establish a treatment plan. And finally, the parents are crucial in the required follow-up after treatment is underway.

Yet parents do not always agree with each other regarding the extent of the problem or the need for treatment in general or medicine in particular. Sometimes this represents an honest disagreement, and other times it represents simply another battleground on which parents can play out their underlying conflict. This highlights the importance of respectful and civil communication, if not agreement, between parents.

Married or not, parents effectively communicating with each other, then acting in synchrony, provide a key element of any treatment, including pharmacological. I often tell divorcing couples: "Parents don't divorce. Spouses divorce. Parents are stuck together forever." This is demonstrated nowhere more vividly than in the decision to use psychiatric medicine. If parents do not act in concert, conflict rules, and the child is left confused and often torn.

> Mr. and Mrs. Jarnow are no longer in the midst of the contentious divorce that rocked their family five years ago. They can now speak in civil tones, at least briefly. The civil tones heat up, however, when they discuss their ongoing disagreement about their son, Timothy's, use of methylphenidate. The mother sees the medicine as crucial and the father sees it as a crutch. Eight-year-old Timothy doesn't understand why he takes his medicine on the mornings he wakes up at his mom's house but not when he awakens at his dad's.

In the best case, parents discuss the clinician's treatment recommendation, then decide whether to follow the recommendation. While communicating with others who know the child might be important in deciding what the next step should be, it is crucial for all involved to remember that this decision-making process takes place within the context of the doctor-patient relationship. The physician's duty, clinically and legally, is to the patient (and, for a minor, this includes the child's parents). With proper consent, other parties are contacted. These people provide invaluable information and often have a sense of what they think the treatment approach should be, for example, whether medicine should be prescribed. Ultimately, the physician cannot do other than what the patient (or parent) permits.

Although the physician should clearly communicate his or her recommendations and do only what good practice dictates, often a physician will allow the patient some leeway in deciding what to do next, with the expectation that eventually the physician's advice will be followed. If the physician feels that the parents are not ready to heed that advice, he or she might wait until they are. The physician's task is not simply to find the "correct" medicine. It is to engage in a respectful, understanding relationship based on ongoing communication with the patient to ensure that the patient will stay engaged in the process of finding a remedy or learning to adapt to a chronic difficulty. While this depends on the clinician's conveying a balanced view of risks and benefits, in today's climate of patients partnering in the treatment decision-making process, the clinician sometimes conveys the information, then allows the patient to struggle with the decision. Nevertheless, remaining available to the patient is best accomplished by perpetuating a trusting, honest relationship.

When proceeding with the recommendation of medicine, the clinician reviews with the patient's parents an explanation of the patient's difficulty and how treatment might help it. In their distress, parents often hope for the medicine to solve a problem that it is not intended to solve or fear side effects that might be unlikely. Realistic expectations of both benefits and side effects must, therefore, be discussed. This lowers noncompliance with medication, an unfortunately frequent occurrence. It also encourages an open dialogue between doctor and patient that is in itself therapeutic.

One common struggle for parents has to do with the length of time the child will be on medication. Parents are usually encouraged to see the medicine as an intervention for the upcoming months or year. Most medicines used in child psychiatry are taken for at least the better part of a year, not a few weeks. Rarely are they needed in an emergency, although certainly there is urgency to some situations. So in most cases, after the child's safety is secured, parents have time to consider carefully the elective use of medicines.

Medicine is presented as a tool to be used within a comprehensive plan. This allows the clinician to continue to emphasize the importance of parenting, school intervention, and other appropriate therapies. I inform parents whether a medicine is FDA approved for the specific condition in a child of that age, but remind them of the limits of FDA approval, namely, that some medicines are very effective but not FDA approved for that age group, and that FDA approval is no guarantee of safety.

An important aspect to communication centers on the need for ongoing follow-up. The effects and side effects of medicine must be monitored, which can be done by eliciting experiences from the patient and observations from parents and teachers. Rating scales can also be used to compare the patient's functioning prior to medication and at different doses. As already discussed, an additional goal of follow-up is the ongoing development of a relationship, particularly with the patient.

There are a number of reasons why follow-up by the medicating clinician is often insufficient, thus inhibiting fruitful communication. These include the financial expense, difficulty finding appointment times because of busy schedules, and the view of some patients that little seems to happen in follow-up appointments anyway. Besides, parents sometimes protest, the patient is already in therapy with someone else, again highlighting the need for adequate communication.

Insufficient follow-up, however, leads to the medicating clinician's not adequately knowing or having a trusting relationship with the patient, something that takes time to build, especially with a child or adolescent.

> Patty is a demoralized, angry 16-year-old who doesn't quite fit the criteria for depression. She also is overly concerned about her weight and runs zealously every day. Sometimes she vomits after she eats. She recently broke up with her boyfriend. She is referred because her therapist thought a trial of an antidepressant would be useful.
>
> The physician agrees but needs to see Patty for follow-up. When Patty comes for appointments, she does her best to summarize what's been going on in her life, but she's not very comfortable yet with the physician, and so there's a lot of "Yeah, I think things are better." The physician wonders what that means. Is Patty over her boyfriend? Has she simply passed through a difficult, but transient, stage of adolescence? Is the medicine working or even necessary? It's very hard to know.

Parents, without realizing, can have undue expectations about the physician's capabilities. When crises arise, the lack of a true therapeutic alliance between doctor and patient is exposed, and communication is compromised.

> *Jeremy is 17 years old and has been followed for years by a physician who has prescribed stimulants for ADHD. Jeremy's mother tries to keep the appointments brief and infrequent. One day she comes across a hash pipe in Jeremy's room. She immediately calls the physician so he can see Jeremy and help solve the problem. As one can imagine, Jeremy is less than happy about seeing the physician, whom he has known peripherally for years, but who today seems more like an inquisitor.*

In a situation like this, the doctor-patient relationship has been minimized and communication compromised. Some wonder if the psychiatrist-patient relationship should be viewed as analogous to calling the pediatrician, who is usually seen annually, when the child develops a rash. The difference is that, as a rule, children who require psychiatric medicine are at greater risk for a host of issues, whether emotional, social, academic, or otherwise. They are thus more likely to require close follow-up. In order to understand the difficulties experienced by these children, a more in-depth interview of the child is often necessary. This is always more effective in the context of a trusting relationship. In addition, many children, and especially adolescents, have strong underlying feelings about psychiatric medicine that they don't have about other medicines, such as antibiotics, often prescribed by the pediatrician. This sometimes leads to resistance or outright refusal to take the medication. At those times, a trusting alliance with the patient is crucial.

## The Child

As we've seen, although parents have responsibility for their child, saying they are always in charge is an overstatement. The increasing independence that comes with development, along with factors such as the child's temperament and the relationships within the family, all affect who is taking control of the decision to use medicine.

The child, of course, stands at the hub of the action. Parents typically make the decision for children, and most children oblige without significant question. If that is not true, as sometimes happens with very oppositional children, a parenting problem is highlighted that requires nonpharmacological intervention. For example, occasionally a child, because of either obstinacy or underlying anxiety, will refuse to take medicine. Parents can usually learn to communicate their insistence about the medicine to the elementary school–age child, and after a few days or weeks, the child simply takes the medicine as part of the daily routine. If not, the clinician must assess why not. Is the patient's refusal reflecting an underlying disagreement between the parents? Is the child pervasively defiant? Is the parent incapable of taking charge because of his or her own depression or anxiety?

Although parents decide for older children as well, those who are cognitively and emotionally capable are best brought into the decision-making process. That is to say, explaining to the older child the reason for medication, discussing the possible common but not overly frightening side effects, and, most important, allowing the child to ask questions sets a tone of respectful communication that conveys to the child that his or her input will be taken seriously.

Children often have fears about the meaning or side effects of the medicine. For example, some children worry that taking a stimulant can have a negative impact on how they are seen by their peers. If the patient is to be on the medicine for years, as sometimes ends up happening, making the patient part of the team when young helps make the patient a more cooperative and responsible team member during early adolescence, when the need to assert one's independence is greater.

> Thirteen-year-old, mildly obese Leila is out of control. Her temper explodes on a daily basis and lands her in the emergency room. She is started on olanzapine. Over the subsequent weeks, Leila gains about 10 pounds. Clearly unhappy, she voices her opinion that this is unacceptable. She says she's looking like a blimp and is going to be mercilessly teased by her peers. While Leila is perhaps overstating her case, her physician and parents listen attentively to her concerns, agree that this is a problem, and try to come up with solutions.

Communicating the risks and benefits to the child in an age-appropriate manner is important. Talking about benefits is fairly straightforward. Without exaggerating the potential benefits, explaining them can be reassuring to a patient such as a depressed adolescent or anxious child. I also stress that the medicine is a tool to be used by the patient, who is still responsible for his or her behavior. Responsibility for one's behavior cannot be excused by a diagnosis or by forgetting to take one's medicine. Patients must grow to accept that they are responsible for caring for their disorder and managing their behavior. By seeing the medicine as a tool, the patient can claim some responsibility for any ensuing success and not see it as caused solely by the medicine.

Being honest about side effects, however, often presents a challenge when one is talking with an adolescent. Because many adolescents, particularly those who are dubious about using medicine, will check out their medicine on the Internet or with friends who have already taken the medicine, being open about side effects fosters a relationship with the patient. This must be done prudently, however, because young patients, especially those with anxiety, often don't have a sense of probability and see any side effect mentioned as likely to happen.

While parents are legally and financially in charge of their adolescent children, the growing need for adolescents to assert independence may limit a parent's influence and control regarding medication. Obviously this depends on the clinical situation, as there is a difference between insisting that a 17-year-old take a stimulant so that he can more productively complete his homework and insisting that he take his antidepressant because he is suicidal. Nevertheless, adolescents often remind their parents who is in charge. And young adults are in fact legally, but often not financially, in charge of themselves. This opens up lines of conflict that vary from case to case. In any event, keeping the adolescent within the communication loop leads to a greater sense of trust and responsibility, and hence compliance.

## The Therapist

Over recent decades, the burgeoning field of psychopharmacology, the specialization within certain types of psychotherapy, and such nonmedical factors as waning insurance coverage have led to the increased use of split treatments. Usually these treatments consist of the physician or nurse practitioner prescribing medicine while a therapist, often a psychologist or social worker, sees the patient in therapy. This relatively new but rapidly growing model can offer the patient better care by a supportive team of specialists who consult with one another to propose a host of ideas about cause and treatment. Or it can offer a disjointed approach by a team of individuals who do not know or communicate with one another and who might even unconsciously resent one another.

For example, uncommunicative professionals risk allowing some patients to portray one as all good and another as all bad, thus stoking a competition for the patient's favor and esteem. Physicians risk feeling resentful because, having once been able to develop meaningful doctor-patient relationships, they now feel reduced to 15-minute office visits during which they write prescriptions that others determine are necessary. And whereas they once had the powerful responsibility of pronouncing the patient's diagnosis, now others can read the criteria in DSM-IV and arrive at a diagnosis themselves. Highly trained therapists with postgraduate degrees may feel resentful that they do the day-to-day work of dealing with patients and their families but must have their judgment validated by a "supervising" physician, whom they need to write the prescription. And they might feel that their experience is more than adequate to challenge the diagnosis arrived at by the physician. These and other conflicts can play out as alleged disagreements about diagnosis and treatment. In these situations, responsible patient care is the loser.

Sometimes, however, real disagreements about diagnosis and treatment occur. When this happens, parents must be presented with the acknowledged difference of opinion in as respectful a manner as possible.

The system works better if professionals know and can communicate with one another. The better acquainted the professionals are, the more confidence they will have in one another's judgment. When professionals know one another, they are less likely to be defensive and territorial. In a field in which uncertainty often reigns, collegial disagreements are usually easily dealt with.

It is important for both therapist and physician to be appreciative of the other's ability and comfortable with the other's judgment. Physicians, for example, want to know that the therapist's judgment can be relied on in dealing with a suicidal adolescent. Therapists want to know the physician is supportive of therapy, respectful of their opinions, and available in an emergency.

This working relationship between therapist and physician rests on ongoing communication. The relationship works best when both parties communicate at least occasionally. This might simply be a brief message left on an answering machine after the patient is seen, or it might mean a periodic extended discussion. Admittedly, finding common convenient times is always a challenge.

## The Teacher

Outside of the family, the adults with whom the child spends the most time and with whom the prescribing clinician must usually have some working relationship are the school staff. Mostly this means the child's teacher, but it often includes the learning specialist, speech or language therapist, and others. Like everyone else involved in treating the child, the school staff, particularly teachers, offer a wealth of observations of the child and a host of insights of their own. Likewise many teachers are receptive to hearing the treating clinician's insights and appreciate practical input regarding managing the child in the classroom. Thus communication with the teacher is very useful, if difficult to schedule.

From the physician's point of view, teachers are invaluable in that they provide observations of the child by a trained professional culled from many hours in the classroom. If gathering the insights of teachers is valuable, talking to the teacher of every child is impossible. Therefore rating scales completed by teachers on which they can also write their thoughts are helpful.

In addition, teachers are crucial in obtaining information about the child who has been started on medicine. This is true of all medicines, but especially true of medicines for ADHD. These medicines cause a distinct change in classroom behaviors, particularly inattention and impulsivity, and the classroom teacher is in the best position to notice any changes. Comparing rating scales completed by the teacher before and after medicine has been started is an efficient way of assessing such changes.

Parents often ask whether they should tell the teacher that they are starting the child on a stimulant. They need to obtain the teacher's feedback, but they are frequently concerned that such information would confirm to the school that their child has a problem and that pharmacology, not good teaching, is the solution. Parents sometimes see informing the teacher about the child's medication status as tantamount to arming the teacher with questions such as "Did you take your meds today?" to be asked when the child is misbehaving.

In general, I try to assure parents that most teachers have their child's best interests at heart. Yet regarding medicine, again particularly medicine for ADHD, my advice is to tell the teacher that medicine is being considered, but that initially the teacher will purposely be kept in the dark about when medication might be started. Then, without knowing the child's medication status, the teacher will be asked for his or her observations.

The purpose of this secrecy is that teachers, like all of us, are prone to interpret rather than report objectively. So, just as throughout this book I have stressed research studies that rely on "blind" observers, in the classroom the same standard should be met. Teachers have their own biases. Some have positive expectations for medicine, and others see medicine as overprescribed and unnecessary.

I also stress to parents, however, that they should assure teachers that they will be informed after the trial of medicine is over and a course of treatment has been decided upon. I explain to parents that most teachers feel a commitment to their students and invest great time and effort in ensuring that each child receives the best education and care. Out of respect for these efforts, they should be acknowledged as an informed part of the team. In addition, since many teachers appreciate any advice for dealing with the difficult child, there is a reasonable quid pro quo within a team working with a common interest.

Many parents accept this advice about informing the teacher, but some do not. This reflects the complex relationship between school and parents, with their seemingly similar but sometimes different goals. Some parents see the teacher as an agent of the school who would be too happy to medicate. In the best-case scenario, parents and teacher see each other as having a common goal. Admittedly, schools represent a multitude of individuals who have contact with the child, many of whom change on a yearly basis. Parents will learn to trust some but not others, and some school staff will forge stronger relationships with the parents than others.

High school teachers are sometimes important sources of information within the school community and are able to inform one of the school mental health professionals of their concerns about a particular child. Yet, because of their limited time with the student, they are often less able than elementary school teachers to offer observations about the efficacy of medicines for ADHD.

## The School Mental Health Staff

The classroom teacher deals with a child on a day-to-day basis. The school psychologist, social worker and guidance counselor are often at the hub of the wheel, connecting, supporting, and educating the various parties who care for and about the child. These professionals deal with the troubled child but also advise the child's teacher about day-to-day management, help the parents relate to the teacher, talk with private therapists, act as liaison between the child psychiatrist who might be medicating the child and the school staff, and present the child to the special education committee.

Of particular note is the relationship between the school mental health staff and the off-premises medicating clinician. While all parties have the child's best interests at heart, this relationship is nevertheless complicated by the fact that they work for different employers. That is, the school clinicians have a professional duty toward the child but are employees of the school. The medicating clinician has a professional duty to the child and his or her family only. This can raise some difficult issues. For example, the school psychologist or social worker feels the pressure of doing what is best for the child but must also take the needs of other students and the teacher into account. The private clinician, while caring about the other students, has a duty only to the particular child.

Medicine can sometimes be the crux of tension between the treating clinician and the school mental health staff. This might revolve around the differences in opinion about whether medicine is necessary or about the different relationship each staff member has with the parents.

> *Everyone agrees that 14-year-old Sophie Janius is depressed. Her psychiatrist recommends treating Sophie with an SSRI but meets with resistance from Sophie's parents. Having previously withheld this painful information, they finally confide that Sophie's grandfather suffered from bipolar disorder and committed suicide when Mrs. Janius was 11. They are worried that the SSRI could precipitate mania and cause Sophie to be suicidal. They do not want the physician to share this information with the school. When the psychiatrist speaks with the school psychologist, he struggles with how to explain the parents' rationale for refusing medication. He knows that he must continue to work with the family to move the process along while keeping their secret from a perplexed school psychologist.*

My experience is that a few rules help the relationship between school professionals and private clinicians. These include acknowledging the limits of one's expertise; respecting the professional credentials and knowledge of the other, particularly in discussions with the child's parents; and fostering communication among the different parties, an admittedly difficult task.

> *Nine-year-old Hayden misses many of the teacher's instructions. He seems distracted. His parents consult a child psychiatrist, who thinks that Hayden has many features of ADHD, inattentive type. She also notes a high degree of anxiety but would rather give Hayden a trial of a stimulant medicine. The school psychologist disagrees. He feels that Hayden's anxiety is the chief problem. The trial of the stimulant fails. The psychiatrist agrees to try an SSRI for anxiety, on which Hayden makes a significant change. The psychiatrist and school psychologist are able to discuss the case without a sense of competitiveness or defensiveness.*

## The School Nurse

Long-acting medicines, especially stimulants, have made the lunchtime lineup at the school nurse's office less common than in years past. Nevertheless, the school nurse is often an integral part of the treatment team. The nurse still doles out psychiatric medicine—sometimes for children who take short-acting medicines at lunchtime and sometimes for those who have forgotten or were unable to take the morning dose. Other children need the school nurse to give them their medication, usually a stimulant, before leaving school so that it's effective for after-school activities. In short, despite the advent of long-acting medicines, the school nurse still dispenses psychiatric medicine.

In addition, the school nurse often provides a haven of safety for the anxious child and thus fields his or her physical complaints. The nurse is also the medical person with the easiest access to the child in case a follow-up pulse or blood pressure measurement is needed. These are some of the reasons why the school nurse should, if the situation merits, be in the medication loop.

> Eight-year old Sarina's anxiety prevents her from attending school. Her parents are considering treating Sarina with an SSRI. With support, she begins entering the school building every morning. She will not, however, use the bathroom, fearing someone will hear her in the stall. Ms. Malone, the school nurse, arranges for Sarina to use the private bathroom in the nurse's office, while Sarina's psychologist works towards helping her lessen her social anxiety.

## The Pediatrician or Family Practitioner

Last, but certainly not least, is the child's primary care physician. Often this part of the team includes the nurse practitioner. Although child psychiatrists are physicians who are specially trained in the psychiatric care of children, including medications, the number of child psychiatrists in the country is woefully inadequate. The child's primary care physician is often left with the responsibility of prescribing psychiatric medicine. To some extent, the suicide controversy associated with the SSRIs led to reluctance by these physicians to diagnose depression or prescribe these medicines (Libby, Orton, & Valuck, 2009). They continue, however, to be involved in prescribing medicine for ADHD, and in many parts of the country they continue to shoulder the lion's share of the care of complex psychiatric patients. In addition, as frontline medical practitioners, they are in a unique position to screen patients and offer initial psychoeducation.

When the child's primary care provider is dispensing medicine, the communication between that provider and the parents, and possibly the school, is crucial. As we saw in the MTA study, one of the differences between the care given by the study's treatment team and that given by the local practitioners was the greater interaction between the treatment team and the school. This led to better outcomes of the treatment of ADHD. Unfortunately, this takes time that the primary care physician often lacks.

When a child psychiatrist dispenses medicine, that physician takes responsibility for the pharmacotherapy and for coordinating care with the school and any other therapist. Nevertheless, it is still important for the primary care physician to know what medicine the child is taking. Often this communication gets lost in the shuffle of busy practitioners. But it should not. The treating clinician should communicate the child's medication plan to the pediatrician. The pediatrician then knows what treatments the child is receiving in case a difficulty arises.

*Chapter 15*

# Evaluating Risks and Benefits: Problems and Pitfalls

Throughout this book I have stressed the need to weigh the potential benefits of medicine against its risks. Unfortunately, that is not as simple as putting weights on a scale. First, the benefits and risks of medicine are always weighed against those of other treatments. How likely is psychotherapy to help the patient? What are its risks, or at least its costs? If nothing else, they include time and money, both finite resources. And what are the chances that an alternative treatment will benefit the patient? And with what risk? And how well is this established?

The benefits of medicine must be weighed against those of other treatments, and these must be weighed against those of not treating. Doing nothing carries its own potential benefits and risks. Those who work with the patient must understand that all potentially therapeutic interventions carry risk. Unfortunately, these are not easily calculated, and professionals and patients alike are prone to miscalculate. This results from over- or underestimating the benefits or the risks.

## Overestimating Benefits

Medicine has come to represent a mindset as much as an actual intervention, namely, the certainty that modern science offers some way to control almost every outcome. While an overstatement, this sentiment does represent many patients' initial feeling when faced with a medical problem and is manifested by the patient's reflexive request for the proper medication.

In child psychiatry, issues of temperament are unwittingly reconfigured as disorders that might respond to medicine. To be sure, the line between temperament and disorder is fuzzy, and the role of medicine in changing temperament is only beginning to be explored. Sometimes, however, medicine is used in an attempt to treat such issues of temperament as low adaptability, when parent counseling would be more to the therapeutic point. Or complex cases are reduced to a list of comorbidities that justify the use of an equally long list of medicines. Using medicine in an attempt to treat complex difficulties is surely reasonable. Sometimes, though, the patient and doctor take a long tour through every available medicine rather than accept that the patient has a malignant disorder whose treatment must be something other than medicine.

And sometimes the demoralization of the average adolescent, albeit one who might be in an acute crisis, is seen as depression and an SSRI is considered, when time or change of circumstance would be sufficient. In such cases, the potential benefit of medicine is overestimated.

The value of medicine is also overestimated when we ignore the potential benefits of other treatments. For example, as we have seen in previous chapters, CBT is a powerful therapy for some conditions, although it takes time, money, personnel, and perseverance—all in increasingly short supply. Bypassing these treatments in favor of medication is a form of overestimating the benefits of medicine.

## Underestimating Benefits

Just as benefits can be overestimated, they can be underestimated too. In general, this is associated with the underestimation of the risks of a disorder. The use of medicine is always weighed against the risks associated with the disorder, particularly if left untreated. As I have tried to demonstrate throughout this book, psychiatric disorders are not benign stages of life. Those who underestimate them do so at the peril of the children for whom they care. Whether the suicidality of those with depression, the dysfunction of those jailed by anxiety, the disruptiveness of those who overwhelm their families with out-of-control temper outbursts, or the legal problems caused by the impulsivity of ADHD, psychiatric disorders disrupt lives and families.

About half of psychiatric disorders are often at greater risk. Clinicians sometimes pursue polypharmacy, not because they have lost sight of all the medicines the patient is taking, but because a combination of medicines is necessary to keep the patient functional. For some, polypharmacy can be life-saving, even with medicines that are being used off-label.

About half of psychiatric disorders begin in childhood and adolescence, and even more begin in early adulthood. Some people might outgrow their disorders. But many do not and are left with a bleak, or at least risky, future. Although it is not always certain that medicine will alter the outcome, that possibility must be considered.

## Overestimating Risks

An overestimation of the risks of medicine usually signals an inordinate fear that is out of proportion to the actual risk. Just as medicine can represent the all-powerful beneficent arm of science reaching out to help control the future, it also conjures images of the flailing arm of science causing unforeseen damage.

This is well represented in the decreased use of antidepressants after the alleged association with suicidality. If the antidepressants are associated with suicidality, it is at an overall low rate of about 1–2% greater than placebo, a figure that represents mostly an increase in suicidal thoughts, not completed suicides. Nevertheless, after the FDA issued a black box warning, its highest cautionary signal for an approved medicine, use of the SSRIs dropped by about 20%. This was associated with an increase in the rate of completed adolescent suicides. Interestingly, the black box warning even seemed to impact the diagnosis of depression, there being a significant decrease in the diagnosis after the warning appeared (Libby, Orton, & Valuck, 2009).

While patients on SSRIs must be monitored, both because of their disorder and because they are on SSRIs, the actual risk of a negative outcome from medicine is minuscule. And while it is not known if the decrease in SSRI use caused the increase in suicide rates, with approximately 2,000 children and adolescents completing suicide each year, every percent change in the suicide rate represents about 20 actual deaths. Yet when the parents of depressed teens contemplate the use of an SSRI, the fear that the medicine may cause their child to commit suicide looms large. In fact, the risks from depression, including the disorder causing suicide, are far greater. This is an example of the benefits of medicine being underestimated and the risks being overestimated.

## Underestimating Risks

Finally, some have become excessively cavalier in the new age of psycho-pharmacology. When pushing to start a medicine or combination of medicines, parents and therapists sometimes casually ask, "What's the worst that could happen?" Without being overly blunt or callous to the concerned parent, I answer this rhetorical question by saying that, though highly unlikely, death is the worst that could happen. This is a sobering reminder that we try to control the future but cannot do so with certainty.

Often, when cautioned about the lack of long-term safety data, parents and therapists who have seen the benefit of medicine resist returning to the possibility of disabling symptoms. A parent whose child is no longer destroying the household, both literally and figuratively, is sometimes apt to ignore the risks of medicine, particularly those that are not definitive. This is most ironic when the parent who once resisted starting the child on medicine now zealously clings to its continued use.

In addition, there is the problem of polypharmacy. Approximately 30–50% of youth who take one psychiatric medicine take more than one (dos Reis et al., 2005; Duffy et al., 2005; Staller, Wade, & Baker, 2005). Although this polypharmacy does not necessarily cause difficulties, we must acknowledge that we are on largely untested ground. While the use of medicine is supported by a fair amount of information, many unanswered questions remain. For example, while the SSRIs frequently cause sexual dysfunction in adults, the mechanism of this common side effect is unknown. How comfortable should prescribers be when giving these medicines to developing children? There is no evidence of their causing any difficulty, but do we really know that they won't?

Last, a significant, but not well understood, group of consequences of all treatments are psychosocial. I use this term to cover the time and money that any treatment costs, as well as the psychological effects on the patient. Does medicine encourage the sick role or the blaming of the disorder for behavior better ascribed to the child's responsibility? Or might it instead encourage viewing oneself as simply having a disorder, no different from asthma or diabetes? Whether this is a risk or a benefit is largely dependent on how the topic is presented to the child. Nevertheless, it is an important consequence of taking medicine.

*Chapter 16*

# Are Psychiatric Medicines Over- or Underprescribed?

As we complete our voyage from studying the workings of the individual neuron to using medicine to change those neurons that go astray, we address a final question, the question that garners the most public attention and anxiety: Are we using these medicines too often or not often enough?

Headlines scream about the overprescribing of psychiatric medicine to children. Many line up squarely on the side of those aghast at the rising prevalence of medication. Others, often those who have benefited from medicine, are equally passionate in the belief that too few parents afford their children the benefits of medicine. How can we make sense of this provocative question?

## First, Some Ground Rules

To discuss this topic, we have to establish a few ground rules. To begin, let's not lump all psychiatric medicines together. We've seen throughout this book that there are many types of psychiatric medicines and they have many purposes. They are not all the same. Let's examine them as groups, such as the SSRIs or stimulants.

Next, let's appreciate that an increased use of any invention is not inherently bad. If you examine automobile use, you'll find a great increase between 1900 and 1920. If you look at cell phone use, you'll find a great increase between 1990 and 2010. That's because new inventions increase in use as people discover them, use them, then decide whether they want to increase their use of them. While this sounds quite obvious, remember that some groups of psychiatric medicines have been around for only about 20 years, and so physicians and patients are still using them in a variety of clinical situations to see if they'll be helpful. If they're meeting a need, then in their initial years there's probably going to be an increase in use. Increased use is not the issue. It is how one decides that medicine should be used.

Last, let's accept that we don't have perfect data. Researchers examining the number of people who take medicine obtain their information from a variety of sources: insurance records, pharmacy records, Medicaid records, and the like. This might tell us the number of prescriptions written in a large sample of the population, but it doesn't tell us if the patient filled the prescription and whether, and for how long, he or she took the medicine. Many prescriptions go unfilled, and many patients stop taking their medicine without telling their doctor. In addition, the studies establishing how many people take medicine cover a variety of groups, including different ages, races, sexes, socioeconomic levels, and settings (urban versus rural) or regions and states of the country. All of these vary and therefore impact the numbers.

## Now, a Bit of Data

Here are the facts as we know them. Most studies show that about 4–5% of children are prescribed a stimulant (Zuvekas, Vitiello, & Norquist, 2006; Visser, Lesesne, & Perou, 2007; Castle et al., 2007). Some studies show rates closer to about 8–10% (see LeFever, Dawson, & Morrow, 1999, for a study in Virginia), and others show rates at about 2% (see Habel et al., 2005, for a study in California). About 2–3% of youth are prescribed an antidepressant (Vitiello, Zuvekas, & Norquist, 2006; Zito et al., 2008), with the rate being about 3–4% among adolescents. About 1% or fewer are prescribed an antipsychotic (Curtis et al., 2005), and fewer than 1% are taking a mood stabilizer (Hunkeler et al., 2005).

Putting aside the fact that many children take more than one medicine and so would be counted twice, if we simply add up these numbers, we see that about 10% (or fewer) of children are taking a psychiatric medicine. Put another way, the overwhelming majority of children do not take a psychiatric medicine.

Nevertheless, these numbers represent a large increase over the past 20–30 years. From the late 1980s through the late 1990s, the number of children taking stimulants roughly quadrupled (Olfson et al., 2002). Then, depending on which years are compared, that number roughly doubled, or was stable for various shorter intervals, during the next 10 or so years (Habel et al., 2005; Zuvekas et al., 2006; Castle et al., 2007). Of particular note, as I'll discuss later, the rate of using stimulants (albeit sometimes obtained from friends, not physicians) is especially high in select populations, such as among college students.

The number of children being prescribed antidepressants also increased significantly from the late 1980s over the subsequent 20 years (Hunkeler et al., 2005; Vitiello et al., 2006). We must take into consideration, however, that, given the lack of evidence of their efficacy in youth, the TCAs were not widely used in the 1970s and 1980s, and the SSRIs were not introduced until the very late 1980s and 1990s. So to say that SSRI use increased from the late 1980s is like saying automobile use increased after Henry Ford introduced the affordable car. Interestingly, as we have seen, after the black box warning about suicidality was added to the antidepressants, the prescription rate of antidepressants actually dropped about 20% (Rosack, 2005).

The number of children prescribed antipsychotics also doubled during the 1990s (Zito et al., 2003; Cooper et al., 2004). But again, we must remember that the FGAs were not commonly prescribed to children during the 1970s and 1980s, and the SGAs were not introduced to the market until the 1990s.

Nevertheless, it is fair to say that although a small minority of children and adolescents use prescribed psychiatric medicines, over recent years many more prescriptions have been written for children and adolescents. Many of these have been written for FDA-approved indications, but many have been written for off-label purposes.

## Why the Increased Use of Medicine?

I believe that a few general themes, not one reason, underpin the increase in the use of psychiatric medicine. First, psychiatric disorders are beginning to be understood in biological terms. In the 1950s psychiatric problems were seen as caused by faulty psychology brought about by a faulty environment. Put much too simply, your difficulties were caused by bad mothering, and the cure was to work out those feelings in psychotherapy. Over the past few decades, the role of biology has gained prominence. Psychiatric difficulties are seen as a function of faulty neurons, which can be changed by medicine.

Interestingly, the frontier of today's research is not in proving nature or nurture but in demonstrating whether and how biological influences interact with environmental stresses, each impacting the other. For example, do certain life stressors, such as child abuse, impact the neuronal development only of those with certain genotypes, thus leading to particular psychiatric disorders in those individuals? Do different combinations of genes interact with different combinations of environments to influence the severity of these disorders? For our purposes, if medicine is seen as a means to change neurons, it is doing so independently of how the neurons became faulty—whether because of genetic influences, environmental influences, or an interaction of the two.

Second, since DSM-III, psychiatric disorders are increasingly recognized by physicians and their patients. Greater recognition of disorders leads to a greater search for treatment. Whether the actual prevalence of disorders has also increased, thus leading to a greater number of people seeking treatment, is more difficult to know.

Third, medicines have increased in use because they work, and with a minimum of side effects. That is not to say medicines are a panacea. Nor is it to say they have no side effects. I hope this book has shown both of those contentions to be false. Nevertheless, I also hope I've shown that scientifically rigorous studies are proving some medicines to be more beneficial than placebo, often with reasonable risk relative to the potential benefit. To be sure, for some uses a substantial placebo effect adds to the perceived benefit in many patients.

Moreover, medicines are sometimes effective for those patients without a clearly diagnosed disorder. Diagnostic criteria can be stretched, and a prescription seems justified on the grounds that it just might work. The hope that medicine might effect some change for their child is sufficient impetus for some parents to request it and physicians to prescribe it. Particularly when a situation is becoming dire and other therapies are proving unhelpful, medicine becomes the "go to" solution.

This brings us to the fourth factor, namely, everyone's expectation that medicine will work. Direct-to-consumer advertising and friends' and colleagues' testimonials convince patients and physicians that benefits can be had. In addition to the glossy advertisements showing people once again enjoying life, physicians are inundated with articles proving (or at least extolling) the benefits of medicine. (The relative absence of published studies demonstrating the ineffectiveness of medicine has been changing over recent years.) Practicing in an environment that lauds the potential of medicine, and supported by their own experience of patients who have been helped, physicians have hopes, bordering on expectations, that medicine will once again save the day.

Fifth, in a world that values time and money, medicine is a relatively cheap and expedient solution. While patients might balk at the effort and expense of useful therapies like CBT, using medicine is fairly easy, and generics are often inexpensive. Insurance companies encourage patients to schedule fewer appointments, so any benefit offered by medicine saves money. With the majority of prescriptions in child psychiatry being written by non-psychiatrist physicians, the busy doctor with minimal time to evaluate and treat can at least write a prescription.

Last, the use of medicine reflects what people value and how they define a problem. People value life. So life-prolonging medicines, such as the antibiotics and those that improve cardiac function, are used to solve the problem of how to extend a person's life. People value freedom from pain and the ability to function. So medicines like the pain relievers and anti-inflammatory medications are used to solve the problem of how to relieve pain and increase function. An increase in the use of any group of medicines should have one wondering what is valued and what problem is being solved.

Like other medicines, psychiatric medicines help solve the problem of how to attain what the patient values. Antidepressants and mood stabilizers prolong life by preventing suicide, end the psychological pain of depression, irritability, and anxiety, and improve family, social, and vocational functioning. SGAs rid the patient of dysfunction-causing hallucinations and minimize the volcanic explosions that threaten the patient and others.

The stimulants can help prolong life (for example, by preventing the child from impulsively running into the street or the adolescent from causing reckless car accidents), but more likely they are used to help attain the level of functioning that patients (or their parents) value. This includes preventing the chronically disobedient child from constantly giving in to the impulse to hit his sister. This includes improving the compliance of the extremely defiant child. This includes smoothing social relationships to prevent social ostracism and, better, allow for the possibility of friendships.

And this includes attaining the academic functioning that many parents see as crucial to their child's self-esteem and future success. My experience is that this rarely means ensuring the stereotypical Ivy League education. It commonly means helping a struggling child reach his or her academic potential. Parents—and schools—value educational achievement. So parents worry that their intelligent child is floundering in school, that with every homework assignment not handed in their child's self-esteem is pummeled, that their child's college and therefore future job prospects are being adversely affected. If the problem is that educational attainment is being threatened, stimulants are seen as a potential answer.

The point is that I believe the increased use of psychiatric medicine reflects an attempt to solve what patients or their parents see as a problem. As I described early in this book, patients determine symptoms. Understanding how child patients and their parents determine what behaviors are problematic, and therefore symptoms requiring treatment, is the interesting part of the story.

## Too Much or Not Enough?

So I've established that medicine use has increased, and I've theorized about some of the reasons for this. The original question is, however, are medicines overprescribed or underprescribed? Medicines are over- or underprescribed if there are more or fewer prescriptions written than ought to be written. How many prescriptions ought to be written? What are the criteria for writing a prescription? Let's assume, for the sake of argument, that the medicines being discussed have been shown to be effective and that no other effective treatment exists. Both of these are, of course, arguable depending on the disorder and the medicine.

If having a diagnosed disorder is the criterion for taking medication, then medicines for both ADHD and depression are underprescribed. Roughly half to three quarters of those with ADHD are prescribed medicine (Rowland et al., 2002; Guevara et al., 2002; Reich, Huang, & Todd, 2006; Visser et al., 2007). And, with fewer than 4% of youth taking an antidepressant (Vitiello, Zuvekas, & Norquist, 2006), about half or fewer of those with depression are prescribed medicine. In fact, Ma and colleagues (2005) found that antidepressants were prescribed in about 50% of visits in which depression was reported. In short, if having a disorder is the criterion for determining who ought to be prescribed a psychiatric medicine, then stimulants and antidepressants are underprescribed.

Perhaps, however, symptoms are the criteria for deciding who ought to be prescribed a medicine. After all, most of us purchase over-the-counter medicines for symptomatic relief, not the treatment of a diagnosed disorder. In this way, stimulants provide the more provocative and illuminating tale of how often disorders and symptoms are treated by prescribed medicines. Reich and colleagues (2006) found that about one third of those who were prescribed a stimulant had ADHD symptoms but did not have ADHD. Jensen and colleagues (1999) found that half of those prescribed a stimulant were symptomatic but did not have ADHD.

So if having a disorder is the criterion for deciding who ought to be prescribed a psychiatric medicine, one could paradoxically conclude that stimulants are overprescribed. In short, medicines are used to treat not just disorders but symptoms.

Would doctors prescribe medicine for the symptomatic who do not fit criteria for a disorder? The answer is an unqualified yes. We've seen that in the studies just mentioned. And McKenzie and Wurr (2004) found that more than 60% of pediatricians and child psychiatrists in Great Britain would write a prescription for a stimulant without the patient's having met the criteria for ADHD. In fact, all doctors commonly treat symptoms without having diagnosed a disorder. Although doctors search for a diagnosis to aid an understanding of the problem, when a diagnosis is elusive, they will often treat the patient's symptoms. It is no different in child psychiatry, where an evolving diagnostic nomenclature is sometimes inadequate to capture some clearly symptomatic and dysfunctional children. If the medicine helps the suffering patient, the doctor will prescribe it.

If a symptom justifies the use of medicine, then perhaps the question is not whether medicines are overprescribed or underprescribed. Rather, the question is what do we value that leads us to consider ourselves symptomatic when we lack it? What motivates us to take medicine? What problem are we trying to solve by using medicine?

These questions will certainly unlock Pandora's box, forcing us to confront what we value. This very theme underlies how we evaluate the benefits and side effects of medicine, which has been the crux of this book. Our values, as demonstrated in the next two stories, determine whether a situation or its treatment is problematic.

*Mrs. Lark's mother committed suicide when Mrs. Lark was a teenager. Now the child psychiatrist is recommending an SSRI to treat Mrs. Lark's daughter, Lana's, depression. In Mrs. Lark's view, the potential for even the slightest increase in suicidality is more than she can bear. She opts for psychotherapy.*

*Mr. D'Antonio is a mason, as were his father, grandfather, and great grandfather. Dom, his son, can't focus in school, but loves working with his hands. The pediatrician recommends a stimulant to help Dom in school. Mr. D'Antonio and Dom both see Dom's future in masonry, not college. Mr. D'Antonio wonders, of what benefit is a stimulant?*

The question of the over- or underprescribing of medicines is a paper tiger. The real question is how do we define the life problems that demand our intervention? And then how do we weigh the risks and benefits of any intervention compared to the outcome of not intervening?

These are the questions that every prescriber, every clinician, and every parent must ask.

# Helpful Websites and Books

## Helpful Websites

Anxiety Disorders of America Association: www.adaa.org
Autism Society: www.autism-society.org
Child and Adolescent Bipolar Foundation: www.bpkids.org
International OCD Foundation: www.ocfoundation.org
Trichotillomania Learning Center: www.trich.org
Children and Adults with Attention Deficit/Hyperactivity Disorder
    (CHADD): www.chadd.org
National Alliance on Mental Illness (NAMI): www.nami.org
American Academy of Child and Adolescent Psychiatry: www.aacap.org

## Helpful Books

Atwood, T. (2007). *The complete guide to asperger's syndrome*. London:
Jessica Kingsley.
As the title suggests, this thoroughly explains and gives treatment recommendations for those with Asperger's.

Birmaher, B. (2004). *New hope for children and teens with bipolar disorder.* New York, NY: Three Rivers.
Of the many books on childhood bipolar disorder, this book by a leading researcher and national expert on the topic is my favorite, in part because of the reasonably high threshold it sets for diagnosing children with bipolar disorder.

Haerle, T. (1992). *Children with Tourette syndrome: A parents' guide.* Rockville, MD: Woodbine House.
This is a comprehensive guide to help parents with the many aspects of Tourette syndrome.

Hallowell, E. M., & Ratey, J. J. (1994). *Driven to distraction: Recognizing and coping with attention deficit disorder from childhood through adulthood.* New York, NY: Simon and Schuster.
This book nicely illustrates the ways ADHD impacts the lives of children and adults and has some handy lists of practical behavioral interventions.

Kalikow, K. T. (2006). *Your child in the balance: An insider's guide for parents to the psychiatric medicine dilemma.* New York, NY: CDS Books.
This book teaches parents and professionals how to decide if psychiatric medicine is the right choice of treatment. New edition forthcoming from W. W. Norton & Company 2011.

Koplewicz, H. S. (1996). *It's nobody's fault: New hope and help for difficult children and their parents.* New York, NY: Random House.
This is a good overview of the various disorders of child psychiatry and emphasizes that they are not caused by parenting.

Koplewicz, H. S. (2002). *More than moody: Recognizing and treating adolescent depression.* New York, NY: Berkley Publishing Group.
This book reviews the topic of childhood depression.

March, J. S., with Benton, C. M. (2007). *Talking back to OCD.* New York, NY: Guilford.
This is a good guide for parents and children to OCD and treatment with CBT.

March, J. S., & Mulle, K. (1998). *OCD in children and adolescents: A cognitive-behavioral treatment manual.* New York, NY: Guilford.
This is an excellent step by step manual teaching professionals how to implement CBT for children with OCD.

Owens, J A. & Mindell, J. A. (2005). *Take charge of your child's sleep.* New York, NY: Marlowe.
This is a user friendly guide for parents to the many difficulties associated with children's sleep.

Mindell, J. A., & Owens, J. A. (2010). *A clinical guide to pediatric sleep: Diagnosis and management of sleep problems.* Philadelphia, PA: Wolters Kluwer.
This book is a comprehensive guide for professionals to pediatric sleep disorders by two of the nation's leading experts on the topic.

Rapoport, J. L. (1998). *The boy who couldn't stop washing.* New York, NY: E. P. Dutton.
This book, by one of the country's leading researchers in pediatric psychiatry, describes OCD in children.

# References

AACAP (American Academy of Child and Adolescent Psychiatry). (2007). Practice parameter for the assessment and treatment of children and adolescents with depressive disorders. *Journal of the American Academy of Child and Adolescent Psychiatry 46*: 1503–1526.

Abikoff, H., Hechtman, L., Klein, R. G., et al. (2004a). Symptomatic improvement in children with ADHD treated with long-term methylphenidate and multimodal psychosocial treatment. *Journal of the American Academy of Child and Adolescent Psychiatry, 43*, 802–811.

Abikoff, H., Hechtman, L., Klein, R. G., et al. (2004b). Social functioning in children with ADHD treated with long-term methylphenidate and multimodal psychosocial treatment. *Journal of the American Academy of Child and Adolescent Psychiatry, 43*, 820–829.

Abikoff, H., Nissley-Tsiopinis, J., Gallagher, R., et al. (2009). Effects of MPH-OROS on the organizational, time management and planning behaviors of children with ADHD. *Journal of the American Academy of Child and Adolescent Psychiatry, 48*, 166–175.

Abma, J. C., Martinez, G. M. , & Copen, C.E. (2010). Teenagers in the United States: Sexual activity, contraceptive use, and childbearing, national survey of family growth 2006–2008. National Center for Health Statistics. *Vital and Health Statistics, 23*(30).

Allen, A. J., Kurlan, R. M., Gilbert, D. L., et al. (2005). Atomoxetine treatment in children and adolescents with ADHD and comorbid tic disorders. *Neurology, 65,* 1941–1949.

Alvir, J. M. J., Lieberman, J. A., Safferman, A. Z., et al. (1993). Clozapine-induced agranulocytosis: Incidence and risk factors in the United States. *New England Journal of Medicine, 329,* 162–167.

Alwan, S., Reefhuis, J., Rasmussen, S. A., et al. (2007). Use of selective serotonin-reuptake inhibitors in pregnancy and the risk of birth defects. *New England Journal of Medicine, 356,* 2684–2692.

Aman, M. G., DeSmedt, G., Derivan, A. et al (2002). Double-blind, placebo-controlled study of risperidone for the treatment of disruptive behaviors in children with subaverage intelligence. American Journal of Psychiatry, 159, 1337–1346.

Aman, M. G., Mitchell, E. A., & Turbott, S. H. (1987). The effects of essential fatty acid supplementation by Efamol in hyperactive children. *Journal of Abnormal Clinical Psychology, 15,* 75–90.

Amminger, G. P., Schafer, M. R., Papageorgiou, K., et al. (2010). Long-chain omega-3 fatty acids for indicated prevention of psychotic disorders: A randomized, placebo-controlled trial. *Archives of General Psychiatry, 67,* 146–154.

Anderson, L. T., Campbell, M., Adams, P., et al. (1989). The effects of haloperidol on discrimination learning and behavioral symptoms in autistic children. *Journal of Autism and Developmental Disorders, 19,* 227–239.

Arnold, L. E., Christopher, J., Huestis, R., et al. (1978). Methylphenidate vs. dextroamphetamine vs. caffeine in minimal brain dysfunction: Controlled comparison by placebo washout design with Bayes' analysis. *Archives of General Psychiatry, 35,* 463–473.

Arnold, L. E., Kleykamp, D., Votolato, N. A., et al. (1989). Gamma-linolenic acid for attention-deficit hyperactivity disorder: Placebo-controlled comparison to d-amphetamine. B*iological Psychiatry, 25,* 222–228.

# References

Atomoxetine ADHD and Comorbid MDD Study Group, Bangs, M. E., Emslie, G. J., et al. (2007). Efficacy and safety of atomoxetine in adolescents with attention-deficit/hyperactivity disorder and major depression. *Journal of Child and Adolescent Psychopharmacology, 17*, 407–420.

Attia, E., Haiman, C., Walsh, B. T., et al. (1998). Does fluoxetine augment the inpatient treatment of anorexia nervosa? *American Journal of Psychiatry, 155*, 548–551.

Beck, A. T. & Steer, R. A. (1987). *Manual for the Beck Depression Inventory*. San Antonio, TX: Psychological Corporation.

Berard, A., Azoulay, L., Koren, G., et al. (2007). Isotreninoin, pregnancies, abortions and birth defects: A population-based perspective. *British Journal of Clinical Pharmacology, 63*, 196–205.

Biederman, J., Monuteaux, M. C., Spencer, T., et al. (2009). Do stimulants protect against psychiatric disorders in youth with ADHD: A 10-year follow-up study. *Pediatrics, 124*, 71-78.

Biederman, J., Petty, C. R., Monuteaux, M. C., et al. (2010). Adult psychiatric outcomes of girls with attention deficit hyperactivity disorder: 11-year follow-up in a longitudinal case-control study. *American Journal of Psychiatry, 167*, 409-417.

Biederman, J., Spencer, T. J., Monuteaux, M. C., et al. (2010). A naturalistic 10-year prospective study of height and weight in children with attention-deficit/hyperactivity disorder grown up: Sex and treatment effects. *Journal of Pediatrics*, on-line, June 7, 2010.

Biederman, J., Spencer, T. J., Wilens, T. E., et al. (2006). Treatment of ADHD with stimulant medications: Response to Nissen perspective in *The New England Journal of Medicine*. *Journal of the American Academy of Child and Adolescent Psychiatry, 45*,1147–1150.

Biederman, J., Wilens, T., Mick, E., et al. (1999). Pharmacotherapy of attention-deficit/hyperactivity disorder reduces risk for substance use disorder. *Pediatrics, 104*, e20.

Birmaher, B., Axelson, D. A., Monk, K., et al. (2003). Fluoxetine for the treatment of childhood anxiety disorders. *Journal of the American Academy of Child and Adolescent Psychiatry, 42*, 415–423.

Birmaher, B., Axelson, D., Strober, M., et al. (2006). Clinical course of children and adolescents with bipolar spectrum disorders. *Archives of General Psychiatry, 63*, 175–183.

Birmaher, B., Ryan, N. D., Willamson, D. E., et al. (1996). Childhood and adolescent depression: A review of the past 10 years. Part 1. *Journal of the American Academy of Child and Adolescent Psychiatry, 35,* 1427–1439.

Black, B., & Uhde, T. W. (1994). Treatment of elective mutism with fluoxetine: A double-blind, placebo-controlled study. *Journal of the American Academy of Child and Adolescent Psychiatry, 33,* 1000–1006.

Blader, J. C., Schooler, N. R., Jensen, P. S., et al. (2009). Adjunctive divalproex versus placebo for children with ADHD and aggression refractory to stimulant monotherapy. *American Journal of Psychiatry, 166,* 1392–1401.

Bloch, M. H. (2009). Trichotillomania across the life span. *Journal of the American Academy of Child and Adolescent Psychiatry, 48,* 879–883.

Bloch, M. H., Landeros-Weisenberger, A., Dombrowski, P., et al. (2007). Systematic seview: pharmacological and behavioral treatment for trichotillomania. *Biological Psychiatry, 62,* 839–846.

Bloch, M. H., Panza, K. E., Landeros-Weisenberger, A., et al. (2009). Meta-analysis: Treatment of attention-deficit/hyperactivity disorder in children with comorbid tic disorders. *Journal of the American Academy of Child and Adolescent Psychiatry, 48,* 884–893.

Blumer, J. L., Findling, R. L., Shih, W. J., et al. (2009). Controlled clinical trial of zolpidem for the treatment of insomnia associated with attention-deficit/hyperactivity disorder in children 6–17 years of age. *Pediatrics, 123,* e770–776.

Boylan, K., Georgiades, K., & Szatmari, P. (2010). The longitudinal association between oppositional and depressive symptoms across childhood. *Journal of the American Academy of Child and Adolescent Psychiatry, 49,* 152–161.

Bradley, C. (1937). The behavior of children receiving benzedrine. *American Journal of Psychiatry, 94,* 577–585.

Brent, D., Emslie, G., Clarke, G., et al. (2008). Switching to another SSRI or to venlafaxine with or without cognitive behavioral therapy for adolescents with SSRI-resistant depression. *Journal of the American Medical Association, 299,* 901–913.

Bridge, J. A., Birmaher, B., Iyengar, S., et al. (2009). Placebo response in randomized controlled trials of antidepressants for pediatric major depressive disorder. *American Journal of Psychiatry, 166*, 42–29.

Brotman, M. A., Kassem, L., Reising, M. M., et al. (2007). Parental diagnoses in youth with narrow phenotype bipolar disorder or severe mood dysregulation. *American Journal of Psychiatry, 164*, 1238–1241.

Brown-Sequard, C. (1889). The effects produced on man by subcutaneous injections of a liquid obtained from the testicles of animals. *Lancet, 134*, 105–107.

Buckley, W. E., Yesalis, C. E., Freidl, K. E., et al. (1988). Estimated prevalence of anabolic steroid use among male high school seniors. *Journal of the American Medical Association, 260*, 3441–3445.

Campbell, M., Adams, P. B., & Small, A. M., et al. (1995). Lithium in hospitalized aggressive children with conduct disorder: A double-blind and placebo-controlled study. *Journal of the American Academy of Child and Adolescent Psychiatry, 34*, 445–453.

Campbell, M., Small, A. M. , Green, W. H., et al. (1984). Behavioral efficacy of haloperidol and lithium carbonate. *Archives of General Psychiatry, 41*, 650–656.

Carandang, C. G. (2006, November 2). Lamotrigine in adolescent treatment-resistant depression. *Child & Adolescent Psychopharmacology News, 11*(2), 1–5, 10.

Carandang, C. G., Maxwell, D. J., Robbins, D. R., et al. (2003). Lamotrigine in adolescent mood disorders. *Journal of the American Academy of Child and Adolescent Psychiatry, 42*, 750–751.

Carlson, G. A. (2005). Diagnosing bipolar disorder in children and adolescents. *Child & Adolescent Psychopharmacology News, 10*(2), 1-6.

Carlson, G. A. (2009). Treating the childhood bipolar controversy: A tale of two children. *American Journal of Psychiatry, 166*, 18–24.

Carlson, T., Reynolds, C. A., & Caplan, R. (2007). Case report: Valproic acid and risperidone treatment leading to development of hyperammonemia and mania. *Journal of the American Academy of Child and Adolescent Psychiatry, 46*, 356–361.

Castellanos, X. F., Giedd, J .N., Elia, J., et al. (1997). Controlled stimulant treatment of ADHD and comorbid Tourette's syndrome: Effects of stimulant and dose. *Journal of the American Academy of Child and Adolescent Psychiatry, 36,* 589–596.

Castle, L., Aubert, R. E., Verbrugge, R. R., et al. (2007). Trends in medication treatment for ADHD. *Journal of Attention Disorders, 10,* 335–342.

Chambers, C. D., Hernandez-Diaz, S., Van Marter, L. J., et al. (2006). Selective serotonin-reuptake inhibitors and risk of persistent pulmonary hypertension of the newborn. *New England Journal of Medicine, 354,* 579–587.

Chang, K., Saxena, K., & Howe, M. (2006). An open-label study of lamotrigine adjunct or monotherapy for the treatment of adolescents with bipolar depression. *Journal of the American Academy of Child and Adolescent Psychiatry, 45,* 298–304.

Chang, K. D., Saxena, K., Howe, M., et al. (2010). Psychotropic medication exposure and age at onset of bipolar disorder in offspring of parents with bipolar disorder. *Journal of Child and Adolescent Psychopharmacology, 20,* 25–32.

Charach, A., Ickowicz, A., & Schachar, R. (2004). Stimulant treatment over five years: Adherence, effectiveness, and adverse effects. *Journal of the American Academy of Child and Adolescent Psychiatry, 43,* 559–567.

Chavira, D. A., Shipon-Blum, E., Hitchcock, C. et al. (2007). Selective mutism and social anxiety disorder: All in the family? *Journal of the American Academy of Child and Adolescent Psychiatry, 46,* 1464–1472.

Chia, C. Y., Lane, W., Chibnall, J., et al. (2005). Isotretinoin therapy and mood changes in adolescents with moderate to severe acne: A cohort study. *Archives of Dermatology, 141,* 557–560.

Clarke, G., Debar, L., Lynch, F., et al. (2005). A randomized effectiveness trial of brief cognitive-behavioral therapy for depressed adolescents receiving antidepressant medication. *Journal of the American Academy of Child and Adolescent Psychiatry, 44,* 888–898.

Coffey, Barbara, J. (2010)."Tics, Tourette's disorder and comorbidity: Strategies for treatment resistance." Advanced Psychopharmacology for Clinical Practice Institute at American Academy of Child and Adolescent Psychiatry Meeting. October 26, 2010.

Cohen, J. A., Mannarino, A. P., Perel, J. M., et al. (2007). A pilot randomized controlled trial of combined trauma focused CBT and sertraline for childhood PTSD symptoms. *Journal of the American Academy of Child and Adolescent Psychiatry, 46*, 811–819.

Colman, I., Wadsworth, M. F. J., Croudace, T. J., et al. (2007). Forty-year psychiatric outcomes following assessment for internalizing disorder in adolescence. *American Journal of Psychiatry, 164*, 126–133.

Conners, C. K., Casat, C. D., Gualtieri, C. T., et al. (1996). Bupropion hydrochloride in attention deficit disorder with hyperactivity. *Journal of the American Academy of Child and Adolescent Psychiatry, 35*, 1314–1321.

Connor, D. F. (2004). Paroxetine and the FDA. *Journal of the American Academy of Child and Adolescent Psychiatry, 43*, 127.

Cook, E. H., Wagner, K. D., March, J. S., et al. (2001). Long-term sertraline treatment of children and adolescents with obsessive-compulsive disorder. *Journal of the American Academy of Child and Adolescent Psychiatry, 40*, 1175–1181.

Cooper, W. O., HIckson, G. B., Fuchs, C., et al. (2004). New users of antipsychotic medications among children enrolled in Tenncare. *Archives of Pediatrics and Adolescent Medicine, 158*, 753–759.

Corkum, P., Rimer, P., & Schachar, R. (1999). Parental knowledge of attention-deficit hyperactivity disorder and opinions of treatment options: Impact on enrollment and adherence to a 12-month treatment trial. *Canadian Journal of Psychiatry, 44*, 1043–1048.

Correll, C. (2007). Weight gain and metabolic effects of mood stabilizers and antipsychotics in pediatric bipolar disorder: A systematic review and pooled analysis of short-term trials. *Journal of the American Academy of Child and Adolescent Psychiatry, 46*, 687–700.

Correll, C. (2008). Antipsychotic use in children and adolescents: Minimizing adverse effects to maximize outcomes. *Journal of the American Academy of Child and Adolescent Psychiatry, 47*, 117–128.

Correll, C. U., & Carlson, H. E. (2006). Endocrine and metabolic adverse effects of psychotropic medications in children and adolescents. *Journal of the American Academy of Child and Adolescent Psychiatry, 45*, 771–791.

Correll, C.U., Manu, P., Olshanskiy, V., et al. (2009). Cardiometabolic risk of second-generation antipsychotic medications during first-time use in children and adolescents. *Journal of the American Medical Association, 302,* 1765–1773.

Costello, E. J., Angold, A., Burns, B. J. et al (1996). The Great Smoky Mountains study of youth: Goals, design, methods and prevalence of DSM-III-R disorders. *Archives of General Psychiatry 53,* 1129-1136.

Cox, D. J., Merkel, R. L., Moore, M., et al. (2006). Relative benefits of stimulant therapy with OROS methylphenidate stimulant versus mixed amphetamine salts extended release in improving the driving performance of adolescent drivers with attention-deficit/hyperactivity disorder. *Pediatrics, 118,* e704–e710.

Curry, J., Rohde, P., Simons, A., et al. (2006). Predictors and moderators of acute outcome in the treatment for adolescents with depression study (TADS). *Journal of the American Academy of Child and Adolescent Psychiatry, 45,* 1427–1439.

Curry, J., Silva, S., Rohde, P. et al. (2010). Recovery and recurrence following treatment for adolescent major depression. *Archives of General Psychiatry.* doi: 10.1001/archgenpsychiatry.2010.150.

Curtis, L. H., Masselink, L. E., Ostbye, T., et al. (2005). Prevalence of atypical antipsychotic drug use among commercially insured youths in the United States. *Archives of Pediatrics and Adolescent Medicine, 159,* 362–366.

Daviss, W. B., Bentivoglio, P., Racusin R., et al. (2001). Bupropion sustained release in adolescents with comorbid attention-deficit/hyperactivity disorder and depression. *Journal of the American Academy of Child and Adolescent Psychiatry, 40,* 307–314.

De Abajo, F. J., & Garcia-Rodriguez, L. A. (2008). Risk of upper gastrointestinal tract bleeding associated with selective serotonin reuptake inhibitors and venlafaxine therapy. *Archives of General Psychiatry, 65,* 795–803.

DelBello, M. P., Chang, K., Welge, J. A., et al. (2009). A double-blind, placebo-controlled pilot study of quetiapine for depressed adolescents with bipolar disorder. *Bipolar Disorder 11,* 483-493.

DelBello, M. P., Findling, R. L., Kushner, S., et al. (2005). A pilot controlled trial of topiramate for mania in children and adolescents with bipolar disorder. *Journal of the American Academy of Child and Adolescent Psychiatry, 44,* 539–547.

DelBello, M. P., Schwiers, M. L., Rosenberg, H., et al. (2002). A double-blind, randomized, placebo-controlled study of quetiapine as adjunctive treatment for adolescent mania. *Journal of the American Academy of Child and Adolescent Psychiatry, 41,* 1216–1223.

DeLeon, O. A. (2000, December). Anti-epileptic drugs in bipolar disorder. *Child & Adolescent Psychopharmacology News, 5*(6), 1–5.

DeVeaugh-Geiss, J., Moroz, G., Biederman, J., et al. (1992). Clomipramine hydrochloride in childhood and adolescent obsessive-compulsive disorder: A multicenter trial. *Journal of the American Academy of Child and Adolescent Psychiatry, 31,* 45–49.

Diamond, I. R., Tannock, R., Schachar, R. J., et al. (1999). Response to methylphenidate in children with ADHD and comorbid anxiety. *Journal of the American Academy of Child and Adolescent Psychiatry, 38,* 402–409.

Dilsaver, S. C., Chen, Y. W., Swann, A. C., et al. (1997). Suicidality, panic disorder and psychosis in bipolar depression, depressive-mania and pure-mania. *Psychiatry Research, 73,* 47–56.

Dion, Y., Annable, L., Sandor, P., et al. (2002). Risperidone in the treatment of Tourette syndrome: A double blind, placebo-controlled trial. *Journal of Clinical Psychopharmacology, 22,* 31–39.

Donnelly, C., Bangs, M., Trzepacz, P., et al. (2009). Safety and tolerability of atomoxetine over 3 to 4 years in children and adolescents with ADHD. *Journal of the American Academy of Child and Adolescent Psychiatry, 48,* 176–185.

Donovan, S. J., Stewart, J. W., Nunes, E. V., et al. (2000). Divalproex treatment for youth with explosive temper and mood lability: A double-blind, placebo-controlled crossover design. *American Journal of Psychiatry, 157,* 818–820.

dos Reis, S., Zito, J. M., Safer, D. J., et al. (2005). Multiple psychotropic medication use for youths: A two-state comparison. *Journal of Child and Adolescent Psychopharmacology, 15,* 68–77.

Duffy, F. F., Narrow, W. E., Rae, D. S., et al. (2005). Concomitant pharmacotherapy among youths treated in routine psychiatric practice. *Journal of Child and Adolescent Psychopharmacology, 15*, 12–25.

Duggal, H. S., & Kithas, J. (2005). Possible neuroleptic malignant syndrome with aripiprazole and fluoxetine. *American Journal of Psychiatry, 62*, 397–398.

Dummit, E. S., Klein, R. G., Tancer, N. K., et al. (1997). Systematic assessment of 50 children with selective mutism. *Journal of the American Academy of Child and Adolescent Psychiatry, 36*, 653–660.

Egger, H. (2010). A perilous disconnect: Antipsychotic drug use in very young children. *Journal of the American Academy of Child and Adolescent Psychiatry, 49*, 3–6.

Elkins, R. N., Rapoport, J. L., Zahn, T. P., et al. (1981). Acute effects of caffeine in normal prepubertal boys. *American Journal of Psychiatry, 138*, 178–183.

Emslie, G. J., Findling, R. L., Yeung, P. P., et al. (2007). Venlafaxine ER for the treatment of pediatric subjects with depression: Results of two placebo-controlled trials. *Journal of the American Academy of Child and Adolescent Psychiatry, 46*, 479–488.

Emslie, G. J., Heiligenstein, J. H., Wagner, K. D., et al. (2002). Fluoxetine for acute treatment of depression in children and adolescents: A placebo-controlled, randomized clinical trial. *Journal of the American Academy of Child and Adolescent Psychiatry, 41*, 1205–1215.

Emslie, G. J., Kennard, B. D., Mayes, T. L., et al. (2008). Fluoxetine versus placebo in preventing relapse of major depression in children and adolescents. *American Journal of Psychiatry, 165*, 459–467.

Emslie, G. J., Rush, A. J., Weinberg, W. A., et al. (1997). A double-blind, randomized, placebo-controlled trial of fluoxetine in children and adolescents with depression. *Archives of General Psychiatry, 54*, 1031–1037.

Emslie, G. J., Venture, D., Korotzer, A., et al. (2009). Escitalopram in the treatment of adolescent depression: A randomized, placebo-controlled multisite trial. *Journal of the American Academy of Child and Adolescent Psychiatry, 48*, 721–729.

Emslie, G. J., Wagner, K. D., Kutcher, S., et al. (2006). Paroxetine treatment in children and adolescents with major depressive disorder: A randomized, multicenter, double-blind, placebo-controlled trial. *Journal of the American Academy of Child and Adolescent Psychiatry, 45*, 709–719.

Faraone, S. V., Biederman, J., Morley, C. P., et al. (2008). Effect of stimulants on height and weight: A review of the literature. *Journal of the American Academy of Child and Adolescent Psychiatry, 47*, 994–1009.

Faraone, S. V., Biederman, J., Spencer, T., et al. (2006). Diagnosing adult attention deficit hyperactivity disorder: Are late onset and subthreshold diagnoses valid? *American Journal of Psychiatry, 163*, 720–729.

Fedorowicz, V. J., & Fombonne, E. (2005). Metabolic side effects of atypical antipsychotics in children: A literature review. *Journal of Pyschopharmacology, 19*, 533–550.

Fiedorowicz, J. G., Endicott, J., Leon, A. C. et al (2011). Subthreshold hypomanic symptoms in progression from unipolar major depression to bipolar disorder. *American Journal of Psychiatry, 168*, 40–48.

Findling, R. L., Johnson, J. L., McClellan, J., et al. (2010). Double-blind maintenance safety and effectiveness findings from the treatment of early-onset schizophrenia spectrum (TEOSS) study. *Journal of the American Academy of Child and Adolescent Psychiatry, 49*, 583–594.

Findling, R. L., Kusumakar, V., Daneman, D. et al (2003) Prolactin levels during long-term risperidone treatment in children and adolescents. *Journal of Clinical Psychiatry, 64*, 1362–1369.

Findling, R. L., McNamara, N. K., Branicky, L. A., et al. (2000). A double-blind pilot study of risperidone in the treatment of conduct disorder. *Journal of the American Academy of Child and Adolescent Psychiatry, 39*, 509–516.

Findling, R. L., McNamara, N. K., Gracious, B. L., et al. (2003). Combination lithium and divalproex sodium in pediatric bipolarity. *Journal of the American Academy of Child and Adolescent Psychiatry, 42*, 895–901.

Findling, R. L., McNamara, N. K., Youngstrom, E. A., et al. (2003). A prospective, open-label trial of olanzapine in adolescents with schizophrenia. *Journal of the American Academy of Child and Adolescent Psychiatry, 42*, 170–175.

Findling, R. L., McNamara, N. K., Youngstrom, E. A., et al. (2005). Double-blind 18-month trial of lithium versus divalproex maintenance treatment in pediatric bipolar disorder. *Journal of the American Academy of Child and Adolescent Psychiatry, 44,* 409–417.

Findling, R. L., McNamara, N. K., Stansbrey, R., et al. (2006). Combination lithium and divalproex sodium in pediatric bipolar symptom restabilization. *Journal of the American Academy of Child and Adolescent Psychiatry, 45,* 142–148.

Findling, R. L., Nyilas, M., Forbes, R. A., et al. (2009). Acute treatment of pediatric bipolar I disorder, manic or mixed episode, with aripiprazole: A randomized, double-blind, placebo-controlled study. *Journal of Clinical Psychiatry, 70,* 1441–1451.

Findling, R. L., Robb, A., Nyilas, M., et al. (2008). A multiple-center, randomized, double-blind, placebo-controlled study of oral aripiprazole for treatment of adolescents with schizophrenia. *American Journal of Psychiatry, 165,* 1432–1441.

Flament, M. F., Rapoport, J. L., Berg, C. J., et al. (1985). Clomipramine treatment of childhood obsessive-compulsive disorder: A double-blind controlled study. *Archives of General Psychiatry, 42,* 977–983.

Fluoxetine Bulimia Nervosa Collaborative Study Group. (1992). Fluoxetine in the treatment of bulimia nervosa: A multicenter, placebo-controlled, double-blind trial. *Archives of General Psychiatry, 49,* 139–147.

Fortinguerra, F., Clavenna, A., & Bonati, M. (2009). Psychotropic drug use during breastfeeding: A review of the evidence. *Pediatrics, 124,* e547–e556.

Freedman, R. (2010). Psychiatrists' role in the health of the pregnant mother and the risk of schizophrenia in her offspring. *American Journal of Psychiatry, 167,* 239–240.

Gadow, K. D., Sverd, J., Sprafkin, J., et al. (1995). Efficacy of methylphenidate for attention-deficit hyperactivity disorder in children with tic disorder. *Archives of General Psychiatry, 52,* 444–455.

Gadow, K. D., Sverd, J., Sprafkin, J., et al. (1999). Long-term methylphenidate therapy in children with comorbid attention-deficit hyperactivity disorder and chronic multiple tic disorder. *Archives of General Psychiatry, 56,* 330–336.

Gamo, N. J., Wang, M., & Arnsten, A. F. T. (2010). Methylphenidate and atomoxetine enhance prefrontal function through alpha-2 adrenergic and dopamine D1 receptors. *Journal of the American Academy of Child and Adolescent Psychiatry, 49*, 1011–1023.

Garfinkel, B. D., Webster, C. D., & Sloman, L. (1975). Methylphenidate and caffeine in the treatment of children with minimal brain dysfunction. *American Journal of Psychiatry, 132*, 723–728.

Geller, B., Cooper, T. B., Sun, K., et al. (1998). Double-blind and placebo-controlled Study of lithium for adolescent bipolar disorders with secondary substance dependency. *Journal of the American Academy of Child and Adolescent Psychiatry, 37*, 171–178.

Geller, B., Tillman, R., Craney, J. L. et al. (2004). Four-year prospective outcome and natural history of mania in children with a prepubertal and early adolescent bipolar disorder phenotype. *Archives of General Psychiatry, 61*, 459–467.

Geller, B., Tillman, R., Bolhofner, K., et al. (2008). Child bipolar I disorder: Prospective continuity with adult bipolar I disorder; characteristics of second and third episodes; predictors of 8-year outcome. *Archives of General Psychiatry, 65*, 1125–1133.

Geller, D., Donnelly, C., Lopez, F., et al. (2007). Atomoxetine treatment for pediatric patients with attention-deficit/hyperactivity disorder with comorbid anxiety disorder. *Journal of the American Academy of Child and Adolescent Psychiatry, 46*, 1119–1127.

Geller, D. A., Hoog, S. L., Heiligenstein, J. H., et al. (2001). Fluoxetine treatment for obsessive-compulsive disorder in children and adolescents: A placebo-controlled clinical trial. *Journal of the American Academy of Child and Adolescent Psychiatry, 40*, 773–779.

Geller, D. A., Wagner, K. D., Emslie, G., et al. (2004). Paroxetine treatment in children and adolescents with obsessive-compulsive disorder: A randomized, multicenter, double-blind, placebo-controlled trial. *Journal of the American Academy of Child and Adolescent Psychiatry, 43*, 1387–1396.

Geller, B., Tillman, R., Craney, J. L., et al. (2004). Four-year prospective outcome and natural history of mania in children with a prepubertal and early adolescent bipolar disorder phenotype. *Archives of General Psychiatry, 61*, 459–67.

Gentile, S. (2010). On categorizing gestational, birth, and neonatal complications following late pregnancy exposure to antidepressants: The prenatal antidepressant exposure syndrome. *CNS Spectrums, 15,* 167–185.

Ghaemi, S. N., Rosenquist, K. J., Ko, J. Y., et al. (2004). Antidepressant treatment in bipolar versus unipolar depression. *American Journal of Psychiatry, 161,* 163–165.

Ghuman, J. K., Aman, M. G., Lecavalier, L., et al. (2009). Randomized, placebo-controlled, crossover study of methylphenidate for attention-deficit/hyperactivity disorder symptoms in preschoolers with developmental disorders. *Journal of Child and Adolescent Psychopharmacology, 19,* 329–339.

Gilbert, D. L., Batterson, J. R., Sethuraman, G., et al. (2004). Tic reduction with risperidone versus pimozide in a randomized, double-blind, crossover trial. *Journal of the American Academy of Child and Adolescent Psychiatry, 43,* 206–214.

Gittelman Klein, R., & Mannuzza, S. (1988). Hyperactive boys almost grown up. III. Methylphenidate effects on ultimate height. *Archives of General Psychiatry, 45,* 1131–1134.

Gleason, M. M., Egger, H. L., & Emslie, G. J. (2007). Psychopharmacological treatment for very young children: Contexts and guidelines. *Journal of the American Academy of Child and Adolescent Psychiatry, 46,* 1532–1572.

Gonzalez-Heydrich, J., Weiss, M., Connolly, M. et al (2006). Pharmacological management of a youth with ADHD and a seizure disorder. *Journal of the American Academy of Child and Adolescent Psychiatry, 45,* 1527–1532.

Goodman, L. S. & Gilman, A. (1975). *The pharmacological basis of therapeutics.* New York, NY: Macmillan.

Goodyer, I., Dubicka, B., Wilkinson, P., et al. (2007, June 7). Selective serotonin reuptake inhibitors (SSRIs) and routine specialist care with and without cognitive behaviour therapy in adolescents with major depression: Randomised controlled trial. *British Medical Journal, 335,* 142. doi:10.1136/bmj.39224.494340.55.

Grant, J. E., Odlaug, B. L., & Kim S. W. (2009). N-acetylcysteine, a glutamate modulator, in the treatment of trichotillomania: A double-blind, placebo-controlled study. *Archives of General Psychiatry, 66,* 756 763.

Greenhill, L. L. (2009). "Update on the treatment of children and adolescents with ADHD". Child and Adolescent Psychopharmacology: Evidence-based Treatments and Beyond. New York, NY. January 23 & 24, 2009.

Greenhill, L., Kollins, S., Abikoff, H., et al. (2006). Efficacy and safety of immediate-release methylphenidate treatment for preschoolers with ADHD. *Journal of the American Academy of Child and Adolescent Psychiatry, 45,* 1284–1293.

Greenhill, L. L., Biederman, J., Boellner, S. W., et al. (2006). A randomized, double-blind, placebo-controlled study of modafinil film-coated tablets in children and adolescents with attention-deficit/hyper-activity disorder. *Journal of the American Academy of Child and Adolescent Psychiatry, 45,* 503–511.

Grella, C. E., Hser, Y. I., Joshi, V., et al. (2001). Drug treatment outcomes for adolescents with comorbid mental and substance use disorders. *Journal of Nervous and Mental Disorders, 189,* 384–392.

Guevara, J., Lozano P., Wickizer, T., et al. (2002). Psychotropic medication use in a population of children who have attention-deficit/hyperactivity disorder. *Pediatrics, 109,* 733–739.

Gutgesell, H., Atkins, D., Barst, R., et al. (1999). Cardiovascular monitoring of children and adolescents receiving psychotropic drugs: A statement for healthcare professionals from the Committee on Congenital Cardiac Defects, Council on Cardiovascular Disease in the Young, American Heart Association. *Circulation, 99,* 979–982.

Haas, M,, Delbello, M. P., Pandina, G., et al. (2009). Risperidone for the treatment of acute mania in children and adolescents with bipolar disorder: A randomized, double-blind, placebo-controlled study. *Bipolar Disorders, 11,* 687–700.

Habel, L. A., Schaefer, C. A., Levine, P., et al. (2005). Treatment with stimulants among youths in a large California health plan. *Journal of Child and Adolescent Psychopharmacology, 15,* 62–67.

Hall, R. C. W. & Chapman, M. J. (2005). Psychiatric complications of anabolic steroid abuse. *Psychosomatics, 46,* 285–290.

Halvorsen, J. A., Stern, R. S., Dalgard, F., et al. (2010, September 16). Suicidal ideation, mental health problems, and social impairment are increased in adolescents with acne: A population-based study. *Journal of Investigative Dermatology.* Advance online publication. doi:10.1038/jld.2010.264.

Hamani, Y., Sciaki-Tamir, Y., & Deri-Hasid, R. (2007). Misconceptions about oral contraception pills among adolescents and physicians. *Human Reproduction, 22,* 3078–3083.

Hazell, P. L., Stuart, J. E. (2003). A randomized controlled trial of clonidine added to psychostimulant medication for hyperactive and aggressive children. *Journal of the American Academy of Child and Adolescent Psychiatry, 42,* 886–894.

Hechtman, L., Abikoff, H., Klein, R. G., et al. (2004a). Academic achievement and emotional status of children with ADHD treated with long-term methylphenidate and multimodal psychchosocial treatment. *Journal of the American Academy of Child and Adolescent Psychiatry, 43,* 812–919.

Hechtman, L., Abikoff, H., Klein, R. G., et al. (2004b). Children with ADHD treated with long-term methylphenidate and multimodal psychosocial treatment: Impact on parental practices. *Journal of the American Academy of Child and Adolescent Psychiatry, 43,* 830–838.

Henderson, D. C., Cagliero, E., Gray, C., Nasrallah, R. A., Hayden, D. L., Schoenfeld, D. A., Goff, D. C. (2000). Clozapine, diabetes mellitus, weight gain, and lipid abnormalities: A five-year naturalistic study. *American Journal of Psychiatry, 157,* 975–981.

Hollander, E., Chaplin, W., Soorya, L., et al. (2010). Divalproex sodium vs. placebo for the treament of irritability in children and adolescents with autism spectrum disorders. *Neuropsychopharmacology, 35,* 990–998.

Hoover, D. W., & Milich, R. (1994). Effects of sugar ingested expectancies on mother-child interactions. *Journal of Abnormal Child Psychology, 22,* 501–515.

Horne, R. L., Ferguson, J. M., Pope, H. G., et al. (1988). Treatment of bulimia with bupropion: A multicenter controlled trial. *Journal of Clinical Psychiatry, 49*, 262–266.

Horrigan, J. P. (1996). Guanfacine for PTSD nightmares. *Journal of the American Academy of Child and Adolescent Psychiatry, 35*, 975–976.

Hughes, C. W., Emslie, G. J., Crismon, L. M., et al. (2007). Texas children's medication algorithm project: Update from Texas consensus conference panel on medication treatment of childhood major depressive disorder. *Journal of the American Academy of Child and Adolescent Psychiatry, 46*, 667–686.

Hunkeler, E. M., Fireman B., Lee, J., et al. (2005). Trends in use of antidepressants, lithium, and anticonvulsants in Kaiser Permanante-insured youths, 1994–2003. *Journal of Child and Adolescent Psychopharmacology, 15*, 26–37.

Jensen, P., Kettle, L., Roper, M. T., et al. (1999). Are stimulants over-prescribed? Treatment of ADHD in four US communities. *Journal of the American Academy of Child and Adolescent Psychiatry, 38*, 797–804.

Jensen, P. S., Arnold, L. E., Swanson J. M., et al. (2007). Three-year follow-up of the NIMH MTA study. *Journal of the American Academy of Child and Adolescent Psychiatry, 46*, 989–1002.

Joffe, H., Cohen, L. S., Harlow, B. L. (2003). Impact of oral contraceptive pill use on premenstrual mood: Predictors of improvement and deterioration. *American Journal of Obstetrics and Gynecology, 189*, 1523–1530.

Joffe, H., Petrillo, L. F., Viguera, A. C., et al. (2007). Treatment of premenstrual worsening of depression with adjunctive oral contraceptive pills: A preliminary report. *Journal of Clinical Psychiatry, 68*, 1954–1962.

Juruena, M. F., Ottoni, G. L., Machado-Vieria, R., et al. (2009). Bipolar I and II disorder residual symptoms: Oxcarbazepine and carbamazepine as add-on treatment to lithium in a double-blind, randomized trial. *Progress in Neuropsychopharmacology and Biological Psychiatry, 33*, 94–99.

Kantafaris, V., Coletti, D. J., & Dicker, R. (2001). Adjunctive antipsychotic treatment of adolescents with bipolar psychosis. *Journal of the American Academy of Child and Adolescent Psychiatry, 40*, 1448–1456.

Kantafaris, V., Coletti, D. J., & Dicker, R. (2003). Lithium treatment of acute mania in adolescents: A large open trial. *Journal of the American Academy of Child and Adolescent Psychiatry, 42*, 1038–1045.

Kaye, W. H., Nagata, T., Weltzin, T. E., et al. (2001). Double-blind, placebo-controlled administration of fluoxetine in restricting- and restricting-purging-type anorexia nervosa. *Biological Psychiatry, 49*, 644–652.

Keller, M. B., Ryan, N. D., Strober, M. et al (2001). Efficacy of paroxetine in the treatment of adolescent major depression: a randomized, controlled trial. *Journal of the American Academy of Child and Adolescent Psychiatry, 40*, 762–772.

Kennard, B. D., Silva, S. G., Tonev, S., et al. (2009). Remission and recovery in the treatment for adolescents with depression study (TADS): Acute and long-term outcomes. *Journal of the American Academy of Child and Adolescent Psychiatry, 48*, 186–195.

King, B. H., Hollander, E., Sikich, L., et al. (2009). Lack of efficacy of citalopram in children with autism spectrum disorders and high levels of repetitive behavior. *Archives of General Psychiatry, 66*, 583–590.

Kirsch, I., & Weixel, L. J. (1988). Double-blind versus deceptive administration of a placebo. *Behavioral Neuroscience, 102*, 319–323.

Klein, D. J., Cottingham, E. M., & Sorter, M. (2006). A randomized, double-blind, placebo-controlled trial of metformin treatment of weight gain associated with initiation of atypical antipsychotic therapy in children and adolescents. *American Journal of Psychiatry, 163*, 2072–2079.

Klein, R. G., Abikoff, H., Hechtman, L., et al. (2004). Design and rationale of controlled study of long-term methlyphenidate and multimodal psychosocial treatment in children with ADHD. *Journal of the American Academy of Child and Adolescent Psychiatry, 43*, 792–801.

Kontaxakis, V. P., Karaiskos, D., Havaki-Kontaxaki, B. J., et al. (2009). Can quetiapine-induced hypothyroidism be reversible without quetiapine discontinuation? *Clinical Neuropharmacology, 32*, 295–296.

Kotler, L. A., Devlin, M. J., Davies, M., et al. (2003). An open trial of fluoxetine for adolescence with bulimia nervosa. *Journal of Child and Adolescent Psychopharmacology, 13*, 329–335.

Kowatch, R. A., Suppes, T., Carmody, T. J., et al. (2000). Effect size of lithium, divalproex sodium, and carbamazepine in children and adolescents with bipolar disorder. *Journal of the American Academy of Child and Adolescent Psychiatry, 39*, 713–720.

Kratochvil, C. J. and Owens, J. (2009). Pharmacotherapy of Pediatric Insomnia. *Journal of the American Academy of Child and Adolescent Psychiatry, 48*, 99–107.

Kumra, S., Frazier, J. A., Jacobsen, L. K et al (1996). Childhood-onset schizophrenia: a double-blind clozapine-haloperidol comparison. *Archives of General Psychiatry, 53*, 1090–1097.

Kushner, S. F., Khan, A., Lane, R., et al. (2006). Topiramate mono-therapy in the management of acute mania: Results of four double-blind, placebo-controlled trials. *Bipolar Disorders, 8*, 15–27.

Lahey, B. B., Pelham, W. E., Loney, J., et al. (2005). Instability of the DSM-IV subtypes of ADHD from preschool through elementary school. *Archives of General Psychiatry, 62*, 896–902.

Lambert, N. M., McLeod, M., & Schenk, S. (2006). Subjective responses to initial experience with cocaine: An exploration of the incentive-sensitization theory of drug abuse. *Addiction, 101*, 713–725.

Law, S. F., & Schachar, R. J. (1999). Do typical clinical doses of methylphenidate cause tics in children treated for attention-deficit hyperactivity disorder? *Journal of the American Academy of Child and Adolescent Psychiatry, 38*, 944–951.

LeFever, G. B., Dawson, K. V., & Morrow, A. L. (1999). The extent of drug therapy for attention deficit–hyperactivity disorder among children in public schools. *American Journal of Public Health, 89*, 1359–1364.

Leonard, H. L., Swedo, S. E., Rapoport, J. L., et al. (1989). Treatment of obsessive-compulsive disorder with clomipramine and desipramine in children and adolescents: A double-blind crossover comparison. *Archives of General Psychiatry, 46*, 1088–1092.

Lewinsohn, P. M., Klein, D. N., & Seeley, J. R. (1995). Bipolar disorders in a community sample of older adolescents: Prevalence, phenomenology, comorbidity, and course. *Journal of the American Academy of Child and Adolescent Psychiatry, 34*, 454–463.

Lewinsohn, P. M., Rohde, P., Seeley, J. R., et al. (2000). Natural course of adolescent major depressive disorder in a community sample: Predictors of recurrence in young adults. *American Journal of Psychiatry, 157,* 1584–1591.

Libby, A. M., Orton, H. D., & Valuck, R. J. (2009). Persisting decline in depression treatment after FDA warnings. *Archives of General Psychiatry, 66,* 633–639.

Lidstone, S. C., Schulzer, M., Dinelle, K., et al. (2010). Effects of expectation on placebo-induced dopamine release in Parkinson disease. *Archives of General Psychiatry, 67,* 857–865.

Liebenluft, E., Charney, D. S., Towbin, K. E., et al. (2003). Defining clinical phenotypes of juvenile mania. *American Journal of Psychiatry, 160,* 430–437.

Lock, J. (2009, October). Eating disorders in children and adolescents. *Psychiatric Times,* 35-39.

Luby, J. L. (2009). Early childhood depression. *American Journal of Psychiatry, 166,* 974–979.

Luby, J. L., Mrakotsky, C., Heffelfinger, A., et al. (2003). Modifications of DSM-IV criteria for depressed preschool children. *American Journal of Psychiatry, 160,* 1169–1172.

Luby, JL: Early childhood depression. *American Journal of Psychiatry 166*: 974-979, 2009.

Lyon, G. J., Samar, S., Jummani, R. et al (2009). Aripipprazole in children and adolescents with Tourette's disorder: An open-label safety and tolerability study. *Journal of Child and Adolescent Psychopharmacology, 19,* 623–633.

Ma, J., Lee, K. V., Stafford, R. S. (2005). Depression treatment during outpatient visits by U. S. children and adolescents. *Journal of Adolescent Health, 37,* 431–433.

March, J., Silva, S., Petrycki, S., et al. (2004). Fluoxetine, cognitive-behavioral therapy, and their combination for adolescents with depression. *Journal of the American Medical Association, 292,* 807–820.

March, J. S., Biederman, J., Wolkow, R., et al. (1998). Sertraline in children and adolescents with obsessive-compulsive disorder. *Journal of the American Medical Association, 280,* 1752–1756.

March, J. S., Entusah, A. R., Rynn, M., et al (2007). A randomized, controlled trial of venlafaxine ER versus placebo in pediatric social anxiety disorder. *Biological Psychiatry, 62,* 1149–1154.

Marcus, S. M., & Heringhausen, J. E. (2009). Depression in childbearing women: When depression complicates pregnancy. *Primary Care, 36,* 151–165.

Masse, P. G., Van den Berg, H., Livingstone, M. M., et al. (1998). Nutritional and psychological status of young women after a short-term use of a triphasic contraceptive steroid preparation. *International Journal of Vitamin and Nutritional Research, 68,* 203–207.

Mataix-Cols, D., Nakatani, E., Micali, N., et al. (2009). Structure of obsessive-compulsive symptoms in pediatric OCD. *Journal of the American Academy of Child and Adolescent Psychiatry, 47,* 773–778.

McCracken, J. T., McGough, J., Shah, B. et al (2002). Risperidone in children with autism and serous behavioral problems. *New England Journal of Medicine, 347,* 314–321.

McGuffin, P., Rijsdijk, F., Andrew, M., et al. (2003). The heritability of bipolar affective disorder and the genetic relationship to unipolar depression. *Archives of General Psychiatry, 60,* 497–502.

McKenzie, I., & Wurr, C. (2004). Diagnosing and treating attention difficulties: A nationwide survey. *Archives of Disease in Childhood, 89,* 913–916.

Melvin, G. A., Tonge, B. J., King, N. J., et al. (2006). A comparison of cognitive-behavioral therapy, sertraline, and their combination for adolescent depression. *Journal of the American Academy of Child and Adolescent Psychiatry, 45,* 1151–1161.

Mendlewicz, J., Souery, D., & Riveli, S. K, (2000, December). Short-term and long-term treatment for bipolar patients: Beyond the guidelines. *Child & Adolescent Psychopharmacology News, 5*(6), 5–11.

Merenstein, D., Diener-West, M., Halbower, A. C., et al. (2006). The trial of infant response to diphenhydramine: The TIRED study; a randomized, controlled, patient-oriented trial. *Archives of Pediatrics and Adolescent Medicine, 160,* 707–712.

Michelson, D., Allen A. J., Busner, J., et al. (2002). Once-daily atomoxetine treatment for children and adolescents with attention deficit hyperactivity disorder: A randomized, placebo-controlled study. *American Journal of Psychiatry, 159*, 1896–1901.

Michelson, D., Faries, D., Wernicke, J., et al. (2001). Atomoxetine in the treatment of children and adolescents with attention-deficit/hyperactivity disorder: A randomized, placebo-controlled, dose-response study. *Pediatrics, 108*, e83.

Michelson, D., Read, H. A., Ruff, D. D., et al. (2007). CYP2D6 and clinical response to atomoxetine in children and adolescents with ADHD. *Journal of the American Academy of Child and Adolescent Psychiatry, 46*, 242–251.

Molina, B. S. G., Hinshaw S. P., Swanson J. M., et al. (2009). The MTA at 8 years: Prospective follow-up of children treated for combined-type ADHD in a multisite study. *Journal of the American Academy of Child and Adolescent Psychiatry, 48*, 484–500.

MTA Cooperative Group. (1999a). A fourteen-month randomized clinical trial of treatment strategies for attention-deficit/hyperactivity disorder. *Archives of General Psychiatry, 56*, 1073–1086.

MTA Cooperative Group. (1999b). Moderators and mediators of treatment response for children with attention-deficit hyperactivity disorder: The multimodal treatment study of children with attention-deficit disorder. *Archives of General Psychiatry, 56*, 1088–1096.

Nemets, H., Nemets, B., Apter, A., et al. (2006). Omega-3 treatment of childhood depression: A controlled, double-blind pilot study. *American Journal of Psychiatry, 163*, 1098–1100.

Newcorn, J. H., Kratochvil, C. J., Allen, A. J., et al. (2008). Atomoxetine and osmotically released methylphenidate for the treatment of attention deficit hyperactivity disorder: Acute comparison and differential response. *American Journal of Psychiatry, 165*, 721–730.

Newcorn, J. H., Sutton, V. K., Weiss, M. D., et al. (2009). Clinical responses to atomoxetine in attention-deficit/hyperactivity disorder: The integrated data exploratory analysis (IDEA) study. *Journal of the American Academy of Child and Adolescent Psychiatry, 48*, 511–518.

Nilsson, M., Joliat, M. J., Miner, C. M., et al. (2004). Safety of subchronic treatment with fluoxetine for major depressive disorder in children and adolescents. *Journal of Child and Adolescent Psychopharmacology, 14*, 412–417.

Nur, M. M., Romano, M. E., & Siqueira, L. M. (2007). Premenstrual dysphoric disorder in an adolescent female. *Journal of Pediatric Adolescent Gynecology, 20*, 201–204.

Nurnberger, J. I. (2009). New hope for pharmacogenetic testing. *American Journal of Psychiatry, 166*, 635–638.

Oberlander, T. F., Warburton, W., Misri, S., et al. (2006). Neonatal outcomes after prenatal exposure to selective serotonin reuptake inhibitor antidepressants and maternal depression using population-based linked health data. *Archives of General Psychiatry, 63*, 898–906.

O'Connell, K., Davis, A. R., & Kerns, J. (2007). Oral contraceptives: Side effects and depression in adolescent girls. *Contraception, 75*, 299–304.

Oinonen, K. A., & Mazmanian, D. (2002). To what extent do oral contraceptives influence mood and affect? *Journal of Affective Disorders, 70*, 229–240.

Olfson, M., Marcus, S. C., Weissman, M. M., et al. (2002). National trends in the use of psychotropic medications by children. *Journal of the American Academy of Child and Adolescent Psychiatry, 41*, 514–521.

Owen, R., Sikich, L., Marcus, R. N., et al. (2009). Aripiprazole in the treatment of irritability in children and adolescents with autistic disorder. *Pediatrics, 124*, 1533–1540.

Papatheodorou, G., Kutcher, S. P., Katic, M., et al. (1995). The efficacy and safety of divalproex sodium in the treatment of acute mania in adolescents and young adults: An open clinical trial. *Journal of Clinical Psychopharmacology, 15*, 110–116.

Pappadopulos, E., MacIntyre, J. C., Crismon M. L., et al. (2003). Treatment recommendations for the use of antipsychotics for aggressive youth (TRAAY). Part II. *Journal of the American Academy of Child and Adolescent Psychiatry, 42*, 145–161.

Patel, N., DelBello, M., Bryan, H., et al. (2006). Open-label lithium for the treatment of adolescents with bipolar depression. *Journal of the American Academy of Child and Adolescent Psychiatry, 45*, 289–297.

Patton, G. C., Olsson, C., Bond, L., et al. (2008). Predicting female depression across puberty: A two-nation longitudinal study. *Journal of the American Academy of Child and Adolescent Psychiatry, 47,* 1424–1432.

Pavuluri, M. N., Henry, D. B., Carbray, J. A., et al. (2004). Open-label prospective trial of risperidone in combination with lithium or divalproex sodium in pediatric mania. *Journal of Affective Disorders, 82* (supplement), S103–S111.

Pavuluri, M. N., Henry, D. B., Carbray, J. A., et al. (2005). Divalproex sodium for pediatric mixed-mania: A 6-month prospective trial. *Bipolar Disorders, 7,* 266–273.

Pavuluri, M. N., & Sweeney, J. A. (2008). Integrating functional brain neuroimaging and developmental cognitive neuroscience in child psychiatry research. *Journal of the American Academy of Child and Adolescent Psychiatry, 47,* 1273–1288.

Paykina, N. & Greenhill, L. (2008). Attention-deficit/hyperactivity disorder. In R. L. Findling, MD, (Ed.) *Clinical manual of child and adolescent psychopharmacology* (pp. 33–97). Washington, DC: American Psychiatric Publishing.

Pediatric OCD Treatment Study (POTS) Team. (2004). Cognitive-behavior therapy, sertraline, and their combination for children and adolescents with obsessive-compulsive disorder: The Pediatric OCD Treatment Study (POTS) randomized controlled trial. *Journal of the American Medical Association, 292,* 1969–1976.

Pliszka, S. R., Matthew, T. L., Braslow, K. J., et al. (2006). Comparative effects of methylphenidate and mixed salts amphetamine on height and weight in children with attention-deficit/hyperactivity disorder. *Journal of the American Academy of Child and Adolescent Psychiatry, 45,* 520–526.

Polanczyk, G., de Lima, M. S., Horta, B. L., et al. (2007). The worldwide prevalence of ADHD: A systematic review and metaregression analysis. *American Journal of Psychiatry, 164,* 942–948.

Pope, H. G., & Katz, D. L. (1994). Psychiatric and medical effects of anabolic-androgenic steroid use: A controlled study of 160 athletes. *Archives of General Psychiatry, 51,* 375–382.

Posey, D. J., Wiegand, R. E., Wilkerson, J., et al. (2006). Open-label atomoxetine for attention-deficit/hyperactivity disorder symptoms associated with high functioning pervasive developmental disorders. *Journal of Child and Adolescent Psychopharmacology, 16,* 599–610.

Poznanski, E. O., & Mokros, H. B. (1995). *Children's Depression Rating Scale, Revised (CDRS-R) manual.* Los Angeles, CA: Western Psychological Services.

Raishevich, N., Pappadopulos, E., Jensen, P. S. (2008). Disruptive behavior Disorders and aggression. In R. L. Findling, MD, (Ed.) *Clinical manual of child and adolescent psychopharmacology* (pp. 99–142). Washington, DC: American Psychiatric Publishing.

Rao, U., Weissman, M. M., Martin, J. A., et al. (1993). Childhood depression and risk of suicide: A preliminary report of a longitudinal study. *Journal of the American Academy of Child and Adolescent Psychiatry, 32,* 21–27.

Rapkin, A. J., & Mikacich, J. A. (2008). Premenstrual syndrome and premenstrual dysphoric disorder in adolescents. *Current Opinion in Obstetrics and Gynecology, 20,* 455–463.

Rapoport, J. L., Buchsbaum, M. S., Weingartner, H., et al. (1980). Dextroamphetamine: Its cognitive and behavioral effects in normal and hyperactive boys and normal men. *Archives of General Psychiatry, 37,* 933–943.

Rapoport, J. L., Gogtay, N., Shaw, P. (2008) Schizophrenia and psychotic illnesses. In R. L. Findling, MD, (Ed.) *Clinical manual of child and adolescent psychopharmacology* (pp.337-373). Washington, DC: American Psychiatric Publishing.

Rashid, H., Ormerod, S., & Day, E. (2007). Anabolic androgenic steroids: What the psychiatrist needs to know. *Advances in Psychiatric Treatment, 13,* 203–211.

Ratzoni, G., Gothelf, D., Brand-Gothelf, B., et al. (2002). Weight gain associated with olanzapine and risperidone in adolescent patients: A comparative, prospective study. *Journal of the American Academy of Child and Adolescent Psychiatry, 41,* 337–343.

Ray, W. A., Chung, C. P., Murray, K. T., et al. (2009). Atypical antipsychotic drugs and the risk of sudden cardiac death. *New England Journal of Medicine, 360,* 225–235.

Reich, W., Huang, H., & Todd, R. D. (2006). ADHD medication use in a population-based sample of twins. *Journal of the American Academy of Child and Adolescent Psychiatry, 45,* 801–807.

Research Unit on Pediatric Psychopharmacology (RUPP) Anxiety Study Group. (2001). Fluvoxamine for the treatment of anxiety disorders in children and adolescents. *New England Journal of Medicine, 344,* 1279–1285.

Research Units on Pediatric Psychopharmacology (RUPP) Autism Network. (2002), Risperidone in children with autism and serious behavioral problems. *New England Journal of Medicine, 347,* 314–321.

Research Units on Pediatric Psychopharmacology (RUPP) Autism Network. (2005a). Risperidone treatment of autistic disorder: Longer-term benefits and blinded discontinuation after 6 months. *American Journal of Psychiatry, 162,* 1361–1369.

Research Units on Pediatric Psychopharmacology (RUPP) Autism Network. (2005b). Randomized, controlled, crossover trial of methylphenidate in pervasive developmental disorders with hyperactivity. *Archives of General Psychiatry, 62,* 1266–1274.

Rey, J. M., Walter, G., & Soh, N. (2008). Complementary and alternative medicine (CAM) treatments and pediatric psychopharmacology. *Journal of the American Academy of Child and Adolescent Psychiatry, 47,* 364–368.

Reyes, M., Buitelaar, J., Toren, P., et al. (2006). A randomized, double-blind, placebo-controlled study of risperidone maintenance treatment in children and adolescents with disruptive behavior disorders. *American Journal of Psychiatry, 163,* 402–410.

Rich, B. A., Schmajuk, M., Perez-Edgar, K. E., et al. (2007). Different psychophysiological and behavioral responses elicited by frustration in pediatric bipolar disorder and severe emotional dysregulation. *American Journal of Psychiatry, 164,* 309–317.

Riddle, M. A., Berstein, G. A., Cook, E. H. et al. (1999). Anxiolytics, adrenergic agents, and naltrexone. *Journal of the American Academy of Child and Adolescent Psychiatry, 38,* 546–556.

Riddle, M. A., Reeve, E. A., Yaryura-Tobias, J. A., et al (2001). Fluvoxamine for children and adolescents with obsessive-compulsive disorder: A randomized, controlled, multicenter trial. *Journal of the American Academy of Child and Adolescent Psychiatry, 40*, 222–229.

Robb, A. S., Cueva, J. E., Sporn, J. et al (2010). Sertraline treatment of children and adolescents with posttraumatic stress disorder: A double-blind, placebo-controlled trial. *Journal of Child and Adolescent Psychopharmacology, 20*, 463–471.

Rohde, P., Silva, S. G., Tonev, S. T., et al. (2008). Achievement and maintenance of sustained response during the treatment for adolescents with depression study continuation and maintenance therapy. *Archives of General Psychiatry, 65*, 447–455.

Rosack, J. (2005, September 2). New data show declines in antidepressant prescribing. *Psychiatric News, 40* (17), 1.

Ross, R. G. (2006). Psychotic and manic-like symptoms during stimulant treatment of attention deficit hyperactivity disorder. *American Journal of Psychiatry, 163*, 1149–1152.

Ross, RG. (2008). New findings on antipsychotic use in children and adolescents with schizophrenia spectrum disorders. *American Journal of Psychiatry, 165*, 1369–1372.

Ross, R. G., Novins D., Farley, G. K., et al. (2003). A 1-year open-label trial of olanzapine in school-age children with schizophrenia. *Journal of Child and Adolescent Psychopharmacology, 13*, 301–309.

Rowe, R., Maughan, B., Pickles, A., et al. (2002). The relationship between DSM-IV oppositional defiant disorder and conduct disorder: Findings from the Great Smoky Mountains Study. *Journal of Child Psychology and Psychiatry, 43*, 365–373.

Rowland, A. S., Umbach, D. M., Stallone, L., et al. (2002). Prevalence of medication treatment for attention deficit–hyperactivity disorder among elementary school children in Johnston County, North Carolina. *American Journal of Public Health, 92*, 231–234.

Russo, R. M., Gururaj ,V. J., & Allen, J. E. (1976). The effectiveness of diphenhydramine HCl in pediatric sleep disorders. *Journal of Clinical Pharmacology, 16*, 284–288.

Rynn, M. A. & Regan, J. (2008). Anxiety Disorders. In R. L. Findling, MD, (Ed.) *Clinical manual of child and adolescent psychopharmacology* (pp.143–196). Washington, DC: American Psychiatric Publishing.

Rynn, M. A., Riddle, M. A., Yeung, P. P., et al. (2007). Efficacy and safety of extended-release venlafaxine in the treatment of generalized anxiety disorder in children and adolescents: Two placebo-controlled trials. *American Journal of Psychiatry, 164*, 290–300.

Rynn, M. A., Siqueland, L., & Rickels, K. (2001). Placebo-controlled trial of sertraline in the treatment of children with generalized anxiety disorder. *American Journal of Psychiatry, 158*, 2008–2014.

Salehi, B., Imani, R., Mohammadi, M. R., et al. (2010). Gingko biloba for attention-deficit/hyperactivity disorder in children and adolescents: A double blind, randomized controlled trial. *Progress in Neuropsychopharmacology and Biological Psychiatry, 34*, 76--80.

Sallee, F. R., Kurlan, R., Goetz, C. G., et al. (2000). Ziprasidone treatment of children and adolescents with Tourette's syndrome: A pilot study. *Journal of the American Academy of Child and Adolescent Psychiatry, 39*, 292–299.

Sallee, F. R., McGough, J., Wigal, T., et al. (2009). Guanfacine extended release in children and adolescents with attention-deficit/hyperactivity disorder: A placebo-controlled trial. *Journal of the American Academy of Child and Adolescent Psychiatry, 48*, 155–165.

Scahill, L. (2008). Tic disorders. In R. L. Findling, MD, (Ed.) *Clinical manual of child and adolescent psychopharmacology* (pp. 301–335). Washington, DC: American Psychiatric Publishing.

Scahill, L., Aman, M. G., McDougle, C. J., et al. (2006). A prospective open trial of guanfacine in children with pervasive developmental disorders. *Journal of Child and Adolescent Psychopharmacology, 16*, 589–598.

Scahill, L., Leckman, J. F., Schultz, R. T., et al. (2003). A placebo-controlled trial of risperidone in Tourette syndrome. *Neurology, 60*: 1130–1135.

Scheffler, R. M., Brown, T. T., Fulton, B. D., et al. (2009). Positive association between attention-deficit/hyperactivity disorder medication use and academic achievement during elementary school. *Pediatrics, 123*, 1273–1279.

Schur, S., Sikich, L., Findling, R. L., et al. (2003). Treatment recommendations for the use of antipsychotics for aggressive youth (TRAAY). Part I. A review. *Journal of the American Academy of Child and Adolescent Psychiatry, 42*, 132–144.

Shaw, P., Lerch, J., Greenstein, D., et al. (2006). Longitudinal mapping of cortical thickness and clinical outcome in children and adolescents with attention-deficit/hyperactivity disorder. *Archives of General Psychiatry, 63*, 540–549.

Shaw, P., Sharp, W. S., Morrison, M., et al. (2009). Psychostimulant treatment and the developing cortex in attention deficit hyperactivity disorder. *American Journal of Psychiatry, 166*, 58–63.

Shea, S., Turgay, A., Carroll, A., et al. (2004). Risperidone in the treatment of disruptive behavioral symptoms in children with autistic and other pervasive developmental disorders. *Pediatrics, 114*, e634-e641.

Sikich, L., Frazier, J. A., McClellan, J, et al. (2008). Double-blind comparison of first- and second-generation antipsychotics in early-onset schizophrenia and schizo-affective disorder: Findings from the treatment of early-onset schizophrenia spectrum disorders (TEOSS) study. *American Journal of Psychiatry, 165*, 1420–1431.

Sikich, L., Hamer, R. M., Bashford, R. A., et al. (2004). A pilot study of risperidone, olanzapine, and haloperidol in psychotic youth: A double-blind, randomized, 8 week trial. *Neuropsychopharmacology, 29*, 133–145.

Silber, T. J., & Valadez-Meltzer, A. (2005). Premenstrual dysphoric disorder in adolescents: Case reports of treatment with fluoxetine and review of the literature. *Journal of Adolescent Health, 37*, 518–525.

Skoog, G., & Skoog, I. (1999). A 40-year follow-up of patients with obsessive-compulsive disorder. *Archives of General Psychiatry, 56*, 121–127.

Snyder, R., Turgay, A., Aman, M., et al. (2002). Effects of risperidone on conduct and disruptive behavior disorders in children with subaverage IQ's. *Journal of the American Academy of Child and Adolescent Psychiatry, 41*, 1026–1036.

Spencer, E. K., Kafantaris, V., Padron-Gayol, M. V. et al (1992). Haloperidol in schizophrenic children: early findings from a study in progress. *Psychopharmacology Bulletin, 28*, 183–186.

Spencer, T. J., Kratochvil, C. J., Sangal, R. B., et al. (2007). Effects of atomoxetine on growth in children with attention-deficit/hyperactivity disorder following up to five years of treatment. *Journal of Child and Adolescent Psychopharmacology, 17,* 689–700.

Staller, J. A., Wade, M. J., & Baker, M. (2005). Current prescribing patterns in outpatient child and adolescent psychiatric practice in central New York. *Journal of Child and Adolescent Psychopharmacology, 15,* 57–61.

Stein, M. A., Sarampote, C. S., Waldman, I. D., et al. (2003). A dose-response study of OROS methylphenidate in children with attention-deficit/hyperactivity disorder. *Pediatrics, 112,* e404.

Steinhausen, H. C., Wachter, M., Laimbock, K., et al. (2006). A long-term outcome study of selective mutism in childhood. *Journal of Child Psychology and Psychiatry, 47,* 751–756.

Stingaris, A., Maughan, B., & Goodman, R. (2010). What's in a disruptive disorder? Temperamental antecedents of oppositional defiant disorder: Findings from the Avon Longitudinal Study. *Journal of the American Academy of Child and Adolescent Psychiatry, 49,* 474–483.

Sundstrom, A, Alfredsson, L, Sjolin-Forsberg, G, et al (2010). Association of suicide attempts with acne and treatment with isotretinoin: retrospective treatment cohort study. *British Medical Journal.* doi: 10.1136/bmj.c5812

Suri, R., Altshuler, L., Hellemann, G., et al. (2007). Effects of antenatal depression and antidepressant treatment on gestational age at birth and risk of preterm birth. *American Journal of Psychiatry, 164,* 1206–1213.

Swanson, J., Greenhill, L., Wigal, T., et al. (2006). Stimulant-related reductions of growth rates in the PATS. *Journal of the American Academy of Child and Adolescent Psychiatry, 45,* 1304–1313.

Swanson, J. M., Elliott, G. R., Greenhill, L. L., et al. (2007). Effects of stimulant medication on growth rates across 3 years in the MTA follow-up. *Journal of the American Academy of Child and Adolescent Psychiatry, 46,* 1015–1027.

Swedo, S. E., Allen, A. J., Glod, C. A., et al. (1997). A controlled trial of light therapy for the treatment of pediatric seasonal affective disorder. *Journal of the American Academy of Child and Adolescent Psychiatry, 36,* 816–821.

Swedo, S. E., & Grant, P. J. (2004). PANDAS: A model for autoimmune neuropsychiatric disorders. *Primary Psychiatry, 11*, 28–33.

Swedo, S. E., Leonard, H. L., Garvey, M., et al (1998). Pediatric autoimmune neuropsychiatric disorders associated with streptococcal infections: Clinical description of the first 50 cases. *American Journal of Psychiatry, 155*, 264–271.

The TADS Team. (2007). The Treatment for Adolescents with Depression Study (TADS): Long-term effectiveness and safety outcomes. *Archives of General Psychiatry, 64*, 1132–1143.

Tanner, S. M., Miller, D. W., & Alongi, C. (1995). Anabolic steroid use by adolescents: Prevalence, motives and knowledge of risks. *Clinical Journal of Sports Medicine, 5*, 108–115.

Tao, R., Emslie, G., Mayes, T. et al (2009). Early prediction of acute antidepressant treatment response and remission in pediatric major depressive disorder. *Journal of the American Academy of Child and Adolescent Psychiatry, 48*, 71–78.

Thiruchelvam, D., Charach, A., & Schachar, R. J. (2001). Moderators and mediators of long-term adherence to stimulant treatment in children with ADHD. *Journal of the American Academy of Child and Adolescent Psychiatry, 40*, 922–928.

Thomsen, P. H., Ebbesen, C., Persson, C. M. (2001). Long-term experience with citalopram in the treatment of adolescent OCD. *Journal of the American Academy of Child and Adolescent Psychiatry, 40*, 895–902.

Tohen, M., Kryzhanovskaya, L., Carlson, G., DelBello, M., et al. (2007). Olanzapine versus placebo in the treatment of adolescents with bipolar mania. *American Journal of Psychiatry, 164*, 1547–1556.

Tourette Syndrome Study Group. (2002). Treatment of ADHD in children with tics: A randomized controlled trial. *Neurology, 58*, 527–536.

Upadhyaya, H. P., Gault, L., & Allen, A. J. (2009). Challenges and opportunities in bringing new medications to market for pediatric patients. *Journal of the American Academy of Child and Adolescent Psychiatry, 48*, 1056–1059.

Visser, S. N., Lesesne, C. A., & Perou, R. (2007). National estimates and factors associated with medication treatment for childhood attention-deficit/hyperactivity disorder. *Pediatrics, 119* (supplement), S99–S106.

Vitiello, B. (2008) Developmental aspects of pediatric psychopharmacology. In R. L. Findling, MD, (Ed.) *Clinical Manual of Child and Adolescent Psychopharmacology* (pp.1–31). Washington, DC: American Psychiatric Publishing.

Vitiello, B., Zuvekas, S. H., & Norquist, G.S. (2006). National estimates of antidepressant medication use among US children, 1997–2002. *Journal of the American Academy of Child and Adolescent Psychiatry, 45,* 271–279.

Volkow, N. D. (2006). Stimulant medications: How to minimize their reinforcing effects? *American Journal of Psychiatry, 163,* 359–361.

Wagner, K. D., Ambrosini, P., Rynn, M., et al. (2003). Efficacy of sertraline in the treatment of children and adolescents with major depression disorder: Two randomized controlled trials. *Journal of the American Medical Association, 290,* 1033–1041.

Wagner, K. D., Berard, R., Stein, M. B., et al. (2004). A multicenter, randomized, double-blind, placebo-controlled trial of paroxetine in children and adolescents with social anxiety disorder. *Archives of General Psychiatry, 61,* 1153–1162.

Wagner, K. D., Jonas, J., Findling, R. L., et al. (2006). A double-blind, randomized, placebo-controlled trial of escitalopram in the treatment of pediatric depression. *Journal of the American Academy of Child and Adolescent Psychiatry, 45,* 280–288.

Wagner, K. D., Kowatch, R. A., Emslie, G. J., et al. (2006). A double-blind, randomized, placebo-controlled trial of oxcarbazepine in the treatment of bipolar disorder in children and adolescents. *American Journal of Psychiatry, 163,* 1179–1186.

Wagner, K. D., Redden, L., Kowatch, R. A., et al. (2009). A double-blind, randomized, placebo-controlled trial of divalproex extended-release in the treatment of bipolar disorder in children and adolescents. *Journal of the American Academy of Child and Adolescent Psychiatry, 48,* 519–532.

Wagner, K. D., Robb, A. S., Findling, R. L., et al. (2004). A randomized, placebo-controlled trial of citalopram for the treatment of major depression in children and adolescents. *American Journal of Psychiatry, 161,* 1079–1083.

Walkup, J., Labellarte, M., Riddle, M. A., et al. (2002). Treatment of pediatric anxiety disorders: An open-label extension of the research units on pediatric psychopharmacology anxiety study. *Journal of Child and Adolescent Psychopharmacology, 12*, 175–188.

Walkup, J. T. (2009). "Treatment of Childhood Anxiety Disorders: The Evidence Base and Beyond". Psychopharmacology Update Institute. American Academy of Child and Adolescent Psychiatry, New York, NY January 23–24, 2009.

Walkup, J. T., Albano, A. M., Piacentini, J., et al. (2008). Cognitive behavioral therapy, sertraline, or a combination in childhood anxiety. *New England Journal of Medicine, 359*, 2753–2766.

Walsh, B. T., Gladis, M., Roose, S. P., et al. (1988). Phenelzine vs. placebo in 50 patients with bulimia. *Archives of General Psychiatry, 45*, 471–475.

Walsh, B. T., Kaplan, A. S., & Attia, F. (2006). Fluoxetine after weight restoration in anorexia nervosa: A randomized, controlled trial *Journal of the American Medical Association, 295*, 2605–2612.

Waschbusch, D. A., Pelham, W. F., Waxmonsky, J., et al. (2009). Are there placebo effects in the medication treatment of children with attention-deficit hyperactivity disorder? *Journal of Developmental and Behavioral Pediatrics, 30*, 158–168.

Weintrob, N., Cohen, D., Klipper-Aurback, Y., et al. (2002). Decreased growth during therapy with selective serotonin reuptake inhibitors. *Archives of Pediatrics and Adolescent Medicine, 156*, 696–701.

Weissman, M. M., Pilowsky, D. J., Wickramaratne, P. J., et al. (2006). Remissions in maternal depression and child psychopathology: A STAR*D-Child Report. *Journal of the American Medical Association, 295*, 1389–1398.

Weller, EB. (2007). Developmental effects of SSRIs on fetuses, children, adolescents, and adults-clinical applications. American Academy of Child & Adolescent Psychiatry-2007 Psychopharmacology Update Institute New York, NY, pp 67-110.

Wenzel, R. G., Tepper, S., Korab, W. E. et al (2008). Serotonin syndrome risks when combining SSRI/SNRI drug and triptans: Is the FDA's alert warranted? *The Annals of Pharmacotherapy. 42*, 1692–1696.

Wilens, T. E., Adler, L. A., Adams, J., et al. (2008). Misuse and diversion of stimulants prescribed for ADHD: A systematic review of the literature. *Journal of the American Academy of Child and Adolescent Psychiatry, 47*, 21–31.

Wilens, T. E., Faraone, S. V., Biederman, J., et al. (2003). Does stimulant therapy of attention-deficit/hyperactivity disorder beget later substance abuse?: A meta-analytic review of the literature. *Pediatrics, 111*, 179–185.

Wilens, T. E., Gignac, M., Swezey, A., et al. (2006). Characteristics of adolescents and young adults with ADHD who divert or misuse their prescribed medications. *Journal of the American Academy of Child and Adolescent Psychiatry, 45*, 408–414.

Wisner, K. L., Sit, D. K. Y., Hanusa, B. H., et al. (2009). Major depression and antidepressant treatment: Impact of pregnancy and neonatal outcomes. *American Journal of Psychiatry, 166*, 557–566.

Yates, T. (2004). Atomoxetine. *Child & Adolescent Psychopharmacology News, 9*(6), 1–5.

Young, E. A., Kornstein, S. G., Harvey, A. T., et al. (2007). Influences of hormone-based contraception on depressive symptoms in premenopausal women with major depression. *Psychoneuroendocrinology, 32*, 843–853.

Zalsman, G., Carmon, E., Martin, A., et al. (2003). Effectiveness, safety, and tolerability of risperidone in adolescents with schizophrenia: An open-label study. *Journal of Child and Adolescent Psychopharmacology, 13*, 319–327.

Zito, J. M., Safer, D. J., de Jong-van den Berg, L. T., et al. (2008). A three-country comparison of psychotropic mediciation prevalence in youth. *Child and Adolescent Psychiatry and Mental Health, 2*, 26.

Zito, J. M., Safer, D. J., dosReis, S., et al. (2003). Psychotropic practice patterns for youth: A 10-year perspective. *Archives of Pediatrics and Adolescent Medicine, 157*, 17–25.

Zuvekas, S. H., Vitiello, B., & Norquist, G. S. (2006). Recent trends in stimulant medication use among US children. *American Journal of Psychiatry, 163*, 579–585.

## Books and articles relied on heavily

American Psychiatric Association. (1994). *Diagnostic and statistical manual of mental disorders*. 4th ed. Washington, DC.: American Psychiatric Association.

Correll, C. (2008). Antipsychotic use in children and adolescents: Minimizing adverse effects to maximize outcomes. *Journal of the American Academy of Child and Adolescent Psychiatry, 47*, 117–128.

Cozza, K. L., Armstrong, S. C., & Oesterheld, J. R. (2003). *Drug interaction principles for medical practices*. Washington, DC: American Psychiatric Publishing.

Diamond, R. J. (2009). *Instant psychopharmacology*. New York: Norton.

Evans, D. L., Foa, E. B., Gur, R. E., Hendin, H., O'Brien, C. P., Seligman, M. E. P., Walsh, B. T. (2005). *Treating and preventing adolescent mental health disorders*. New York: Oxford University Press.

Findling, R. L. (2008). *Clinical manual of child and adolescent psychopharmacology*. Washington, DC: American Psychiatric Publishing.

Greenhill, L. L., & Osman, B. B. (1991). *Ritalin: Theory and patient management*. New York: Mary Ann Liebert.

Greenhill, L. L., Pliszka, S., Dulcan, M. K., et al. (2002). Practice parameter for the use of stimulant medications in the treatment of children, adolescents, and adults. *Journal of the American Academy of Child and Adolescent Psychiatry, 41* (supplement), 26S–49S.

Julien, R. M. (2001). *A primer of drug action*. New York: Henry Holt and Company.

Practice parameter for the assessment and treatment of children and adolescents with enuresis. (2004). *Journal of the American Academy of Child and Adolescent Psychiatry, 43*, 1540–1550.

Practice parameter for the assessment and treatment of children and adolescents with attention-deficit/hyperactivity disorder. (2007). *Journal of the American Academy of Child and Adolescent Psychiatry, 46*, 894–921.

Practice parameter for the assessment and treatment of children and adolescents with depressive disorders. (2007). *Journal of the American Academy of Child and Adolescent Psychiatry, 46*, 1503–1526.

Schatzberg, A. R., Cole, J. O., & DeBattista, C. (2007). *Manual of clinical psychopharmacology*. Washington, DC: American Psychiatric Publishing.

## Major Sources on Sleep

*The international classification of sleep disorders, revised: diagnostic and coding manual*. (2001). Westchester, IL: American Academy of Sleep Medicine.

Mindell, J. A., & Owens, J. A. (2010). *A clinical guide to pediatric sleep: Diagnosis and management of sleep problems*. Philadelphia, PA: Wolters Kluwer.

Owens, J. A. (2009, February). Pharmacotherapy of pediatric insomnia, *Journal of the American Academy of Child and Adolescent Psychiatry, 48*(2), 99–107.

## Major Sources on Alternative Medicine

Flanagan, J., & Jurgens, T. (2000, June). KAVA: Piper methysticum. *Child & Adolescent Psychopharmacology News, 5*(3), 7–11.

Flynn, R. (2000, October). Evening primrose oil. *Child & Adolescent Psychopharmacology News, 5*(5), 10.

Murphy, A. (1999, December). Remembering gingko. *Child & Adolescent Psychopharmacology News, 4*(6), 5.

Rey, J. M., Walter, G., & Soh, N. (2008). Complementary and alternative medicine (CAM) treatments and pediatric psychopharmacology. *Journal of the American Academy of Child and Adolescent Psychiatry, 47*, 364–368.

White, K. (2000, February). St. John's wort. *Child & Adolescent Psychopharmacology News, 5*(1), 4.

# Index

Note: Tables are noted with a *t*.